D1534696

Musical Echoes

REFIGURING AMERICAN MUSIC

A series edited by Ronald Radano and Josh Kun

Charles McGovern, contributing editor

Sathima and Abdullah with Boots the dog in Central Park, mid-1960s. *Collection of Sathima Bea Benjamin.*

Musical Echoes

South African Women Thinking in Jazz

CAROL ANN MULLER & SATHIMA BEA BENJAMIN

Duke University Press Durham & London 2011

Duke University Press gratefully acknowledges the
support of the LLoyd Hibberd Endowment of the
American Musicological Society, which provided
funds toward the publication of this book.

Short audio clips of Sathima Benjamin's music are
available for listening at http://www.africanmusical
echoes.org/ as is information on purchasing tracks
from *Cape Town Love* and other Benjamin recordings.

TO OUR CHILDREN

Tsakwe

Tsidi

Zachary

Jasmine

A Diasporic Generation

Contents

LIST OF FIGURES   ix

PREFACE   xiii

ACKNOWLEDGMENTS   xxiii

A TRIBUTE BY ABDULLAH IBRAHIM: "Sathima"   xxxi

SATHIMA: My Life's Journey as a Jazz Singer   xxxiii

1. Beginnings   1

2. A Home Within   11
   CALL: Recollecting a Musical Past   11
   RESPONSE: Entanglement in Race and Music   33

3. Cape Jazz   53
   CALL: Popular Music, Dance Bands, and Jazz   53
   RESPONSE: Imagining Musical Lineage through
   Duke and Billie   95

4. Jazz Migrancy   128
   CALL: Musicians Abroad   128
   RESPONSE: A New African Diaspora   167

5. A New York Embrace   189
   CALL: Coming to the City   189
   RESPONSE: Women Thinking in Jazz, or the Poetics
   of a Musical Self   217

6. Returning Home?   242
   CALL: *Cape Town Love* / An Archeology of Popular Song   242
   RESPONSE: Jazz History as Living History   260

7. Musical Echoes   271
   CALL: Sathima's Musical Echo   271
   RESPONSE: Reflections on Echo   274

8. Outcomes — Jazz in the World   283

NOTES   297

SELECTED REFERENCES   325

INDEX   337

Figures

1. Cover of the CD *A Morning in Paris*. xii
2. Sathima in her apartment at the Hotel Chelsea, 1991. 4
3. Sathima and Carol at Penn Station, July 2010. 4
4. Sathima Bea Benjamin as a baby. 16
5. Sathima, her sister Joan, and a cousin. 16
6. Benjamin family, Sathima as a baby held by Ma Benjamin. 18
7. Two couples in ballroom attire. 57
8. Cape Town Jive Band. 59
9. Jimmy Adams's Swing Band. 63
10. Sathima's mother at the piano. 68
11. Golden City Dixies deplaning in South Africa. 75
12. Jimmy Adams with American School of Music jacket and Sathima's sister Edith Green, 1996. 79
13. Harold Jephthah, December 1999. 79
14. Sathima singing at a nightclub, late 1950s. 81
15. New lineages in Paris with Duke Ellington, Dollar Brand Trio, and Billy Strayhorn, from the CD *A Morning in Paris*. 97
16. Sathima singing at the Antibes Jazz Festival with the Dollar Brand Trio. 111
17. Sathima singing, with Abdullah Ibrahim on piano. 150
18. Sathima's and Abdullah's son, Tsakwe. 157
19. Abdullah and Sathima meet President Samora Machel of Mozambique and his then-wife, Graça. 161
20. Sathima and Abdullah Ibrahim on their wedding day in London, 26 February 1965. 171
21. School picture of Sathima's daughter, Tsidi. 192
22. Sathima's son, Tsakwe, in the early 1990s. 194
23. Sathima singing at Sweet Rhythm. 211
24. Sathima's favorite bass player, Buster Williams. 211
25. The bass player Buster Williams and the drummer George Grey play at Sathima's seventieth birthday at Sweet Rhythm. 212
26. Sathima singing at Sweet Rhythm, with Stephen Scott on piano. 212
27. Sathima with her daughter, the hip-hop artist Tsidi Ibrahim, aka Jean Grae, at Sweet Rhythm. 213

28. Sathima's sister Joan Franciscus at Sweet Rhythm.   213
29. Cover of Sathima's CD *Cape Town Love*.   244
30. Sathima's African diasporic lineage in jazz, from an early Benjamin record cover.   261
31. Cover of Sathima's CD *Musical Echoes*.   272

Musical Echoes

1. Cover of the CD *A Morning in Paris*.

Preface

Feeling like intruders, we witness a moment of encounter captured in a photographic image on the slipcover of a compact disc titled *A Morning in Paris*. Taken many years earlier and made public for the first time in 1997, the close-up in black and white of the two faces exudes a feeling of familiarity, even intimacy, in the way in which the eyes interlock. These are two unlikely subjects: a young woman of ambiguous racial marking and an older man in a brightly lit public space. He occupies the left of the frame, she the right. We see only one side of their faces. The partial shadow that covers the man's cheek darkens his complexion, and then we notice the detail in the hair: this is definitely a man of African descent. His ear catches our attention. It is poised to hear. The light casts less shadow on the woman's countenance: dark, straight hair with deliberate curl, fine features, and distinctive eyebrows. We are given few clues about the nature of the encounter between these two people. Her head is tilted up toward his, he tenderly returns the gaze. The mouths of both are slightly open: neither seems to speak, except perhaps in whispered tones.

The woman's imprint: her handwriting is superimposed in white on the mechanically reproduced title in indigo, white, and red: *Sathima Bea Benjamin, A Morning in Paris*. A block of the city skyline underscores the text. A European city, a woman's name, Sathima, not recognizably European, but no further clues about origins or community. Snippets of the fleur-de-lys are inserted below. Is she French? Algerian perhaps? He looks familiar but lacks a name. Should we know who he is?

A Morning in Paris was launched on 23 February 1997, in Carnegie Hall in New York City. Thirty-four years after it was recorded, and well after the death of the man in the photograph, the woman, South African–born Sathima Bea Benjamin, celebrated the rediscovery of the tapes from her studio session in Paris in 1963. Finally she had proof of her first personal encounter with the man whose music she had come to know among passionate jazz fans and performers in Cape Town, in the mid- to late 1950s. Though he had never traveled to South Africa in person, the young woman felt she already knew him because she had worked so intensely with his music through close listening to records, seeing him on the movie screen, and hearing his music played by local musicians. He was the jazz composer, arranger, and pianist Duke Ellington. His was the other face in the photograph.

The recording was made at the now-defunct Barclay Studio in Paris. Fortuitously, a photographer who dropped by the studio where Ellington was producing for Reprise Records, Frank Sinatra's label, began shooting, and several of those images were inserted inside the liner notes to the CD when it was released in 2006. After the tapes were discovered, Sathima tracked down the photographer, who had still photos of the meeting of musicians: a close-up of Billy Strayhorn behind dark glasses, one of Gerhard Lehner, the German engineer, and a medium-range shot of the South African musicians—Dollar Brand, who later became Abdullah Ibrahim, Makhaya Ntshoko, and Johnny Gertze—in the studio with Ellington. Svend Asmussen, the Danish violinist heard playing pizzicato lines around Benjamin's melody, had already left the studio because by the time the photographer arrived Sathima had finished recording. There is no picture of Sathima Bea Benjamin in the studio: she wasn't self-assured enough to insist that the archive of the encounter include pictures of her next to the better-known male musicians.

In fact, the photograph on the front cover was not taken at that historic meeting of African American, Danish, and South African musicians in Paris. The picture comes from a shared moment in the airport in Copenhagen almost a year later. Historically inaccurate in terms of place and time, it nevertheless provides the necessary evidence: the image is the testament to the musical relationship that existed between the South African singer and one of the greatest figures in jazz. While the photograph is spot on, until the discovery of the tapes in Paris by the journalist and Strayhorn biographer David Hajdu of New York, the content of the image was insufficient. To assert a rightful place for herself in the annals of American jazz history, the South African singer needed the tapes.

Truthfully, then, the photograph has nothing to do with that particular morning in February 1963. But perhaps it is just as well there were no pictures taken of Sathima that day because while she recalls the grandeur, generosity, and kindness of Ellington and his musical partner Strayhorn, it is unlikely the photographic evidence would have conveyed the profound sense of connection the image on the CD cover portrays. "When Ellington looked at you, it was as if he saw right through you," Benjamin recalls. Such recognition and insight could hardly have been captured in the visual record amidst the uncertainty of first personal encounters or of the awe the South Africans felt being in the presence of Ellington and Strayhorn.

A Morning in Paris is a compelling piece of the larger story told in this book of how American jazz traveled to South Africa in the twentieth century and was imaginatively incorporated into the lives of many South Africans in the post–Second World War era. The story is told from the perspective of one woman, Sathima Bea Benjamin, and her musical peers—all men—inside South Africa, but also as she has traveled from South Africa to Europe, Brazil, Mozambique, Australia, and the United States over the last fifty years. Sathima is a woman who felt called to jazz, a music claimed as America's classical music, though she has never thought of herself as American. (Sathima was given a U.S. passport in the 1980s, though like others, she thinks of herself more as a New Yorker than an American. Her South African citizenship was revoked at about the same time because of her involvement in the anti-apartheid movement in New York City. As several cities around the world are, New York City is thought to be the space of refuge and "strategic retreat" more than the United States as the country of sanctuary.) Her childhood and young adult memories are situated in and shaped by her family history, the city of Cape Town, where she was raised, and the people who nurtured the qualities of courage, strength, and love that characterize her approach to life and to jazz itself. This book also tells of a formative period in Cape Town when the singer began to find a place for herself in the world through the books she read—books about the struggles in society of Africans in America, who were called both colored and Negro. One story in particular, that of Billie Holiday, a woman and a singer of mixed racial heritage also called colored, was particularly important. She began to hear Holiday's voice on records owned by members of an international community of jazz fans who participated in the local jazz scene in Cape Town. And she moved toward the music of Ellington.

If you are a reader who has only ever thought of jazz as American music and of race as drawing no distinction between coloreds and Negroes this is a story that will require you to rethink prior assumptions about the given-ness and certainty of many social categories and of twentieth-century music making. This story fundamentally challenges the contours of ownership, categorization, and place, and, indeed, of just what music scholars mean when we talk about American music, popular music, or jazz as specifically American music. In this book we are proposing a sense of American music different from the more conventional, place-based familiarity of sound, style, and community characteristic of the jazz canon, and indeed in much contemporary scholarship on allegedly American music. In this book America's music has traveled the world over. As it has traveled it has been translated into local music histories and scenes giving rise to new musical communities and histories. Such travel suggests that the time is right for us to devise mechanisms for broadening the perspective beyond the United States in a more direct conversation with those inside its borders to constitute a worldwide, comparative, and more equitable representation of jazz historiography. We hope the book will gently persuade readers to move into these new ways of thinking.

This book is about individual and collective musical experiences chan-neled into and through real and imagined acoustical—mostly jazz—worlds from the middle years of the twentieth century to the present. It is a set of reflections on the feminized dimensions of jazz and popu-lar music history and culture—interiority, the senses, the voice, dreams, visions, compositional process—generated by the story of an extraordi-nary woman singer, composer, producer, recording artist, independent record company director, mother, wife, and, in Gramscian terms "organic intellectual," whose recording ventures were financed by her husband in return for the launch of his international career as a jazz pianist that she facilitated. It was, after all, her persistence with Ellington in Switzer-land in January 1963 that resulted in the Ellington recording session men-tioned earlier.

Our book engages interrogatively with U.S.-centered jazz historiogra-phy by proposing new ways of thinking about these bodies of knowledge by inserting a local-global versus universal model of understanding into jazz scholarship. In other words, this is a particular story told from what were the margins of jazz performance, which intentionally engages with the American master narrative to extend jazz historiography into other places in the world. This is also different from the comparative project ethnomusicologists implicitly engage with, in which musical cultures of the world are read in parallel. Our project strives to put jazz cultures in dialogue with each other.

Such a position is one consequence of what Dipesh Chakrabarty calls "provincializing Europe," or the United States in this instance (2003). So, for example, while this is a book focused on a particular strand of jazz history and practice, it strives to extend that story out to those often marginalized by jazz history — women, non-Americans, and those whose recordings have not traveled to the U.S. center. While it is a story about racial struggles, it does not always treat race in the way it has been written about in the United States or Britain, the two sites where the most prolific theorizing has occurred. The primary source materials emerge out of the life experiences of an individual, but this book is not only biographical. Because Sathima is not popular in the sense that Ella Fitzgerald or Sarah Vaughan were, I was told early on by a representative of another academic press that the purely biographical wouldn't sell. The book had to be more than biography. Thus the ethnographic narrative and theorizing generated by these materials is multisited and, quite literally, international.

Theoretically, while the narrative is about African diaspora, it bears little resemblance to the diaspora that brought West African slaves to the Americas. Instead, this is a mid-twentieth-century African diaspora from the southern reaches of the continent. It is a story of the dispersal of American sound and experience in objectified forms — films, recordings, books — through the channels of the global entertainment industry to all corners of the earth, and the responses of one community of listeners to that process, a significant group of whom traveled to the metropolitan centers of jazz history and performance to meet and play with key African American jazz musicians in Europe and the United States.

This book is written in a way that is different from the small but significant literature on jazz communities outside the United States. By narrating Sathima's side of the jazz story, the book strives to put American jazz scholars and their work in dialogue with other communities. The intention is to disrupt the one-dimensional relationship non-Americans have had with American-generated jazz in the twentieth century, in which it is almost always the other who knows something about what is happening in American jazz, while many American jazz musicians, critics, and writers know little about jazz elsewhere. At the end of the book I argue that there is an ethical imperative to strive for greater inclusiveness in the writing of jazz history, to recognize that jazz has come of age in many parts of the world: it is critical that its history be treated as a truly world-wide narrative in the twenty-first century. As I do so I am aware that there is a dilemma in calling for these transformations when it has taken the academy so long to acknowledge and incorporate African American music, history, and culture, and jazz specifically, into its curriculum and to value the larger African American contribution to American music as a whole. While the challenge for those of us from places other than the United States is to begin to demand a larger lens of understanding, one with a truly global comparativist reach, it is important to do so without displacing the central place of African American creativity in this larger jazz history.

Further, in the last decade South African studies has come into its own in the global community of scholars. The transition to democracy in the 1990s liberated South Africans in many ways, not least in terms of the archives made newly available and the kinds of scholarship that began to be produced, expanding outward writing about race, gender, class, democracy, modernity, and so forth from a South African perspective. And my own priorities as a scholar of South African music, like so much else, have changed in the last twenty years, both inside South Africa and in the world at large. As the political climate in that country has undergone major transformation, the published literature on South African jazz has begun to shift and grow into new interpretive possibilities and areas of intellectual exploration. In a postapartheid era the ability to frame the artistic output of South African musicians is no longer dependent on the same kind of political message or politicized interpretation of the work with the kind of pressing urgency sensed during the apartheid regime. In the last few years, I have begun to think more about the relationship between beauty or deeply felt emotion and social justice (see, for example, Chakrabarty [2003], especially "Nation and Imagination"; Scarry [2001]; Nussbaum [2003]; Nuttall [2007]; and Nakedi [2006]); about what my responsibility as a writer might be. How do I present Sathima's life and music in a rhetoric that is evocative, pleasing to the eye and to the ear, wondering why our presentation of scholarly ideas often reads in such monotonous tones? In this spirit I have taken some liberty in experimenting with expressive and poetic possibilities in this book.

So while our book is generated out of the conversations and contemplation of two women, we trust that we have reached a place in the struggle by women and other minorities all over the world for visibility and academic credibility, that the book will be read as a substantive contribution to the reformulation of jazz studies in the twenty-first century by many, particularly jazz critics and scholars. We urge you to join us in that exploration into a world of new ways of thinking about some very familiar subjects with a spirit of openness and adventure.

Perhaps the greatest challenge in writing this book has been an organizational one: the research and conversations with many people in various places have generated an extraordinary amount of information and kinds of texts over the years. In addition, Sathima's life story, the music she sings, and the recording projects she has produced over the last three decades open themselves to new ways of thinking about the world of music as we conventionally know it, though few know her story or her music. Writing that narrative has required both the biographical and the reflective to coexist in a single space—to make sense of the scholarly reflection one needs first to read the story. Then, because Sathima and I have worked together over an extended period of time, our knowledge and stories have become intertwined. On the one hand, while I am clearly the author of the written rendition of the book, Sathima's thinking has profoundly shaped the way in which I have come to understand her life and music. I have also had to probe the commonly held beliefs about exile, diaspora, race, gender, South African history, and the use of the imagination. On the other hand, while it is obviously Sathima who knows the contours of her life story, there are parts of her life experience she simply has not been able to remember. It didn't matter how many times I asked or how much I prodded, until I found archival evidence, interviewed some of her old friends, or read the Rasmussen books on Cape jazz I could not recuperate key pieces of the biography. In fact, the most comprehensive list of all the musicians who have played a part in her life is to be found in the people she acknowledges at the beginning of the book. She provided that list for me in August 2009, at the end of my research, not the beginning. She simply couldn't recall many of those names when we started out.

The question has been how to write the book to allow for these quite different kinds of knowledge to coexist, without one being silenced or overridden by the other. How do we retain the linear chronology of her life story while opening up moments for the reader to pause and ruminate on the poetic and intellectual implications of this narrative? The solution has been to articulate in the very structure of the book the idea of the musical echo as a kind of call and response. Call and response is how Sathima has conceptualized her relationship to the world of jazz from the outset—she heard the call of jazz in South Africa and has responded in a variety of ways over her lifetime. The musical echo is Sathima's more recent extension of the call and response idea, and it exists now as a song, the title of a recording, and here in book form.

The book is divided into eight chapters. The first and last chapters work as bookends: "Beginnings" and "Outcomes." Each of the six chapters in between is organized into two parts: the "call," which is Sathima's life story woven into the larger political and musical contexts of that story; and the "response," my reflections on the contours of that story. As I have suggested above, while the calls provide the content of Sathima's life story, they are not written in the first person—I am the book's writer; and the responses, which are my reflections, have been shaped in conversation with Sathima.

The first chapter outlines the three-pronged project undertaken here: first, to tell Sathima's story; second, to reflect on the contribution this story makes to an understanding of processes like race, gender, diaspora, and history in jazz studies; and, third, to suggest a paradigm for the worldwide study of the past in jazz. In chapter 2 the call tells the story of Sathima's traumatic childhood and music as a form of escape, solace, and space of imaginary play; it extends into her teenage and young adult years, a period in which she expressed her love for music through popular song. The response ruminates on race under apartheid, on "Cape Colouredness" specifically, and on Sathima's experience of racial categorization; then I reflect on race and jazz in the postapartheid era. The call in chapter 3 outlines Sathima's move into greater political consciousness, her awareness of herself as a person of color, and her shift into the world of jazz and a discourse of musical freedom. My response fleshes out ideas about musical lineage manifest in the virtual presence of both Duke Ellington and Billie Holiday in postwar South Africa and in Sathima's life specifically. The call in chapter 4 narrates Sathima's experiences, musical and personal, as she moved out of South Africa to Europe, England, the United States, and back to southern Africa and ultimately settled in New York City. In this period she married Abdullah Ibrahim (twice); recorded with Ellington and Billy Strayhorn; met other South Africans in exile; encountered the free jazz movement in Europe; had two children, Tsakwe and Tsidi; witnessed the Soweto uprising of 1976; and started to compose her own music. My response reflects on the methodological challenges inherent in diasporic research and posits four new ways of thinking about African diaspora and exile in the contemporary world. The call in chapter 5 outlines the period of "strategic retreat" when Sathima and Abdullah openly declared their opposition to the apartheid regime, had their passports revoked, took up U.S. citizenship, and moved into the Hotel Chelsea in Manhattan. The couple began to work and perform for the ANC in exile. Sathima thinks of this time as the moment of personal reinvention of herself as a woman in jazz. She started her own record company and produced several recording projects in which she acted as bandleader. In my response I position Sathima in a wider network of women in jazz and reflect on ways in which she thinks in and about jazz. In chapter 6 the call discusses in some detail Sathima's return to South African musically in her recording *Cape Town Love* (1999). The recording works as a kind of palimpsest of Anglo-American popular culture. In my response I play with ideas about living history. The call of chapter 7 starts with Sathima's recording *Musical Echoes* and moves in the response into a discussion of the echo as acoustical, mythical, musical, and political phenomenon. I situate her voice and presence in the field of jazz studies through a discussion of Elaine Scarry's essays about beauty and social justice, suggesting that beauty, like jazz, inspires the desire for the copy, for expanding on exact replication into an aesthetic realm that enables the constitution of beautiful things and sounds, much like the music of Ellington and Holiday did for Sathima early in her life. I propose that her voice opens up new possibilities for a jazz poetics, one which includes the more feminine domains of jazz performance—beauty, love, creativity, spontaneity, healing, and the voice itself. In the final chapter we reflect on new directions for a worldwide study of jazz. I suggest the echo is a useful metaphor for conceptualizing the global travel of jazz as a historical and comparative project, drawing on the South African case study, of which Sathima is the central actor.

Acknowledgments

SATHIMA BEA BENJAMIN

Here are my acknowledgments to the folks who inspired, encouraged, and supported my lifelong trip through this wonderful music called jazz. When Carol asked me to do this list, I knew I had to think long and hard and go back to the beginnings of my musical love affair with interpreting life and love through poems and song. My cousin Basil Rich (now deceased) was the first to tell me I had a beautiful voice. He played guitar and on Saturday afternoons we would go to Aunt Ethel's home in the Cape Town suburb of Woodstock. Along with his friend Lennie Daniels, a pianist, we would have a really great time working on popular music so I would say first on my list of thanks are Basil Rich and Lennie Daniels. I should mention that during the week, while I was cooking with Ma Benjamin, my grandmother, the radio played the BBC. The country at that time was called the Union of South Africa. She would let me run to the radio, where I had pen and paper to write down whatever words I could catch. I listened to Nat "King" Cole, Frank Sinatra, Ella Fitzgerald, Sarah Vaughan, Perry Como, Vera Lynn, Gracie Fields, Duke Ellington, and Frankie Laine, among the popular singers of the day.

Later, when I moved to my mom's house in Athlone, Cape Town, I did some singing with my mom and my sister Joan at local bars, concerts, and cinemas. I was invited to a jazz gig by Bernie Smith, where I was introduced to Anthony Schilder, the pianist. I think I also met Leslie Cedries, the drummer, and the bassist whose name I have forgotten. Word got around that I was a great jazz singer. I was introduced to all the musicians who were working most of the time in the white nightclubs. This included folks like the guitarists Louis Schouw and Kenny Jepthah; the saxophonists Harold Jephthah and Jimmy Adams; the bassist Basil Moses; the pianists Henry February, Arthur Gilles, Vincent Kolbe, Sammy Hartman, and Mervyn Jacobs; and the drummer Louis Cedrus. I was taking lessons from Mervyn Jacobs, and I had just a few lessons when he suddenly had a heart attack and died. Then there was the Schilder family of musicians — Chris, Phillip, Jackie, Richard, and Anthony. And, of course, Sammy Hartman. Later on there were others who supported me when things were difficult in Cape Town: Rafik Fris and Trevor Stone, who gave Abdullah and me a place to stay, and Mike Kemp, who was a dear friend and fan. And Howard Lawrence, friend and reporter for the *Golden City Post.*

I need to thank my Mom, who encouraged me to follow my heart and do the music. I was a schoolteacher during the week and singing in clubs on weekends. She helped me to follow my dreams. Thanks go to the Swiss graphic designer Paul Meyer, who introduced me to Abdullah — then called Dollar Brand; to Dave Saunders, owner of the dance club called Ambassadors, where I met and started working with Abdullah. We worked together on Ellington's music using my mother's piano in Athlone.

More recently, I need to thank folks who have recorded with me: the drummer Lulu Gontsana; all those at Milestones Recording Studio in Cape Town, especially the engineer Murray Anderson; the photographer George Hallett; Rashied Lombard who invited me to bring my trio to the Cape Town Jazz Festival; former president Thabo Mbeki, who presented me with the Ikhamanga Award for jazz singing in South Africa and abroad. And thanks to Abdullah Ibrahim for inviting me to sing with my New York Trio at the Spier Jazz Festival in Cape Town. Over the long term I would like to thank Jimmy Adams, the saxophonist and my companion for protecting and looking after me on that horrendous trip to the former Rhodesia with *Coloured Jazz and Variety.* Thanks to Vincent Kolbe, who worked at the library and gave me all the books on jazz he could find, even Billie Holiday's book.

For the European experience, thanks to Abdullah for rehearsing me with the trio so I could be as perfect as possible in the studio in Paris with Ellington and Strayhorn. Abdullah was very strict with me — in terms of beginnings, endings, and smooth delivery. That's when I became a professional act, and that impressed Ellington when we did the recording of *A Morning in Paris.* Thanks to Club Africana for letting me perform with the trio anytime I wanted to, even though I didn't have a real gig there. Thanks to the Club Montmartre and the Golden Circle in Copenhagen for letting me sing, even if it was the late night show.

Most of all I just need to thank Abdullah Ibrahim for his wonderful arrangements of the songs I sang and for accompanying me. It was always a challenge for me and a thrill. He brought out the best in me.

Then I need to thank Duke Ellington, Billy Strayhorn, and Gerhard Lehner for *A Morning in Paris*. Thank you for making the secret tape of our recording session, Gerhard, and giving it to me thirty-four years later. I am so blessed to have had Duke Ellington in my life musically. In 1965 he brought me to the Newport Jazz Festival in Rhode Island. I performed with the Ellington band, no rehearsal. He suggested New York City would be a good place for us to live. Along with a letter from him and one from his friend Langston Hughes, we managed to get green cards, and, five years later, U.S. citizenship. Our South African passports were taken away because of our anti-apartheid involvement. Specifically, I remember with great warmth our comrade and friend the African National Congress leader Johnny Makatini, who made sure I joined the ANC and did liberation concerts for them. Thanks to Ruth Ellington, who found us an apartment in New York.

I have always loved New York City, where the musicians are. I want to express my gratitude to my longtime friend Barbara Serlin, who introduced me to James Brown, the owner of Sweet Rhythm (now closed). That became my performance room for several years, where I felt so at home when I performed. I have to thank all the musicians I have worked with: Onaje Allan Gumbs, Kenny Barron, Larry Willis, Marcus McLaren, George Grey, Ricky Ford, Victor Lewis, Billy Higgins, Ben Riley, and Stephen Scott, my absolutely most favorite pianist. I have recorded in Rudy Van Gelder's wonderful studio in Englewood Cliffs, New Jersey. When I thanked him for recording me and my trio so beautifully, he graciously replied that I have excellent microphone technique!

Thanks to two very important people: the Danish used book dealer and Cape Town jazz fan Lars Rasmussen, for loving my work and using his personal funds to produce *Embracing Jazz*, and David Hajdu, professor at Columbia University, who, in researching *Lush Life*, went to Paris and met Gerhard Lehner, who made those secret tapes.

I have to thank my two children Tsakwe and Tsidi, who encourage me to perform and let me know they are proud of my efforts. And then there are the three women who help me when I sing: Julia Meissenheimer, Joanna Klein, and Kate Smith. I could not perform without them because I get nervous and am quite difficult in those moments. Of course, there is my sister, Edith Green, pragmatic and loving. Thank you, Carol, for doing this book with me, for acknowledging my work, for our warm friendship, and for the way we have bonded over the years. Finally, I have probably left some folks out, and if I did I apologize deeply. At my age I can't remember everything.

CAROL ANN MULLER

This book has traveled a long and circuitous path to publication. It probably began in the 1980s, when I was an undergraduate student at what is now the University of KwaZulu Natal. That was a remarkable place, particularly for its time. I had some extraordinary teachers: Christopher Ballantine, Darius Brubeck, Veit Erlmann, Jim Kiernan, Deborah James, Eleanor Preston-Whyte, and Kevin Volans. For graduate school I moved on to New York University, where there were some equally important instances of intellectual and musicological growth: Kay Shelemay made my graduate studies happen at NYU; the visiting scholars Allen Feldman and Nadia Serematakis and the anthropologists Bambi Schieffelin and Faye Ginsberg were awesome; Stanley Boorman, Edward Roesner, and Robert Bailey opened up the source studies approach to historiography for me. Coming out of South Africa, where history in school had been so ideologically driven by the apartheid regime, I recall the sheer joy of accessing historical archives through their teaching. This was also where I connected with a quite stunning community of graduate students — we represented most regions of the world, many of which were going through unprecedented political transformation while we studied in New York City — Su Zheng (Beijing), Tomie Hahn (who was visiting Budapest as the revolution unfolded), Maria Theresa Valez (from Colombia, where the U.S. government was at war with drug lords), a woman from the former Yugoslavia, and I was from the rapidly changing apartheid to-postapartheid South Africa. They were quite thrilling, if uncertain, times.

I began this project at NYU and met Sathima and Abdullah in New York City. Inspired by the political transformation in South Africa, I actually contemplated changing dissertation topics from my planned work on Shembe to a dissertation on musicians in exile. I talked briefly with Abdullah Ibrahim about my ideas: at the time he didn't believe South African jazz musicians would work with me. The dynamic of a white researcher and black musicians just didn't seem viable at the time. This was before Sathima suggested we work together.

Teaching at the University of [KwaZulu] Natal in the mid-1990s, I began to be exposed to black South African jazz musicians; the Music Library held several of Sathima's recordings. But the project with Sathima took off only after I presented a paper at a conference in Cape Town where I was accused of being racist because I represented a field called *ethno-musicology* and probably had much to learn about those called Cape Coloured. While ethnicity is a key defining character in the United States, it had been used by the apartheid regime in brutal ways against South Africans. That moment gave me pause. And it seems Sathima sensed the turbulence: she called my home while I was still at the conference. We talked a few days later, and she suggested we write a book together. That was in 1995.

In 1996, before returning to the United States, I spent about a month in Cape Town working in the South African Library scanning newspapers and whatever else I could locate pertaining to South African jazz history in the postwar period. I am grateful to all who assisted me both in Cape Town and at the State Archives in Pretoria in 1999. I spent the academic year 1999–2000 as a Fellow at the National Humanities Center (NHC) in Research Triangle Park, North Carolina, with a fellowship from the National Endowment for the Humanities. It was the dedicated time I needed to undertake the reading and explore the ideas that would begin to form the core of this book. I am deeply indebted to the staff and directors of the National Humanities Center: to Associate Director Kent Mullikin, the librarians Eliza Robertson and Jean Houston; the wonderful intellectual interaction with all the other Fellows at the center that year. I would like to acknowledge the generosity of the National Endowment for the Humanities, which funded the fellowship at the NHC, and the University of Pennsylvania, which released me for the fellowship just a year after I arrived there as an assistant professor. Thanks to Gary Tomlinson, Jim Primosch, and then–Associate Dean Rebecca Bushnell, who provided the necessary time and support. I also had a grant from the Research Foundation at the University of Pennsylvania to undertake fieldwork trips to South Africa and a recent publication subvention from the Research Foundation. Thank you to the American Musicological Society, Bob Judd and his committee, for a publication subvention from the Hibberd Endowment for the musical examples on the accompanying website.

The first graduate seminar I taught at the University of Pennsylvania in 1998 was "Reading Women in Jazz." There were some very smart students in the group: out of that seminar, three related research projects emerged. Elaine Hayes wrote a wonderful dissertation on Sarah Vaughan, Hilary Moore has published a book on British jazz, and Laura Lohman pursued postdoctoral work on the music of Umm Kulthum in the Arab world. It was an inspiring moment for me as a scholar and teacher. Like my own project several years earlier, both Laura's and Elaine's work was expanded by a field trip we made to the Rutgers Jazz Archive in Newark.

Having exhausted a good portion of my doctoral research material on the Shembe community and women, I finally began to turn my attention to Sathima's project in 2004. I taught another seminar on women in jazz and published a variety of journal articles, both on Sathima individually and on South African jazz more generally. There is a chapter on this material in the first and second editions of my book on South African music (2008), among other places. At about this time I met Professor of Classics Ralph Rosen, who introduced me to free jazz, the music that had a profound impact on Sathima and Abdullah in the early 1960s and that continues to be performed in Philadelphia. The kindness of Associate Dean Joe Farrell and Department Chair Jeff Kallberg provided me some leave in the fall semesters in 2005 and 2006 through a Weiler Faculty Fellowship. The time given made it possible for me to begin to put Sathima's life and music in book form. More recently, Associate Dean Ann Matter has been a wonderful colleague in so many ways.

In 2005 Ron Radano heard a panel on Women in Jazz that featured Hilary Moore, Elaine Hayes, and me. Soon after that he asked me to contribute to the "Refiguring American Music" Series. I completed the first draft of a manuscript in October 2006. Steve Feld read and responded to it at the time. I am deeply grateful to Steve and equally so for the support of Ron Radano and those at Duke University Press — Ken Wissoker, Leigh Barnwell, and Courtney Berger — and the four anonymous reviewers who were thoughtful and generous with their advice. Thank you also to those who have assisted in the production of this book, including the copyeditor Lawrence Kenney. Several of our graduate students (some have now graduated) have read and commented on this manuscript — Gavin Steingo, Jennifer Kyker, Garry Bertholf, Charles Carson, John Myers, Jennifer Ryan, Darien Lamen, and Ian MacMillen. That was the version those who evaluated my dossier and wrote letters in support of my promotion to full professor also read — I don't know who you are, but you must have liked what you read because the promotion was successful! Thank you to all of you.

I have prevailed upon a few colleagues to read through a series of sup-posedly final versions — Gavin Steingo and Gwen Ansell. I cannot thank them enough for the time they have given to me. (Thanks to Gwen An-sell, too, for filling in missing information about Chan Parker's gift to Harold Jephthah.) Lars Rasmussen, whom I know only through email and his amazing work, provided a cornerstone for my writing. Along the way I presented a paper at the Society for Ethnomusicology annual meet-ing in Hawaii on Jazz in Denmark that focused on Sathima and Abdul-lah in that country, which helped me realize there was a whole new story to tell about South Africans in exile in Europe that differed from the Makeba–Masekela experience in the United States. The discovery of the Transcription Center archive so late in my writing meant that I had to rely on a recent graduate student to do the research. Kate Thomas just happened to move to Austin at the time I needed someone to scour the archive. She was awesome, efficient, and seemed to know just what I needed. And, by extension, thank you to the librarians who compiled the list of Transcription Center contents at about the same time. Fortu-itous to say the least! My colleagues Tim Rommen, Farah Griffin, Rita Barnard, Demie Kurz, and Kofi Agawu have been wonderfully supportive of this work.

It goes without saying that my gratitude to Sathima, Abdullah, Tsakwe, and Tsidi runs deep and wide. You opened yourselves to a white South African academic when few others would have. You have confided in me; let me into your lives in ways that cannot always have been easy. And you have taught me much. I hope I have done justice in telling a piece of your story, at least from Sathima's perspective. But surely it is my small family that has borne the full burden of my writing. Writing eats up so much of one's presence of mind, sleep time, and creativity. It is hard for chil-dren to always understand. My husband, Eric, is amazing in his support and in the ways he keeps the children busy on weekends and so often in the summer. My mother arrived from South Africa recently: it was my father who made sure her long-awaited visa finally came through. She has carried our household several times and, along with my father, done bas-ket after basket of laundry, among other things. So to all of you, THANK YOU, for the beautiful love and tireless support you have given over the years, and particularly as I have worked to complete this book.

"Sathima"

Sathima Bea Benjamin is undoubtedly
a great jazz singer and composer.

She had that rare quality of being able to interpret and
articulate the deeper nuances of lyric and melody with a natural
and impeccable sense of rhythmic timing.

She imparts to a listener — in understated tones — her life's
experiences — love, pain, social commitment — a constant reminder
of elusive, innate hidden beauty within everything.

An arduous path to follow — for those who choose it —
not expecting anything in return — only the constant striving
for excellence and unattainable perfection.

17 February 2009

This book/life and music is all very overwhelming for me, for it has been in some way (for me anyway) a trip about my own take on what it is to live intuitively, and one thing leading to another. All the time it works like that. In my life and this story, I have not been afraid of being honest and so totally dedicated to this music. The music has stood by me, and kept me strong and inspired—most of all—liberated me from all that is mundane and ordinary in this life.

The music within, our expression as song, my own compositions or so-called jazz standards have given me my own understanding of *Freedom*. It presents endless ways to improve your imagination and talent. I have been blessed with a big dollop of courage to take risks, and because it comes from my heart, so deep within, I trust my instincts without question and live intuitively. I make sure that if the compositions are not mine and I'm singing someone else's song that if the composer heard it, he or she would not mind the little changes I make and would be pleased.

The musicians I choose to record or perform with are those I'm sure will let me into their hearts and minds and let the music touch and affect them. That way they go with me into their musical echoes—my home within—and the call and response, which is the basis of this music, comes into play. That, I believe, is how the quartet I put together—the trio and me—becomes one beautiful voice.

—Sathima Bea Benjamin to Dr. Carol Muller, 20 November 2005
"For BOOK to be written sometime-SOON"

.

Beginnings

It was a simple telephone call at a highly charged moment of South Africa's political history that made this book possible: hoping for an interview I called the home of the South African jazz pianist Abdullah Ibrahim in New York City on 9 February 1990, three days after State President F. W. de Klerk had announced he would lift the ban on South Africa's "liberation movements"—the African National Congress (ANC), the South African Communist Party, and the Pan-Africanist Congress. The release of perhaps the most famous political prisoner of the twentieth century, Nelson Rolihlahla Mandela, seemed imminent. Stunned by the sudden reversal of apartheid policy, hundreds had gathered at Riverside Church in New York City on 6 February to celebrate a moment few had believed they would see in their lifetimes. Several South African musicians who had lived for decades in cultural and political exile outside of South Africa performed at the church that evening. Ibrahim was there, and so was his wife, the jazz singer Sathima Bea Benjamin. She answered the phone when I called to speak to Abdullah: he was in India.

I first came to know the music of Abdullah Ibrahim (earlier known as Dollar Brand) in an undergraduate seminar run by Christopher Ballantine, then a Marxist musicologist of rare vision and courage at the University of (KwaZulu) Natal in 1984. Ibrahim and his music were banned in South Africa at the time, along with that of Miriam Makeba, Hugh Masekela, Sathima Bea Benjamin, and others. But we listened to some of their music in the early 1980s in Durban, South Africa, and read about many of its makers in that seminar. The learning was partial because there was scant recognition of women in South African or any other jazz history in that period. Looking back, I realize that the listening was also always comparative—everything South African was heard in relation to jazz generated in the United States. While the University Music Library held the long-playing (LP) records in its collection, we students were not permitted to listen to these supposedly dangerous sounds at will. Close accounting was kept of every track each student listened to. Officially, we were not permitted to make copies of the records. Unofficially, however, I recall obtaining duplicates of Abdullah's music and spending an entire weekend listening closely to the tapes. I read the short pieces written about his early life and specifically his conversion to Islam. Here was a South African whose music and spirituality were inextricably intertwined: he had found a way to make his Muslim belief work musically. This seemed an unusual position in the world of Islam.[1] I emerged from that solitary weekend mesmerized by the music and creative output of a man I imagined would be impossible to ever meet in person. In retrospect, I realize that this is probably how Sathima felt about Duke Ellington when she first heard and fell in love with his music in Cape Town, never dreaming she would actually come to know him, let alone record with him.

In 1989, as a graduate student at New York University, I took a seminar with the jazz historian Lewis Porter, who required his students to visit the Institute of Jazz Studies at Rutgers University in Newark, New Jersey, in order to construct discographies and biographies of jazz musicians. I selected three non-Americans, the South Africans I knew best: Abdullah Ibrahim, Hugh Masekela, and Miriam Makeba. Tied to Ibrahim's files were those of Sathima Bea Benjamin. I was aware that these two musicians were living in New York City, but I also remembered from my South African jazz seminar in 1984 that Ballantine had warned that they (or any people of color) would not talk with white South Africans. Longing for some kind of contact and hoping to gather more materials on these musicians without being intrusive, I found a telephone number in Sathima's files for Ekapa, the name of the independent record label she and Ibrahim established in the 1980s to distribute her recordings. I called the number. "Salaam," a deep, male voice responded. I am not sure who I thought would answer, but this was not the voice. "Is that Ekapa Records?" I asked nervously. Suddenly I realized that the voice on the other end *was* that of Ibrahim. Independent labels are often run from musicians' homes — how had I not made that connection earlier? He proceeded to interrogate me: suspicion characterized many of the encounters between South Africans across racial divides, even those abroad. At the end of the call, Ibrahim promised to call me back a few days later, which he did. Perhaps satisfied that I was not a South African government informer or a member of the CIA, we agreed to meet a week or so later in the Green Room after one of his performances at Avery Fisher Hall in Lincoln Center.

Meeting Abdullah Ibrahim in person was an awesome moment—something I never really believed would happen, and it took place in the presence of many exiled South African musicians and theater people who also came to the Green Room to meet the pianist. I recall waiting right to the end and letting everyone else who seemed to know Ibrahim personally, greet him before me. After about an hour, I finally came face to face with the man whose music had so deeply moved me in South Africa several years before. It was close to 1 A.M. by then. I left Lincoln Center and ran back to catch the last train out of the city that evening amazed that I had finally come to meet Abdullah Ibrahim in person.

We could never have imagined it would be less than a year before we would gather again in such a radically transformed political moment. In stark contrast to the feeling of uncertainty and fear that had characterized my first conversations with Ibrahim by telephone in 1989, we embraced on the street outside Riverside Church in February 1990, unsure about the future as South Africans but holding onto the possibilities of freedom that had opened up with de Klerk's globally disseminated message earlier that day. Nine months after my seminar assignments were due Ibrahim agreed to talk. He suggested I call the following week.

Just before Sathima answered the phone when I called to speak to her husband she had spoken with someone from the ANC's culture desk, and she was angry because it seemed as if those organizing the anti-apartheid events in exile had slighted her, again. They regularly invited Abdullah to represent the liberation struggle abroad, but she, they said, didn't sound "African enough," and she performed with American musicians. She insisted (and her story told here demonstrates) that she had paid her dues with the ANC, working and performing for them while she lived in exile in New York City. At first I thought her marginality in anti-apartheid musical events was linked to her musical style—she is so clearly a jazz singer, and jazz after all is American music. I have come to understand (as I explain in this book) that the exclusions might equally be about racial identities, about gender, and about the language she sings in: she is of mixed race, or what the apartheid regime classified as Cape Coloured, she is a woman singer, and she sings in English rather than in one of the more exotic-sounding African languages popularized internationally by Makeba.

Still holding the phone, I did some quick thinking. I was becoming

2. Sathima in her apartment at the Hotel Chelsea, 1991.

3. Sathima and Carol at Penn Station, July 2010.

Both photos by Carol Ann Muller.

more interested in the untold story of women musicians, and this was probably not a good moment to ask to speak to her husband. "Abdullah told me to call this week, but since he is away, I wonder if you would talk with me about your music?" I asked. "When?" she replied. "Whatever works for you," I said, stunned that she was so willing. We agreed on a time and a place. "You may not bring a tape recorder," she stressed. "You may not record this interview. You must ask me the questions, come with questions. Meet me at the Chelsea, and we can go together from there."

I spent the rest of the week scouring my files — these were pre–World Wide Web days — figuring out what I needed to know and what questions I wanted to ask. Early in March 1990 I went to the Hotel Chelsea on West 23rd Street with a list.[2] Once we were seated in a neighborhood diner I asked my first question. There was scant need for further inquiry: Sathima Bea Benjamin had an extraordinary story to tell, and she was an artful narrator. After about ninety minutes of listening I stumbled out into the street, my head swimming with words and images: some exhilarating, others drenched in pain and struggle. We had agreed to meet again. Thankfully, from then on Sathima allowed me to bring a recording device!

Finding Common Ground

Both Sathima Bea Benjamin and I spent our childhoods in Cape Town, a port city that has profoundly shaped our sense of place in the world. Nestled between the Cape Fold Mountains and the Indian and Atlantic oceans, Cape Town since the mid-seventeenth century has become home to people from a wide range of perhaps unexpected places, including Indonesia, Sudan, Turkey, India, China, Russia, and Europe. All have come and intermingled with the Khoisan- and Xhosa-speaking peoples who traversed the mountains and coastline of the Cape.

Despite our common point of origin our engagement with Cape Town was fundamentally different. Sathima was born Beatrice Benjamin in 1936, twelve years before what became known as the apartheid government came to power. That was the year my parents were born. I was born in Cape Town in 1963, just shy of three years after the infamous Sharpeville massacre and a year after Sathima had left for Europe. The 1960s was the decade of what has become known as grand apartheid, in which the laws put in place from 1948 through the end of the 1950s were implemented. The Group Areas Act was the centerpiece of this era. The act legislated that all people of the same race or "tribe" or both were to live together in the same place, and those South Africans who were of the so-called wrong race or tribe were to be forcibly removed to the right places. It effectively denied citizenship in white South Africa to all people of color, requiring them to live in their own homelands, or Bantustans, unless they were employed in so-called white areas. A host of additional laws supported the basic idea of separate development, including the Mixed Marriages Act, the Immorality Act, the Color Bar Act, the Land Act, the Pass Laws, and the Separate Amenities Act. I was born into that world of grand apartheid.[3]

While there are many places Sathima and I remember in common, racial difference fundamentally informed our knowledge and understanding of the world. Born white, I grew up in a working-class suburb called Mowbray in the period after those classified as Coloured had been moved from Mowbray to other parts of the city. Sathima's home, the one originally owned by her grandmother Ma Benjamin, was in a more respectable suburb, but it was on the wrong side of the railroad tracks, that is, the Coloured side. The Benjamin family lost their home under the Group Areas Act. A few years ago Sathima returned to Cape Town and went to find that home. She struggled to identify the exact house because, though she knew the road, when she was young the houses had been identified by name and now they were numbered. Since her family had been forced to sell the house and leave the area under Group Areas legislation the house had had a makeover. Their neighborhood had been "Chelseafied" and become a place for middle-class whites only.

Though we came to live in New York City for different reasons — I for graduate school, Sathima because that was where Duke Ellington had suggested she and Abdullah would be able to survive playing the kind of jazz they did — both of us carried vivid memories of and love for the sheer beauty of Cape Town, the Mother City. New York City is equally cherished for its sheer size, energy, and sense of possibility it gives to artists, intellectuals, and musicians. To Sathima New York is a vast urban space she has come to know and love because of the lived experiences she has etched upon its landscape. It is the "ultimate in freedom," she says. You can be as connected to or as distant as you want to be from the thousands of people walking in the streets each day. My own knowledge and love of New York is similarly marked by a profound sense of the freedom to be, but it has also been formed by the many conversations I have had with Sathima and the rare, remarkable performances I have witnessed featuring her and her trio over the years. When I taught at New York University, Marymount College in Tarrytown, New York, and, more recently, at the University of Pennsylvania, Sathima has visited my classes. Over the years we have spent many hours in recorded and telephone conversations. We have both subsequently returned to South Africa on numerous occasions, each of us pulling out our very distant recollections of a bygone era, united in travel by our common love of jazz, particularly in its South African inflections.

When Sathima suggested to me in 1995 that we write a book together, I jumped at the idea. "Women writing culture" at last—a joint project on which we could work in partnership to write the book and fulfill the ideals expounded in the seminal text *Writing Culture* (1986), and the gendered response to that book, *Women Writing Culture* (1996) and their offspring. Sathima could tell her story in the way she wanted to with the support of my research and publishing expertise. The idea seemed full of promise. Such a book, however, was not to be. Time, place, resources, family demands, and individual availability just never seemed to coincide to make it possible for Sathima and me to sit down together in the same room and write her story.

One should not despair, however, about the potential for collaborative scholarship between the scholar and the singer because in producing this book we have both had a hand in contributing to its content, in shaping it contours, and giving life to its story. Perhaps by default there has been a clear division of labor, each according to her realm of expertise. While I have done the usual scholarly things like record and transcribe interviews; read a vast corpus of primary materials and secondary literature on a wide array of subjects—from Islamic recitation through birthing narratives, cosmopolitanism, and forgiveness to race and historiography; write and present papers; talk to publishers; and produce this book, Sathima has done the talking, rehearsing, singing, recording, and packaging of her recordings. Several years ago she put me in touch with her family and friends in Cape Town and New York City. In 1996 Abdullah kindly drove me around Cape Town, from one home to the next in between calls to prayer, so I could interview her extended family from St. Helena and others who had known Sathima in her youth and early adult life. Sathima's sister Edie Green arranged all the interviews. I simply arrived to conduct them according to her program. The timing was fortuitous, as most of those I spoke with are no longer alive. I am forever indebted to Abdullah and Edie for their generosity and time.

Relative to other books, even those in the academic world, this one has been a long time in coming. Though my work with Sathima Bea Benjamin was my first major research project as a graduate student, I have completed three books on other materials in the interim principally because I have struggled to locate what the feminist philosopher Lorraine Code calls the appropriate "rhetorical space" for the kinds of material the research has generated (1995), a struggle often paralleled in Sathima's career as a musician in the world of jazz, and similar to my own as a scholar of this music. Since my move to the United States it has taken some time for me to find a scholarly voice that incorporates my own kind of diasporic living and experience into my writing and thinking about jazz.

Sathima has read and responded to everything I have written about her over the last twenty years. For the most part her responses have concerned factual corrections, and although I have pressed her to critique what I have written she has refrained from doing so. She has left the writing to me. When I completed a draft of three chapters of the book I mailed the work to Sathima in New York City in August 2006. About a week later she called and left a message on my cell phone. She told me she had taken the padded envelope and walked to the park close to the Hotel Chelsea, where she had sat alone and read the three chapters from start to finish. And she had wept. This woman who had her own catalog of recordings, was the founding director of her own record label, and a South African singer with Grammy recognition had been in tears because as she read she had been overcome by the material evidence, the written story of her life.

It is easy to devalue the singer by suggesting her tears were predictable, perhaps even inevitable: after fifteen years of conversations with me and ten years of waiting for a book version of them, here at last was the evidence that a monograph was in the making. As I have thought further about both Sathima's emotional response and its ramifications, I have come to a different understanding of the sentiments she expressed as she read the chapters about her life. Her tears, I think, speak to the sense of loss and alienation that typically accompany contemporary experiences of living in diaspora and political exile.

Listening to Sathima's Voice

For readers who have not heard Sathima singing live or do not own one of her recordings, her online music may begin to fill the gap. If you imagine an African singer, you may be surprised at what you hear, and you may initially have difficulty placing her. This seems to have been her struggle with the ANC's cultural organization, though her experience in the United States has not been that different: one prominent African American jazz musician dismissed her a few years back by saying she couldn't possibly come from South Africa. If she were singing jazz in this way, he told her, she must really be from the American Midwest or somewhere. When she and other South Africans traveled and performed in Europe in the 1960s and 1970s, there was the same lack of recognition. Seeing her in person, they have struggled to match her appearance with the stereotype of a South African: they have simply expected a more African sound or a darker complexion.

And yet Sathima's is a characteristically South African musical story. Like many of her generation, Sathima, after honing her vocal skills on white English and American "girl singers" of the 1940s, borrowed American-made jazz as her musical home in the late 1950s because it provided a space for the individual voice in a collective fabric, for expressive freedom, and for her growing political consciousness of the plight of people of color in South Africa and the world at large. I say *borrowed* because, as is amply demonstrated in this book, for Sathima and the music community she inhabited in the forties and fifties popular music, swing bands, the music of Ellington, and the more experimental jazz world were the acoustical discourses completely naturalized through radio, film, sound recordings, and live renditions of the American-derived repertory.

Since the late 1950s Benjamin has applied the principles of jazz performance to a peculiarly South African songbook, songs that intermingled in her home and community from the 1930s to the 1960s, drawn from local renditions of British music hall, American Tin Pan Alley, and, increasingly, her own compositions. This complicated identity of much music making in twentieth-century South African popular music and jazz performance is poignantly articulated in her LP *Memories and Dreams* (1983), her third recording on her Ekapa label. Side A contains her composition titled *Liberation Suite* comprising three separately composed pieces: "Nations in Me—New Nation A'Comin'," "Children of Soweto," and "Africa." Side B has four songs drawn from Hollywood musicals and jazz standards from the 1940s and popular in her youth. It is hard not to see her "memories" as American and the "dreams" as her originals, projecting forward to a new South African nation and society.

Tension between views of jazz and its ancestral repertories in or by South Africans as belonging versus being borrowed has plagued the composition, performance, and reception of Sathima's music, regardless of historical or physical location. Because she and others left South Africa in the early 1960s, her story is not always remembered or recognized in contemporary South Africa. In reality, much of her energy in exile in the United States from the mid-1970s on has been spent trying to help the larger jazz world see the connections between the pasts in jazz from a U.S. perspective and those from its distant musical kin in the southernmost part of the African continent.

Proving legitimate membership of the African diaspora has been a part of that struggle: Sathima Bea Benjamin's is a voice that is incessantly in exile. Over the years she has wrestled with the lack of a clear sense of place in the world of jazz. As a result, each of her recording projects, and the words she spins around them, tells a piece of her story. And in many ways this book is written in response to the persistent confusion listeners and musicians express in terms of who she is, where she comes from, and what she chooses to sing.

2

A Home Within

Recollecting a Musical Past

Guthrie P. Ramsey Jr. introduces *Race Music* (2003), his collection of essays on African American music, with a personal narrative about the musical memories of his childhood and young adult life in Chicago with his extended family. Ramsey says he reflects on his past so that his readers might understand the questions he strives to address in the book. There is surely a larger issue: the reality that many people remain ignorant about the kinds of musical experiences that might have characterized those of African American families in the mid-twentieth century.[1] His past is not as self-evident as one might presume, and it is this absence of a more broadly known archive of musical experience that propels Ramsey to insert his personal memories into a more generalized narrative. Looking back on that musical past in Chicago, Ramsey implies a fundamental difference in upbringing between himself and others in the American academy.

Like Ramsey's introduction, this chapter is a retrospective narrative about South African popular culture and ultimately jazz performance, constituted from the remembrances of Sathima Bea Benjamin, her family, and her friends from about the 1930s through the early 1960s. Sathima has lived an extraordinary life. It is a life that had humble beginnings but was nevertheless drenched in musically rich experiences. She has traveled more miles in her life than entire communities of people will collectively cover in a similar period of time. These experiences shaped who Sathima became as a singer, what repertory she selected to sing, and the manner in which her style and repertory continue to reflect a transnational and local sound in jazz, and they sustained her through years of displacement and travel. In other words, the narrative, while not comprehensive, is an original: there is no parallel account of popular music and jazz performance in Cape Town in the postwar era.[2] Whether she liked it or not, as a woman classified as Cape Coloured in postwar South Africa, the personal has become deeply implicated in the political. Had she been born in another moment of South African and African American history, her story may well have been strikingly different.

The goal in writing this chapter and the next is not to constitute a definitive historical account so much as to provide one solution to the challenge of writing a past for non-American jazz in places that do not have large recorded archives but that rely instead on personal memories and local print media for constructing narratives of a past in jazz. In the words of Abdullah Ibrahim, in South Africa "generations of information have been lost" through death, destruction, and a desire by the apartheid state to suppress all activity that promoted interracial interaction.[3] This is one attempt to recuperate such knowledge. It tells one story about the emergence of jazz as a way of life, as an approach to musical performance, a form of political consciousness, and indeed as one piece of a global history of style.

This call outlines the story of Sathima's early life in Cape Town (1936–62), and it is divided into three large parts. The first introduces Cape Town and its history as one implicated in South Africa's peculiar ties to sea routes and slave trades. The second is centered on live performances and the radio in Sathima's grandmother's home; and the third is concerned with school, film music, and live dance band performances in public places. In many ways chapters 1 and 2 provide the most cohesive sense of place and community in the book because despite the traumas of apartheid—forced removals and the destruction of communities inside South Africa—the story is located in identifiable places: Cape Town and Johannesburg (briefly), with a few shorter excursions to other cities in southern Africa.[4] Once she leaves the country in 1962 it becomes more challenging to narratively reconstruct her life chronology, and it is in this context that she begins to imagine the contours of her musical upbringing for the world at large as a "home within." She does so in response to the constant pressure to justify herself as a singer of jazz who came from South Africa and not the United States.

Describing the City

Cape Town is a beautiful place, with mountains, the sea, a perfect climate, exotic birds, flora and fauna, and gorgeous sunrises and sunsets. There seemed to be music in the air, always. Is that possible, or is that just the memory I carry? — Sathima Bea Benjamin to Lee Hildebrand, 25 January 1987

There was music everywhere. First you would hear the horses coming down the street and then you'd hear them shouting, "Aartappels en uiwe" (potatoes and onions). They're singing the price and everything. There was always so much music, people just using their voices naturally. It was everywhere. — Sathima Bea Benjamin, 16 March 1990

Those who visit Cape Town, the port city in the southernmost part of the African continent, cannot help feeling in awe of the sheer physical beauty of the place. Situated in the area where the Indian and Atlantic oceans meet, the Cape and surrounding coastline have been explored and written about since the Portuguese first encountered it in the late fifteenth century, though Bushmen paintings and archeological findings in the interior mountain ranges point to a much older history of human presence in the area. Founded as a refreshment station called the Cape of Good Hope by the Dutch East India Company in 1652, the city is nestled between the ocean and the mountains. Those who live in the city have long demonstrated enormous pride in belonging to and coming from this place. For many who were born there in the 1930s and 1940s and who left during the apartheid era, Cape Town is also remembered as being a place filled with melodious strains, not just on stage or over the radio but in the streets themselves. This memory of the vibrancy of the musical sensibility of Cape Town is reflected in the wide range of acoustical activity written about and advertised in South African newspapers of the time.

The cosmopolitan and creolized nature of Cape society as it developed from the mid-seventeenth century to the present is complex and instructive. The major European forces that colonized and inhabited the Cape were the Dutch, the English, the French, the Portuguese, and the Germans, although until 1948, when the Afrikaner Nationalist government took power, it was largely the Dutch and English (1795–1803 and

1806 until 1910, respectively) who competed for control of what has become the city of Cape Town. Both were seeking a halfway house on the
sea route from Europe to the East. While Cape Town's liberal tradition
has a reputation among some for being more tolerant than other places,[5]
the cultural and political history of the city is nevertheless woven out of
narratives of slavery, colonial immigration, the decimation of indigenous
peoples through warfare and disease, an ongoing interaction between
Islam, Christianity, and indigenous beliefs, racial and nationalist power
struggles, and the emergence of the South African language of Afrikaans
and of annual rites of celebration.[6]

Family Ties

Beatrice Benjamin, often called Beatty by friends and family, and later
changed to Sathima was born to Edward Charles Benjamin and Evelyn
Henry in Johannesburg on 17 October 1936. Edward had gone to Johannesburg to find work, so when she was seven months pregnant Evelyn
boarded the train in Cape Town and headed north to join him there.
Baby Beatty was born in Johannesburg more than a month early and
weighed just four and a half pounds. "You were born like Jesus," Sathima's
mother later told her. "We had no clothes for you." The woman who
ran the boardinghouse where Evelyn was staying had torn a sheet into
long strips and wrapped the newborn baby in swaddling clothes. Disappointed that she was not a boy, Sathima's father refused to look at her for
the first two weeks. When he did finally look, he saw a similarity between
his new daughter and his sister, also named Beatty. So the newborn was
named Beatrice, later shortened to Bea.

Little is known about the family heritage of Sathima's mother, Evelyn
Henry. Sathima's maternal grandmother, Francesca de la Cruz, was of
Filipino descent. She had come to Kimberly with the diamond rush in
the 1880s or 1890s. Traveling by boat, she would have landed in Cape
Town and probably met her husband Robert Henry in the port city on
her way to Kimberly. They married and had two children, Robert and
Evelyn. Both parents died in the influenza epidemic of 1918, and their
orphaned children were sent to live with an Aunt Connie in Cape Town.
Aunt Connie and Sathima's grandmother Eva Thwaites Benjamin were

close friends, which is how Edward and Evelyn met. Evelyn became pregnant, and his mother insisted Edward marry Evelyn.

Theirs was a turbulent marriage. Only after the birth of Bea, Joan, and a younger son, Maurice (who died as a child), did Evelyn realize her husband, something of a ladies' man, had been having an affair with another woman for many years. Sathima recalls waking up in the middle of the night when she was about four years old. A violent storm was raging outside the house. She was lying next to her baby sister Joan, and her mother had gone to find her husband. The two girls were terrified and huddled together. Evelyn Henry remained out all night until she found her husband at the home of his longtime lover, Hettie van Vuuren. Evelyn decided to leave Edward, escaping with the three children. They walked all the way from Claremont to Athlone, where she had a friend, Aunt Helen, who took them in. Edward Benjamin wouldn't divorce her, so she got pregnant again, this time with Edward Green. Sathima's father reluctantly agreed to divorce her mother, after kidnapping the three children one afternoon while they were playing outside their home in Athlone. The case went to court, where the judge ruled that Evelyn Henry was too poor to take care of her three children. They were put in the custody of their father and his girlfriend Hettie van Vuuren, who then became his new wife. Evelyn married a second time and in her two marriages bore eight children, two of whom died in childhood.

Sathima recalled quite unexpectedly, as the memory flashed before her in a diner in New York in 2008, that her new stepmother, Hettie van Vuuren, "was half white, German. I don't know where my father found her. I had a wicked stepmother, and that story must be told." Her voice choked as the images came back. "Nobody will believe it, but how could I make it up—like having your hands and feet tied at night?" Hardly able to utter the words, Sathima spoke in whispered tones as she remembered that the wicked stepmother would come into Joan's and her rooms at night, after they were in bed. Their father wasn't the kind of man who came to say goodnight. He would see them at the dinner table. Joan would have bruises on her body or a black eye, and occasionally her father would ask what had happened to her. She was a strong-willed child, and they often attributed her wounds to her supposedly difficult personality. But, Sathima remembered, it was the wicked stepmother. There were high walls at the house. The stepmother would push Joan off the walls and

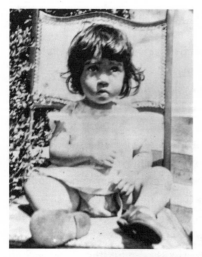

4. Sathima Bea Benjamin as a baby.

5. (*left to right*) Sathima, her sister Joan, and a cousin.

Both collection of Sathima Bea Benjamin.

then tell the father she had fallen down. "She would push us down, then tell us we were naughty children. We weren't naughty, it was she who hurt us."

Sathima paused. "I can't remember everything, but she had a ritual with us, a way that started early in the morning. More happened to Joan than to me, but she made me watch. She would tell me I must count while she hit Joan with a skipping rope or a piece of wood. My father was a carpenter and he used to bring the wood home. I had to count. It was supposed to be a hundred strokes, though I never got that many." This pattern of abuse continued until the school contacted Child Welfare. Joan continually arrived at school with bruises and marks on her body. One day Sathima was called into the principal's office and asked what was going on at home. She was too afraid to say anything for fear of the stepmother's retribution. "She would tell us, if we told anybody what she did she would kill us. She would get a bread knife and pretend to cut Joan's head off. I used to stand there and think I would see her head come off. What would make me think that this wouldn't happen if I told them about her? I was only seven or eight years old." They assured Sathima she would be protected. In fact, Sathima remembers that their story was reported in a local newspaper. Child Welfare arranged for the two girls to move out of their father's house and live with their paternal grandmother, Ma Benjamin, who had a large house in the middle-class but racially segregated suburb of Claremont in Cape Town. Sathima was nine years old.

On occasion Sathima and Joan would visit their mother, Evelyn, on Sunday afternoons. She lived some distance away from Claremont in a small apartment in Kew Town, in the historically Coloured area of Athlone. Losing their mother and going to live with their stepmother had a profound impact on the two girls. And it almost broke their mother's heart. But Evelyn Green (nee Henry) was a fighter, even if she often had to pay the price for her very tenacious personality.[7] The loss of the girls' mother at such a tender age made Sathima determine that when she had children of her own she would always be there to care for them, a resolution that would have an impact on her career once she moved to New York City in the late 1970s. "I wanted very fiercely to be a mother because I didn't have one, she didn't raise me and wasn't there," she recalled in April 2006.

Life improved significantly with the move to Ma Benjamin's because

6. Benjamin family, Sathima as a baby held by Ma Benjamin.
Collection of Sathima Bea Benjamin.

the home was filled with extended family — several of the girls' aunts and uncles boarded with the older woman. In her sixties at that time, Ma Benjamin had raised ten children on her own after her husband died. "I am very old-fashioned," Sathima reminds me, "and I got that from Ma Benjamin. She taught me to stay the course and finish whatever I started." Ma Benjamin was not an emotionally demonstrative woman, but she loved the girls in a "Ma Benjamin sort of way," and she certainly never beat them. "Nobody ever asked how you were feeling," Sathima recalled, but she felt safe in the household, and that she valued. "My grandmother was very strict, very British in her ways, and very dark in complexion." The girls were taught to be subservient to men, to cook and clean in the afternoon after school. Sathima, who was more compliant than Joan, had the inside chores, and Ma Benjamin taught her to cook traditional St. Helenian dishes like tomato bredie and potato stew. Joan, who was more rebellious, worked outside feeding the chickens and weeding and watering the garden. It is quite striking that these early domestic patterns shaped how the girls would imagine themselves as adults. Sathima, who was always in the kitchen and listening to music on the radio, still inhabits that realm, and Joan works in a flower shop.

The weakness in the Benjamin family was gambling on horses at the Kenilworth racetrack. Every Thursday night Ma Benjamin would send Sathima to the corner store run by the Muslims, who never gambled themselves, to buy the horse-racing book for the week. On Friday nights she had to cut the racing tips out of the newspaper. "Ma Benjamin never read the newspaper, she bought it for gambling," said Sathima. On Saturday mornings, all the working adults in the family would pay Ma Benjamin for board and lodging, a good portion of which would be gambled on the horses. Every Saturday afternoon Ma Benjamin would dress herself—she cut quite a stunning figure in the young girl's mind—and Sathima, Joan, and her cousins would be sent to the movies while their grandmother made her way to the racetrack.

It was often the house money that was gambled away at the track. "That was when I learnt to buy on credit," Sathima reflected. "If Ma Benjamin's bets were unsuccessful, I would have to go to the local store—like Wellingtons—for food and ask to pay the next week. Everyone in the neighborhood knew Ma Benjamin because she was the woman people called when someone died. She would lay them out and see them off. She would say, 'I've got to go and see so-and-so off.' My mother had that role too, it must be a gift." Ma Benjamin was not the only one who gambled; Sathima's father inherited the habit. The girls knew when he won big because he would go out and buy a new car. It was always a Chevrolet, though the cars were reserved for his girlfriends. Neither Sathima nor Joan recalls ever riding with their father.

Schooling for Coloured children in Cape Town in the 1940s was limited to what the Christian missions provided, even in Claremont. Sathima remembers very little from her early schooling except another traumatic experience. Because they could not afford public transport many Coloured children would walk to and from school. One afternoon Sathima was walking home alone, taking her time as she wandered across a field close to Ma Benjamin's house that had wild berries she loved to eat. Lingering a little, she was suddenly confronted by a man who began to molest her. She panicked and screamed loudly enough that a couple walking by took notice and intervened before the man could rape her. Like many young girls who were molested, Sathima never told anyone at home what had happened for fear of getting into trouble for walking home too slowly.

Sathima's memories of her secondary school days resonate with those of many others classified as Cape Coloured because there were only two high schools for Coloured students in Cape Town in the 1940s: one in District Six, near the city center, and the other, Livingstone High, in Claremont. Livingstone High continues to occupy a significant place in educating Cape Town's youth. Founded in 1926 by concerned parents and leaders of the Coloured community, it started off in three stables renovated as classrooms for seventh grade students. Formed in defiance of the British and then of the apartheid government's neglect of Coloured education, Livingstone educated many leaders, artists, and intellectuals from the start.[8] When Sathima and Joan joined the school, many of its teachers were politically active, questioning the increasing discrimination meted out by the apartheid regime toward their communities.[9]

Sathima met Ruth Fife, who would become a close friend, at Livingstone. The Fife household was Sathima's first encounter with a politically engaged family. Ruth's family descended from both St. Helenians and the Scottish. She remembers that Ruth's brother was a teacher at Livingstone. He was in a relationship with a woman of Indian descent, an illegal partnership under the Immorality Act of 1950. He was arrested and forced into exile because he and others had been handing out leaflets on the streets of Cape Town in protest against the Van Riebeeck Day celebrations held annually on 16 April until 1990.[10] Sathima studied at Livingstone through the tenth grade, and when she left the school, it gave her a Jaycee certificate that entitled her to enter the Battswood Teachers' Training College in Wynberg, one of the few institutions of tertiary education available to Coloured students at the time.[11]

Sathima was the first woman in her family to go to teachers' college, and she remembers how supportive Ma Benjamin was. If she was studying she was relieved of her household chores, a privilege few others were given. Ma Benjamin was extremely proud of her granddaughter—everyone else in the family was an upholsterer, cabinetmaker, or factory worker. Sathima would become a teacher. She attended Battswood until she completed her teaching certification, at which point she started working at a school in Athlone, close to where her mother lived.

The longing to be with their mother became acute for Sathima and Joan in their teenage years. Joan always seemed to be in trouble with her father, so she was the first to leave the Benjamin household and go to live with her mother in Kew Town. Sathima followed soon after. She remembers the day she went to tell Ma Benjamin she had decided to live with her mother. Ma Benjamin didn't express much emotion, but it was clear the older woman was devastated. Sathima, after all, had become indispensable to her grandmother: for eight or nine years she had been her daily household help, cooking, cleaning, caring for, and supporting the older woman. Her departure would be deeply felt. Struggling to hold back the tears and feeling torn by her decision, Sathima knew she had to go.

Overwhelmed by her unresolved anger toward the wicked stepmother and by the guilt of leaving Ma Benjamin, a guilt reinforced by her father, who was angry that she had left, Sathima had a nervous breakdown. She cried uncontrollably for weeks on end. Eventually her mother took her to a doctor, who recommended Sathima leave town for a few weeks to recover. She was sent to her mother's extended family, still living in Kimberley. The aunts and uncles were kind to the young woman, and she began to heal. One of her friends from Cape Town, Mary McGregor, who later left South Africa for Australia, visited her while she was in Kimberley. After three months away, she was able to return to Cape Town. She no longer felt the need to harm Hettie van Vuuren. Further, by that time she was beginning to move into the wider jazz community. Jazz would become the agent of the young woman's healing and recovery.

Sathima never returned to live in the Benjamin home because the family subsequently lost the house when Claremont was declared a suburb for whites only, markedly increasing the sense of loss and longing among Cape Town's Coloured community. Ma Benjamin refused to allow the government to take her house and decided to sell it herself. Family members dispersed to various parts of Cape Town, but no one moved out to the Cape Flats, where the state provided housing for the Cape Coloureds forced to move. With the idea she will return to South Africa to live out her last days, Abdullah purchased an apartment for Sathima in the historically white part of Claremont, an important mechanism for reclaiming a place for herself in postapartheid South Africa.

Music at Home

There is only a small body of writing about Coloured social life and music making in twentieth-century Cape Town, most of it centered around the city and District Six specifically.[12] Located on the perimeters of the city, District Six was a cultural space that paralleled Harlem in New York City with its historical mix of working-class immigrant, freed, and indigenous peoples. District Six was razed in the 1960s, and its varied communities moved into areas outside the city assigned by the Group Areas Act. People's memories of the place, its mix of people and vibrant sense of belonging and cultural experimentation, are often tinged with a deep nostalgia and pain for the devastating loss of community.[13] Stories that are told about District Six invoke a particular kind of cosmopolitan sensibility, one generated by the extraordinary range of people living in that inner-city community, including Russians, Germans, Jews, Muslims, Christians, Xhosa-speaking people, and Coloureds.[14] Located close to the harbor, District Six was a social space that lent itself to racial, cultural, class, and gender crossovers, and people recall the openness to and tolerance of difference. Some have suggested that the district created a prototype of what South Africa could have been without apartheid.

Growing up Coloured and St. Helenian in Claremont, Sathima was shaped by a cosmopolitan sensibility that was distinctively English rather than, as in District Six, racially and linguistically mixed in orientation. Correspondingly, those who have written about St. Helenians on the island argue that this small community remains the most loyal of all British subjects to the British Crown. Clinging to English ways through a language of respectability, civility, and culturedness were mechanisms St. Helenians in the 1940s and 1950s harnessed to keep themselves as far as possible from the domination of Afrikaner nationalism, the language of Afrikaans, and the politics of mixedness and hybridity that being classified Coloured in Cape Town invoked.

English culture was well represented in live and mediated forms in the Benjamin household. Sathima recalls, for example, that as a young girl she heard and sang early twentieth-century British popular music with the St. Helenian part of her family who gathered at Ma Benjamin's house in the forties and fifties. On Friday nights the adults played gin rummy together, while Sathima and Joan made savories in the kitchen: crackers with tomato and cheese, fish paste, and sardines, which they served until late into the night. On Sunday nights, family members sang the popular songs of the 1920s and 1930s, accompanied on the piano by a family member.

During the week, while she undertook her household chores, cooking, cleaning, and ironing in the kitchen, Sathima remembers hearing Ma Benjamin humming the old British tunes she played on a phonograph she had in the house. Many of these melodies, like "Ah! Sweet Mystery of Life" and "The Roses of Picardy" had been popular in Ma Benjamin's youth: they derived from light operetta and British music hall repertories. Occasionally, the family would gather for a more spirited celebration and dance the night away to the sounds of these old tunes streaming out of the gramophone.

Sunday was the day Sathima and Joan participated in another repertory of English and American-derived music: that of the Wayside missionaries who held Sunday school classes in Ma Benjamin's garage. All the neighborhood children attended Sunday school with Sathima, Joan, their cousins, and the two white missionaries from America.[15] After lunch the children would join the congregation for the eventide service at the St. Savior's Anglican Church in Claremont.[16] Sathima recalls the wonderful melodies of the old English hymns "Onward Christian Soldiers," "The Church's One Foundation" (which she now hears in her mind as a jazz tune), and "Joy, Joy, Joy, With Joy My Heart Is Ringing." Though Ma Benjamin never attended, she insisted that the girls go regularly to church.

While many who attended St. Savior's remember that the church community included people from a wide range of backgrounds in terms of race, class, and nationality, Sathima's recollections of the church are bittersweet.[17] She fulfilled her church duties until she was about fifteen. Typical of both cinemas and churches in Cape Town at the time, seating arrangements were segregated inside St. Savior's church building. Whites sat in the front and Coloured members sat farther back. One day Sathima decided she would sit in the forbidden white zone. Perhaps predictably, she was immediately informed that she should either move to the appropriate place for Coloureds or leave the building. Stunned by the cold reality of racism in the church community, Sathima left and never returned. A decade later, Coloured parishioners felt the same kinds of pressures to keep to their own communities, some left the church with forced removals, while others continued to travel in town for the Sunday services. In 1999 Sathima went back to that church with a Cape Town filmmaker to reflect on her experiences as a young woman and was once again denied permission to enter—this time because the pastor would not allow the filmmaker to record Sathima's experiences of discrimination on church property.

Once again, District Six provides a contrasting narrative. Several of the musicians I have interviewed recall the church there as being a more supportive, tolerant space.[18] The Cape Town librarian and former District Six resident Vincent Kolbe and the saxophonist Jimmy Adams both remembered the Catholic Church in District Six. Adams told me that in 1958 the jazz group at the Church of the Holy Cross in District Six used to run a weekly poll that measured audience opinion about the most outstanding players in the Cape.[19] Kolbe said that the church also hosted variety shows and talent contests and often functioned as a rehearsal and training space for aspiring dance band and jazz musicians.

Sathima was perhaps more fortunate than many of the jazz musicians she later performed with. For about two years her father paid for conventional piano and theory lessons for her and Joan. There were no teachers of jazz piano available to these young women—first, because it would not have been deemed a socially acceptable form of training for girls and, second, because most lessons were in syncopation (that is, a more British style of playing popular melodies) rather than in jazz per se. When her father left Cape Town for London in the late 1940s, the lessons stopped. Sathima recalls that she preferred to express herself in songs she had heard others singing rather than sitting at the keyboard reading music. The words and music of popular songs were her real passion, so the rest of her musical training was more compatible with that of her friends, most of whom were self-taught and learned by careful listening and imitation. In her late teens Sathima even took opera lessons, but the style did not appeal to her sense of a good singing voice. She found the vibrato too contrived, preferring what she calls a more natural-sounding voice.[20]

Kolbe tells quite a different story about his early musical training. He began to play an instrument when he was quite young simply because everyone around him did too, and there was always someone, a neighbor, a family member, or a friend, who played in the New Year's Coon Carnival. Instruments were plentiful in the community, and he remembers that musicians were more than willing to share their knowledge with neighborhood kids. You learned some chords or bass lines, and that prepared you to play on the weekends.[21] In a similar manner, Sathima's cousin Basil Rich first encouraged the young girl to sing. The extended Benjamin family often spent Christmas vacations together at the coast in tents on the Hout Bay and Kommetjie beaches. Basil would bring his guitar, and Sathima would sing. In those years the two Benjamin sisters, Sathima and Joan, formed a group called the Melody Five, with Vincent Hester, Neville de Vries (who was killed in a car accident while a member of the group), and another musician called James.[22] They performed whenever and wherever they could: at concerts, community events in churches, theaters, and in the town hall. Joan recalled their repertory was drawn largely from the radio and the old sheet music they found around the house.[23]

Sathima's first exposure to the European classical repertory was through the Fife household, where it was preferred over jazz and popular music. Yet Ruth Fife recalled that it was the music of Nat "King" Cole that opened up the world of American popular music to her mother.[24] As he was for the jazz pianist Henry February and others discussed later, Cole was the bridge between the world of European classics, light operetta, and American popular music of the postwar era. At home, however, Ma Benjamin would not allow the girls to listen to anything classical, as she wanted to hear only the popular tunes of the day.

The streets themselves were a source of all kinds of music, music made by people and by the natural environment. In addition to the tuneful renditions of men and women selling flowers, fish, and vegetables on the street, Christmas and New Year's were the times set apart in Cape Town for street processions and musical performances. Like her peers, Sathima would watch the live performances of Coloured street bands and choirs at Christmas time and over the New Year holidays. There were Malay choirs and brass bands called Christmas choirs and minstrel groups who are still known locally as the Coons. She remembers following the groups as they paraded through town between Christmas and New Year's. She was so engaged with the music she would get lost in the city as she did so. There was something so magical about these processions that musicians and followers alike often experienced the performances in trance-like states. S. D., an elderly retired fruit hawker from District Six, recalled, "I tell you, when we were little we would follow [the bands and choirs] to wherever they went . . . we would try to get near to them and walk with them. They sang up close to us. . . . I wanted to touch [them]. . . . They was something, really beautiful, they wasn't far away on radio. They was here, our choirs, singing for us."[25]

The impact of this music on the sounds and rhythms of dance band and jazz performance and on discourses about them is articulated in the ways in which musicians talk about dance band performances. For example, when the carnival troupes marched in the Coon Carnival from the center of the city, they had to walk directly uphill to Schotsche's Kloof. As they struggled up the steep incline, the bandleader would call to the group, "Heuwel op!" (Go up the hill!)[26] Kolbe explains that *heuwel op* translated musically: "It can mean 'heavy' or, musically it means you've got to really pump now because you're going uphill now . . . but I know the old band leaders on the dance floor would now shout to the band, 'Heuwel op!' Which means, you know, the drummer does something to the beat, you know. The after-beat is either sooner, or the after-beat is delayed. And that actually was reflected in the dance halls as well, in the movements. . . . This affected the way you created your rhythm and the way you created your melodies, you created your accompaniment and you arranged your instrumentation and things like that."[27] The Cape Town rhythm (*ghoema* or *klopse* rhythm, as it is known locally) has become a signature feature of many of the layers of sound created on recordings by Abdullah Ibrahim and Sathima Bea Benjamin as a key musical marker of individual history and a distinctive sign of musical place.[28]

Mediated Music

The Benjamin family network as well as others was deeply enmeshed in a range of live musical activities in the forties and fifties at home, at church, at school, and on the streets. But in the twentieth century an entirely new world began to form as a result of the worldwide dissemination of popular music through radio broadcast, popular films, and sound recordings. A song first heard in a movie on a Saturday afternoon might be heard repeatedly the following week. One might hear it again on radio, on record, and performed live in a cover version by local dance bands, in subsequent talent contests held at the cinema, and at fundraising events organized in churches and community halls. In the Benjamin household radio was the primary medium of foreign and local musical transmission.[29]

In 1950, when Sathima was fourteen years old, Springbok Radio, the first commercial radio station in South Africa, was initiated by the South African Broadcast Corporation (SABC). It broadcast in English and Afrikaans.[30] In 1952 a rediffusion service was established for broadcasting in three Bantu languages to the township of Soweto, west of Johannesburg. From the early 1960s a concentrated effort was made by the SABC to control the black population by infusing the airwaves with the kind of programming that would keep all listening very localized and traditional. By the mid-1960s the SABC provided regional services in several local languages, including Tswana, North Sotho, Zulu, Xhosa, Venda, and Tsonga.

It seems from what Sathima remembers that it was not to the local stations that the Benjamin household was tuned for their daily consumption of radio fare. She has suggested that they listened daily to the South African commercial station, Springbok Radio, or the BBC; it may also have been Lourenço Marques Radio (LM Radio) because Springbok Radio began broadcasting on 1 January 1950, at least five years after the young girls had moved into their grandmother's home. LM Radio, which beamed out of the capital city of Lourenço Marques (present-day Maputo) of neighboring Mozambique, was the primary format for popular music consumption in South Africa in the thirties and forties. Initiated in 1933, LM Radio was supported by South African interests from its earliest days. It broadcast largely in English and fostered a transnational community through its programming. First, LM Radio brought in personnel from numerous places around the world, Europe and Australia in particular. Many of these men and a few women had had wartime radio experience, had lived in a variety of countries, and had worked in a range of broadcasting organizations. Second, music was the mainstay of LM Radio programs. Under the direction of David Davies, LM Radio garnered considerable fame for the excellence of its popular music programming. Newspapers, magazines, and the radio shows of the postwar period regularly ran comparative tables of hit tunes on LM Radio, Springbok Radio, England, and the United States, meaning that listeners of these stations rarely inhabited a single geographical space in the virtual world constituted through the radio waves. Third, the regular programming of serials, the familiarity of the voices of announcers, and so forth produced clear messages of predictability, pleasure, and comfort. As a result many English-speaking South Africans who were not specifically interested in the SABC focus on apartheid ideology that infused its broadcast policy or in its focus on elite culture felt that LM Radio was all there was to listen to in the postwar era.[31]

These radio formats provided the kind of music and radio programming young Sathima absorbed every day of her childhood. While radio music constituted the background to household chores, Ma Benjamin never intended that the music be copied and performed in public, as her young granddaughters were doing without her knowledge. Sathima recalls that her grandmother would become so exasperated with the pull of radio music on her granddaughter that she would tell her to just get right inside the box! But Sathima knew she had to keep listening in order to create a repertory of songs for herself. From the age of about ten she used to keep a pen and notebook hidden in the windup gramophone cabinet so she could write the words of the songs she heard on the radio, phrase by phrase. She could not afford to buy the sheet music, sound recordings, or fake-books — books used by popular and jazz musicians to learn melody, text, and chord progressions — so she painstakingly copied the words and memorized the melodies of tunes as they were broadcast daily. When Sathima performed she always made her sister and cousins promise not to tell Ma Benjamin.

For this young girl living apart from her parents and often being reminded by the extended St. Helenian family of her status as a charity child, the popular songs of love and romance, even of broken hearts and desperation, sung by English and American women like Doris Day and Joni James provided affective pathways to a world beyond the local into which she escaped each afternoon. Coloured girls like herself were rarely allowed to move around the streets of Cape Town alone, and they spent the day doing domestic chores. In the kitchen, with the warmth of the sound streaming from the radiogram, Sathima and girls like her could daydream themselves into fantasies of familial love, warmth, and intimacy through the words and melodies of women they had never met but felt they knew by way of the airwaves transmitted directly into their homes.[32]

In addition to the radio and the windup Victrola in her grandmother's home, going to the cinema, or the bioscope, as it was more commonly known, was closely tied to Sathima's memories of family life with Ma Benjamin. The bioscope brought the magic of faraway people and places close to home. The first movie the young girl ever saw was Disney's *Snow White*, which she remembers seeing with the whole family. For the next seven or eight years Sathima accompanied her sister and cousins to the bioscope every Saturday.

The magical world of the cinema was the place to feast their eyes and to dream while they feasted on candy, potato chips, and *biltong* (dry, salted beef). "Saturday was your big day for the movies," Sathima explained. "That's where you would get your big dollop of American culture. I saw the musicals, the westerns. It was almost as if you had no choice. My grandmother went to the [horse] races, the whole big house closed down for the afternoon. . . . We had three movie houses: one was in Lansdowne, which wasn't too far, we had to walk. In Lansdowne it was called the Broadway, and Claremont was called the Orpheum, and Wynberg was the Gaiety."

Ma Benjamin never went to the movies, either with the children or with her friends. "She was a very strange woman," Sathima remembered:

> She went to the movies once in her life. She came back and she said, "What a waste of time, how stupid was that! A guy falls off his horse down the mountainside and he's still got his hat on his head. And I just slip over the step and I break my leg!" Ma Benjamin said the movies were far-fetched and never returned to the cinema. Actually, I remember when I was at Livingstone High School we did this play "San Merino Island," and I was a vampire. I was very pleased: I got my grandmother to come. It was performed at the Rondebosch Town Hall, and I said she must come. Ma Benjamin sat in the front, I was so proud. We were in this high school play. I had to pull my skirt up and pull the dagger and then I stabbed. My grand-mother was so upset. She said, "You had me go to this thing that was so ridiculous. I am not going to these things!" She was a horse-racing person.

For aspiring teenage performers like Sathima, Hollywood films were vivid models of popular performance by people of color. By going to the movies, Sathima and her friends deepened their knowledge of jazz and dance band performance specifically. *Cabin in the Sky*, starring Lena

Horne as the singer and Duke Ellington as the bandleader, and *Stormy Weather*, featuring a range of African American jazz performers and variety entertainers, were two of the most popular movies shown in South Africa in the mid-1940s. But there were many others in which people like Billie Holiday, Cab Calloway, and the Ink Spots appeared.

After the Second World War the bioscope came to play a central role in the life of Cape Town's Coloured communities.[33] In contrast to the more controlled audiences in white theaters[34] going to the movies was a ritualized, often boisterous communal activity in Cape Town's "dream palaces" in the mid-1940s to late 1950s. The historian Bill Nasson writes, "The local 'bioscope' was a place to which both adults and children went in order to be cocooned in the dream world of the flickering screen. Attendance was regular and habitual, as films continually widened their audience appeal and imaginative power to transport people out of themselves, and the humdrum confines of their work and domestic lives at least once a week. . . . While [cinemas] tended to be fairly small and unpretentious in appearance, their names, the Star, the West End, the Empire, the British Bioscope — dripped with the promise of glamour or old imperial splendor."[35]

Even though some theaters were segregated, and exclusively white theaters definitely more plush than those for Coloureds only, these were places where the entire community gathered. The cinemas were noisy because people often talked back in the middle of a movie. Sathima remembers that if one character was about to kill another, the audience would call out and warn of the impending assault. If a male character was cheating on a woman, the audience would offer sympathy and advice to the female character. Some would read the subtitles out loud for those who couldn't read. And audiences brought their children, even babies accompanied their mothers. Couples would kiss, and gangs would sometimes stage fights in the middle of the film. And there was the smelly food. Many brought fish and chips and other kinds of food with them. Some spent the entire evening at the movies. Kolbe remembers he would escort his mother to the movies. They would dress for the occasion and take a thermos of tea and sandwiches. The evening's program included a newsreel, cartoons, and two movies.

In the increasingly monitored public environment, the movies were perhaps the only space that allowed some freedom of social and romantic interaction between Cape Coloureds in Cape Town in the 1940s and 1950s. In no other contexts were young Coloured girls permitted to appear in public without their parents. With its mix of reality and fictional material, the program at the theater, much like television in the United States and Britain in the same period, kept the community in touch with the outside world. The darkness of the cinema allowed audiences to sit back and open their eyes to an otherwise inaccessible world of glamorous enchantment or else to keep them closed and to dream. The South African actor John Kani recalls "[sitting] in this dark place, and magic takes place on the wall. For a moment, we forgot apartheid, we forgot there was another world that wasn't good, we sat there and were carried away by the dream of these American movies."[36]

There was a well-established tradition among Coloured movie audiences in Cape Town in which live and mediated experience coexisted inside the walls of the theater. Audience members recall singing along with the popular songs that accompanied Tom and Jerry cartoons, for example. At the time, the words and music appeared on the screen, encouraging collective participation. "Just a Song at Twilight," a tune Sathima vividly remembers from her childhood, was one of these songs. Many local theaters also staged elaborate live variety acts and hosted talent competitions. The Gaiety Bioscope ran an advertisement in 1936 that read, "The Gaiety Bioscope will have a real Gala Week for their patrons and predict full houses. It is advisable to be early to secure seats. Chandu the Magician and the Western drama, Sharpshooter [will be the features]. . . . The Two Black Crows [clever, eccentric dancers and singers] in their tap dancing and singing will entertain in a clever interlude. . . . The Moffie Concert Party will appear on Wednesday evening."[37]

Sathima's First Talent Contest

Sathima entered her first talent contest at the Gaiety one Saturday afternoon (the contests took place during intermission). Urged to sing by Joan and her close school friends, Sathima made them promise that if she did so they would not tell Ma Benjamin. Sathima won. The prize was eight free tickets to the movies. This was the first of many talent contests she would enter in her teenage years in which she was awarded first prize. At the time she sang the popular songs of largely white singers like Doris Day, Joni James, and others. "Mr. Wonderful" and "Somewhere over the Rainbow" were her two signature tunes for admiring followers. Even though Sathima was singing a cover version of the song, Ruth Fife recalls that when she heard her at that first talent contest it was clear that even if she was using the words and melodies of others Sathima already had a distinctive style. Her lifelong friends Sam Isaacs, Henry February, and Jimmy Adams all agreed that the young singer had a sound of her own right from the start.

Film music was reenacted in local variety and talent shows as well. "You had Cape Town's Perry Como, Cape Town's Louis Armstrong. The moffies, the gays, always had Cape Town's Marilyn Monroe, Cape Town's Brigitte Bardot. It was all a kind of stage entertainment. Anytime a school or a church had a fundraising thing, the community would get up there and perform. You just had to," recalled Kolbe. The cinemas provided opportunities for working adults and children to make new music "or even [enjoy] the thrill of being lionized by local audiences as popular performers in their own right."[38]

Sathima suggests there were three levels at which American and British films shaped her individually and musically. She identified with child stars of the movies and recalls that her aunt even braided her hair in the style of girl stars of the period. Film culture inculcated a particular notion of romance and romantic love, one that, even if she was never to really find it in daily relationships, she could express desire for in song. For the young Sathima, the emotional force of romantic love she witnessed in the realistic images of the cinema was enhanced by the rich sounds of film melodies.[39]

Cape musicians also recall watching the occasional film about the lives of American jazz musicians in this period, though the pianist February was dismissive of the content: too much love, sex, and drugs and not enough music in the films, was his opinion. With great laughter he told me of a day when the Benny Goodman film was being shown in Cape Town. It must have been in the mid-1950s when Sathima was performing with February's Nat "King" Cole Trio. The guitarist Kenny Jephthah told February the film was showing at the Gem Theater nearby. "So we took a break—you know how long our break was? The whole *Benny Goodman Story!*"[40] Adams didn't remember watching very many films as a child and young adult, though he did remember seeing *The Glenn Miller Story* when it was showing in Cape Town.

Sathima carries in her memory a whole archive of tunes from radio, film viewing, live performances at home, and Saturday night dancehalls. She has incorporated them into a peculiarly South African version of the American songbook repertory popularized by Ella Fitzgerald, Vera Lynne, Sarah Vaughan, and Carmen McCrae in the mid-twentieth century: "You see, one thing about these melodies from the twenties and thirties, they were wonderful melodies. . . . Having grown up in Cape Town where I heard these melodies being played, you see, the melodies remain very real with me. They played in my head."[41] In 1999 she returned to Cape Town to record eleven of these songs with a Cape Town trio, but in a jazz rather than straight style of performance. Eight of the songs appear on *Cape Town Love* (1999) (see chapter 6 and www .africanmusicalechoes.org for streamed excerpts of the songs and liner notes).

Musicians and consumers in Cape Town listened to jazz and popular music with finely tuned ears and great expectations because for some the music made in America by African Americans, like jazz, signaled models and possibilities for musically imagining oneself part of a larger, international movement for political, racial, and economic equality and freedom. This was certainly true for individuals in the Coloured and black South African communities. For some, it was the sound of the music, the warm, even romantic sentiment of its texts, which initially captured their hearts and ears: it remained a music that brings pleasure to its listeners. For others, this foreign music disseminated locally in the postwar era in South Africa in its popular and jazz forms served to nurture the emotions and ultimately instill a political consciousness in many.

RESPONSE

Entanglement in Race and Music

Nations in me, I have so many nations in me;
Looking at my family tree, I can see that I'm the fruit of their love.
In the land of my birth they say you're of no worth

If you're black or have nations in you.
So much humiliation and pain, but we know it's their loss and our gain
For the struggle will not be in vain.
For there's a new nation a'comin'
There'll be no talk about color
We won't be concerned about race
For we're building a new nation with just one beautiful face.
—Sathima Bea Benjamin, *Memories and Dreams* (1983)

Taking a professional risk in New York City in the 1980s, Sathima wrote
the song "Nations in Me, New Nation A'Comin.'" It is one of the few explicitly political songs she has written (see chapter 5). Composed after
she had been living in exile for several years and more than two decades
in South Africa, "Nations in Me" speaks to the issue of being racially
mixed by subverting its common representation as shameful miscegenation. I heard "Nations in Me" on record when I first met Sathima, though
she has not sung the song at a single live event that I have attended in the
twenty years I have known her.

In this song Sathima's portrayal transforms shame into a humanity born
out of love, family, and lineage. The words honestly reflect on Sathima's
family history, a history the apartheid regime had made people of mixed
race ashamed to interrogate or make public.[42] The lyrics of Sathima's
song convey a powerful political and personal position: after the honest acknowledgment of her mixed racial heritage, she contrasts the positive perspective on her heritage with disdain of the apartheid regime, the
"humiliation and pain" inflicted on all people of color, whether of mixed
or African descent. And then the singer presents a vision of a new nation,
a vision few singers had the insight or courage to articulate musically in
the 1980s, but one consistent with ANC politics and its Freedom Charter:
a nonracial democratic nation with no talk of race or color.

Gesturing toward the humanity of all South Africans, Sathima meta-
phorizes the nation through the image of a single "beautiful face."[43] It
is significant that Sathima sings of both those who are black and those
who have "nations inside" because it resists the anti-apartheid position
of Coloured rejectionism, that is, denying the creation of the racial category of Coloured as an apartheid invention.[44] Even though she was performing and working for the ANC in exile when she wrote the song, she

insists there are two categories—and both have been wrongfully treated by the apartheid regime. Not everyone is subsumed under the category of black.[45] There are individual family lineages that suggest alternative narrations of belonging beyond the categories of the apartheid regime. It is these lineages that point to the particular history that being labeled Coloured in South Africa created.

Coloured by History

In the United States, where African Americans are an English-speaking numerical minority among a white majority and mostly descendants of African slaves, subsuming Coloreds into the larger category of black or African Americans has probably been good political strategy. In South Africa, where those called Coloured mostly speak English or Afrikaans—they are closely aligned linguistically with white South Africans—and are mostly descendants of non-African slavery, there has often been real resistance to being absorbed into the category of black South Africans. The first democratic elections in 1994 made this resistance patently clear in the Western Cape province. Cape Coloureds did *not* vote the ANC into power, but supported the Afrikaner Nationalists instead. Those on the political left and those who had supported the anti-apartheid movement abroad were shocked at the elections results: they had long rejected the label Coloured, preferring black South African.

The refusal of Cape Coloureds to vote for the ANC opened the door to a flurry of academic conferences, research, and publication about those who in the 1990s identified themselves, or at least had been classified, as Coloured by the apartheid regime. Two important collections of essays emerged out of this burst of scholarly inquiry, much of it pertaining to issues of identity politics and collective history: the sociologist Zimitri Erasmus edited *Coloured by History, Shaped by Place* (2001), and the historian Mohammed Adhikari published both a monograph, *Not White Enough, Not Black Enough: Racial Identity in the South African Coloured Community* (2005) and his edited volume *The Burden of Race: Coloured Identities in Southern Africa* (2009). This work provides a useful entry into a discussion of Coloured as a racial category.

In Erasmus's eclectic volume contributors examine Coloured identity formation in the postapartheid era as a historical and contemporary practice. Erasmus reminds readers that being Coloured has never been defined as a positive identity. Rather, paralleling the idea of miscegenation, from the perspective of white supremacy Coloured was defined as the unfortunate result of the mixing of two purer forms, black African and white European. Such mixing was considered immoral, promiscuous, illegitimate, impure, and productive of only a residual or bastardized identity. "Coloured people don't know where they come from" and "They have no culture of their own" were statements I often heard growing up in South Africa. Such uncertainty of place and identity put Coloureds in an impossible position under apartheid.

Being categorized as a single racial group called Coloured by the apartheid regime erased prior histories and heritage, when in fact those labeled Coloured were less a homogenous racial category than a class defined by a variety of individual and family histories. While hair and skin marked difference inside the Coloured community, they were not adequate identifiers of blood lineages and certainly not of race. As a result, some rejected the category and sought to pass for white or to identify through other social groupings, including class and education. Some in the Coloured community stressed their European biological heritage,[46] while others, in the 1970s and 1980s, embraced the South African black consciousness movement and identified collectively as black, though they were often considered to be "Blacks of a *special* type by many in the anti-apartheid movement."[47]

In the South African context, racial mixing between whites and others created unease, a third space, and the interstitial, and some believed it even induced a state of madness.[48] Erasmus writes against reducing Coloured identity to racial mixture without rigorous inquiry into the conditions of the making and remaking of that identity over the last four hundred years. Coloured identities, she argues, have always been constituted in contexts of domination and a lack of access to the means of self-representation. Rather than turn exclusively to African American writings on race, she looks to the Caribbean, as others have done, in thinking about mixed race histories and senses of belonging.[49]

Erasmus invokes Edouard Glissant's notion of the "cornered community" and the idea of "entanglement" to restore a place for collective and individual history to those called Coloured in South Africa. A cornered community has "had its cultural histories and institutions eradicated," on one hand, but in South Africa these identities have been formed in the "context of racialized relations of power and privilege."[50] Both Coloureds and whites have historically constituted the African as other, although by living as inferior to whiteness, Coloureds have often complied with or been entangled in white domination.[51] Entanglement is a key trope in Erasmus's writing: it urges Coloured South Africans to honestly assess what it has meant to be Coloured. Erasmus argues that this requires one to recognize complex forms of social and political entanglement. Instead of denying a Coloured history and identity formation, she urges scholars of Coloured identities to uncover hidden histories and memories of encounters with difficulty, the difficulty of being and living as Coloured in South Africa.

Adhikari's (2009) collection on Coloured identity focuses on constituting a historical narrative about Coloured politics and experience in South Africa and the southern African region, all subject to British colonialism. Like Erasmus, Adhikari explains that Coloured in southern Africa refers to those of mixed racial identity[52] rather than those identified as black, and references those intentionally engaged with Europeanor Western culture and resistant to all things African. In reality, Adhikari argues, those who identified as Coloured in the past felt they were never white enough, and indeed many ruefully acknowledge that now they are not sufficiently black to gain in any significant way from the postapartheid political dispensation. In other words, to identify as Coloured has meant occupying an interstitial position between those classified as white and those as black African. Both because of their racial mix and relatively smaller numbers everywhere except the Western Cape, the Coloured community in South Africa has therefore historically occupied a marginal political place—under both colonialism and apartheid and now in the postapartheid era.[53]

Marginal in the nation but, Adhikari insists, never lacking a measure of individual and collective agency, the Cape Coloured community was from the outset a heterogeneous group of people from a range of places in the world. Sometimes included in this classification were the hunter-gatherer Khoekhoe and pastoralist San, who had been present in the region for thousands of years prior to colonial conquest. People of color and of mixed race emerged in the Western Cape with the arrival of the

Dutch in 1652 because the Dutch East India Company, which, as noted, settled the first Europeans in the Cape, introduced slaves and political exiles from the East to provide labor for their representatives. Slaves were imported to the Cape from India (Bengal, Malabar, and Coromandel), the East Indies, Ceylon (present-day Sri Lanka), Mozambique, Madagascar, the East African coast, Malaya, and Mauritius. Estimations are that sixty-three thousand slaves came to the Cape between 1658 and 1808, with many more slaves born into slavery. At its peak, the slave population numbered forty thousand, a small number relative to other sites of slavery but a group that far outnumbered the European population in the Cape at the time.

The diverse places of origin of Cape slaves meant there was almost no cultural or linguistic homogeneity. Rather, the mutual incomprehensibility between slaves and their owners supported the development of a lingua franca in the Cape, first called *Kaaps* and later Afrikaans. Ironically, Afrikaans, the language used by white Afrikaners to oppress black South Africans and underscore apartheid in the twentieth century, was first spoken among slaves who did not learn Dutch, and it was initially written down in Arabic script because many slaves were Muslim in religious practice. Slaves introduced Islam, Hinduism, and Catholicism to the Cape.

Historians of Cape slavery argue that there is no comparable diversity among slave populations elsewhere in the world and that there is no parallel slave constituency in which a local colonial community was shaped as much by slaves as in the Cape.[54] Cape Town's traditional cuisine is attributed to the origins of its slave community; its characteristic architecture, the original fishing industry, particular forms of furniture making, and the competence of tradesmen derived from what Indian and East Indian slaves brought to Cape Town. The New Year's festivals, music, and ceremonies that have become a central part of Cape culture — including the Cape Minstrel, or Coon, Carnival, the Malay and Christmas Choirs — trace their origins to slavery. Finally, slaves were crucial to the survival of what was initially a fragile economy in the Cape.

Until the abolition of slavery in 1834, all children born to European men and slave women were regarded as the children of slaves — they followed the matrilineal line, which meant their white fathers were not held responsible for their well-being other than as their slaves.[55] Adhikari argues that it wasn't until the discovery of gold and diamonds from the 1860s onward that the idea of a self-identified, separate community of Coloured people began to form among the descendants of slaves and exiles in South Africa. These discoveries created the conditions for the industrial revolution in South Africa, a revolution that required large numbers of laborers for the mines. With slavery abolished, black South Africans were forced into such employment through a series of taxes imposed by the colonial government. It was at this moment that the descendants of slaves and exiles from the east who had resided mostly in the Cape came into contact with black South Africans, and in response they increasingly identified themselves as Coloured peoples in an effort to retain a certain privileged status inside the white colonial regime. Adhikari describes the group as an "emergent community of assimilated blacks" of relatively low social status because of their color and prior history as slaves and prisoners or political exiles from Asia, Cuba, and other places.[56]

In 1903–5 the South African Native Affairs Commission (SANAC) report was assembled to delineate racial groupings and enhance administrative control over people of color and the so-called native races of South Africa. The report gave an overview of the natives in each area of South Africa and attempted to define each of those groups by region. Thiven Reddy remarks that those of mixed race or mixed blood occupied an ambiguous place in the SANAC report, a fact that shifts markedly by 1950, when the Population Registration Act naturalized all racial categories as fixed and real.[57]

Bernard Magubane argues that it was the British who formalized Coloured as a separate ethnic group in 1909.[58] British High Commissioner to South Africa Lord Selbourne spelled out a position in a letter to Gen. Jan Smuts in this period. He argued that the Coloured community should act as a buffer zone between Europeans and Africans. He suggested that the British cultivate a close relationship with Coloured people so that they wouldn't create political alliances with and provide leadership for the natives, or Bantu-speaking peoples. Selbourne further urged Smuts to publicly stress the European and not the native blood in those categorized as Coloured and as much as possible not to differentiate between the treatment of Coloureds and Europeans. In contrast, natives, that is, black, Bantu-speaking South Africans were to be taught to work (for whites). Implicitly consolidating the ties between whites and Coloureds against black Africans in 1927, the British implemented the first Immorality Act, which forbade sexual intercourse between white and native. Racial purity being its purpose, the apartheid regime would amend the Immorality Act in 1950 and again in 1957 to forbid any sexual encounter between white and nonwhite, including those categorized as Coloured. In 1959 the apartheid regime amended the Population Registration Act with a detailed subdivision of those classified as Coloured into "Cape Coloured, Cape Malay, Griqua, Indian, Chinese, 'other Asiatic,' and 'other Coloured'" (Reddy 2001, 75).

In the first decades of the twentieth century, the period of British-imposed racial segregation, or what Sathima described as "relaxed apartheid," those known as Cape Coloured lived in the western and northern parts of the Cape, and they were characterized by a strong sense of local community.[59] Sathima recalls that two social principles were inculcated into her as a child of mixed race: know your place and do not look for trouble. There was always pressure to be respectable. Her family and friends knew where they were positioned in the racial hierarchy and rarely moved beyond their home communities into white or black African communities. Until she moved into the world of jazz, Sathima had very little daily experience with anyone who was not recognized as Coloured. In some areas of the city, like District Six and Windemere, mostly working-class people lived side by side, regardless of race or religion: those were the areas destroyed by the apartheid regime. The exiled Coloured musician Brian Isaacs talked of growing up in the years of segregation in the town of Vrededorp, just outside of Johannesburg.[60] He recalled that the town was divided into three racial groups by street number. The first set of streets were occupied by whites, the Coloureds were the buffer in the second set of streets, and black South Africans lived in the third set of streets. But even though they were segregated by place of residence children knew each other and played together.

From 1948, when the British were defeated in the whites-only election, these principles of racial segregation quickly became apartheid law under Afrikaner nationalism and were enforced in the 1950s and 1960s. Rationalized through the ideology of "separate development" for all race groups, segregation was institutionalized discrimination increasingly maintained in ruthless and cruel ways by the state. In 1984 Sathima eloquently explained to the American writer Sally Placksin the changeover from the period of segregation to what seemed like the overnight implementation of apartheid rule:

> In a strange kind of way apartheid was always there. Even though South Africa was ruled by the British, it was basically in peoples' hearts, and in any case, when you came from the Black or so-called Coloured or mixed-race communities, you never just had money to go where White people went. We were already living in our own areas, without it being made an issue. . . . You couldn't implement a system that just put up signs over night. . . . I really do remember. I had to take a train to school and I remember suddenly there were signs on the train saying "Whites" and "Non-Whites," and you had to get in a certain place on the train. You saw it everywhere. You were just aware of signs telling you Whites and Non-Whites. Benches, movie houses, just everywhere you looked, signs that weren't there before. I don't know how long they took to prepare all these things, but it was all ready almost over night. Busses, all means of transportation—the only time you didn't see it was when you went shopping. But the minute you came out you were aware of it again. Even in church.[61]

The demarcation of racial differences that Sathima describes was the outcome of two cornerstones of apartheid legislation: the Group Areas Act and the Population Registration Act, both passed in 1950 (amended in 1966). The Population Registration Act divided residents of South Africa into racial categories: whites, natives, and Coloureds;[62] the Group Areas Act told them where they were to live within those racial categories. Both acts had particularly severe and painful ramifications for those identified as Cape Coloured. The Population Registration Act required the creation of a national register that recorded every person living in the country, classified by race. Classification boards were established to facilitate division by race, and, instituting a system that would reveal the sources of miscegenation, they classified everyone as individuals, not by family or lineage. This meant that brothers and sisters, husbands and wives could be classified in different racial groups depending on the tone of their skin color and curl in their hair. Once classified, everyone was required to carry an identity document containing their racial classification.

Racial categories were created in the context of social Darwinism and racial eugenics, but there was little that could be defined as scientific in

the application of the label Coloured under apartheid. Put simply, Coloureds were defined as persons who did not look like or were not known
to be native or European or as persons who had married someone classified as Coloured. Chinese were included in the category Coloured, while
Japanese and some other Asians were classified as "honorary whites" because the apartheid government had diplomatic ties with Japan and Tai-
wan. Indigenous peoples, such as the Khoekhoe and San, were sometimes called native, sometimes Coloured.[63] For those who were mixed or
came from families whose genetic ancestry was racially mixed, the classification process was quite traumatic. Basically, if you looked white and
your hair was straight, you were classified as white; if your skin was dark
and your hair couldn't pass the "pencil test," you were classified as native
or Bantu. The pencil test was particularly worrisome for those who self-
identified as Coloured. Isaacs explained that if an apartheid official ran
a pencil through your hair and it passed through without getting caught
in the curl, you were considered white or Coloured enough; if it was too
curly, you were classified as native or black. Isaacs laughed when he recalled that those who were worried about being classified as black shaved
or cut their hair before going before the classification board. Family photos from Sathima's childhood, for example, show that her extended family
represents a wide range of shades of brown and kinds of hair.[64] These
were the individual features by which race was supposedly measured
by the regime. There were also several hair moments in Sathima's early
life—having straight hair and light skin, she was thought to be not African enough.[65] In fact, as a teenager she had her mother cut her long locks
because of the taunts her fellow musicians in the Cape subjected her to.

For the St. Helenian community that Sathima's father's family belonged
to, the process of being classified as Cape Coloured was slightly different.
They were not Cape Coloureds in the historical sense of the term, that
is, tied to a Cape history of slavery or political exile, although their identity as racially mixed meant they were categorized as Cape Coloured by
the apartheid regime. In the 1890s Sathima's father's family had left the
British-controlled island of St. Helena in the South Atlantic, an island
with a long history of racial mixing. The Benjamins arrived in Cape Town
on the Conway liner boat in search of work and settled among other St.
Helenians.[66] St. Helenians lived in three places in the city: District Six,
the then–racially mixed Rondebosch-Claremont suburbs, where Sathima

spent her early childhood, and Athlone, a Coloured area where she lived in her late teens and early twenties with her mother.[67] St. Helenians of her father's generation kept themselves apart from others in Cape Town. Carrying British passports, they were proud that their birth certificates identified them as mixed St. Helenian rather than Cape Coloured. Unlike the Coloured working class, who spoke Afrikaans and danced to live band music on weekends, St. Helenians aspired to participation in a milieu of English-language cosmopolitanism and respectability.[68] They created their own associations and gathered the extended family and friends to play cards and sing around the piano. Most were church-going Anglicans. This would change with Sathima's generation, which sought to assimilate into Cape society, popular music and jazz being an integral dimension of such integration.

Despite St. Helenians' best efforts to separate themselves from the others called Coloured, everyone was forced into state-imposed categories according to the Population Registration Act. Sathima vividly remembers how it happened. She was nine or ten years old and living with her father's mother, Ma Benjamin, on the day an apartheid government official came around to the house with census forms and required the elderly woman to sign a document stating that she agreed to be classified as Cape Coloured. Proud of her St. Helenian roots, Ma Benjamin refused to sign. She came in tears to Sathima and asked her if she would please sign the piece of paper. Ma Benjamin was told she would have to sign because in the eyes of the government, "mixed St. Helenian" no longer existed. Everybody who was not white or African would now be in the same boat: the Coloured one.

Sathima recalls that she didn't fully understand the politicized nature of these issues at the time, or why becoming Coloured seemed to disturb her grandmother. In Sathima's mind, she herself was already a Cape Coloured because she attended a Coloured school, lived in a neighborhood of people of mixed race, and was interacting with Coloured children every day. But she remembers the emotional weight of the moment because she had never seen her Ma cry before. Sathima obediently signed the paper. Under the Population Registration Act of 1950, the St. Helenian side of the family officially became Cape Coloured. From that time on they were required to carry identity cards naming them as Cape Coloured.

Both the Population Registration and the Group Areas acts targeted the Coloured communities in the Cape, many of whom lived alongside white South Africans.[69] The Group Areas Act resulted in the forced removal of many in Cape Town's Coloured communities in the 1950s and 1960s. If there were people living in one area who were not of the assigned racial category for that location, the apartheid regime forced them to move from their homes and relocated them to the area assigned to their race. Cape Coloureds were sent to live in places like the Cape Flats, Mannenberg, Bonteheuwel, and Athlone. Between 1957 and 1985, some 150,000 people classified as Cape Coloured were forcibly removed by the apartheid regime to what have become known as Coloured townships.[70]

Numerous published accounts by South African writers living in exile and, more recently, oral history projects, documentary films, and so forth, in which those who were forcibly removed witnessed their neighborhoods and homes be destroyed, recall the trauma of the Group Areas legislation and its impact on people's lives. In his autobiography, *Sophiatown: Coming of Age in South Africa* (1987), Don Mattera narrated his experience of the destruction of Sophiatown, a racially mixed community in Johannesburg, by the apartheid regime; Richard Rive recalls growing up in District Six in *Writing Black* (1981) and *Buckingham Palace: District Six* (1986); in her autobiography, *The House in Tyne Street: Childhood Memories of District Six* (1996), Linda Fortune recalls her family home in District Six, which was destroyed by the regime. *Sala Kahle District Six: An African Women'sPerspective* (2001), by the black South African Nomvuyo Ngcelwane, and *Shadow People*, a novel by Shunna Pillay (2007), contain rich descriptions of jazz performance in District Six. Joe Schaeffers, a former resident of District Six, takes visitors to the District Six Museum around the remains of his home community and evokes the district's vibrant community in a documentary film titled *District Six: The Colour of Our Skin?*, which is sold at the museum. The historians Sean Field and Henry Trotter have engaged in oral history projects concerning this experience of forced removal among those called Cape Coloured.[71]

Other legislation that had a significant impact on Sathima and others called Coloured included the Immorality Act, which, as noted, included a ban on interracial marriages and made all sexual relations across what was called the color bar illegal; the Separate Amenities Act (1950), which mandated racial segregation in all public venues, including jazz clubs and nightclubs;[72] the Suppression of Communism Act (1950) and the Unlawful Organizations Act (1960), both of which prohibited organizations deemed to be threatening to national security, a characterization that eventually encompassed any interracial gathering (many jazz and religious events during that period were attended by people of diverse races). For musicians, the legislation that finally put an end to interracial audiences and performances was the Publications and Entertainments Act of 1963, which essentially outlawed all performances involving more than one of apartheid's racial groups in the same place. This law sounded the death knoll for the jazz avant-garde in Cape Town.

Within the space of about fifteen years, 1950–65, Cape Town, the Mother City, changed for people of color from evoking a profound sense of place and home to a space of exclusion, fragmentation, transgression, and boundary marking. Newspapers from the fifties and early sixties are replete with articles expounding on the implications of apartheid legislation for Coloured people. Ultimately, these kinds of racial categories worked themselves out in painful ways in their communities. These included forced divorces, the break-up of families because some members were classified as Coloured and others as European or black/native. Sathima recalls what it meant to be racially classified as Cape Coloured:

> You know the regime was always separating the races. . . . They used the so-called Coloured people as a buffer between themselves and the Africans, and for so long my own people lived in that twilight zone and never came to the realization of exactly who they are. You have to know that there were just two experiences: one was a White and one was a Black one. It didn't matter if you're "Black, Brown or Beige," it was the same thing.[73] And you had to unite as black people because unity was strength in the struggle against apartheid. But there was always discrimination, always. You just didn't get into trouble [before apartheid] if you didn't obey. On the other hand, you didn't care to [disobey] because you went where everybody else went; you were happier with your own. They could never have turned that country around like that if it wasn't there to start with.[74]

How were those classified as Coloured to respond? Some of the elite chose political opposition, while others refused to engage politically, fearing state reprisal.[75] This was the case with musicians, some of whom stayed inside their communities, performing in religious groups, minstrel troupes, Christmas choirs, and dance bands; in the late 1950s others began to cross over into genres like jazz that included people of all racial groups. Like her peers, Sathima hoped the world of jazz would enable her to transcend the categories imposed by the regime. She explained that move to me a few years ago:

> I just don't want to be part of the so-called Coloured thing. You are living in the world, in a global village, and you just have to be yourself, whoever that is. You should be happy to be yourself, whoever you are. This is the pain of denial that a lot of people experience. I told myself a long time ago that I wanted to be somebody other than what the government classified me as. I made that the rule of my life, the rule by which I live. You get past being that way. It happened to me in Europe. That is where I came to terms with who and what I was and what I was supposed to be doing.[76] It's about family, and family to me is the jazz family. Wherever you will find them—and they are all over the world now—whether it be a fan, a critic, or a writer who is just writing about jazz because they love the music. Basically, it's about a way of life, it's about taking risks.[77]

Postapartheid Entanglements

Drawing on the writings of a wide range of scholars, including Erasmus, the South African literary and cultural critic Sarah Nuttall suggests that the idea of entanglement is rich with possibility for addressing the post-apartheid present, above all in literary and cultural domains. Entanglement, she writes, is "a condition of being twisted together or entwined, involved with." It may gesture toward social relationships that are "complicated, ensnaring, in a tangle" but that also signal a human foldedness. Entanglement works with "difference and sameness, but also with their limits, their predicaments, their moments of complication."[78]

While acknowledging the histories of violence embedded in systemic articulations of difference on the basis of race in places like South Africa and the United States, the idea of entanglement allows one to seek out more complex readings of the past and the present, readings that allow for overlaps, convergences, and intersections in political processes, temporalities, people, and things. In this sense, the idea of entanglement urges one to seek out points of intersection, even complicity, in possibly unexpected but certainly imaginative and freshly conceived ways. While there is, as Nuttall concedes, a certain utopian dimension to such a perspective, the notion of entanglement provides a vehicle that allows one to move beyond apartheid, to "unexplored terrain of mutuality, wrought from a common, though often coercive and confrontational, experience."[79]

Following Erasmus and Nuttall, I suggest that entanglement is a productive image for reflecting on the relationship between Sathima and me. Prodded by questions from anonymous reviewers of the manuscript, I recently asked Sathima if racial differences between us had ever felt like a problem to her. She was a little surprised by the question. "I left South Africa because I didn't want to live that way," she reassured me. "I wanted to transcend all that apartheid stuff. But let me ask you, then, why do you have the family that you do?" I hesitated, not really wanting to write about my own family. My children are young, and I would prefer to protect them from scrutiny. But my family is what Americans call a racially blended family: we are impossible to categorize by just one race, and we are not really multiracial. Between the four of us—me, my husband, and our two children—our lineages cover four continents: Africa, the Americas, Europe, and Asia. Why had I chosen that route for a family?, Sathima asked. "Since adoption was our only option for a family," I answered, "it was the birth mothers who chose us. We had no racial preference for a child, and we knew that children of mixed race were harder to place than those who were clearly white or black." Looking back, I suppose having lived through the apartheid years and its transformation, like Sathima, I just wanted to be free of racism at the very core of my sense of self. This doesn't mean my family and I don't encounter it often in the ways people respond to us, but it does require us to live free of it in ourselves. Knowing and living that kind of freedom is something we all strive for every day.

The common desire to transcend race that Sathima and I share does not directly address how white South Africans like me have come to terms with the weight of being white under apartheid.[80] There was a poignant moment in the writing process that illustrates one dimension of the postapartheid burden of a white-dominated past. In 1999, as a Fellow at the National Humanities Center in North Carolina, I began to do the broader reading that would enable me to transform Sathima's memories of the past into this monograph. At the time I searched hard for writing about South Africa's Coloured community, and it seemed that much of the material that existed was written with an interest in supporting the apartheid regime. *Outcast Cape Town*, by the American sociologist John Western, provided a useful distance on the subject. As I read Western's narrative I was struck by the information about the impact of the Group Areas Act on those classified as Cape Coloured who had lived in the suburb of Mowbray, the suburb where I had spent my early childhood from the mid-1960s through 1972. While I had returned to Cape Town many times after leaving, it was always to my extended family that lived on the other side of the mountain or in the northern suburbs, so I rarely went back to Mowbray.

As I read I found myself struggling to locate in my mind places discussed by Western. He wrote about a mosque that had existed in Mowbray. And almost like a computer searching for lost files, I scanned my memory, trying unsuccessfully to visualize that mosque. He also wrote about Kew Town, which I remembered being mentioned in interviews I had conducted in Cape Town in 1996. Fragments of places and words from signs popped up in my mind's eye: I could see the bus ranks, the double-decker buses, and it's possible I could imagine seeing Kew Town as a destination for one of the buses. Perhaps I did not remember simply because Kew Town was a place whites couldn't visit when I was growing up. I was struck once again by how differently those of us who lived there in the past now relate to the City of Cape Town. I wondered how many other spots on the map don't resonate for me because they were not white destinations.

Sitting in an office at the National Humanities Center, I felt an urgent desire to return to Mowbray, not so much to the place of my childhood as to a place remade. Disturbed and unsettled by Western's account, I felt a longing to give Mowbray a postapartheid makeover, to reinsert the people who had been forcibly removed, to rename the old sites, to quite literally recover the landscape. The apartheid way was all I had known in my childhood. But now that there was some distance between that era and the present, I longed to turn back the pages of the past. I wished we could restore what had been wrongfully taken away. There was no hint of nostalgia about my childhood: only a longing to write a different story, to reconstitute a less violent past for those who had endured what apartheid had dealt them.

Such a vision of return to a pristine, preapartheid state is an individual expression of longing and desire to make things right because apartheid's workings and systematic destruction are now apparent to all. In reality, however, we have to live with the ruptures of memory: the stability of a white childhood in the Cape remade with the disturbing knowledge of Coloured removal, community destruction, and white occupation. Home and childhood have been tainted with the knowledge of state abuse, punishment, harassment, and unjust practices. Memories of home and childhood have become what Veit Erlmann called "unhomely."[81] And the burden of race doesn't just disappear in the postapartheid context. We South Africans continually trouble over how to move beyond apartheid, recognizing that even if not intentionally we were all entangled in its impact and history.

There is a rapidly growing body of writing that explores what it means to be South African, to have lived through the years of apartheid, to be classified by race, and to experiment with the consequences of freedom that the postapartheid era has given to all its citizens. And in the same period there has been a growing corpus of writing on being of mixed race outside of South Africa, in the United Kingdom and the United States particularly.[82] Often this body of work combines the biographical with the scholarly, an approach that parallels what we have done in this book. In retrospect, one of the more effective pathways I have found to address the burden of having been white under apartheid has been through my scholarly reading, research, writing, and teaching. I have found that such activity has become a way of knowing what we have done, where we are, and how we might imagine a more socially just future. While we suspected that the apartheid regime was committing atrocities when I was growing up, we could never really be sure. Fear and the state-controlled media made sure of that.

In the last two decades I have found that I can come to terms with apartheid as ideology and distortion with greater certainty by assembling an archive, interrogating its assumptions, constructing a series of narratives about the multiplicity of pasts that constitute the history of musicians and music in South Africa, and sharing it with readers and students. These processes have opened to me an understanding of the apartheid past that living through its atrocities never enabled.

This book is not intended to be a project about identity formation, a process that dominates postapartheid and ethnomusicological literature as a whole. Because I have lived inside and outside of South Africa for equal periods of time, I feel less bound to geographically specific places and communities. I am more motivated to come to some deeper understanding of what it meant to have lived under a regime that discriminated, to have witnessed its undoing, and then to wonder what we all might learn from the peculiarities of South Africa's history, and the response of its musicians to that historical condition, and how to proceed together in the present.

I have long believed in the value of fieldwork as a mechanism for interracial dialogue. The ethnographic method requires that its practitioners listen, that their interlocutors be heard and equitably represented in their writing. To me, a white South African woman working in the apartheid years, ethnographic listening provided an extraordinary, if politically contested, opportunity to begin to understand personal experiences across racial divides. It required me to move out of my comfort zone and to seek out the other side of white privilege: racism and poverty but also the richness of cultural, musical, and religious practices inside South Africa. As a person of faith, I grew up knowing we were to love our neighbors—in apartheid South Africa just who our neighbors were was a political issue. The biblical story of the Good Samaritan, of the politically despised individual who assisted the wounded man left on the side of the road to die after the powerful had passed him by, made me think hard about where moral capital and true humanity were to be found in South African society. I grew up increasingly convinced that a life focused on racial difference was futile; that South Africans had to seek out the capacity for finding common ground. The question was, how to proceed as a white woman when the law ruled against crossing over? Like other white South Africans at the time, I found a way through my university training: I traveled to the township of Umlazi and learned to gumboot dance during states of emergency in 1985; and I undertook research in the Inanda Valley, one of the most heavily armed areas in South Africa in the early 1990s. In the postapartheid moment, I wonder how we might begin to imagine a world in which race doesn't persistently define the mode of social and intellectual engagement? What are the possibilities for human interaction across communities that aren't first and foremost about difference? Can we ever truly move towards a nonracial democracy?

Jazz Entanglements

In bringing this reflection on entanglement and narratives about race and its mixing to conclusion, it strikes me that encountering jazz as an improvised musical discourse produces feelings of uncertainty and anxiety in the ears of the jazz novice that parallel first meetings with people of mixed race. This was certainly how I first encountered jazz as a student in South Africa. I never listened to the music as a child — it wasn't played much in my world. And when I began to listen to jazz I couldn't figure out the relationship between title and tune — when I heard "My Favorite Things," for example, it didn't sound familiar at all. To my teenage ears, jazz was too dissonant, its rhythms always displaced. I couldn't make sense of its incessant improvisation, harmonic substitution, and melodic elaboration. What was the underlying logic, the internal structure? How would I know when the piece would end? Why did audiences applaud or laugh when they did?

This confusion and reluctance to listen began to shift in my undergraduate years at the University of KwaZulu Natal, where I was exposed to the sounds of jazz history, the European and South African avant-garde, on one hand, and, on the other, to a strident critique of apartheid ideology on campus and through my academic work. My undergraduate experience was a radical confrontation with both apartheid reality and with jazz. Opening myself to these two worlds in the late 1980s meant embracing the new and sometimes experimental. It built the capacity for uncertainty, noise versus silence, risk, relentless improvisation, and dissonance. The unexpected combinations of sounds and textures enabled me to live with the possibilities of musical and political change and to allow for creative exploration; to take risks, to expand my horizons, to live with the unknown, and indeed to cross over into unfamiliar and, on occasion, dangerous terrain. During this period I was first exposed to the possibilities of what was, at the time, the unwritten history of South African jazz.

At present jazz studies in the United States occupies a very different place from what it does in South Africa. Some might even argue that American jazz studies has reached a state of equilibrium and that the future of jazz studies lies in writing a globally distributed versus U.S.-centered historiography. South African jazz history has begun to be written, though much of its narrative circulates exclusively around the notion of a homogeneous black South African jazz. There is little sense in South African music of a mixed racial heritage in jazz. How to proceed? I am suggesting that one possible path is for jazz studies to follow trends in contemporary studies of race outside of the United States. This includes, for example, work on the black diaspora in Britain, which incorporates the Asian and Caribbean diasporas into its domain; the important scholarship on issues of mixed racial identities and histories; and the literature that has emerged in postapartheid South Africa, especially the new directions in writing a past for those of mixed race as a history of entanglement.

The idea of entanglement in jazz studies requires one to focus on musical forms and processes that avoid the pressure to highlight ideals of purity, authenticity, harmony, sameness or difference, and singular origins (as race studies have done) by privileging instead the processes of hybridity, creolization, and blurred boundaries. Such a shift could well reveal a surprising number of cornered communities and secret histories in all racial groups that otherwise might remain hidden from view. Perhaps music scholars take on the metaphors by which Coloured history and ways of being in the world have been explained, as resonant conduits for opening up the boundaries of American jazz to incorporate other performers, performances, and even histories elsewhere in the world.

At the very least we might begin to inquire how jazz the world over has played with and against the natural categories of race by harnessing discourses of entanglement embodied in *inter*cultural, *inter*personal, and *trans*national engagement. We might interrogate how such engagement has worked to constitute interracial communities, even nonracial constituencies as jazz has assumed a global presence from the mid-twentieth century to the present. This is how the community of progressive jazz musicians and listeners imagined itself in Cape Town and Johannesburg in the late 1950s. It was an interracial, international gathering of people who were passionate about the possibilities — musical, political, and societal — embodied in the sounds of American-generated jazz produced locally.

3

Cape Jazz

Popular Music, Dance Bands, and Jazz

In South Africa after the Second World War *Cape jazz* was not the term used by South Africans to describe the music composed and performed in Cape Town. While South African jazz seemed to have moved from the sounds of *marabi* and so-called African jazz made in the townships near Johannesburg toward Cape Town and its interracial community, there was no conception of a specific brand of jazz belonging to the Cape or even to the Coloured community in Cape Town.[1] Many South Africans were still listening closely to American jazz on records, and musicians used that language to explore the possibilities of a local sound. There certainly was disagreement in the local press about whether the center of that exploration was located in Cape Town or Johannesburg. This would change when musicians began to leave the country, and audiences abroad wanted to hear more specifically South African sounds in their jazz. Musicians like Abdullah Ibrahim and Johnny Dyani, from the Western and Eastern Cape, respectively, incorporated memories of the music they recalled hearing in their childhood days to create what would come to be marketed as Cape jazz.

Five decades later, in the world music marketplace and in postapartheid South Africa the notion of a distinctive style called Cape jazz is generally assumed, if not universally accepted. This is not to suggest that all musicians from the Cape play an identifiably local sound. Some who remained in the country were invested in a more universally recognized form of jazz, while others explored the integration of local musical languages in their performances. On the one hand, the veteran pianist Henry February laughed when I asked him if there was a specifically Cape Town sound in jazz. "No," he replied, "jazz is a universal language." On the other hand, the Cape jazz label now used does reference the musical creativity and innovation of several musicians led locally and internationally by the pianist and composer Abdullah Ibrahim, and it began in the post–Second

World War era. Those who forged this distinctive sound with Ibrahim in the 1950s–1970s in South Africa include Robbie Jansen, the late Basil Coetzee, the bass player Paul Michaels, the drummer Monty Weber, and the saxophonist Morris Goldberg, of *Graceland* fame. They inserted into the fabric of jazz performances references to local music, some of it derived from so-called Coloured music making—the Cape minstrels, Christmas and dance bands—but also from more general South African sounds like marabi, mission hymnody, Cape Muslim music, and so forth.

To make this strand of South African jazz history audible to the world, the independent label Mountain Records published a CD compilation called *Cape Jazz* in 1993. The disc included tracks of the principal players who forged this style. Ibrahim does not perform on the recording, although the echoes of his sound and style are quite clear in the music of those who do.[2] The label Cape jazz was forged out of market concerns and audience expectations both at home and abroad. And yet, as Sathima's narrative in this chapter suggests, the story of Cape Town jazz is so much more than a handful of men who performed together and recorded there from the late 1950s through the mid-1970s.

Sathima moved away from the confines of Ma Benjamin's household in the mid-1950s because she sensed there was much to learn outside the home: there were many friends to make, musicians to meet, and so much music to experiment with. As she extended her circle into the wider world of Cape Town, the apartheid regime was increasing its demands of racial separation through surveillance, police harassment, and the threat of arrest. Sathima wasn't more than fifteen or sixteen when she began to rebel against these restrictions, a rebellion she fueled by reading books and listening to music by and about African Americans in the United States. Her sister Joan and then her mother were her musical companions in those heady days. They set out to explore this world of music as it happened live and mediated in the city of Cape Town, in its dance halls, hotels, churches, nightclubs, and other ports of call until she met Abdullah Ibrahim (or Dollar Brand, as he was known at the time).[3] Venturing out was much more common among her male friends than among the women in her community.

From the outset she demonstrated real courage as she increasingly confronted the uncertainty of apartheid, on one hand, and the sense of possibility embodied in the music coming from the United States, on the other. From that point on, Sathima's life and family relationships changed dramatically because few could understand the powerful call to the music that seemed to have possessed her. What follows is an account of Sathima's gradual move out into a wider world of Cape popular music, jazz, and politics from the early 1950s through 1962, when she and Abdullah left South Africa for Europe and the United States.

Sathima participated in several jazz worlds in Cape Town in the postwar period. Common to both the elite and the working class in the Coloured communities in Cape Town was Saturday night social dancing to music made by live dance bands. Until the early 1960s these same Coloured musicians were hired to play in the commercial nightclubs — some were for white patrons exclusively; others were completely interracial; and there was township jazz in the African townships like Langa and Nyanga. Many of the musicians who played in dance bands one weekend would cross over into the white nightclubs the next. Occasionally a black South African would perform in a Coloured band, or a Coloured musician in a black township. The Cape musicians Jimmy Adams, a saxophonist and big band arranger, and Tem Hawker both played a pivotal but, for its time, controversial role as musical and cultural brokers between the black and Coloured communities in the 1950s. Finally, in the late 1950s, there was the jazz avant-garde, which consisted of improvising jazz musicians striving to learn from American styles while searching for a local jazz sound. The two most important groups that coalesced around these goals were the Jazz Epistles and the Blue Notes, both of whom developed an intimate knowledge of Ellington and the hard bop styles of the period.

The postwar period was also important for the opportunity given to black and Coloured South Africans who joined traveling variety shows. Modeled on a handful of films like *Cabin in the Sky* and *Stormy Weather* that featured light-skinned African American musicians and dancers, these traveling shows were intended to showcase local talent in the black and Coloured South African communities. Several of these shows had extended runs, some traveled around the country, and a couple went into southern and central Africa. The names of the shows included *Township Jazz, African Jazz and Variety* (later called *African Follies*), *Sponono* (1961), *Dingaka, Shebeen,* and *Mr. Paljas*. Two in particular, *King Kong* (1959) and the *Golden City Dixies* (formed in the mid-1950s) traveled overseas. The shows provided training and experience for many black and Coloured

musicians and functioned as launching pads for careers, some successful, some less so, both in South Africa and abroad. Sathima auditioned
with the *Golden City Dixies* when they traveled to Cape Town and then
joined a show of the Australian impresario Arthur Klugman, *Coloured
Jazz and Variety*, modeled after the impresario Alf Herbert's *African Jazz
and Variety*. Both of these productions toured southern Africa in the mid-
1950s. By the early 1960s all of this activity was foreclosed by the apartheid regime through police surveillance, death threats, and harassment
and through the undisciplined behavior of some of the artists, who it
seemed were always on the brink of financial collapse.

Ballroom and Langarm Dances

Dancing to live bands was a vital dimension of social life for many in
Cape Town's Coloured community for much of the twentieth century.
Such dances served a variety of purposes: they could be used to raise
money for charity, to aid the war effort, to build community halls, to
purchase hospital equipment, or to support the indigent; in the 1940s
the Communist and Socialist parties in South Africa used dances as a
locus for building membership and support for their causes.[4] Churches
hosted social dancing, as did sports associations and schools. Even the
St. Helenians, who had their own sports club, the Suburban Harriers,
founded by Steven Regan, held an annual ball.[5] Social dancing was central to the Coloured elite, who called their events ballroom; and they
were equally important to the Coloured working class, whose events
were called *langarm* (literally "long arm," a reference to the style of ballroom dance, like the tango, performed to this music). Dance bands were
expected to perform similar music for both kinds of dances, regardless
of social class. Denied access to political and even religious leadership
and participation, it was especially on the dance floor or performing in
the band that the tiny gradations of social status within Coloured communities were created.

During the week Coloured men and women were carpenters, factory
workers, upholsterers, store owners; they worked at the dry cleaners and
in the harbor; they were truck drivers and janitors, and some were domestic workers and gardeners in white homes. On Saturday nights the

7. Two couples in ballroom attire. *Courtesy of District Six Museum.*

working class was completely transformed. Until communities were broken up and moved under the Group Areas legislation, people mostly lived
close to their places of employment, which meant there was time on the
weekends to socialize. People joined sports clubs or a dance band, went
dancing, or spent the evening at the movies. For those who didn't want to
cause trouble and those who knew their place in a European-controlled
society, ballroom and langarm dancing provided the means to imaginatively remake oneself for the night. Vincent Kolbe described, for example,
the Cinderella-like transformation of young women at Saturday evening
dances: "Women would work a whole week in a factory, and Saturdays

go to a dance with this gown, golden shoes, and a cigarette holder as they had seen in the movies. Young women fantasized on the weekend about being a 'princess for the night.' Men dressed up too—they would wear bow ties and black suits."

Sathima recalls that in her teens in the 1940s she went to dances every weekend, venturing out with Joan. They rarely went with partners, but the two girls were passionate about the music and dancing. No singers performed with these dance bands, but, as Sathima told me in the early 1990s, "the saxophone was always out front playing the melody. Ooohh, those melodies, they just did something to me, you know there was magic in those melodies. I used to listen to the way the saxophone bent the notes. The big intervals I use when I sing now come from the way those musicians played their instruments. And I phrase my melodies from the sense of timing I heard consciously and unconsciously at those dances: I hear the strict rhythm for the dancing in my head as I start singing some-where between beat 1 and 2—that is where I began to develop my style as a singer. In the dance halls."

In addition, many in the community fondly recall dancing at bob parties, or what Adams (who began playing at these gigs in his father's band when he was nine years old (ca. 1938) called bob bops, in the neigh-borhood and, in Sathima's case, among her peers from Battswood Teach-ers' College.[6] Bob parties were like African American rent parties, a bob equaled ten cents and was the price one paid to enter the house of the party giver, who often had a live band or at the very least a piano player to entertain the guests. All proceeds from the party were used to pay rent or to cover household expenses. The squares, the waltz, the foxtrot, and the samba were some of the dance styles played by live bands or on record. Those rhythms shaped Sathima's sophisticated yet quite relaxed sense of musical time.

The Bands

The early history of jazz in Cape Town is a history of dance bands, on one hand, and, as mentioned earlier, of working-class minstrelsy, on the other. Dance band history in South Africa can be traced back to the Victorian era. Such ensembles were certainly not new to the Cape in the period after the Second World War, though the instrumentation and repertory

8. Cape Town Jive Band. *Courtesy of District Six Museum.*

had changed from what they had been before war. Kolbe's grandmother told him that musicians went to serve in the Second World War carrying stringed instruments and returned with brass instruments. Born in 1929, Adams remembered that when he first played in his father's band in the late 1930s, it was a string band, mostly violins. Adams played banjo, cello, bass, and eventually even the drums for his father. When he was in his late teens they used to perform regularly in the Drill Hall in Cape Town — the band was seated on a stage in the middle of the hall, and everyone would dance around the band.

The father of Sathima's cousin John Samuels had one of the elite dance bands in the 1920s and 1930s, the Ed Samuels Orchestra, also a string band. Samuels remembered that when he was a child there were seven violins in his home available for anyone to learn to play. With great pride he showed me programs from his father's performances of the time. In 1931 he played at the Cinderella Dance at the Rondebosch Town Hall, and on another occasion at the Owl Sporting Club. The proof of Ed Samuels's prestige in the Coloured community, however, was the fact that he and his son were invited to one of the two balls held in honor of the British royal family's visit to Cape Town in 1947. One ball was for whites and the other for elite Coloureds. Because Ed Samuels had once worked alongside Steven Regan, cofounder of the first Coloured political party, the African People's Organization, he received an invitation to attend the ball with British royalty.

Adams recalls that on some occasions in the 1940s six or seven dance bands played in a single day, starting early on a Saturday night and going right through to 2 A.M. the next morning. At one such event in the Sea Point Town Hall in 1946, Adams first heard Hawker's African dance band from Langa Township. The music it played was completely different from that of Coloured dance bands—there were three saxophones playing in harmony together. Jimmy insisted that his father introduce him to Tem. Hawker had a remarkable life, having learned jazz arranging while traveling the world in the South African navy. One day Adams arrived at his father's barbershop to find Hawker waiting to meet him. Adams subsequently spent many weekends in Langa Township with Hawker and his musicians, teaching drumming in exchange for being instructed in jazz arranging from Hawker.[7]

Even though black South Africans had organized big bands in the 1930s and 1940s, Adams had the first Coloured big band in Cape Town.[8] For five years or so he arranged music, much of it first heard in single men's hostels in Langa Township, where his band rehearsed nightly. In the early 1950s Adams secured a five-year recording contract with the South African Broadcast Corporation (SABC) for their Transcription Series, that is, everything recorded would be aired on radio. He took his big band to the SABC to record these new sounds he knew were popular because they had played live in various places. In the apartheid mindset, however, the music sounded too black and not Coloured enough for SABC producer Gerry Bosman, who was white: they wouldn't record it. There was no capacity for racial or musical crossovers in this period, as there would be in postapartheid South Africa.[9] Adams was so frustrated he refused to work with the SABC any longer, breaking his contract. It was a tough decision to make because SABC was almost the only place to get one's music recorded in Cape Town at the time.

A few months later Adams's entire body of work, five years' worth of musical arrangements, was stolen at the Snakepit in the Cape Town City Hall during a fundraising performance. Adams recalled that shortly thereafter several black South Africans were recorded by the SABC in Johannesburg, and their *kwela* recordings became a huge hit both in South Africa and abroad.[10] When I spoke with Adams in 1996 he was quite bitter about the blatant racism of the SABC and the opportunity he missed for popularizing his arrangements of kwela-style big band music.

Many of Cape Town's most popular band leaders of the period had either performed as musicians in the war effort or had been trained by those who had "gone North," that is, to North Africa in the Second World War. Kolbe explained: "In the army, they learnt music. They could read music. They played in the band. They had a kind of education that other people didn't have. They had a kind of sophistication about them. And lots of these original bands, at least the ones I learnt from, were guys that had actually been in the army. They were interesting to talk to, and they were very skillful and talented and we learnt our music from them. We would play in bands where the bandleader was a sergeant major in the army: he was disciplined and he'd count. 123 or quickstep you know. And he would read. And he demanded the best out of you. There was a kind of pursuit of excellence. The world we lived in was full of hope."

Kolbe's view on the war as a force for shaping local culture is corroborated by a key institution in the Coloured community of Cape Town: the Cape Corps Military Band. Formed during the First World War, it was at that time a mix of white and Coloured musicians. The founder of the band was Irish, and he espoused the values of the working class: promoting musical excellence and social respectability.[11] As social dancing did for young factory workers, the Cape Corps Military Band enabled the transformation of working-class individuals into a citizenry that was beautiful, regal, and respected in its community for the sound of their music and their ability to read scores rather than just play by ear. Although located in the Cape, the group nevertheless carried cosmopolitan memories of wartime travel and transnational engagement through musical performance.

As suggested earlier, when those who had performed in the Second World War entertainment units returned to Cape Town, Coloured dance bands adapted the stringed sounds onto brass instruments, the saxophone in particular. This is where the wailing sound of the alto saxophone in Cape Jazz developed. One of the most important postwar bands (which is still in existence, with different personnel) is a group called the Philadelphia Rhythms. They play langarm. There were many others, like Alf Wylie's dance band, Willie Max's band, and the Tem Hawker band. And there were the elite groups, like the Spes Bona Orchestra.

These military musical experiences were critical for Coloured musicians because no local schools of music taught young Cape Tonians this style. The older musicians would pass their knowledge on to the younger ones. Kolbe recalls,

> There were always churches and church youth clubs where you learnt all kinds of things like dancing and table tennis and what have you, and we would have social evenings with the glee clubs and there was a piano there, and my friends and I had a little band. Then invariably some old-timers or some other members of the church or some ex-musicians would join us and we'd get to know them and they'd pull out their fiddles and they'd show us some things they used to do in their days. And I often wondered why they kept saying to us, "You guys play too fast. Your tempo is wrong." They insisted on this tempo. "Timing! Timing!" they'd say.
>
> I realized in later years that we were just a young, jiving, rock'n'rolling crowd, you know, and we were more energetic. But there was this emphasis on rhythm and on good timing—a good swing. The older people would always complain that our timing wasn't good. They would dance more elegantly, they would dance with . . . how can I say it? It's like a delayed movement. You don't really put your foot down on the beat. Good ballroom dancers don't and good jazz musicians don't, you know. And I find that totally missing in today's disco-oriented music.[12]

While the rhythms were oriented to dance steps, Cape musicians borrowed melodies for local dance band performances from the Hollywood movies they watched in movie theaters. Kolbe recalled that when he was not accompanying his mother to the movies, he and a friend would be given money by one of the local bandleaders to go and see the newest musicals as soon as they arrived in the theater. The boys were instructed to watch the movie over and over until they had memorized the words and melodies of a song sung in the movie, for example, by Nat King Cole. They repeated what they memorized to the bandleader. The next Saturday night Cole's newest song would be played at social dances for the

9. Jimmy Adams's Swing Band. *Courtesy of District Six Museum.*

Coloured community. In the dance band context, the tunes were played straight to sustain regular rhythms required of ballroom dance. It was in the live renditions of dance band performances rather than through the recordings that the majority of Cape Town's Coloured community remember hearing the sounds of Hollywood and American swing.

It wasn't just the music that Cape musicians admired and copied, note for note, on Saturday nights. They also drew on the images on record covers to construct the perfect replica in hair and clothing styles. So if you were performing as Cape Town's Dizzy Gillespie you would take the record cover of Gillespie to the barber and get the appropriate haircut. Then you would proceed to the tailor, who would cut you an outfit that duplicated what you could see on the album cover. In the increasingly repressive political environment, Hollywood images of American entertainment and of African American navigation of that world operated in stark relief to what was happening in South Africa. Lena Horne, Dorothy Dandridge, Duke Ellington, and Harry Belafonte were the obvious models of upward social mobility achieved through excellence in the performing arts. And for those classified as Coloured in the Cape these lighter-skinned performers offered models and hope for similar upward social mobility and social integration in the Cape through musical performance.

Dance bands played a varied repertory that sought to articulate and keep up with the tastes of their clients. Kolbe recalled that the band repertories reflected the diverse histories of the Coloured community with "Muslim songs, Jewish songs, Afrikaner songs, Portuguese songs, French songs." The bands could expect to play for a varied clientele. That said, elite people would hire a local band with the understanding that they "could play carnival [that is, working-class] music. It might be a bow tie and black suit sort of occasion. These people would be very elegantly dressed. It would be all very respectable people. At the end of the evening the band would be expected to play a selection of music in what Kolbe described as a "raw and raunchy style." It was the wild working-class style of dancing at the end, when people had been drinking a little, which blurred the social distinctions conventionally drawn in the Coloured community between the elite and working classes.

Developing a Personal Style

While there were no singers performing with these dance bands Sathima recognizes that her musical style was shaped by the melodies of the saxophones and the feel of dancing herself. Archived in bodily memory is the strict sense of timing required for good dancing, on one hand, and the "just between the beat" feel of the old-time dancers that Kolbe talked about, on the other. Once Sathima moved into the world of club and jazz singing, she had to give up Saturday night dancing because she began to position her voice in a different place in the musical fabric. Her vocal lines replaced the saxophone out front, bending notes, expanding the pitch, playing in a subtle but respectful way with timbre, texture, timing, text, and tune. In talking about her work with specific musicians she uses the metaphor of dance — the American bass player Buster Williams, for example, she imagines as a wonderful dance partner in the way he can "take the corner" on his instrument.

In addition to learning from the dance bands, Sathima was first exposed to the world of jazz performance in Cape Town when she met the jazz drummer and music teacher Sam Isaacs in 1952. Sam was doing an extra year of study at Battswood Teachers' Training College when Sathima encountered him. She was sixteen, he twenty-three and she vividly remembers the first time she saw him: he was leaning against a wall smoking a cigarette. "I was so taken with his savvy and worldliness," she commented. "He reminded me of those tough guys in the movies in the way he carried himself. I was so enthralled and impressed I fell head over heels in love with him. Sam was the first man who truly fell in love with me, and it was a love that endured through good times and bad."

At the time Isaacs had a regular gig at a white ice-skating rink, playing drums in what he said was a "George Shearing–style" trio.[13] Though she was not allowed inside because she was Coloured Sathima would sit outside the rink and listen to the music through the windows. Sam would come and meet his new friend at intermission. I was fortunate enough to talk with Isaacs in 1996 in Cape Town. In the course of our conversation he reflected on the ironies of living under apartheid. He told me that at the time he was seeing Sathima he often performed in white-owned nightclubs with white strippers and a white clientele. The club would hire Coloured bands to play because the musicians would play for less money and were considered more reliable than the white bands. Because the strippers were white, the Coloured musicians were hidden behind a curtain when the club was open so they couldn't see them. In rehearsal, however, race didn't seem to matter because there was no curtain then. He laughed at the silliness of it all, but even in 1996 it didn't seem all that funny.

Battswood Teachers' College was important musically in Sathima's growth as a singer for another reason. As she had done at Livingstone High, she joined the school choir at Battswood College. Despite her strong voice she was never asked to perform solos in the cantatas and light operettas the choir sang. When she asked the instructor, Dan Ulster, why this was so, he said she "scooped" too much with her voice. An emotional trademark of her style and the way she imaginatively played with the music in her head, scooping was not good practice in choral performance, but she hadn't realized that. Fortunately, Ulster kept her in the choir, although she always was placed in the back row. Sathima would later identify a similar quality in Billie Holiday's vocal style.

When Sathima and Joan moved in with their mother Evelyn Green in Kew Town, they discovered that she was a ragtime pianist. It was she who encouraged Sathima to pursue her growing passion for singing. Sathima's half-sister Edith Green remembers that when Joan and Sathima came to live with them their mother purchased a piano. The instrument became the center of wonderful evenings spent with Sathima and the group of jazz-loving friends she began to gather around her. The move out of Claremont and into Athlone connected Sathima to the more public world of popular music performance and to the vibrant community of jazz fans and performers. She is convinced that had she stayed in Claremont she would never have ventured into the public world of musical performance.

When Sathima began to sing publicly there were many places to perform, including charity evenings in churches, nightclubs, cinemas, after-hours events, and as the local talent in traveling shows. In the staged performances, she recalls, "you would be on the same bill as local tap dancers, acrobats, it could be anything that people found entertaining. But there were a lot of singers, both male and female, not just in the jazz vein, but doing songs that were popular at the time. There were people there who could play Errol Garner's solo to every note that Errol Garner played. Cape Tonians are very good at imitating. Excellent. We always had the Cape Town Jerry Lewis, the Cape Town Bing Crosby. I think for a while I was either Doris Day or Joni James, before I went into jazz."[14]

Sathima remembers that there was one man, Joey Gabriels, a gifted member of the Eoan Opera Corps of Cape Town, who sang "Come Back to Sorrento."[15] Gabriels changed his name to Giuseppe Gabriello when he left South Africa to study opera in Italy and at the Juilliard School in New York City.[16] Sathima distinctly recalls Gabriels's appearance in the theater:

> When the emcees would call Joey Gabriels, he would come on stage and the emcee would announce, "And now for Cape Town's very own Mario Lanza" or it could have been Caruso or some other popular European

voice. And Joey would walk. Everyone else would be waiting their turn backstage and just walk on the stage and go to the microphone (which probably wasn't working or working and making squeaks). Joey was different. He would present himself, not from backstage. When they announced him, he came from the back of the cinema. He puffed out his big chest, so pretentious, pompous, and full of conceit. It was all part of the act. He'd arrive at the stage and walk to the middle. Then he would quite deliberately take the microphone stand and walk over to the side of the stage and put the mic stand in front of the curtain wings. He was clearly telling his audience "Joey Gabriels does not need a microphone." He'd just stand there in the middle of the stage with his gorgeous looks and tenor voice. It was always the same thing, every time he performed. He never disappointed because people always wanted the same thing. They'd give him these standing ovations.

On occasion the three, mother and two daughters, would go to local hotels, the Athlone being their favorite because there was always a piano and a place to sing. This was a new possibility in postwar Cape Town, allowing women into the lounges of hotels to socialize without male presence. Self-taught, Evelyn Green could play only in the keys of C, F, and G, and she always played the melody of old songs like "Up a Lazy River," "Chicago," "Come Back to Sorrento" and "Ah! Sweet Mystery of Life." Joan recalls she was the seamstress for these events, making dresses according to their sense of fashion. "We were quite popular, the three of us," she told me in 1996. The girls' mother willingly accompanied their friends as well. Joey Gabriels was one of the singers Evelyn Green accompanied in that period.

These live renditions of popular music received little press coverage. People knew about Sathima's vocal abilities and the talents of others by word of mouth. She sang all over: in hotels, clubs, school, and at jazz concerts. Very few recordings of Cape Coloured music made a musician famous, and even if Coloured musicians did record, few acquired copies from the SABC or Gallo Records. What is remembered more is the live music. It was the audiences who were the strongest critics. They were very quick to judge the performance and would let performers know if they were not up to standard. "'Oh no, you're singing *that*!' They would throw things at you, you know," Sathima told me in April 1990. "You really had to be very careful because they could take you off and replace

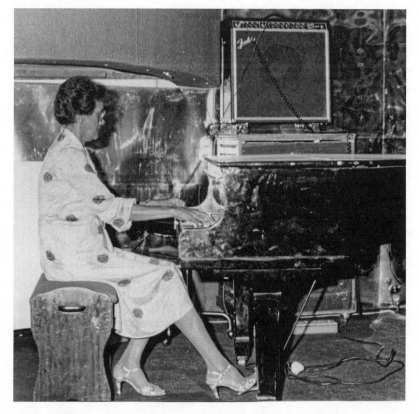

10. Sathima's mother at the piano. *Collection of Sathima Bea Benjamin.*

you with someone else who would really do something beautiful. So it was really a tough but beautiful audience. You could almost hear them breathing with you. That's the way it was. It was always such a rewarding experience."

On the Road with Jazz and Variety

We already know that the Cape Corps Military Band formed as a band during the First World War, a core institution in Coloured musical performance history in Cape Town, and the training of dance band musicians. The Second World War continued this training and introduced an additional musical institution: the traveling jazz and variety show, featuring black and Coloured South African talent. *Zonk!*, the first of these shows, was the product of the Union (of South Africa) Defence Force Entertainment Unit led by Maj. Myles Bourke.[17] This unit entertained troops in the African and European theaters. Some of the best jazz musicians, black and Coloured, were sent to entertain black units of the Allied troops. On their return, Lt. Ike Brooks, a white, created a variety show with these musicians, and they traveled around the Union of South Africa entertaining audiences of all racial groups. The show was extremely popular and opened the way for several similar kinds of productions over the next fifteen years or so.

A review in the largely white Cape newspaper *The Argus* in December 1944 described *Zonk!* as a "nationally celebrated African revue" when it performed in the Cape Town City Hall. The reviewer praised the show for its originality and the performers for their talent and versatility and for being "better than their American prototypes," a common comparison. "There is some excellent tap dancing, a first-rate band, some Negro spirituals; in short, almost a surfeit of good things. The performers, without a single exception, have amazing stage presence and present their various turns with verve and evident enjoyment," wrote the reviewer.

Zonk! has archival significance in the present because not only was it performed live, but a film about the show has been reissued on video. The reissue opens a rare window onto black and Coloured performance cultures of the mid-twentieth century and the kinds of variety performances Sathima and her peers would have participated in. *Zonk!* was intended to showcase black and Coloured talent, to get it out of the townships and present it to a wider public. The stage setting in *Zonk!* references the context of the film *Cabin in the Sky*, which was shown in South Africa in the late 1940s. The film version comprises fifteen individual acts introduced by an emcee. The acts represent working-class and elite black and Coloured cultures and are performed in several South African languages, including isiZulu, English, Afrikaans, and seSotho. The emcee occasionally reflects on the specific nature of the performances and their relationship to images and sounds that South Africans have borrowed from record, radio, and film.

Despite the film's claims, what is perhaps most surprising is the apparent lack of African traditional content. Instead, *Zonk!* the film presents a modern display of black and Coloured South African performance culture: the urbanized performing arts written about so eloquently by David Coplan, Christopher Ballantine, Lara Allen, and others. In the words of the pianist Henry February, "If you could sing like a current pop singer, [these shows] grabbed you, you see. Now they give you a record of the singer, now you must sing it, like clones . . . now if the singer is doing this [he breathes] then you must do the same thing. . . . It wasn't artful, it was just copying, you may just as well have played the original record."[18]

Zonk! opens with a jazz singer supported by a close harmony male vocal group and a jazz ensemble. They perform a song of praise to the film producers and to *Zonk! The African People's Magazine,* the film's sponsor. The opening and closing cuts provide the most obvious examples of the influence of nineteenth-century minstrelsy on black South African performance.[19] The second act is a rendition of "Deep River," the song made famous by Paul Robeson, but it is performed here by South Africa's version of Paul Robeson.[20]

In the third act a male vocal trio sings in English and Zulu about the "Copper Colored Girl" in the style of a "Happy Days Are Here Again" rendition. The singer is accompanied on piano and bass and intersperses a tap-dancing routine. The fourth act represents elite culture: a black woman rocks her baby to sleep while singing a Brahms lullaby accompanied by an offstage organ. The emcee introduces the song with a narrative about composers of beautiful music who are "better known to some than to others" distinguishing between those exposed to the European classical tradition and those who were not. In the fifth segment, the emcee code switches into Afrikaans as he introduces the Cape Coons from Hanover Street in District Six. These twelve men, who wear soft white shoes also used by isicathamiya performers, sing in a mix of English and Afrikaans and represent the Coloured working class from the Cape. The sixth segment features Abafana Kumnandi, a close harmony vocal quartet singing in the "Manhattan Style." They sound like Glenn Miller's "In the Mood" with a Zulu language text focused on the theme of *isitimela,* the train.[21]

The seventh act represents the traditional migrant worker singing longingly about his rural home. The backdrop is a painted rural scene, with a Sesotho man singing a very slow ballad about traditional life in a deep, Robeson-like timbre. The eighth act features the Zulu Melodians, who sing a moral ditty about the vices of alcohol to the accompaniment of an eleven-piece jazz band. The ninth act is an early gumboot dance called *isicathulo*, presented in the context of a worker's home-style restaurant. The dancers are accompanied by Zulu *maskanda* guitar playing in the *ukuvamba* style (vamping).[22] In the tenth act Richard Majola, the tap dancer, sings and dances to jazz ensemble accompaniment. He references Harlem in the song text. The contrast between this and the previous cut suggests class distinctions: tap dancing was for the elite, and gumboot was the style of migrant workers. The tenth act consists of a langarm dance band performance in Cape Town. The singing is in Afrikaans, with the characteristic saxophone lineup.

An attractive blues and jazz singer introduces the final portion of the film by paying tribute to the sponsor. She sings "The Girl on the Cover of *Zonk!*" This clip demonstrates the two venues of jazz performance, the elite ballroom dance and the more rowdy working-class environment. The same singers and instrumentalists frequent both sites, though what is required musically is quite different in each context. The emcee in act twelve informs the audience in an ironic tone that the black singer Skip Mphahlane will sing "September in the Rain," a song made famous by a white man imitating the black man. The grand finale features the *Zonk!* female singer, who is joined by the jazz band as the entire cast enters and performs together. As a final gesture, and with visual flashes of African rural life, the cast sings "Nkosi Sikelel' iAfrika," the anthem of the African National Congress, which was banned by the apartheid regime but became an integral part of the new national anthem in the 1990s.

Like most of South Africa's black and Coloured performers of the era, Sathima participated in a couple of the local commercial jazz and variety traveling shows prevalent in the country before the state clamped down on the freedom of movement of people of color. Most were collaborative projects between white, black, and Coloured South Africans. Conceived as one of several white liberal oppositional moves to the growing pressure from the apartheid regime, these shows were among the first instances of interracial collaboration in South Africa. Created to showcase black talent to the world they often generated controversy among performers, who claimed exploitation by white impresarios, frustration with the lack of artistic direction in some, frequent unfulfilled promises of overseas travel, inadequate compensation, and too much repetition in show content. Despite the obvious difficulties, these venues did pro-vide the only experience and training available to black and Coloured South Africans. Probably the most successful regional production was Herbert's *African Jazz and Variety*, which ran for eight years, traveling in South Africa, Zimbabwe, Zambia, Mozambique, and central Africa.

As noted, Sathima auditioned unsuccessfully at Weissman Hall in Cape Town for a part in the *Golden City Dixies*, one of the first shows to tour the country. In 1957, at the age of twenty, she joined Klugman's *Coloured Jazz and Variety* as a singer. I have found no mention of *Coloured Jazz and Variety* in the local press, and Sathima's recollections are a little vague. The acts and personnel she told me about included Tommy Jewel, who bal-anced a bicycle on his chin; the Laughing Policeman; a woman tap dancer called Kathleen Eunoch; there was Ayisha Isaacs, a Muslim girl who sang Portuguese songs; Douggie Noble was Cape Town's Bing Crosby; some-one played the part of Elvis Presley; the two Moffies (cross-dressing per-formers) who performed the Dances of the Seven Veils; Piper Laurie and another man called Joey; and Sathima the singer.[23] They performed in local hotels, movie theaters, and community halls before going on tour in southern Africa in 1956 and 1957.

More variety than jazz, *Coloured Jazz and Variety* was a critical resource for developing Sathima's sense of improvisation, as much a musical as a life skill because big ideas and financial failure were not uncommon features of these shows. Sathima met Adams when she joined *Coloured Jazz and Variety*. Traveling with few resources, financial or otherwise, and being endlessly on the road had its stresses. Jimmy cared for Sathima, ultimately starting a relationship with her. After traveling for several months, they reached Zimbabwe and the Hwange (formerly Wankie) Game Reserve, where Sathima and Jimmy celebrated her twenty-first birthday on 17 October 1957, with a meal of soup and bread. The bus they toured in regularly broke down, and in the end the musicians were left stranded in Mafeking, a town on the South African border. Penniless, several of the performers had to entertain local people in order to be fed and housed. Jimmy and Sathima have warm memories of the hospitality of the people of Mafeking at the time. The gig they organized was en-thusiastically supported, giving them just enough money to buy trans-portation back to Johannesburg. Jimmy and Sathima had heard there was work in the African townships and Portuguese nightclubs in Lourenço Marques (now Maputo), Mozambique, so they traveled to Mozambique to perform in the hotels for the Christmas holidays. Sathima remembers having to learn "an African song," which she sang over and over that Christmas. Adams recalls that the musicians spiked his drink, causing him to pass out at one of the performances. He ended up in the hospital, eventually waking up to find Sathima at his side.

When they returned to Johannesburg, the two lived with a group of gangsters in Malay Camp, a housing settlement for black, Coloured, and Indian South Africans in Johannesburg. Sathima recalls that people would come in and out of their room all night long as they all lay sleeping on the floor. But these people loved artists and musicians, and so she and Adams would sing and perform for their hosts. On occasion they would be performing when the gangsters arrived with their axes and other weapons: "They would have you singing and musicians couldn't stop until they told you to stop," said Sathima. Back in the city, Adams and Sathima often visited the Bantu Men's Social Center (BMSC)/Dorkay House,[24] an institution that holds an important place in black South African performance history. Jimmy remembers going into one of the rooms at the BMSC and seeing a series of holes in the walls with gramophones inside each hole. The musicians were sitting in front of the gramophone players, listening and copying what they heard. The BMSC was also where Adams and Sathima met the renowned South African saxophonist Kippie Moeketsi. Knowing they had no regular income, Moeketsi would press a pound sterling into Adams's hand every time they visited the BMSC. "That kept us alive," Adams told me. "For a year Kippie gave us money for food." The couple finally made their way back to Cape Town in late 1957.

There were other traveling shows featuring black South African and Coloured talent launched in this period, though Sathima didn't perform in them. *African Jazz and Variety* (as noted, it was later called *African Follies*) originated in Johannesburg in 1954 under the direction of Alf Herbert, and, with a cast of forty, traveled through South Africa, Zimbabwe, Zambia, Mozambique, and the Congo. It was still on the road in 1962. South Africans who made careers in South Africa and throughout the world out of *African Jazz and Variety* include Miriam Makeba, the trumpeter Hugh Masekela, and Sonny Pillay in the United States, Gene Williams, who traveled to Britain to work with the bandleader Jack Parnel, and Jeff Hujah, Brian Isaacs, and Gambi George in Sweden.[25] Some, like Abigail Kubeka and Dolly Rathebe, stayed in South Africa to pursue solid careers as singers in that country.[26] Following the success of

African Jazz and Variety, the newly formed Union of Southern African Artists organized the now well-known Township Jazz concerts in white areas, recordings of which have been reissued by Gallo Records (South Africa).

Similarly, the *Golden City Dixies* was one of the few such ensembles to travel internationally. The trip was described in *Zonk!: The African People's Magazine* in April 1959:

> At last, after many years of having farewell concerts and publicity about going overseas, a show is really going overseas, and our congratulations and good-luck wishes go with the Golden Dixies, a live vital coon show which has left by air for a tour of Britain and the Continent, the first entertainment group from the Union [of South Africa] to tour overseas. They will give concerts and have been booked to appear on television. . . . Corrine Harris and Elizabeth Julius, both polished performers, are the female contingent of the show. Arthur Gillies, the wizard of the keys, is on the piano. Gambi George, South Africa's king of the drums, handles the percussion; Shimmy Peter Radise, tenor sax master; Graham Tainton is show compere and other famous artists such as Jusuf Williams and Brian Isaacs go to make up a very competent group of performers.

Subsequent to the success of these two performances, *King Kong: An African Jazz Opera* was written and produced. In March 1959 the South African Mike Phahlane commented that *King Kong* marked a shift in local performance:

> The days of imitating (often poor imitations) American artists have passed. This era of show business certainly served its purpose, it spotlighted the latent talent possessed by our African artists, it also went to show that we were capable of great things, but let's face it, it was not our own—there was nothing African about our theatre. . . . Now after hard work and plenty of courage, the *King Kong* team has come up with something that is really our own, really African and above all real theater. . . . There are many bouquets to be handed out—the whole conception of the show is remarkable and what *Porgy and Bess* means to the Negro of America, *King Kong* will mean to us. Todd Matshikiza's compositions, Spike Glazer's direction of the band, Harry Bloom's scripting, Leon Gluckman's production and the cast itself all deserve the highest praise![27]

11. Golden City Dixies deplaning in South Africa.
Courtesy of District Six Museum.

As suggested earlier, the international success and local pride achieved with *King Kong* and the *Golden City Dixies* were bittersweet: with travel overseas came the opportunity for several of the performers to remain in Europe and the United Kingdom. Some never returned home.

Creating a Modern Jazz Community

It is hard to know just who initiated the modern jazz movement in Cape Town as a whole, but everyone I spoke to concurred, and the archival evidence supports the claim: this was an extraordinary period of musical passion and activity. The South African press aimed at "non-white" readers — *The Golden City Post, Zonk! The African People's Magazine*, and *Drum Magazine* — all contained regular reviews of recordings, those locally produced (mostly of local music in vernacular languages) and those that arrived from Europe and the United States. A single page of one of these publications could include commentary on traditional and modern African and Coloured music, including Zulu guitarists, concertina players, choral groups, dance bands, and popular and jazz recordings mostly from the United States. Often reviewers would include tidbits of information about recordings and musical life in Britain or the United States. There were film reviews, biographical pieces, and interviews with British and, in the case of jazz, African American musicians.

The newspapers feature extended articles on Duke Ellington, Louis Armstrong, the blues singer W. C. Handy, Sarah Vaughan, Billie Holiday, Ella Fitzgerald, Lena Horne, the folk singer Harry Belafonte, and the popular artist Sammy Davis Jr. On occasion a South African visiting London or New York would meet an artist. Armstrong was interviewed in London during this period, and there are reports of his visit to what is now Zimbabwe on a U.S. State Department tour. Armstrong met the South African Armstrong sound-alike Ben "Satch" Masinga on that trip. There are also articles on South African musicians who were leaving or had left for overseas, with regular commentary about the biggest star of them all, Makeba, who by the early 1960s, with Belafonte as her sponsor, was living and singing in New York City and fraternizing with the African American entertainment elite.[28]

Vincent Kolbe organized the first jazz concert in District Six in Cape Town. The jazz gatherings came about because in 1955 the student Rag committee at the University of Cape Town decided to include a jazz concert in its program.[29] In conversation with me, Kolbe surmised that it was probably an imitation of Dave Brubeck's *Jazz Goes to Campus* idea from the United States. It took place at Weizmann Hall in Sea Point, a venue owned by a Jewish family known for its openness to racial mixing. Keeping the hall integrated constituted an oppositional stance toward the growing presence of the apartheid regime. Unfortunately, the Rag committee asked white musicians only to perform jazz—no Coloured musicians were included. And they were angry. Those "white racist musicians who never really jammed, though they could read very well, [dominated] the show," Kolbe explained. "They eventually formed an all-White Musicians' Union later. And Harold Jephthah, who was the best of our guys, sat with his sax completely ignored." An active member of the Holy Cross Catholic Church community in District Six, Kolbe decided that something had to be done about racism in jazz.

Kolbe approached the priest at Holy Cross, who agreed to let the Coloured musicians use the church hall on Wednesday nights. They would charge "5 bob a head," and whatever was taken at the door would go to the church. This started a regular gathering of jazz musicians and included a host of big bands, including the Merry Macs and Dougie Erasmus's Big Band: "It was such a massive success that people are still talking about it. At the wake for Dougie Erasmus in September 1995 all the guys were there and recalled that concert."[30]

Sathima became more directly connected to that modern jazz world in Cape Town one day after returning home from teaching school. She was picking out a Doris Day tune on her mother's piano and singing along when amateur singer Bernie Smith came to the door selling brushes. He told her he thought she sounded like a jazz singer. The very first jazz concert in Athlone at the Glemore Town Hall was about to take place, and Smith invited her to go and sing with the band, promising to introduce her to the musicians. Sathima was thrilled at the invitation and decided to go. But she remembers being really nervous when she went up to perform. She closed her eyes and, with her heart pounding, began to sing "Don't Blame Me." The saxophonist Harold Jephthah was particularly taken with her singing and told her there were several bands working in the clubs in and around Cape Town. "If I wanted to come and work there, I should just turn up," Sathima said. So she went along to Jephthah's rehearsals and began to sing with the musicians.

Sound recordings became a primary mode of musical immersion for Sathima as she moved more definitively into the jazz scene. She never owned recordings herself because she couldn't afford to buy them. Adams never bought them either because he feared if he listened too closely he would lose a sense of his own particular sound. In fact, that is exactly what happened to him once—he had listened closely to Lee Konitz's recording of "All the Things You Are" and faithfully transcribed the entire arrangement note for note. When Adams arrived at the rehearsal, his musicians could not see what was so special about his arrangements. Failing to recognize the excellence of his aural and arrangement skills, the musicians commented: "You sound just like Lee Konitz." "When will they hear Jimmy Adams and not Lee Konitz?" wondered the frustrated Adams.

February, Adams, and Sathima all agreed: there was no point in just copying the recording because all performance had to come from the heart. "It is better to do what your heart tells you than to copy someone else," was February's advice when I spoke with him in 1996. Many people did buy recordings, however, so Sathima heard blues and jazz performed on records belonging to the male musicians and record collectors she began to associate with, especially in the after-hours gatherings in local clubs and community halls. There was a real passion for the music.

Several musicians interviewed in the last decade talk about how far they would go to hear a particular recording—quite often they didn't even know the person who owned it, they just wanted the chance to hear it. And they would walk for miles to listen to a recording. Jephthah, who, according to his friends, had the largest record collection of anyone in the group, recalled that he would do *anything* to find the money to purchase the latest 78s from the local record store. "I lived in the record shop," Jephthah told me laughingly. "I remember one day I had a toothache, and my mother gave me money to see the dentist. Instead of going in the direction of the dentist's office, however, I walked straight to the shop and bought the latest Coleman Hawkins recording." In fact, Jephthah listened so carefully to recordings of Charlie Parker that when he left South Africa in the early 1960s he actually played in a Parker tribute recording in Europe. Parker's wife, Chan, gave Parker's horn to Jephthah, saying he was the musician who best captured her late husband's musical spirit.

After the Glemore jazz event sometime in 1954 Sathima began to

12. Jimmy Adams with American School
of Music jacket and Sathima's sister
Edith Green, 1996.

13. Harold Jephthah, December 1999.

Both photos by Carol Ann Muller.

moonlight in a range of the less elite clubs in Cape Town. People remember the Tombs, the Catacombs, the Vortex, Darryl's Nightclub, the
Balalaika, and the Navigators' Den. Hardly any of these clubs existed for
longer than a few years because it became impossible to keep anything
open when apartheid legislation began to be enforced. But in the late
1950s there seemed to be plenty of opportunity for Sathima. Kolbe, who,
in his own words, "played some piano," would often invite Sathima to
come and sing to his accompaniment, as did Kenny Jephtah, the guitarist.
Sometimes she would sing with her guitarist cousin Basil Rich. For a few
years the clubs provided musicians with the chance to try out new materials, to explore new musical possibilities, and to begin to really improvise. All that changed in the 1960s, when no more mixing in public places
across the color bar was permitted, and white clubs began to import Portuguese and Greek musicians in place of the Coloured performers.

The more Sathima ventured out into public life as a musician, the more
she was confronted with the new realities of the laws of apartheid, in her
personal experience and in her reading. She began to ask a new set of
questions about what it meant to be called Coloured or St. Helenian of
mixed heritage. Kolbe again occupied a pivotal place in Sathima's education about jazz as music and lifestyle and about its ties to an African
and Coloured diasporic consciousness. He nurtured her growing political awareness of issues of race and jazz, of musical and political freedom. While living with her mother, Sathima spent many evenings in the
Kew Town library located just outside her mother's apartment block.[31]
Under Kolbe's leadership that library was the hub of social and artistic activity. He described the community as bohemian, with a small but
significant group of Coloured intellectuals and artists, among them the
photographer George Hallett, whose photographs appear on the covers
of Sathima's two South African recordings, *Cape Town Love* and *Musical
Echoes* (see figures 29 and 31 on pages 244 and 272).

Kolbe also ran a Jazz Appreciation Club that met at the library. It is
possible Sathima first heard Billie Holiday through this club, though she
thinks it was a little later on. Regardless of the specific details, this was the
time when Sathima began to work more closely with the music of Duke
Ellington (see response below). She began to read about the African
American experience because Kolbe provided her with books by Richard
Wright, Langston Hughes, W. E. B. Du Bois, and others. He passed onto
her the early autobiography of Holiday, *Lady Sings the Blues: The Searing*

14. Sathima singing at a nightclub, late 1950s.
Collection of Sathima Bea Benjamin.

Autobiography of an American Musical Legend (1956) before the apartheid regime banned it. As she began to question her identity, she read of the experience of a people called Colored in the United States.[32] This was a turning point for Sathima because in her mind those the regime had called Coloured were not alone in their experiences of the harshness of racism. There were others, like Billie Holiday, called Colored in her book, who had found a place for themselves as people of color and seemed to be successfully navigating the world on musical terms.

While Sathima was still teaching, a reporter from the *Golden City Post* arrived at the school looking for the young jazz singer because he wanted to photograph and write an article on a jazz singer who was also a teacher, an unusual combination at the time. This was just too much for the school principal: he was already keeping close tabs on Sathima. Every Monday morning he would come into her classroom to check that she was prepared and present. She was always there: she was an excellent teacher and loved her students. If her dual occupations — teacher of the young, which required a morally upright young woman, and singer of jazz in nightclubs, hanging out with the socially and politically transgressive — were made public the principal and his school would probably get into trouble. He was uneasy about the publicity an interview would generate. She spoke to the reporter, and the article and photograph came out on 26 August 1958:

HER NAME SPELLS J-A-Z-Z

Around Cape Town's sleepless night-spots the name of Beatrice Benjamin spells J-A-Z-Z. It is jazz in its careful, sophisticated moods. Jazz wrapped up in glamour, jazz sung delicately, teasingly, and lovingly. For 'Beatty' Benjamin, as hundreds of her fans know her, has a way of using her face, her body and hands, to sing a song, thereby enriching its message.

Recently 'Beatty' went to the Naaz — Cape Town's plushiest, jazziest, all-race nightclub. Her voice, deceptively dreary, sometimes smoky and sad, reached out to the customers as she sang: "It Could Happen to You."

Then galloping away with "Fine and Dandy," Beatty whooped it up, eyes closed, forgetfully alone, in a packed nightclub. The applause at the end was worth it, for "Beatty" Benjamin has just made her finest statement.

At her most original "Beatty" breaks up the pace of the song and its lines, never losing the beat, and achieves a wonderful personal style that taps the true sources of her power.

Beatrice teaches school by day and sings by night. She has a heart too. Once she sang for a POST charity show to help neglected mental cases.

The fact that she gets engagements in all-White clubs hasn't gone to Beatty's head. On Saturdays and Sundays you can see her, working hard at the "Ambassador's Club" rehearsing. This chocolate gal is just "Fine and Dandy!"

Sathima was told she had to make a choice between teaching and singing. She couldn't understand what the fuss was about and invited the principal to come to the jazz gatherings. He refused. The school pleaded with her to choose teaching, but she decided it was time to follow the music. To some extent, being forced to choose was a gendered issue. Her cousin Basil Rich, who was a schoolteacher and guitarist, performed six nights a week at the Navigators' Den, a harbor hangout for jazz musicians and American sailors in Cape Town. He never needed to make the choice between teaching and performing because he never appeared in the newspaper and also, he thinks, because there was a significant physical distance between his daily and nightly workplaces. He wasn't as exposed as his female cousin.[33]

Sathima left the relative security of the teaching profession for the more adventurous but uncertain world of jazz performance. It was a decision that cost her financially and socially. Her family, particularly her father, was frustrated with her. When I talked with Rich in 1996, he told me that from that point on Sathima moved in very different circles from the rest of the extended family: "She moved with the musicians, the jazz people. These people were a complete mixture: Whites, Blacks, Coloureds, Indians, whatever. There it was an advantage to be Black. Like, we weren't black enough, if you get what I mean."

Sathima began to perform with several elite ensembles and pianists in white nightclubs in the Cape Town area. February had a trio with the guitarist Kenny Jephthah and a bass player. Kenny enthusiastically recommended Sathima to February. At first, Henry told me, he hadn't wanted a singer because he thought they weren't real musicians, just imitators. But he agreed to hear Sathima sing and immediately decided she could be a female Nat King Cole, so he modeled his group on the Nat King Cole trio. February, who was married with children, was a wonderful mentor. He was the first to teach Sathima how to handle herself professionally with the band and, significantly for Sathima, unlike the other musicians he never flirted or came onto her sexually. She would repay her old teacher in 1999 by featuring him on *Cape Town Love*.

While she was making the club scene, Sathima met the Swiss graphic designer and jazz and blues record collector Paul Meyer, who had lived for a time in Johannesburg but had migrated down to Cape Town. Meyer was one of several international visitors in Cape Town's modern jazz community, and it was he who introduced Sathima to Abdullah. He also surfaces in the autobiography of Hugh Masekela in an account that discusses Meyer's record collection. Masekela's account concurs with how Sathima remembers her meetings with Meyer in Cape Town sometime later, and it raises an interesting concern about the relationship between jazz and race at the time. Masekela wrote, "Paul was from Basel, a short, blond, blue-eyed man with a film star's looks. He was extremely friendly and spoke with a strong German accent. . . . I drank beer with him, which was illegal for Africans at the time. In fact, Miriam [Makeba] and I had no business being with Paul at all, because it was illegal to socialize with Whites and, with an African woman in the room, we were actually 'conspiring to contravene' the Immorality Act. But I didn't care. I was in music heaven. Paul Meyer had every record ever made by Louis Armstrong, Jelly Roll Morton, Ma Rainey, Bessie Smith . . . Count Basie, Sy Oliver, Duke Ellington and more." [34]

Masekela remarks that it struck him at the time that Meyer had no white jazz artists in his collection. Meyer explained to his guests that

he knew deep down in his heart that jazz was the music of Black folks, and regardless of how much they excelled, White people could never in their wildest dreams capture the true essence of jazz. Paul Meyer's analysis of White people's jazz capabilities really surprised me. I had never heard this angle before. My music colleagues and I had never discussed American or South African music from the perspective of race. We had equally admired Glenn Miller and Count Basie, Benny Goodman and Duke Ellington, Ella Fitzgerald and Rosemary Clooney, . . . Clifford Brown and Miles Davis—it made no difference to us. . . . If anything we were encouraged that music was being used as a weapon for eradicating racial stereotyping. Paul Meyer's comment burst my little bubble of hope. [35]

Whatever his personal views on the relationship between jazz and race in 1958, Meyer was a core organizer in Cape Town of large-scale benefit performances featuring many of Cape Town's finest musicians. Performing for charity was the only way to charge an admission fee and avoid paying the excessively high entertainment taxes levied on all live performance in South Africa. Meyer helped organize several such charity events, one in the Woodstock Town Hall in aid of a mental health institution (called the Snake Pit), and the other titled *Just Jazz Meets the Ballet*, at which Sathima and Abdullah performed.[36] The *Golden City Post* described the affair:

> *The Big Jazz Show Has All the Talent*
> Jazz fans were treated to some high-octane music at the Woodstock Town Hall during the week when five leading jazz groups broke loose with a concert in aid of various Peninsula youth clubs. But if you missed the session, not to worry. All these artists have offered to play for "Post's" big jazz night in the Cape Town City Hall in a few weeks' time. EVERY PENNY RAISED GOES TO THE CAPE MENTAL HEALTH SOCIETY TO START A BUILDING FUND. ALL WILL BE THERE.
> [Picture of Sathima Bea Benjamin].
> Blues Buck up Beattie: Beattie Benjamin, another of the artists at the Woodstock show gives with "Mr. Wonderful." Beattie loves singing, especially the "blues" for it does things for her emotions. "Try singing the blues," she advises. It works wonders for you (*Golden City Post*, 30 April 1958).

> *Just Jazz, Just Great: Post Show Aids Kids.*
> The city's biggest and best jazz show ever. [Picture of Beattie Benjamin] Blues singer Beatrice Benjamin had the boys swooning. The Jimmy Adams big band played as well (*Golden City Post*, 20 July 1958).

Sathima recalls traveling from her mother's place in Athlone to the elite white suburb of Camps Bay in Meyer's Triumph convertible to hear the recordings of Billie Holiday. In terms of the Group Areas Act, it was illegal for her to be in Camps Bay as a Cape Coloured woman, except if she were working as a housemaid; and fraternizing with a white man could be interpreted as a contravention of the Immorality Act. But she was so desperate to hear the music she was willing to take the risk. On one of those evenings, in a room filled with candles, Meyer had pressured her to take the relationship to the next stage. Sathima remembers she burst into tears. "I didn't want that," she told me. "I just wanted to hear the music.

Just then there was a knock on the door. I was terrified it could have been the police. But it wasn't. It was Abdullah Ibrahim." He had arrived at Meyer's home hoping to spend the night there because he was living on the streets at the time. Sathima begged Abdullah to persuade Meyer to drive her home — otherwise she would have to get the bus at dawn and risk arrest. Meyer eventually took her back to Athlone.

By that point Sathima had become increasingly disillusioned with the popular music and jazz scene in the clubs because, it seemed, as a woman she always had to pay a price for male musical accompaniment: the constant pressure to sleep with the musicians. She reached the end of her tether after she refused to shack up with the talented pianist Arthur Gilles of *Golden City Dixies* fame. Gilles accompanied Sathima on piano soon after she refused him and, she commented despairingly, "he deliberately started me off in a key I could not sing in. I was so humiliated that at that point I decided to give up performing in public." Sathima was truly wary of the sexual pressure when she got a call from Meyer, who was organizing a jazz show and wanted her to sing: "I didn't want to perform with any of the local pianists, but Paul persuaded me to go along. He told me that Dollar Brand [Abdullah Ibrahim] would be accompanying the performers, and convinced me that Abdullah would not be interested in me. So I agreed."

Sathima remembers that all the performers had to rehearse at the Ambassadors ballroom dance studio. She had been working on a song by Ellington, "I Got It Bad and That Ain't Good," and was hoping to sing it in the show. Abdullah was sitting at the piano, rehearsing all the singers and dancers. Then it was her turn: "I have to admit I was quite intimidated by this tall, lanky man with the huge brown boots. He didn't have a reputation for warmth and friendliness. 'And what is it that you want to do?' he asked me. 'Well, I am working on an Ellington song, I Got It Bad,' I said. Abdullah blinked twice. It was the same piece he had been working with himself. 'And what key do you want to sing it in?' 'D flat,' I answered. I always seem to sing on the black notes." They worked at it for awhile, but Ibrahim admitted he would have to figure out how to accompany her in that key. She invited him to visit her mother's home and to use the piano there to practice. They began to meet regularly from then on. Sathima's mother was uncomfortable with the relationship that soon developed between the two. Though Abdullah's grandfather was a white

Scotsman, Abdullah may have looked too dark and his hair may have been too curly for him to be warmly welcomed by the wider family. But it also involved the fact he was, in John Samuels's words, "a local," whereas Sathima descended from St. Helenians. "You speak about people integrating and stuff, that is what she's done," Samuels explained. "At that time we used to keep together as a community, that is not the case now."

Sathima and Abdullah performed together at Meyer's charity event, and a report on Sathima's singing came out on 29 January 1959, in the *Golden City Post*: "There is no doubt about it, Beatrice Benjamin is the mostest, the greatest and the most appealing girl singer in the Cape, whispers Howard Lawrence. What she did to the audience at Post's show, "Just Jazz Meets the Ballet" was wow. I got it bad when she sang 'I Got It Bad.' Everybody else got it bad too and they kept shouting for more of that *feeling*. Most promising singer for 1959. Agreed." Sathima has vivid memories of the audiences at those performances, a wonderful community of people who loved the music, who got involved. "This music just naturally brought people together," she said.

It wasn't long before it was clear that Abdullah was in love with Sathima. After Adams, Sathima had returned to her relationship with Sam Isaacs. He had waited patiently for her while she had traveled southern Africa and become stranded in Johannesburg. How would she tell him she was moving on again, this time with a man who could hardly support himself? But Abdullah gave her an ultimatum. She had three days to decide what she wanted out of a relationship and to either go with Sam or commit to him. She knew that if she said no to Abdullah, she would also be turning down the deep sense of calling she felt inside for the music. So she ended everything with Isaacs.

Living as a professional musician was almost unheard of in Cape Town in the 1950s. There was no steady income, and by this time Sathima and Joan had moved out of their mother's home. There were no hotels for Coloured people, so they lived off the goodness of friends, sometimes sleeping in the streets. On one occasion she and Joan were renting a place that didn't allow any additional people, so they used to sneak Abdullah into the building: he either climbed in through the back window or came through the front door dressed in painting overalls pretending to be a contract worker.

Jazz Clubs

The new jazz scene of the late 1950s (actually 1958–62) found its opera-tional base in the clubs of Woodstock, a suburb just outside the city center, which was something of a racially mixed, or "grey" area. In and around the city as a whole there were clubs like the Naaz, the Mermaid, the Restaurant Club, the Vortex, The Navigator's Den, the Three Cellars, the Balalaika, the Catacombs, the Brown Horse, and the Zambezi. The Naaz sponsored racially integrated groups. Kolbe recalled,

> Richer people came to slum in Woodstock. There were quite a few wealthy White jazz fanatics who spent heavily there. They brought their friends. They looked very casual but we knew they were rich. . . . The only previ-ous mixing I was aware of was in the Communist Party, but that was all quite "Camps Bay"—really quite elite. In '50s jazz culture it was a differ-ent kind of thing.
>
> In the clubs there was mixing to the point of contravening the Im-morality Act! Not only was mixed clubbing a problem for the apartheid government, but they targeted individual relationships as well. Maude Damons became a prominent jazz singer from District Six. She ended up in London as the cops were after her and her White lover. Hotep Galeta (Christian Barnett) had an older German girlfriend and they had to leave the country. Had it been left to itself, this jazz scene could have developed into something remarkable. . . . It was an apartheid casualty.[37]

When I asked Adams, who used to attend these jazz clubs, particu-larly the club that met weekly at Holy Cross Catholic Church in District Six, he said that that started as "a Coloured thing" but quickly began to include Africans and whites: "I am sorry to say this, I don't like this politics business, but anyway, it's all there. We had a nightclub here that was very famous, the Naaz (in Woodstock). We had the Mermaid (in Sea Point), you know. And these Whites used to come to these clubs and interfere with our women. That is how they closed down the clubs." Adams recalled one club in particular: "After the Mermaid closed down, I heard that some [white] Parliament members came in there dressed up as ducktails, came to sit around and see what is going on there. . . . Ja, when the *Whities* started moving in with us, that's when everything started going [crazy]. And they closed down all the clubs. They threw us all out of the White clubs."[38]

Sathima concurs with Adams: "The regime wouldn't let us work in the White clubs on weekends anymore. We lost so many people. It was their loss, and it really wasn't our gain. We didn't have our own clubs: we needed those White clubs to stay open. So life really changed." The growing repression of the apartheid regime coupled with her reading and listening meant that Sathima's performance in this period expanded from being a vehicle of emotional outlet and a longing for love to becoming infused with a political consciousness. She was keenly aware that racism was not just a South African problem, and to resist its force musicians would need to make themselves part of an international movement. For Sathima and her peers, the blues was not simply a discourse about individual struggle and pain, but a means to articulating collective social pain. The world of jazz performance was both exhilarating in the way it challenged racial discrimination and insisted upon ideals of freedom, equality, and nonracialism, but equally dangerous because of its integrated community.

Sathima has told me that it was at this time she was drawn to the music of Duke Ellington because it allowed her to imagine new ways of being musically and provided alternative modes of group identification. Challenging but beautiful to Sathima, Ellington's melodies wrapped themselves around emotionally evocative and heartfelt words. It was through Ellington's song "I Got It Bad" that Sathima and Abdullah came to know each other musically. It was Ellington's music that would join their lives together and give them the chance to record in Paris on 23 February 1963, and indeed it was Ellington who opened doors to the world of jazz for both Sathima and Abdullah.

Jazz Ambassadors

Soon after they began their relationship, Abdullah started the Dollar Brand School of Music, the first of several music schools he founded. Sathima gave him money she had saved from her teaching days to initiate the school, which was located on Hanover Street in District Six, right across the road from the Zanzibar Nightclub and a few doors away from the offices of the *Golden City Post*. Abdullah and Sathima lived in that rickety old school building, sleeping on the floor. The school had a piano and some chairs. But, Sathima reflected, she didn't think anyone was ready to embrace the kind of music Abdullah was creating at the time, and so the school was not a success.

In late 1959 and 1960 the two musicians each recorded an LP. Meyer was responsible for the first known LP record of South African jazz: *My Songs for You by Beatty*. Abdullah was the producer, but the record was never released.[39] Soon afterward, Sathima remembers, she and Abdullah "half-walked, half-rode a train" to Johannesburg, where they lived and performed for several months. While in Johannesburg, Abdullah formed a jazz group he named the Jazz Epistles with the alto saxophonist Kippie Moeketsi, the trumpeter Hugh Masekela, the trombonist Jonas Gwangwa, and himself on piano. They went into the Gallo recording studios and recorded *Jazz Epistles: Verse One* around September 1960. Despite being an extremely important development in South African jazz history, the group disbanded soon after the recording when Moeketsi and Gwangwa were offered the chance to travel to London with the *King Kong* musical in 1961.

In Johannesburg, Sathima and Abdullah lived in a Coloured township with a guy called Leon, and they survived for weeks on milk, liver bologna, and bread. They did some "real starving for the music," Sathima commented. Then they moved to one of the black townships, where they lived with the journalist Mike Phahlane, his mother, and a friend named Mike Campbell. Mike's mother had a shebeen, a shack made of corrugated zinc sheets where she let Sathima and Abdullah have the couch. "That's when I remember connecting with the soul of an African Mama," Sathima said. "She didn't say much, but she had this unconditional love that just shone through. She never complained, and I am sure her life was difficult. There was this little girl in the house called Tintinyana—that's why Abdullah wrote that song titled 'Tintinyana.'"[40] Sathima remembers they would travel into the black townships to perform with musicians living there. On a couple of occasions they were arrested because they were traveling into areas they did not have permits to enter. The police "couldn't understand what we wanted in the townships. What we wanted was to make music together." That was when Sathima met Moeketsi for a second time.

Sathima was back in Cape Town at the time of the Sharpeville Massacre in Johannesburg in March 1960. Abdullah had traveled to Johannesburg to perform with the Jazz Epistles. The apartheid regime declared the first of many States of Emergency. It was a frightening time for Sathima because suddenly Abdullah disappeared. It seems there was a group of musicians hiding out in the house of members of the Communist Party in Johannesburg. Life suddenly became dangerous, and Sathima remembers going to stay with Joan and her friend Billie Daniels. While in hiding, Abdullah had an affair with one of the white women in the Communist Party: there were plans for all in their group to leave the country. It was traumatic for Sathima, who had come to regard Abdullah as being above the run-of-the-mill musicians she knew. He had a certain aura and was brilliant, creative, and strong-willed, so she was devastated by the affair. She couldn't believe that someone she had given up so much for was as human as everyone else. But she would realize over and over that this was the price she paid for his love. It would be many years before she recognized that she didn't have to be what the Benjamin's had called the "charity child" in relationships, taking only what was handed out to her.

Sathima and Abdullah were both in Cape Town in 1961. Though they had performed in all the white-owned Cape nightclubs, the place they ultimately created for jazz as a progressive musical form was the Ambassadors. There are three accounts of this musical configuration: an evocative rendering by a reporter from *Drum Magazine* in 1961, a counternarrative by the photographer Hardy Stockman (who wrote it just before he died in Bangkok), and Sathima's own story. First, the beautifully written *Drum* version:

> The naked light bulb, like the mood, is blue. The only other illumination in the place comes from the glowing ends of cigarettes, or maybe a stray moonbeam filtering down the slopes of Table Mountain and in through a back window.
>
> The chairs are arranged carefully, like pews, and the congregation is as devout as any other Sunday night gathering. In the darkened corner the tall, thin guy with the tight jeans and the size 12 army boots is leading his group through an original composition. The long, bony fingers slide or thump, caress or squeeze the notes out, and the horn, the bass, and the drums, catch the message and pass it on.
>
> Dark as it is, the Dollar is gleaming tonight. This is the real stuff, the pulse beat of the jazz world in the Cape, and Dollar Brand and his group are pumping it out—though this is their night off from six days of cafe-capers with the beatnik gang.[41]

From this center of the jazz scene, which is up an iron staircase near where the Cape's trolley buses get their nightly wash and brush-up, the music world stretches far down the Peninsula, and every other month some new guy with a horn or an alto sax or a bass is coming up from the shadows to catch the ear of the people who know their music.

In the past few years, the Cape has taken over as THE place for music, snatching the laurel from the backrooms and cellars a thousand miles north in [Johannesburg]. Dollar was in at the start of the move south, but he doesn't understand how it happened. Anyone who has been around the Cape long enough to know his music remembers the Big Band age just after the war. But they were all African, fifteen or more, beating it out like ebony Dorseys and Goodmans. Maybe it's the changing mood of South Africa that African music—Cape-wards, anyhow—has faded to no more than a township tin lid. So the Coloreds have taken over, and the mood is softer, sweeter, and more serious.

Dollar and his group are the lone wolves of the Cape Tin Pan Alley, dedicated jazz men all. They play it their way—and if the customers don't like it then that's tough on the customers. . . . "Jazz is the real classics," he says. "It's all here, at the Cape. The place is dripping with talent and I'm not sure I ever want to be anywhere else."[42]

Sathima described the club as follows:

The guy who owned [the Ambassadors] was Dave Saunders, and he was a friend of Abdullah's. He had this lovely space in Woodstock. You had to climb these stairs. He had this space and he had a piano. And Abdullah started. We had thirteen people the first week—we used to do it only on Sunday nights. And after a couple of weeks, we couldn't contain all the people. It was just a place where you went and you sat down and listened. There was no dancing, no food, nothing. And, as I said, there was too much mixing going on at the time when they didn't want people to be mixing. So we had to close that down.[43]

One jazz fan, the late Hardy Stockman, recalls that when he moved to Cape Town in 1959, he

started looking for this guy Dollar Brand I heard about in Jo[hannes]burg. I found that he played Sunday nights at the Ambassador, a ballroom danc- ing school for "Non-Whites," right on the Main Road in Woodstock. Off I went climbing up the outside iron staircase, [and] got the surprise of my life. I was stunned. Dollar was on the piano, Johnny Gertze played the bass and Makhaya Ntshoko was the percussion wizard. The trio was producing sounds — and an atmosphere — I had not encountered in Africa before . . .

But that wasn't all. The place was over-crowded. The bands and audience were composed of Black and White and *anything in between*, mingling freely like nowhere else in the land. This was all the more surprising as there was no dancing and neither food nor drink was available. You either played or you listened. There was nothing else. I felt great. Finally, I had arrived "home."[44]

These three narratives, articulated four decades apart, describe the Ambassadors as they simultaneously bear witness to a pivotal moment in South African jazz history: the late 1950s and early 1960s in Cape Town. Sathima Bea Benjamin and Abdullah Ibrahim were central actors in the musical movement that constituted a feeling of home even for those, like Stockmann, who had recently gone to South Africa from a range of places abroad.[45] As he begins, the *Drum* reporter's tone is less ethnographic and more tied into the universal rhetoric of jazz writing. "Table Mountain" is the first marker of place, the first sign that we are not in the company of Americans, for example. Then again, we feel we are part of a transnational community of listeners — the mood is blue, the composition original and with a message; we read of the "Dollar" as proper name, of beatniks, jazzmen, Big Bands, and Tin Pan Alley — all very familiar categories. But with repetition of "the Cape" we come to realize that the writer is deeply embedded in a place and a community of jazz musicians and fans we know very little about. The "ebony Dorseys and Goodmans" suggest it is one where the categories of race and racial identification through musical performance become complicated. The other two accounts are more ethnographic, focused on the local contours of this particular community.

The Ambassadors lasted for several months, providing a place for musical exchange not only between the finest musicians in Cape Town, but also with those who came down from Johannesburg. Sathima recalls the days when Moeketsi came to perform with Abdullah in Cape Town. When Moeketsi played, "I mean it was so beautiful, there was such a connection. It was like a fever that hits, and then you just have to put the fire out," Sathima told me in 1990. This brief moment of musical connectivity locally and diasporic identification with African American jazz history internationally was short-lived.

In the aftermath of the Sharpeville Massacre in 1960 and the State of Emergency declared by the government life changed drastically for all jazz and dance band musicians. The state clamped down on all performance that catered to mixed ensembles, audiences, or clientele. It became clear to Abdullah and Sathima that it would be impossible to survive as creative artists in South Africa. Jazz performance, with all its mixing of people, had become a dangerous activity, monitored and raided by security forces. Sathima had never really thought about leaving South Africa. But it all happened quickly: "And that is when we moved. We would either have to shut up completely or we'd have to leave. And that's when we decided to leave, in 1961, because it became impossible, not only to do jazz. To do any kind of music. It became very repressive," she recalled.

Abdullah and Sathima would have to move a long way from the intimacy and warmth of the Cape Town jazz community if they were to grow or even just survive as professional musicians. In 1962, as the apartheid regime restricted all interracial performances, especially of jazz, the couple, literally starving for lack of opportunities, traveled to Switzerland, where Meyer had promised to help them find work and suitable housing. Jazz had become a tenuous passport to the transnational community of artists in Europe and the United States for these musicians from Cape Town. They followed several South Africans who had left before them, including Makeba, Masekela, and "Satch" Masinga. Sathima and Abdullah went to Europe.

For musicians, one of the most devastating pieces of legislation was the Publications and Entertainments Act, no. 26, of 1963, which established a Publications Control Board to censor perceived undesirable entertainment. The board had the power to prohibit any entertainment deemed to be undesirable; which offended the religious convictions of any section of the Republic's inhabitants (and this included only white people); and anything that propagated or promoted "communism," as it was defined in the Suppression of Communism Act of 1950.[46] This expanded the Entertainments (Censorship) Act, no. 29, of 1931, which was concerned with the control of film and stage entertainment. That act had included the right to control any allegedly offensive matter, in scenes purporting to illustrate "night life"; scenes referring to international or controversial politics; scenes representing antagonistic relations between capital and labor; scenes of pugilistic encounters between Europeans and non-Europeans. The brief description of this single piece of legislation cannot begin to convey the force of its impact on South Africans, particularly because each law operated in concert with others already in place. Suffice to say, that the apartheid regime targeted all interracial gatherings and performances, silenced all sounds and voices. They harassed the families of musicians who went abroad. And they began to take away the rights of citizenship to those who left and spoke out about the regime. In 1963 Makeba addressed the United Nations in New York on the subject of apartheid. She lost her rights to South African citizenship as a result, as did several other South African musicians living abroad.

Makeba, Masekela, and Gwangwa's ties to New York City and Belafonte, Sathima's imagined connection to the deceased Holiday and her in-person meeting with Duke Ellington and Billie Strayhorn, the community built with American free jazz musicians in Europe, and the invitation to a variety of jazz festivals in Europe and the United States in the 1960s would create a strong sense of continuity in racial struggles against white oppression for these South Africans as they moved out into a wider world of jazz performance. These partnerships induced powerful diasporic sentiment between African Americans and the South Africans coming out of Africa in the early 1960s.

RESPONSE

Imagining Musical Lineage through Duke and Billie

Lineage: a group of people related by descent from
a common ancestor.

For us in the Cape, Duke Ellington was never an American: he was just the grand old man from the V/village. —Abdullah Ibrahim, interview on North Carolina Central University radio, recorded in Dakar, Senegal, circa 2000

Though I'd been playing African music for a long time, here at last I was in Africa. —Duke Ellington (1976 [1973]) on his arrival in Senegal

My singer from Africa. — Duke Ellington on Sathima Bea Benjamin at the Newport Jazz Festival, 1965

While admitting the obvious influence of American jazz on its South African counterpart (it is impossible to discount the tremendous impact of Ellington alone), South African jazz has a character and expression of its own. — Richard McNeill in a 1963 newspaper article, quoted in McGregor (1996), 35–36

"Lineage," writes Roland Barthes, "reveals an identity stronger, more interesting than legal status — more reassuring as well, for the thought of origins soothes us."[47] Anthropologists and musicologists have regularly invoked the notion of lineage to explain social and musical relationships, patterns of reproduction or transmission, as well as rules of inheritance, obligation, and expectation between groups and individuals. In social anthropology, the related positions of lineage and affine defined by blood and marriage ties, respectively, have been conceptualized as the foundational mechanisms of social structure in large- and small-scale human groups around the globe. As such, they have been useful tools in the comparative analysis of such communities. Conceived of as internally cohesive, typically located in a single geographic site or, as in marriage, between two identifiable structures inhabiting sites in close proximity, lineage has been the mechanism that has rationalized variability in family relationships.

Similarly, in writing about musical communities, lineage typically signals the ancestral line through which musical craft, talent, or heritage is passed from one human generation to the next. This has been common, for example, in discussions of West African griots and the caste system for musical transmission in India. In a perhaps less socially binding use of the word in the European classical tradition, *lineage* has been used to trace style and its transformation through a discourse of influences or musical resemblances often crossing several places in Europe. One looks for the stylistic residue of one composer in the works of another. These kinds of narratives are typically about people who lived prior to the twentieth century, when concern about ownership, copyright attribution, and royalty payments to living musicians and their estates began to increase. They are mostly situated in a unified field called Europe and written about by those claiming a European cultural heritage. Similarly,

15. New lineages in Paris with Duke Ellington, Dollar Brand Trio, and Billy Strayhorn, from the CD *A Morning in Paris*. *Collection of Sathima Bea Benjamin.*

classical performers earn a pedigree through a lineage of teachers. For example, Tunde Jegede, the British-born cellist of African descent who is also a composer and *kora* player, establishes an authentic place for himself as a classical musician in the European tradition by explaining that his cello teacher had been a student of the world-renowned musician Pablo Casals.[48]

The rapid expansion of the popular music industry from the late nineteenth century on fundamentally dislodged ideas about the local interconnectedness of people and their music through bloodlines, identifiable cultural cohesion, and geography to stories about encounters between strangers, disembodied tracks of sound, across borders, languages, and currencies albeit in a so-called global village. In this context the concept of lineage seems to have lost its analytical value. It has been replaced, for example, by Michel Foucault's notion of the archeology of knowledge[49] — or music production, as per Steven Feld's writing on "Pygmy Pop" and the multiple mutations in unexpected venues and formations of the Solomon Island "Rorogwela Lullaby."[50] In popular music, lineages have been traced in terms of marketing crossovers—from the blues to rock'n'roll, from so-called Gregorian chant to *Chant*, the previously classified classical album that behaved like a popular item when it was repackaged, freshly marketed worldwide, and sold more than three million copies in a six-month period in the 1990s.[51] Veit Erlmann's notion of the "global imagination" is another example of the local thinking beyond the nation.[52]

The bulk of these narratives focus on the migration of musicians, styles, performance practices, and repertories from one place in the world or category in the marketplace to another rather than the centeredness and stability of music over time. Out of a fixed and secure feeling of home and identity, music and musicians have moved into a more uncertain universe. Some have retained a sense of place in the global market through a continuity of style or lineage while others have resulted in new forms, variously labeled as syncretism, blending, and musical hybridity.

As I and others have suggested, jazz has similarly functioned as a transnational musical entity, something acknowledged more by jazz critics and journalists than by jazz scholars. Nevertheless, as a scholarly enterprise American studies has begun to examine more closely the problem of the transnational.[53] Because Sathima and I presume a transnational character and narrative of twentieth-century jazz in this book, I want to reinstate the notions of musical kinship and lineage, concepts that are necessarily read in relation to the ideas of diaspora, musical surrogacy (see the response in chapter 4), and living history (see the response in chapter 6). Musical lineage or kinship as a transnational musical process describes new social formations forged out of a belief in common ancestry, sometimes defined by race, mostly revealed in the lived experiences of social, economic, and political oppression.[54] More poignantly, these ties are manifest in the sound of music itself and of jazz performance specifically. Social and political resemblances are expressed in the musical connections, as an individual asserts his or her own voice in the very process of making the music. These connections are often relationships constituted over long distances, imagined into being by consumers of this music, though in some instances they are also solidified via person-to-person interaction.

In the South African story, musical lineage or kinship is a flexible term

that incorporates the kinds of bonds many South Africans imagined between themselves and African Americans in the postwar period through
the music they heard and the performances they experienced on record,
radio, and film. Some in America similarly fashioned ties to living representatives of their centuries-old African ancestry. Through the course
of their lives, first in South Africa and then as they moved into a state
of musical diaspora and political exile from that country, Sathima and
Abdullah have incorporated themselves into a range of musical lineages.
These have varied according to the particular details of their biological
family trees and according to the family resemblances that their musical
performance exhibits in terms of other lineages.

   In *Abdullah Ibrahim: A Brother With Perfect Timing*, a documentary film
released in 1989 (and as a DVD in 2005), the lineages articulated by the
Cape Town–born pianist range from the local to the diasporic.[55] Filmed
while he and Sathima were living in exile in New York City, this documentary shows Abdullah performing exclusively with African Americans.
In one part of the film he teaches a group of African American singers
some traditional songs from the Coloured community he grew up in, and
the singers learn to sing in at least two African languages in the process;[56]
the members of his septet, called Ekaya, are also African American. He
recalls religious musical lineages traced through his grandmother, a
founding member of the African Methodist Episcopal (AME) church in
Cape Town, and his mother. Both women were pianists in the church,
so those sounds are among the deeply embedded memories he carried
into exile. This musical relationship is traced back to the Mother Bethel
church in Philadelphia, the first African American independent church in
the United States, founded by Richard Allen when his members were refused a place in an all-white congregation.[57] Such transnational connections cycle back and forth between the African continent and the United
States. In a documentary entitled *The Struggle for Love* (2004), Ibrahim
tells the story of one of his musicians, the saxophonist Horace Alexander
Young. Young had a relative, Bishop Young, who was sent to Cape Town
by Mother Bethel church early in the twentieth century to establish the
AME church.

   Interviewed in the documentary, Young says that when he auditioned
for Ibrahim's band he didn't know about his family ties to the AME church
in South Africa and, by extension, to Abdullah, whose grandmother was

an AME church pianist in Cape Town. But as he listened to the music he realized there was a deep feeling of connectedness between Ibrahim's sound and the hymns he had heard in his home church. When he performed with Abdullah's group in South Africa in the 1990s, he met some of the distant members of his family and religious lineage in Cape Town, bringing the parallel experiences of African Americans in South Africa and South Africans in the Americas full circle.

Elsewhere in the film Abdullah talks about his music and explains how it comes to sound the way it does. He invokes another diasporic musical lineage as he talks of the impact of three hundred Angolan slaves bought by the Portuguese and then captured by the Dutch and brought to Cape Town in 1658. This happened just a few years after Jan Van Riebeeck established a refreshment station for the Dutch East India Company. If you want to know the complete story of the musical ancestry of what people think of as Brazilian samba, Ibrahim argues, you need to look to the branch of the family tree extended by those seventeenth-century Angolan slaves in the Cape. Then Ibrahim invokes family resemblance between the sounds of mid-twentieth-century Khoisan music and current rhythmic practices in the Cape. Elsewhere in the film Ibrahim explains a core sound of much South African jazz by tracing it through a set of family resemblances articulated in the early twentieth century through the South African genre called *marabi*.[58] The simple three-chord progression, I IV and V, Abdullah explains in terms of the nuclear family: I as father or heaven; V as the dominant or the mother and the earth; and IV as the child. Finally, in *The Struggle for Love* Ibrahim talks of the replication of nature's "formless forms" in the irregular metrical patterns of his music.[59]

Ibrahim sums up the importance of reflecting on the conceptual premises of contemporary American-centered jazz scholarship in terms of imagined lineage ties in a conversation with an African American journalist from WNCU, the radio station of North Carolina Central University:

Abdullah: Ja, you are treading very dangerous ground here, where you are talking about American musicians. You know we never regarded those people as "American" musicians, you see, Ellington, Ellington, Duke Ellington for us was just the wise old man in the village. I think there is a strong misconception here, or let me put it this way. We have yet to discover this deep relationship that there is between Africa and especially for us in South Africa and black America. So, there's a deeper relationship between families, rather than separating and saying that it's "American" and "South African." Whereas there are much deeper ties, closer ties you see.

Interviewer: Let's forget the term "American:" just tell me who were some of your influences. I am sure you, you mentioned the great Duke Ellington, apparently he was one of your inspirations.

Abdullah: Well, the people who really influenced me when I started off if I mentioned names — were names you wouldn't really know who they are, because in South Africa they were never given recognition. And this is another legacy of the apartheid era that we have lost almost generations of information.[60]

Sathima's musical lineages are quite different because of the distinctive set of musical experiences and memories she carried as a woman of St. Helenian and Filipino descent living in Cape Town. Just after the launch of *Cape Town Love* in Cape Town, Sathima talked of the bond between her own family and that of Duke Ellington registered in a range of coincidences or "magical connections." She starts her story with the Cape Town pianist Henry February and moves on to Ellington: "So I am just realizing when we went to pick Henry up, he said he lives on 'Beatty' Street. Beatty Street, what I used to be called, and he's the one who absolutely refuses to call me anything else. And do you know, February, I got married in February, my two children were conceived in February, I met Duke Ellington in February, I recorded with him in February, and now his [Henry the pianist's] name is February."[61]

I asked Sathima about the origin of the surname February. She replied she didn't know, but that her mother's last name had been Henry: "Before she married Benjamin, she was Henry. Now I am only realizing, my father's name is Edward, and so is Duke Ellington's. Duke Ellington lived with a lady in his last years her name, he called her Bea, but her actual name was Evie, which was my mother's name. He had a sister called Ruth, and I have a sister called Ruth. I have an aunt Violet Kennedy, she's a clairvoyant on my mother's side, my mother's cousin is Violet Kennedy.[62] She reads tea leaves, like a clairvoyant in the family. I don't think she's alive anymore, Auntie Violet, these are my mother's relatives. So even when it comes to names and places and months of the year, there are these, I can't call them coincidences. . . . the thing is I unknowingly sort of move into these things and then it comes to me afterwards when I look at it."[63]

In August 2006 she told me there was a further extended family connection. Her godfather, a Muslim man from Turkey who lived in Cape Town, had been a Freemason and, the story goes, so had Ellington. On another occasion she talked specifically of Ellington as a father figure: "So Duke Ellington was like my real grandfather." And of the family that jazz provides for her, she commented, "I want to go and hear music that ignites there on the spot, as I am sitting there. . . . I come away thinking and feeling that I have family, that's the thing. That's the thing, the family for me is jazz."[64]

In one of the first conversations Ellington had with Dollar Brand and Bea Benjamin, he constituted himself as a kind of gentle father figure to both of them. Sathima remembers Ellington asking her the million-dollar question: would she be willing to travel with his band? As soon as he had asked the question, he realized it was inappropriate. Sathima recalls that she could never have ventured out so soon, not with the whole Ellington orchestra. She was too young and inexperienced to have gone on tour with complete strangers. But that was not the only reason—there was also Abdullah, her South African musical mentor and lover. So, Ellington inquired, what was the relationship between them—were they engaged, married? "Neither," Dollar replied. "Well then," Ellington advised Dollar, "you had better marry this woman before someone else snatches her away from you." Dollar heeded the warning, and the two were married six months later in London.

The musical and personal ties between South African and African American musicians in this period were not unique to the Ellington-Ibrahim-Benjamin trio. The *King Kong* star and Xhosa traditional singer Miriam Makeba had left South Africa in 1959 to travel to the Cannes Film Festival as one of the featured actors in *Come Back Africa*, a film made secretly in South Africa by the American filmmaker Lionel Rogosin. Makeba was introduced to Harry Belafonte, a singer and actor deeply immersed in the civil rights struggle in the United States and at the time increasingly aware of the plight of South Africans living under apartheid. Belafonte took her under his wing. Through another series of transnationally connected anti-apartheid activists, Hugh Masekela was sent a trumpet with the letters *LA*, Armstrong's initials, engraved on the side by Louis Armstrong's wife Lucille. The trumpet was a gift to Masekela by way of British Anglican priest and outspoken activist Father Trevor Huddleston who visited the United States in 1956. One evening, rather like Sathima would do a few years later, Huddleston went to hear Armstrong perform in Rochester, New York. He went backstage to tell Armstrong about the Huddleston Jazz Band, in which Masekela was trumpeter.

Armstrong's trumpet became a much-publicized gift, and Masekela recalled the effect the gesture had on his sense of connection to African American jazz musicians: "When I opened the package and handled the horn, I was overjoyed. I was seventeen, and for the first time I felt something like a spiritual connection with Satchmo and those musicians back in the States that I idolized to my core. This horn was my connection not just to Armstrong; but also to a long, powerful tradition that had crisscrossed the Atlantic from Africa to America and back. It was a sign my direction in life was cemented."[65]

The evidence of a deep feeling of connection between the old and what is increasingly called the beginnings of the new,[66] or what Abdullah calls a contemporary African diaspora that "took place in cities" is rich and compelling.[67] The question remains, nevertheless, why we should call these ties transatlantic musical *lineages* rather than mere social networks? or why not just allow the musicians to be named individually within the parameters of the music they made and recorded and let the connections remain embedded inside the autobiographical weave? How is the musical connection sensed between postwar musicians of color in South Africa and African Americans different, for example, from Feld's archeological digging into the use of "Pygmy" sounds in American popular music? or from the controversial so-called collaboration between Paul Simon, Ladysmith Black Mambazo, Masekela, and Makeba in the *Graceland* project of the mid-1980s?[68]

This might be the quintessential question that this book and other work concerned with this period in South African and American history strives to address. Sathima recognizes that she is a product of a particular moment in history—had she been born at any other time, her story would have been a very different one. In this reflection on the notion of musical lineage, I cannot account for all of that history, so a gesture toward the poetic will have to suffice, and it is taken from Es'kia

Mphahlele's autobiography, *Afrika My Music*. "Oh, the tyranny of time, the tyranny of place," the writer repeatedly laments. As Sathima's constituted memories of the postwar period suggest, to be a person of color—black or Coloured—in South Africa in the fifties and sixties was to have been born into an increasingly brutal and divided society. It was a period in South African history in which all people of color were born into the wrong race, in the wrong place, at the wrong time. They were categorized as *non*-European and, later, as *non*white. Increasingly exiled inside the boundaries of their birthplace, they continued to form new, more modern South African selves inside the movie dream palaces of Cape Town and Johannesburg, feeding the imagination with the images and sounds of Africans in America: Ellington, Armstrong, Dinah Washington, and Lena Horne were among those who modeled a particular kind of sophisticated social and musical modernity for people of color in South African cities.[69] It was a kind of Black and Coloured modernity, a form of the "global imagination" that translated easily into local musical traditions and performance histories.[70]

Apartheid dislodged continuities, fragmented communities, and silenced dissent. The trauma of this period stirred a diasporic consciousness—people changed their names and reinvented themselves, while some passed for white, and they began to think of leaving the country. It is in this context one understands the radical political, musical, and social message jazz performance engendered. To play this music among a racially mixed community of people, to insist on the freedom of expression that individuals assumed as they performed, was to foster a profound sense of musical kinship and belonging. It was often only in the act of performance and to a lesser degree in the poetic rendering of the spoken word that visions of a fully democratic, nonracial society could be realized.

Jazz, its racial mixing, and growing diasporic consciousness embodied the politically transgressive: the Group Areas Act, the Immorality Act, and the Freedom of Association Act were contravened each time this nonracial community gathered around the music. As a result, many who participated in this world were increasingly alienated from their blood kin. This was certainly true for Sathima and Abdullah. Both came to rely on the sentiments of belonging, the "brotherhood of breath," as Chris McGregor named his group, which South African jazz communities enabled. Once they left South Africa, Sathima and Abdullah carried memories of these signs of belonging, recollections of a warm, passionate, and vibrant experimental jazz community, and the hopes for connection through the extended family of musicians, the distant musical relatives they had not met but felt they knew so well from listening to their music and living in Europe and the United States.

Ellington in South Africa

I am not really sure when Sathima first heard Ellington's music and don't believe she recalls a particular moment either. The uncertainty is no cause for concern; on the contrary, it seems a particular kind of vagueness contributes to qualities of the ineffable, the mystical and magical—words Sathima uses in conveying her relationship with the American master musician. What is certain, however, is that from the interwar years through the 1960s, Ellington's music was real and present for many in South Africa across all racial categories. It is possible that his initial appearance in that country came in an early film like *Murder at the Vanities* or *Belle of the Nineties* (both 1934), in which Ellington appeared with Mae West, or perhaps even *Symphony in Black* with Billie Holiday in 1935.[71]

The pivotal movie most black South Africans cite is Ellington's act as bandleader in *Cabin in the Sky* (1943), a film many musicians fondly remember watching in their formative years. Unlike the prior productions, and as controversial as many black critics in the United States thought the film, *Cabin in the Sky* and its companion *Stormy Weather*, featuring Cab Calloway rather than Ellington and released in the same year under similar conditions in the United States, appear to have resonated in the black and even Coloured communities in postwar South Africa. *Cabin in the Sky* was released by MGM Studios in Hollywood in response to pressure brought to bear by the Roosevelt administration and Walter White on behalf of the NAACP to make films with black actors and casts because so many black Americans were fighting and dying in the war effort. Hollywood reluctantly agreed to the request, and *Cabin in the Sky* was chosen because it had already had some success in live theater. It was not widely accepted by the black critics because the story it told continued to convey a tension between the folkloric figures of the plantation darkie and the suave sophistication of urban styles of blackness. "At its most basic," writes Krin Gabbard, "the film opposes the values of simplicity, religion, and the country to those of big city sophistication and decadence. . . . God himself demands that black people sing in church rather than dance in nightclubs. In *Cabin in the Sky* this dichotomy is played out in clearly racist terms."[72]

Despite the critique of its black stereotypes—the religious mammy figure played by Ethel Waters and the boyish husband figure performed by Eddie "Rochester" Anderson—*Cabin in the Sky* is noteworthy in a faux ethnographic way for its capacity to showcase the best in black performance in the 1940s.[73] While it conveys ideas about African Americans prevalent in Hollywood in its era, retrospectively it provides a remarkable historical document of the performances of Armstrong, Ellington and his band, Waters, and Horne, all in a single venue. Each figure represents a particular kind of musical or dance performance, and, by extension, each provides a rich palate of possible ways of performing one's racial identity.

In a spirit similar to the ways in which we reflect on Holiday's autobiography (see below), what is relevant here is not so much the truth or fiction of the story told or the appropriateness of the representation of African American characterization. Rather, we seek out the insights we might gain from how South Africans who saw *Cabin in the Sky* in the 1940s interpreted the film. What images, sounds, and practices resonated with South African audiences and why? What influence did this document of African American style—of music, dance, and fashion—exert on local South African culture in the same period? And what place did Armstrong, Waters, Horne, Nicholas, and, most important, Ellington assume in that process?[74]

Answers to these questions have already been provided in a general way in what others have written about the influence of American culture on black South African performance. In the sheer fact that the film is exclusively about people of color *Cabin in the Sky* validates black South African performance by its presence in Hollywood. The musicians in the film made their own music for their own people, with all the signs of urbane sophistication in the shadows of mission Christianity but without any visible signs of white interference. Even the walls of the club are painted with images (albeit caricatured) of African-ness, signaling it is a place of their own.

Having viewed the film again recently, I was struck by the idea that many of the themes that create discomfort for present-day viewers, especially in terms of representation of African Americans, may in fact have been the themes that resonated most closely with black and perhaps even Coloured audiences in South Africa in the 1940s. If they were not totally embraced, at least they would have felt familiar. Such themes include the central tension created in the film between rural and urbanized images of blackness; between opting for either respectability or the underworld, or at least a life associated with thugs and pimps; the key place of the Christian church in shaping the lives of some, especially black women;[75] and the draw many felt to the signs of the good life: money, convertible cars, beautiful women, and the pleasures of the night and of clothing and style.

Ellington and his band rise above the crowd of other actors. Ellington's presence transcends the binary between rural and urban; between the underclass and the sophisticated; and ultimately between good and bad. In selecting Ellington and his band to perform in the movie, the director, Vincente Minnelli, was clearly committed to a discourse of an Africanism that was chic and sophisticated.[76] The musicians are boldly announced outside the nightclub called Jim Henry's Paradise as "Duke Ellington and his Band" for "Tonight Only." The audience hears Ellington's music before it sees him, and his band appears in the second number, one named for the film itself. Thereafter, the audience hears his music only as background to the extraordinary performances by Horne, Waters, and the crowd portrayed in the club. The music, nonetheless, is present for an extended period of time.[77] Without doubt Ellington is the figure "beyond category."[78] He is immaculately dressed in a sparkling white suit, his hair beautifully styled, oiled, and combed back; and while he doesn't speak, his music communicates most eloquently for him to the crowd in the club and to his film audiences. He acts as both pianist and bandleader in the film, occupying a central place not only in leading his musicians, but also in orchestrating the movements of the crowds in the nightclub itself. And Ellington is associated with wealth and the good life. So, for example, when the dubious character Domino Johnson, played by Johnson, returns from prison and enters the nightclub, he comments, "Duke Ellington's Band, where did all this prosperity come from?"

While the audience never sees Ellington performing with Waters or Horne inside the camera frame, his music accompanies their singing

on the film's soundtrack. We catch a brief glimpse of Ellington standing by as Johnson begins his song and dance routine. There is no doubt
in viewers' minds that the famed bandleader, arranger, composer, and
pianist performed with both kinds of singers: the asexual mammy figure
of Waters and the more seductive and glamorous character played by
Horne. Though Sathima has not specifically accounted for this film in our
conversations, I know from oral testimony that the likes of *Cabin in the
Sky* and *Stormy Weather* certainly shaped public performances among the
community she associated with in the mid to late 1950s and early 1960s in
South Africa. In this sense, these kinds of films must have both impacted
her sense of the possibilities of public performance for women of color
in ways not permitted locally—she would chisel out a place somewhere
between the extremes of Waters and Horne—and opened her ears and
mind to the music of Ellington, the man who would become her American musical mentor.

In this regard, numerous accounts from South African musicians name
Ellington as formative in their musical exposure, training, and senses of
themselves as musicians of color in the early to mid-twentieth century.
In his autobiography Masekela writes of the virtual presence of a lineage
of American musicians in his early childhood in towns around Johannesburg in the 1940s: "We were surrounded by music, everywhere we
went. . . . Many homes back then had gramophones . . . they all blasted
their music at high volume—especially on weekends . . . I spent many
an hour leaning against the fence of someone's home, listening to their
records. . . . The music of Louis Armstrong, Louis Jordan and his Tym-
pany Five, Count Basie, Duke Ellington, Cab Calloway, Glenn Miller,
Benny Goodman, and Tommy Dorsey, who were all the kings of the
swing era, had a very big influence on South African big bands at the
time."[79] Masekela listed some of the local South African bands, arguing
that they played the songs popularized by American orchestras, including "Take the A Train," "Tuxedo Junction," and "In the Mood." "These
African bands," he wrote, "sported the same fashions as the Americans
and read music from orchestral arrangements by Chappell Music, which
were available at the music shops in the main cities and towns."[80] Finally,
the late singer Dolly Rathebe from Johannesburg remembered that "we'd
ask the owner of the cinema—I remember it was the Reno Bioscope—to
please, please bring us American films and we would pack that cinema.
I remember *Cabin in the Sky*, where Lena Horne sang "Salt Lake City

Blues" . . . and then when we were going home we'd rehearse the song to get it right."[81]

Similar accounts suggest that Ellington's music was often featured at local Saturday night dance events in Cape Town, at after-hours gatherings, and in local jazz appreciation clubs held weekly to listen to sound recordings imported from Europe and the United States. As Masekela and others suggest, in the prewar days in Johannesburg and Cape Town, it had been Miller, the Mills Brothers, the Inkspots, Armstrong, Count Basie, early Ellington, and others whose music was copied in local big band performances. In her teenage years in the late 1940s and early 1950s Benjamin definitely sounded more like Doris Day, Joni James, and Ella Fitzgerald when she performed at intermission in the local movie theaters. There is no doubt, however, that in the postwar period among the small but intense modern jazz circles whose musicians moved regularly between Cape Town and Johannesburg, Ellington was the focus of repeated listening and close musical analysis. Ellington's music provided models for jazz arranging and was a center of musical admiration and activity. Ibrahim was a central figure in that community, taking Ellington's lead but striving to find a musical voice that resonated with local experience and sound, as Ellington had done for African American music.

Sathima Bea Benjamin marked her membership in the American jazz family through the resonance she felt between herself and Billie Holiday. When she read the life story and heard the voice of Holiday, a singer she would never meet in person, she felt a deep sense of connection because she was already performing in this way and had personally lived in part the life Holiday had written about. Others played a similar role in the lives of South African musicians. Nat "King" Cole, for example, was a key figure in postwar Cape Town: Sathima cites his singing as her model for clear diction. As a pianist listening closely for sophisticated jazz harmony, February created a Cape Town ensemble he named the Nat King Cole Trio. Sathima often sang with the trio. But there were many more: in numerous quotes from oral history interviews, my own and those of others, South African musicians rattle off litanies of names. And as I have already suggested, it was Holiday who made the most profound impression on Sathima, and who shifted the male-centered narrative of South African jazz oral narratives from Ellington, Coltrane, Monk, and Gillespie to a more woman-centered perspective.

Billie Holiday: "Lady Day"

Lady Day, she had her special magic, Beautiful Lady Day! With her unique touch, she sang of love and life: of all its joys and all its pain. From her heart she'd give you the sunshine; when she sang the blues you could feel the rain. Oh, but it's her sound, her sound I hear again, and again, in the echoes, in the echoes of all this music that we play. Lady Day. — Benjamin's tribute to Billie Holiday, recorded on *Windsong*, Ekapa Records, 1985

Must the woman orchestrate your cry, Billie Holiday, now a long time gone but still grinding the blues for us? Can she say to her man, Love some other spring, sun shines around me. . . . No. Deep down in her heart it's cold. Her story has been told millions of times. It's the long black song. — Es'kia Mphahlele, *Afrika My Music*, 1984

In "Lady Day," a song first recorded in 1985, Sathima pays tribute to Holiday, more lovingly remembered by many as Lady Day, the name invented for the singer by her close friend the saxophonist Lester "Pres[ident]" Young. In the song Sathima paints a moving portrait of Lady Day, a woman whose voice touched so many, a woman also known more for her self-destructive habits than for her ladylike qualities. But Holiday was a lady to Sathima because of the resonant sound of her voice, the palette of musical tones she drew on, her emotive treatment of the text, and the sheer power of her words: she was an institution, a force of history, a singer whose sound continues to echo through generations of singers who have listened closely to the pathos of her voice and life story.

A number of voices have acknowledged the force of Holiday's music in their lives. Robert O'Meally (1991), Farah Griffin (2001), Angela Davis (1998), and Stuart Nicholson (1996), among others, have published monographs; a major documentary film called *Lady Day: The Many Faces of Billie Holiday*, has been produced; most of her recorded legacy has been substantially reissued; and numerous poems have been written.[82] Sathima's song, composed years earlier than these works, was recorded by the engineer Rudy Van Gelder and featured the pianist Kenny Barron, the bass player Buster Williams, and, on drums, the late Billy Higgins. It took a South African singer living in New York City to lead

16. Sathima singing at the Antibes Jazz Festival with the Dollar Brand Trio.
Photographer unknown.

the way in paying tribute in song to Holiday as a blues woman and an artist of color.

Sathima has long acknowledged the importance of Holiday as a figure in her first exposure in Cape Town in the 1950s to the literature and recorded music of the African American jazz community, yet it is perhaps surprising that she recorded two albums that paid homage to important people in her life—*Sathima Sings Ellington* (1979) and *Dedications* (1982)—without giving a place to Lady Day on either record. Three decades after first encountering the Holiday autobiography, Sathima inscribed her tribute on her LP disc titled *Windsong*. The third cut on side A, "Lady Day" is preceded by a haunting voice-percussion rendition of the old spiritual "Sometimes I Feel Like a Motherless Child" on the first cut and by Sathima's composition "Windsong" on the second. In juxtaposing these three performances, Sathima poetically makes visible the connections she senses between the old African diaspora and its more recent manifestations. In the context of, first, the cry of "the motherless child" reinvented as a woman longing for her homeland, for lineage, and for a feeling of belonging and then of the homage paid in "Windsong" to the "resilient, remarkable, and courageous mothers and daughters of the struggle for peace and liberation" in the South Africa of the 1980s, Holiday finds her place in a peculiarly South African–American musical lineage and Pan-Africanist political history.[83]

I shall probe a little deeper into the nature of the connection Sathima sensed between herself and Holiday as she read the autobiography and later listened to the sound of the American singer with her friends. My method is somewhat unconventional for ethnomusicology because it is largely concerned with the realm of memory, literature, and social history: the material is substantiated by an accumulation of many years of personal interviews, conversations, and archival research.[84]

In my very first conversation with Sathima in New York City in 1990, she talked about her virtual encounter with Holiday as a formative moment in her consciousness of herself as a woman of color and her development as a singer, though she has always insisted that she never modeled herself on Holiday's performance. Nevertheless, the full extent of the influence, or at least who Sathima imagined Holiday to be, has remained elusive. With the publication of Griffin's work on Holiday and Sherrie Tucker's call for a greater focus on women as agents of jazz history, I decided to look more closely at Sathima's encounter with Holiday as a virtual versus a person-to-person meeting of women through music and life experience.[85] Early in 2005 I told Sathima I needed greater clarity about the extent to which she had been influenced by Holiday. I purchased copies of Holiday's autobiography, Griffin's meditations, and David Margolick's biography of Holiday's signature song, "Strange Fruit," for Sathima and asked her to look again at the texts to see what we could recover of her encounter with Holiday's life and music more than four decades after the initial reading. I was hoping that Sathima's rereading of the autobiography and her introduction to Griffin's reflections on Holiday's impact would prod her memory. Reconnecting a living reader with her original text seemed to me to provide a rare ethnographic opportunity for historical recovery.

I went to New York in May 2005 with the specific intention of recuperating that moment in Sathima's life and development as a singer. We found a quiet place in a Japanese restaurant close to Sathima's home and ordered lunch. The conversation about Holiday didn't start out that well. We talked first about nonmusical matters and, after about twenty minutes (all recorded), I asked Sathima if we could focus more specifically on the Holiday materials. "Wait," she replied. "When I am ready." So the conversation ran on. We talked about Jean Grae, her daughter the hip-hop artist, about Jean's recent visit to Hawaii, and about being of mixed race. "She called home and told me that in Hawaii, people asked her the same question they always ask me, who are you and where do you come from? She is the same as me," Sathima ruefully remarked. "I told her that we were the people of the future. In the distant future, everyone will be mixed like us, but not for a very long time."

After about an hour, she switched direction, commenting that she hadn't read the book again and that Holiday was perhaps not that important in shaping her musical sensibilities. I pushed her a little more: what was it about the book that had seemed so significant then? "Her picture on the cover," replied Sathima.[86] Clearly refusing to be pinned down, these were nonetheless her first words ever about Holiday's physical appearance.[87] It was a significant moment because it made me realize that Sathima's sense of connection to Holiday had been more than an acoustical one, even though Sathima vividly recalls the moment she heard Holiday's voice a few years after reading the autobiography. It was in the sonic encounter that she realized that while she had already been singing with a similar set of vocal skills and emotional depth, there was someone out there, someone more known in the world—a woman identified as Colored—who had already forged a path for singers like herself. She didn't have to sound like the white pop of Day and James, and she didn't need the virtuosity of Vaughan or the sweetness of Fitzgerald. Her sound had a place of its own in the world of jazz.

Well into our lunch, Sathima finally turned to the point of our meeting by asking,

And so what else now do you want to ask me about Billie Holiday? The most important thing you should know is that *I felt so good when I heard her* ... not that anyone should ever dare to think, to say, or even go there, that you sound like Billie Holiday. I don't want to sound like her. I could not sound like her. I sound like me. But I felt good that she put her heart on her sleeve, my God, more than any other singer. She just put it out there. *That is what hit you the most, that emotive quality that touched you.* I was busy with that and was not sure if it was a good approach. Is this not a little bit too much here, maybe you have got to be a little bit more fancy. I don't know, be more tuneful. . . . But after hearing her I felt assured that this is fine. I can do this. Express yourself, use all your emotions, that is quite fine. And jazz music allows you to do that.[88]

Lady Sings the Blues: The Searing Autobiography of an American Musical Legend, the controversial narrative written by Billie Holiday with William Dufty, was published by Doubleday in 1956, three years before Holiday died and almost a decade before Sathima came to the United States. Sathima recalls that she read the book when she had begun the move from amateur singing of popular songs, emulating the likes of Day and James, to the exciting but far more risky world of African American jazz and literature. She read Holiday's autobiography in tandem with the works of African American writers like Richard Wright, Langston Hughes, and James Baldwin. There were almost no books written by people of color in the English language in South Africa at the time, and those that existed were regularly banned by the state and were not locally available anyway.[89] She recalls the librarian Vincent Kolbe calling to ask her to return the book because it had become illegal to read or have in one's possession. Reading the book was a transformative experience for Sathima, at the very least because it may have been one of the few books available to South Africans written by and about a woman of color, and a musician at that.

I use the written word to provide the scaffolding into which I will insert the visual and acoustical as appropriate to three major themes I have selected that register in the autobiography. These three articulate strong points of congruency between the lives of the two women at the moment Sathima read the book for the first time: these are race and gender, childhood and young adult experiences, and a particular approach to music.[90] The difference is articulated largely in the infrastructure of the recording industry available in the United States that was not available to women of color in South Africa, especially those who sang in English. We know that Sathima is believed to have recorded the first LP jazz record in South Africa, *Beatty Benjamin, My Songs for You*, which was never released commercially.

To convey something of the resonance Sathima may have sensed in Holiday's life story and the social and political environments she worked in (and having had no luck in getting Sathima to reread it), I reread the "searing autobiography" myself in order to highlight what are quite remarkable moments of intersection in the life stories of the two women. It has been an instructive exercise because of the ways in which the more recent reading has been thickened by my knowledge of Cape jazz history and practice in the period. I have mapped out moments of identification that the young South African may have sensed between her story and that of the illustrious African American singer, though there are also distinctive points of divergence.

Much has been written about Holiday's autobiography. How much of it was the real story of Holiday's life and how much was fabricated either by herself or by Dufty, whose name appears with Holiday's on the cover, is uncertain. Readers are well advised to follow the lead of O'Meally and Griffin and to think of Billie Holiday as a woman with many faces or as having several versions of a life story, versions that parallel the many renditions of an individual song on record.[91] My concern is with how young women of color, women like Sathima Bea Benjamin, read and interpreted the book in the 1950s without ever having met Holiday in person or seen her perform.

From the outset, what appears to lure the reader into believing the story is more Holiday's than Dufty's is the rhetoric of its narrative voice: the clear first person perspective and the casual introduction to the intimate details of Holiday's home life, family, and friends. The opening line, "Mom and Pop were a couple of kids when they got married," establishes the informal tone. Like the voice of Holiday as reported by friends and fans, the rhetorical "she," which Griffin suggests is a performed self, draws the reader into her story, enabling each to feel he or she has come to know her as an individual. And her narrative deals with the wider jazz community in a similar manner, revealing in the frankest of terms who performed with whom, how they got along, and how drugs, violence, and sex were integral parts of the experience. Intertwined in the story are descriptions of a series of racially charged experiences, which may have fostered feelings of connection between Billie Holiday's life story and parallel conditions South African readers of color knew from their own life experiences.

Formative Experiences

Billie Holiday, born Eleanora Fagin in 1915, and Sathima Bea Benjamin, born Beatrice Benjamin in 1936, were both given new names by male saxophonists later in life: already called Billie, she was renamed Lady Day by Lester Young;[92] Beatrice was renamed Sathima by Johnny Dyani, the South African saxophonist who was part of the South African jazz community in exile in Europe in the 1960s and 1970s.[93] Neither Billie nor Sathima had a particularly happy childhood, and both spent time in the homes of relatives, one of whom — Sathima's stepmother — used to physically beat them. In both narratives there is an underlying thread of longing for motherly love — Billie for her mother, who left home and went to New York and Philadelphia to work as a housemaid, Sathima for her mother, who left and remarried when her husband abandoned her for another woman.

There is little sense of a durable feeling of home in Holiday's narrative. It is hard to find explicit talk of politics in the childhood narratives of either singer, though there is acknowledgment of racial issues in Billie's autobiography. Both girls nurtured their love for jazz by hearing it performed in dance bands in their neighborhoods, and both were severely reprimanded for doing so. Neither girl heard jazz at home, though both felt called to its rhythms and would do almost anything to find a way to listen to it. Billie worked at the local brothel, one of the few places one could hear the voices of Armstrong and Bessie Smith, her two musical heroes. As a young adult, Sathima heard jazz records at the homes of friends who owned them, particularly in the after-hours gathering of musicians, but there was always risk involved in listening to this music.

Conveyed through the stories of both women are lives that are materially impoverished but musically abundant and artistically gifted. In summing up the "many faces of Billie Holiday" O'Meally writes that the truth of her life may not have been anything Holiday would have contested. Rather, what mattered was the music: "That was 'all she had,' all that really mattered — the precious thing was . . . what she had in place of freedom. As a very young singer, she had developed a gift for looking at a song's lyrics, listening . . . to its melody, and then transforming both until they were hers."[94] Similarly, from her first performances in local movie theaters in Cape Town, Sathima's peers consistently recall an individuality of style and voice they heard even in the popular renditions of the young singer. But it is as an alternative economy, with music as the currency of exchange and personal growth, that Sathima and others begin to define for themselves in the late 1950s. It is music that motivates, not money. In fact, Sathima has often told me that her music is all that her children will ever inherit from her. Similarly, Abdullah has often told interviewers that it is the music that has actually saved him.

Race and Gender

The world we lived in was still one that White people made.
—Billie Holiday, *Lady Sings the Blues* (1956)

There are obviously significant parallels between the experiences of musicians of color in the United States and in South Africa. One moment of a real-time connection in the Holiday account occurs when she is in prison for drug possession and is reported to have received supportive letters from around the world, none of which she was allowed to read. The writers are from a range of places, including at least one from Cape Town. Undoubtedly, having her hometown appear on the list must have touched Sathima.

It is evident in Sathima's personal narrative that her encounter with Holiday coincided with a period of individual struggle: a growing awareness of herself as a woman of color living in a world that was becoming increasingly hostile to people like her. It was as a South African woman classified as Coloured that she identified with Holiday.[95] Progressive jazz was viewed by St. Helenians as a dangerous activity because it transgressed the racial boundaries established both by the apartheid regime and by people within the Coloured community, who identified culturally as European, that is, English. Outside of accompanying elite and working-class social dancing, jazz could only lead to trouble. When Sathima moved into the interracial world of late 1950s jazz, many of her childhood friends felt that she had gone mad. Madness is associated with miscegenation.

The lived distinction between Coloured and Bantu or African peoples in South Africa surfaced in Sathima's reading of literature coming out of the United States and indeed in the image of Holiday on the cover of her autobiography. This picture, like most of the photographs of the singer, is in black and white. The shot is of her face in profile, showing the left cheek in full. She is seemingly lost in the emotional intensity of song performance: her eyes are closed, and her mouth is open. She wears a sleeveless black gown, closely fitted to her lean body. Her left arm is bent at the elbow, and there is a ring on her fourth finger. What looks like a large diamond pendant appears from under the sleek black scarf draped around her neck. Her hair is pulled back, revealing a long diamond drop earring in her left ear. The image of Holiday is repeated on the back cover, this time showing her alone in an oval frame. The text beneath the portrait reads, "She sang of love and loneliness with a power and presence that few other performers have ever possessed," a phrase that could as easily describe the song performance of Sathima Bea Benjamin.

A powerful spotlight illuminates Holiday's face in the photograph, enhancing the lightness of skin tone. How might Sathima have read the image from this perspective?[96] Recalling our earlier discussions of the category of Cape Coloured, it is most likely that for a woman striving to find a place for herself in the world, a place in which her family history would fit, Holiday's light skin tone resonated in Benjamin, even though, like the jazz lineage itself, her extended family bore traces of a range of mixed relationships in the wide array of skin tones individual members carried. Holiday's hair may have signaled a further possibility of kinship. In that her hair is pulled back away from her face, the viewer is not as aware of difference in hair texture in ways that were deemed so important in Sathima's experience among the St. Helenian and Coloured communities in Cape Town.

The image that most closely parallels Holiday with the younger Sathima is one taken in July 1963 at the Festival du Mondial du Jazz Antibes at Juan-les-Pins in France. This black-and-white photograph shows Benjamin singing with the Dollar Brand Trio, Abdullah on piano, Johnny Gertze on bass, and Makhaya Ntshoko on drums. Sathima is out front, facing her audience. As in the Holiday image, she appears in left profile, and, like Holiday's, her eyes are closed, as they often are when Sathima sings. She is minimally jeweled and coiffed; her dress is made of a light, soft fabric and is tight fitting and heavily gathered from the hips down. A long scarf attached to the dress descends behind her the full length of the garment. Not shown in the glare of a spotlight, Sathima's skin looks much like Holiday's in complexion. The similarities between the two singers are striking, however, for if one looks through Benjamin's smaller archive of photographs it is clear that she, like Holiday, has several faces.

Placing herself racially through the image on the book, Sathima recalls identifying similarly with what might seem to be a small detail in word choice that she noticed in the African American literature she read. This emerged when, for example, authors from the early twentieth century highlighted distinctions between those called Colored and those called Negroes. In Holiday's autobiography there are a few places where this difference is suggested. First, Billie herself has a mixed lineage: she traces her family history to her great-grandmother, a slave woman who had borne sixteen children by an Irish slave owner named Charles Fagin.[97] Later in the book, Billie recalls working as a prostitute at "Florence's place" and refusing to service "a Negro cat" called Big Blue Rainier. "What the hell good is she?" he hollered at Florence. "She's the only *colored* girl in the house and she won't take *Negroes*?"[98] The problem was not that Sathima wished to reinforce these kinds of differences—so much of her move into music, and jazz specifically, was motivated by a desire to transcend the categories imposed.

The matter of categories was the most obvious common ground that Sathima discovered in Holiday's book, though in a more general way Holiday outlines the struggles of being a woman of color, which Sathima must surely have read with real empathy. Even if she had been protected by the insularity of the extended family from some of the daily hazards written about in Holiday's text—rape, prostitution, drug abuse, and other forms of exploitation—she surely recognized the nature of the experiences, the risks and the problems of being a woman of color singing jazz, sometimes with an all-white band, in the early to mid-twentieth century. These include the striking similarities between places in New York City—black areas like Harlem and the whiter areas of midtown Manhattan—and the Group Areas of apartheid cities; the differences between African American and white liberal social styles; and so forth.

Accounts of Holiday's experiences traveling in the southern and midwestern parts of the United States parallel Sathima's experiences in Cape Town and then traveling with *Coloured Jazz and Variety* and back and forth to Johannesburg with Ibrahim in the early 1960s. In one of my early interviews of Sathima, she commented that reading about Holiday's experiences resonated closely with what happened to Coloured and black South African musicians who performed for white audiences: everyone sat in the kitchen or even outside the building at intermission, forbidden from mixing socially with white South Africans. "Just like black Americans," she commented in April 1990.[99]

A section of the Holiday story reads as follows: "You can say all you want about the South, and I've said plenty. But when I've forgotten all the crummy things that happened on the road, I'll still remember Fox Theatre in Detroit, Michigan. What Radio City is to New York, the Fox was to Detroit then. A booking there was a big deal."[100] The show the group did the first night at the Fox included the jazz band with a chorus line of bare-legged white girls kicking like the Rockettes. The chorus girls had a black band on their legs, however, and that created havoc in the audiences, who demanded the show be changed. Holiday continues: "They did both their numbers in black masks and mammy dresses. They did both their numbers in blackface and those damn mammy getups."[101] The situation worsened when the light-skinned Holiday also came under attack: "Next day they told Basie I was too yellow to sing with all the Black men in his band. Somebody might think I was White if the light didn't hit me just right. So they got special dark grease and told me to put it on."[102] Later in the book, she recalls working a radio gig with Artie Shaw in New York City and being told she had to use the back door to enter the hotel. She also recalled a Kansas sheriff who told her outright he didn't like Negroes — she appreciated his candor if not his sentiment.[103] Racial mixture creates confusion about the freedoms and privileges denied people of darker hue in both South Africa and the United States in the postwar era.

Near the end of the autobiography Holiday writes, "I've fought all my life to be able to sing what I wanted the way I wanted to sing it."[104] What Holiday wanted to sing was the white popular song repertory, which she transformed into her own style. "Holiday," Angela Davis argues, "recontextualized these formulaic ditties mass-produced on the Tin Pan Alley assembly line, in a specifically African-American cultural tradition, while simultaneously extending the boundaries of that tradition."[105] Her style was black originality offered to mainstream white culture. In a similar vein, Sathima takes what was a white repertory, namely, the old songs of British music hall and American Tin Pan Alley, and made them her own. The twist in Sathima's St. Helenian story was that these songs were already once removed from whiteness. Passing through the island of St. Helena and traveling onto Cape Town, South Africa, they might be British, but they were certainly not white in cultural memory and style.

Finally, while any discussion of race and Holiday's music should reflect on her performances of the song "Strange Fruit," it is not clear Sathima would ever have heard the song in South Africa—all local live and foreign imported culture was heavily monitored and censored by the state—except perhaps in the private collections of foreigners living in Cape Town. Nevertheless, there are obvious links between Sathima's own political songs in her "Liberation Suite," Holiday's "Strange Fruit," and the "Freedom Now Suite" by Abbey Lincoln and Max Roach.

Musical Approach

The whole basis of my singing is feeling. Unless I feel something,
I can't sing.—Billie Holiday, *Lady Sings the Blues* (1956)

Despite the twenty years that separate Holiday and Benjamin in age, both women operated in or recall a musical world in which the oral and aural was the primary mode of transmission. Improvisation was shaped out of a musical environment in which musicians didn't read music but played by ear, allowing for a different set of musical skills and possibilities than with the adherence to music literacy, complex written arrangements, and so forth.[106] Billie contrasts her 1950s musical experiences inside recording studios, which she characterized as overly complicated, with what seemed to her a simpler past, when musicians could really "play the music." And here she introduces the idea of spontaneity made possible by a certain lack of detailed planning, an absence of overly rehearsed recordings, and the quality of surprise in musical processes, a dimension of jazz performance Sathima truly relishes. Recalling her days with the Count Basie band in the 1930s, Holiday recollected that

> I often think about how we used to record in those days. We'd get off a bus after a five-hundred-mile trip, go into the studio with no music, nothing to eat but coffee and sandwiches. Me and Lester would drink what we called top and bottom, half gin and half port wine. I'd say, "What'll we do, two-bar or four-bar intro?" Somebody'd say make it four and a chorus—one, one, and a half. Then I'd say, "You play behind me the first eight, Lester." . . .

Now with all their damn preparation, complicated arrangements, you've got to kiss everybody's behind to get ten minutes to do eight sides in. When I did "Night and Day" I had never seen that song before in my life. I don't read music, either. I just walked in, Teddy Wilson played it for me, and I did it.[107]

Later she noted with deep nostalgia, "With Basie we had something no expensive arrangements could touch. The cats would come in, somebody would hum a tune. Then someone else would play it over on the piano once or twice. Then someone would set up a riff, a ba-deep, a ba-dop. Then Daddy Basie would two-finger it a little. And then things would start to happen. . . . Everything that happened, happened by ear. For the two years I was with the band we had a book of a hundred songs, and every one of us carried every last damn note of them in our heads."[108]

Both singers stress, as do many others in jazz, the inextricable ties between jazz performance and everyday life, an approach to singing that Sathima categorizes as natural. Each recalls the central importance of films and recordings played on the Victrola that shaped their early yearnings for a life in song. Both sing with a deeply felt emotional sensibility — over and over Holiday stresses that she cannot sing a song unless she can feel it, unless she has lived the emotions conveyed in the words of the text. Both women compose a body of songs that emerge directly out of the poignancy of lived experience, not songs self-consciously constructed while sitting at a keyboard with a blank page that is gradually filled. Rather, both women sense a song coming, often with words and music, and then request the help of a male musician who can write music to transcribe it and perhaps even fill in the harmonic support. This characterizes Benjamin's compositional process to this day.

Holiday tells the story behind "God Bless the Child," a song she wrote after a conflict with her mother over money: "One day a whole damn song fell into place in my head. Then I rushed down to the Village that night and met Arthur Herzog. He sat down at the piano and picked it out, phrase by phrase, as I sang it to him. . . . I couldn't wait to get it down and get it recorded. I told him about the fight with Mom and how I wanted to get even. We changed the lyrics in a couple of spots, but not much."[109] Sathima uses a similar frame for talking about compositional process: the unexpected emergence of words and melody.

Holiday talks regularly in the autobiography about her relationship to saxophonists and about the oft-cited view that jazz singers sound like saxophones. On the road with Young and the Basie band, she recalled, "Lester sings with his horn. You listen to him and you can almost hear the words."[110] She rails against the idea, however, that the singer is like a saxophone: "If you don't sound right, you can't go out and get some new reeds, split them just right. A singer is only a voice, and a voice is completely dependent on the body God gave you. When you walk out there and open your mouth, you never know what's going to happen."[111]

With the deterioration of Holiday's body after years of substance abuse and other kinds of mistreatment, her voice had changed significantly by the end of her life: some read the mutation as maturation, while others have suggested it was the inevitable consequence of substance abuse. Still others argue that Holiday's more mature sound speaks of the depth of voice and intensity of life experience. Sathima's voice is different. Even though she is in her seventies, those who hear her singing are struck by the youthfulness of the voice. A useful comparison would be, for example, the sound of her voice on *A Morning in Paris* in 1963 and *Musical Echoes* (2002) or even the *Song Spirit* retrospective (2006) forty years later. Furthermore, as a young woman she traveled throughout South Africa with Adams in *Coloured Jazz and Variety* and lovingly recalls how Parker's sound inspired Moeketsi in those days. And she warmly recalls the sound of Cape Town's saxophone lineups in dance bands, and more experimental jazz performances of the period. Some argue that the way in which the saxophone is grouped and played in Cape jazz, its intensity and particular tone, distinguishes it from all other jazz elsewhere in the world.[112]

European Travel and the U.S. vs. the South African Recording Industry

The two most striking differences between Holiday's experience and the South African jazz context of a woman like Benjamin in the 1950s are, first, access to a music and film industry infrastructure — Holiday's voice and image were circulated beyond the confines of the local environment whereas Benjamin's were not; and, second, the two women's views on Europe's relationship to the world of jazz.

In contrast to the rather active recording career of John Hammond, be-

ginning in 1933, there was almost no industry infrastructure or state support for women of color who sang jazz in South Africa. Basically, there
were two institutions that recorded South African music in the 1950s.
The first was the state-controlled SABC, which played a central role in recorded transcriptions of local music. SABC's focus was on the music and
languages of black South Africans or Afrikaans-speaking peoples, music
that could not be imported from elsewhere and that, from the 1960s on,
became an indispensable tool in the instilling of apartheid values in rural
and urban communities. Few Coloured musicians in Cape Town were
ever recorded, though musicians remember the Alf Wylie band, which
did regular gigs for the SABC, and the Cape singer Zelda Benjamin recalls
a recording session with February at some point in the postwar period.[113]
No one actually has any copies of the recordings made. The second con-
trolling institution was a commercial record company that worked hand
in hand with official policy, Gallo Records. Over the years, Abdullah did
some recording with Gallo starting with the Jazz Epistles in 1959, though
generally musicians recall that when they did record they were never paid
royalties, only flat fees for recording. The disadvantages of working inside
the recording industry are well known. Holiday recalls her frustrations:
"People don't understand the kind of fight it takes to record what you
want to record the way you want to record it. I've fought as long as ten
years to get to record a song I loved or wanted to do. . . . Royalties were
still unheard of. I didn't know there was such a thing."[114] Holiday likens
making a record to making a film and handling a camera crew: "They're
like the boys in the control room when you're making records. You can
turn in the best performance in the world, but if those cats in the control room aren't with you when they turn those little knobs or twist those
little dials, you might just as well have stayed in bed, Jack."[115]

The two women's experiences of traveling in Europe were markedly
different also. "I guess every Negro performer dreams of going to Europe.
Some of them have gone over and never come back," mused Holiday.[116]
She made her first trip to Europe in 1954, performing forty gigs in thirty
days. She remembered all the friends she made while there. In particular,
she talked about Berlin and the young guy who ran the only swing band
in the city: "I was never so happy in my life. They were the swingingest
cats I ever heard. All they have is American records. The latest American
sides they had were from '49 and '50, but those cats can blow. And they

had to work to get that way. They're lucky enough to have no American radio or TV, where some promoter can push a button and within a week every damn body is brain-washed and listening to the same stuff like 'Doggie in the Window.'" She continues paying tribute to the musicians, who in her mind didn't have the music in them intuitively but rather they had to really work to capture sound and skill. "It's culture to them, and art, and it doesn't matter whether it's Beethoven or Charlie Parker, they got respect," she writes. And she compares the European reception to that in the United States, where she posited that the only respect for jazz derived from those who could profit from its performance.[117]

Traveling to the continent in the early 1960s, Sathima was much less enthusiastic about the European continent (see chapter 4). Sathima contrasted the sense of comfort musicians could find in Europe with the importance of the jazz community in New York City: "This is very, very different. You need the vitality, all the musicians are here, you need the feeling that the energy is there. So I mean I have a love-hate relationship with New York City. Who doesn't? But, it is a good place to be if you're doing this kind of music. You will never become complacent about yourself."

Lineage and Place

"Who are you and where do you come from?" a reiteration of the question that echoes from mother to daughter, jazz singer to hip-hop artist. The response of mother to daughter to their mixed racial identity can be traced back one further step in their musical lineage to the artistic kinship Sathima imagined out of her consumption of the written word, the visual image, and the emotional resonance she heard in the sound of Holiday's voice. And yet if there is one theme that consistently emerges in every interview I conducted with Sathima's peers in Cape Town, it is that from the outset Sathima had her own style: a naturalness of voice, a deeply felt emotion in the sound; she was willing to play around with the melody and the beat, and that music was her calling. In several moments in the autobiography, Holiday stresses the importance of an individual voice—no two people are the same, all have lived different lives, so each brings a unique quality to their performances. "No two people on earth are alike, and it's got to be that way in music, or it isn't music," comments Holiday.[118] Holiday thereby constitutes the singer as the source, the original, in every sense of the word.

The literary critic Susan Stewart concurs: the sound of the voice defines the person: it is the aural imprint of the "reservoir of life experiences" of the speaker.[119] In its most natural form, the "particular timbre, tone, hesitations" speak of the peculiarity of individual history and human connectedness. We attach specific memories, expectations, and responses to the tone of the human voice. And it is with this sense of Holiday's vision of the individuality of the singer, her life experience, and her sound that one arrives at a deeper understanding of the relationship Benjamin imagined with a woman living a long way away from the her own home, but whose presence was deeply felt and richly imagined in its disembodied representations.

The matter of difference in the African diaspora is not straightforward, however. In contrast to the profound sense of connectedness among those in the old African diaspora, whose first language is English, black South Africans of the more recent diaspora, including singers like Makeba, Letta Mbulu, Thuli Dumakude, and others, measured difference in the novelty of culture and language, as vestiges of an African [American] past pertinent to those in the first African diaspora.[120] This is evident in the recording of Makeba's performance in 1960 at Town Hall in New York City, the "Click Song" being the key sign of difference.[121] Unlike Benjamin, whose repertory and sound resonate with a transnational audience and consumer body in musical and spoken language, Makeba's uniqueness is constituted in the exoticism of tonal languages, like Zulu, with its three clicks, and Xhosa with one more. While Holiday values difference at the level of life experience and emotional expressivity, the South African exile Lewis Nkosi wrote rather disparagingly about the inability to be "cosmopolitan" if one was a black South African abroad.[122] The black, racialized body signaled the first degree of separation, language and culture, and song the next.

In the absence of similar signs of cultural differentiation, Holiday comments, your feelings are the answer: "Everybody's got to be different. You can't copy anybody and end up with anything. If you copy, it means you're working without any real feeling. And without feeling, what you do amounts to nothing."[123] Even if one is singing someone else's song, performing from the heart and inscribing one's own emotion into the articulation of each musical note is what sets one person's rendition apart from that of another. This is what many in postwar South Africa believed about the power of music in their lives. And so it is that Sathima has made a place in the lineage of African diasporic jazz through a highly particular discourse of deeply felt emotion conveyed in the style of a foreign musical repertory made by those of similar skin color, emotional vocabulary, and life experience.[124]

A certain focus on emotional vocabulary of twentieth-century jazz singing makes me wonder if an archeology of emotion might not be key to understanding how popular music became the universal language of the twentieth century. Could it be argued that the emotional resonance heard in the sound of the voice engenders possibilities for some forms of cross-cultural, intercontinental dialogues between singers and their audiences in the transnational consumption of twentieth-century popular music? Might emotional resonance be the metaphor scholars use to productively judge the power of popular music in the twentieth century, much like beauty was used (and abused) in the visual domain?[125] Perhaps it is time for us to constitute new reflections on emotion or beauty in musical expression, perhaps even with socially just outcomes, much as Elaine Scarry has recently posited for the idea of beauty.[126]

In mid-June 2005 Sathima left a message on my cell phone. Despite her protestations about having modeled herself on the life and musical performances of Holiday, there was something deeply mystical that was emerging from our conversation about Holiday. She wanted to tell me that since we had talked, she had had a call from some filmmakers, prodded I believe by Griffin herself, who were making a documentary on Holiday. They wanted to talk with Sathima, to interview her for the film, to record her in performance, and finally to use the song she had written in tribute to Holiday, called "Lady Day," in the soundtrack for the film itself. The journey of voices connecting virtually or mystically was coming full circle. Holiday was once again at the center of a significant moment in the life of the South African singer. This time, however, it was Benjamin's original song and particular quality of voice rendering the music.

4

Jazz Migrancy

Musicians Abroad

It is unlikely Sathima would have left South Africa on her own: leaving was definitely more Abdullah's decision than hers. Writing in 1966 to *Drum Magazine*, Ibrahim reflected on his reasons for leaving: "Night club owners were hostile and avoided me and my music like the plague. The feeling was mutual, though, because I had decided long before, they were not going to turn me into another juke-box . . . the kind of musician they tuck away in a dark little corner of a dingy cellar and who has to pound his soul away into the bleak hours of the morning over their cheap perfumed, whiskied, cigarette smoke, endless babble and false laughter. A black juke-box. The scene was a mess and after long hours of discussion with Bea Benjamin and close friends one fact emerged, we had to go."[1]

Feeling pushed out of South Africa by the increasingly repressive political engineering of the apartheid regime and motivated by the desire to extend their musical horizons through the contacts made with European visitors to the Cape Town jazz scene, Sathima and Abdullah performed at several events held to raise money to enable them to travel to Europe in 1962. By February they had enough cash to buy one-way tickets to Zurich, where, until they found a way to survive through their music, they would stay with Paul Meyer. The trauma of Sharpeville, the state of emergency declared soon after, and the growing forcefulness of the apartheid regime made leaving the country seem to be the only way to continue performing and creating. There were few alternatives at the time.

The contrast between the warmth and excitement of the community left behind and the coldness of Europe, however, was stark for these two South Africans. "We went to the unknown," Sathima recalled. "It was so shocking. It was so rough and cold. And we had to keep moving to survive. Zurich was our base, and we moved out from there." At the beginning Sathima and Abdullah had to work the nightclub circuit, performing whatever was required to eke out an existence. "We even did cha cha

cha at some places," Sathima told me. They moved into a single room in a house with a group of international students that included the Dutchman Rafik Fris and his Danish wife, Tove, whom they had first met in Cape Town. Rafik would act as point man in finding work for the South Africans.

Several months later, with the help of Meyer and Fris, Abdullah secured a 4½-month-per-year contract for three years at the Africana Club in Zurich. "The Africana Club was one of the best in Europe at the time," commented the South African bass player Johnny Dyani in October 1983, shortly before he died. "A lot of music happened there. The Club no longer exists, and hardly anyone ever mentions it, as if it was just a building. But that was a house of Culture! Every time I pass there I see the people and I hear the sounds in my mind. It's still alive."[2] Abdullah quickly persuaded the owner of the Africana to fly the drummer Makhaya Ntshoko and the bass player Johnny Gertze to Switzerland. They joined Abdullah and became the Dollar Brand Trio. Sathima would sing with them on occasion, but in jazz the singer was never really considered a core member of the ensemble.

The Club Africana was important for another reason: that was where Sathima and Abdullah first played for Duke Ellington. The story has been told many times, and it runs something like this. One cold night early in February 1963 Sathima heard that Ellington was performing in the neighborhood of the Club Africana. Instead of singing with the trio that night, she decided to seek him out because she was determined to introduce him to the South Africans. Sathima walked to the venue where Ellington was playing and made her way backstage. She was lucky that night. Ellington was in his dressing room, but he saw her lurking at the door, called her in, and talked with her a little. When Ellington and the band went on stage, he offered her a chair and suggested she watch the show from the wings. She remembers that during one of Sam Woodward's solos Ellington came over to where she was seated and asked her if she and Ibrahim were signed to a record company. She told him they were not. "Wait until the end of the show and I will talk further with you then," said Ellington. Sathima lingered for about an hour until he came toward her. The maestro took her arm, and they walked together to the Africana.

When he saw the Ellington entourage, the owner of the Africana, who had already closed up for the evening, allowed the South Africans to perform. Ellington stayed for a couple of numbers and then turned to the young Benjamin. "And what is it that you do? Are you the manager, are you married to one of these guys?" he asked. "No," Sathima answered, "but I sing sometimes." Ellington urged her to sing. "That was a real surprise, and I wasn't prepared for it at all," Sathima told me, "but when Duke Ellington tells you to do it, you just do it. I didn't sing any Ellington things. I think I sang, "I'm Glad There is You.""[3]

The next day Ellington met with the South Africans in his hotel in Zurich. At the time he was an artists and repertoire person for Frank Sinatra's label, Reprise Records, and he had come to Paris to perform, record, and scout for talent. In this capacity, Ellington told the South Africans that he liked what they were doing and wanted to record them. They were to contact his accountant for train fare and meet him in Paris three days later. Ellington was scheduled to perform in Paris on Saturday evening, and on Sunday morning he met with Sathima, Abdullah, Makhaya, and Johnny in the Barclay Studios. Sathima vividly recalled that day in the studio with Ellington and Billy Strayhorn. Ellington arrived with a woman on one arm and Strayhorn at his side. He introduced Strayhorn: "This is Bea, this is Billy, and you should get to know each other, and we'll start with you."[4]

"I must say that the Ellington session was completely spontaneous. Completely from the get go, it was just, 'Here's so and so, what are you gonna do?' Nothing was planned."[5] "At a certain point I started doing Ellington songs, and then he came out of the recording box and said, 'Wait, those are my tunes, so I have to sit down at the piano.' I couldn't believe that—he played for me," Sathima remarked to me.[6] Soon after the release of her album with Ellington in 1997 she reflected again on that moment in the studio: "Even when Ellington ran out of the recording booth and said, 'That's my song' and sat down and did it, Abdullah stunned him with what the key was. It was 'I Got It Bad and That Ain't Good.' Then he said, 'Oh no, ok, you had better play this.' And Abdullah took a backseat. He said, 'No sir, it's your song.' And you can hear, because we didn't do two takes, you hear that Duke is letting me sing first, and then, 'Where is it? Ok, that is where she is going.' When he got it, it was over," she told me in April 1997.

The Danish violinist Svend Asmussen, who was in town to record with Stephan Grappeli the day before, dropped by the studio.[7] Sathima remembers Duke saying, "Gee, just the person I am looking for. You sit in on this." He told Asmussen not to use the bow because, he said, "'she's the melody. I just want you to fill in the gaps. I don't want you to go anywhere she goes.' Poor Svend Asmussen said, you know his fingers, his fingers were, never in his life had he played so much pizzicato, never ever," Sathima commented.[8]

The German recording engineer Gerhard Lehner was working at the Barclay Studios on 23 February 1963. Lehner had fought in the German army during the Second World War and was taken prisoner by U.S. forces in Russia. He had been persuaded to work for the U.S. Armed Services Radio in Munich. He was subsequently hired as the chief engineer at the Barclay Studios and had been involved in recording many of Ellington's and Strayhorn's musical sessions. He was particularly drawn to the singer that morning. Lehner reminisced about the session in the liner notes to *A Morning in Paris*:

> As we began to balance the first theme, I was instantly fascinated by this South African singer who had fled from apartheid. Not only was I taken by her exceptional beauty but most of all by her extraordinarily subtle voice. The lyrics of the ballads in her repertory were simply sublime, outstanding. The soft lighting in the studio, the attentiveness of Duke Ellington and Billy Strayhorn in the booth (and sometimes on piano), the delicate pizzicati of violinist Svend Asmussen, the generous chords of Dollar Brand, all combined to create a magical atmosphere. I whispered to my assistant as discreetly as I could, asking him to record the session on a 19cm/7.5 inch recorder so that I preserved these magical moments of absolute beauty for myself. This sin, for which I hope I will be forgiven, is the reason why you can listen to this album today.[9]

It is not clear why Ellington spent time with the South African musicians, although it seems that South Africa had been on his mind. Quite by coincidence, just prior to this meeting Ellington had been asked by the U.S. State Department to travel to South Africa on tour; or at least this is what he told the young South Africans sometime later. Ellington refused the offer because he would have had to perform before segregated audiences.[10] It is possible, nevertheless, that meeting the South African musicians made him realize the extent to which his music had traveled around the world and been lovingly consumed by people as far away as

South Africa. Soon thereafter he left on the first of several State Department tours he would undertake.[11]

The Recordings in Paris

About six months after the recording session in Paris Ellington released *Duke Ellington Presents the Dollar Brand Trio*, which included eight of the thirty tracks made that day. Much like the showcasing that has opened doors for world musicians in partnership with American and British producers since the 1980s, Ellington's lending of his name to Abdullah launched his jazz career internationally, particularly in Europe, where he began to perform regularly at festivals and in clubs. The same did not hold true for Sathima. "Not commercial enough," was Sinatra's opinion. While the styles of the two singers are distinctive, one can't help wondering just how different her career might have been had Sinatra decided to release that recording three decades earlier.

Ultimately the Reprise label was sold, and the tapes seemingly disappeared. Sathima told me in 1990 that she had tried very hard to track down the original tapes, had written letters, begged, and pleaded without any luck.[12] While traveling in Italy, Abdullah happened to hear Sathima's voice ringing out at a restaurant, but he couldn't seem to find out who owned the prized originals. "The industry was controlled by the mafia at the time," Sathima commented to me awhile back. The tapes surfaced in July 1994, when she met with David Hajdu, the journalist, professor, and Strayhorn biographer. While doing research for *Lushlife*, his book on Strayhorn, Hajdu had tracked Lehner down in Paris. Lehner gave Hajdu the tapes for Sathima. It would take more than two years before she was able to release twelve tracks of that historic morning in Paris at a recital in Carnegie Hall.

After publishing the compact disc, Sathima was invited to perform with local musicians at a small jazz club in Paris in April 1997. Once again she traveled to Paris to sing with complete strangers. This time, however, she recalls that the old-timers in the audience left the club humming the tunes of songs they remembered from their own pasts in cities and towns far from the humble beginnings of the South African singer, much as she remembers old-timers had done when she was a young woman in Cape

Town. Lehner, his wife, and several friends were in the audience for both the Friday and Saturday evening performances more than three decades after what Sathima calls that first "magical encounter" in the studio in Paris.

The Recording Session

Lehner's copy of that session from 1963, given to Sathima by Hajdu, captures a sense of the first encounters in the studio on the unpublished tracks transcribed below.

Key to Transcription

TAKE ONE, TWO, etc.: separate takes according to when songs are repeated or started over.

BUZZER: the actual sound of a buzzer one hears on the tape, indicating the start of another take.

Song texts are given in italics. To avoid copyright problems I have not cited complete songs texts. Musical and extra musical activity is indicated in parentheses.

Conversation between musicians is given in plain text cited after each person's name.

TAKE ONE
BUZZER
Sathima (begins alone, on a sustained): *I*
Duke (interrupts): Once more.
Sathima: *I should care* (Ntshoko enters with a slow, even tentative, walking bass line).
Duke (interrupts): Excuse me, rest the first beat on the *"care." "I should"* REST boom boom boom.
Makhaya: OK.
Sathima: *I should care* (the bass responds as Ellington suggested),
    I should go around weeping (Asmussen responds with bowed melody on violin).

(They continue, Sathima singing the words, Asmussen responding with exquisitely bowed melodies, bending the pitch, sometimes interspersed with the walking bass of Ntshoko. Sathima completes a complete run through of the song.)

TAKE TWO

BUZZER

(Sathima asks Asmussen to give her the note. They go again, this time with a little more certainty, the pace a little quicker. Once again she proceeds all the way through the song.)

TAKE THREE

BUZZER

(This time with pizzicato violin, the bass is still somewhat tentative. Again, Sathima completes one run-through of the song. Occasionally Ntshoko strikes the high hat but mostly the percussion is silent. There is no piano here. Sathima's voice is strong, resonant, supple, and full of color. She draws out the lyrics: she is deeply respectful of the words and explores a particular quality of voice to convey the words.)

NEXT SONG: TAKE ONE

Sathima: *I'm glad there is you.*

BUZZER

Sathima: Are you playing?

Duke: Watch your *p*'s.

Sathima: My *p*'s and *b*'s.

BUZZER

SAME SONG: TAKE TWO

Sathima: *In this world of ordinary people* (bass responds)

  Extraordinary people (pizzicato violin)

  I'm glad there is you (violin and bass)

(She completes a run-through of the song, repeating the chorus. As she ends Ntshoko strikes the high hat four times.)

TAKE THREE

BUZZER

They run through *I'm Glad There Is You* again.

NEXT SONG: TAKE ONE
BUZZER
Sathima: *If they asked me, I could write a book*
  About the way you walk and whisper and look . . .
(When she repeats the words, the song moves into a propulsive swing.)
  If they ask me I could write a book
  About the way you walk and whisper and look (she continues until)
  And the simple secret of the plot
Ellington: Hold it. Somebody is sharp, . . . flat
(Ibrahim plays some piano, somebody hums a note.)
TAKE TWO, HALFWAY INTO THE SONG
BUZZER
Duke: Try it again.
(Somebody hums.)
Duke: This is on tape, I think you should start that on the second verse,
  leave off that.
Sathima: *If they asked me*
Duke: Stop.

NEXT SONG: TAKE ONE
BUZZER
(Strayhorn on piano, with Asmussen on violin)
Sathima: *Your love has faded*
  It's not what it used to be . . .
(They go through the song once.)

TAKE TWO
BUZZER
(Piano and pizzicato violin do introduction)
Sathima: *You love has faded . . . into the night.*
(The song ends with an exquisite closing performance on piano by Stray-
horn.)

This transcribed excerpt represents some of the unreleased tracks of
the morning's recording, the tentative moments of first encounters. A
group of musicians, all experienced in their own right, had nonethe-

less not been together in a studio before, and some had never heard the music of the others prior to this occasion. The session continues for just over forty minutes on tapes I heard.[13] In November 1963 Jack Lind, who took the picture on the cover of *A Morning in Paris*, published a piece about the recording session. He remarked that the song by Strayhorn, "Your Love Has Faded," had not been recorded in a long time, as Ellington had struggled to find the right voice for the music, and that Sathima had never heard it aired in South Africa. Strayhorn provided words and melody twenty minutes before they began recording. Similarly, Sathima had never sung "In My Solitude"; she didn't know the words of that song either. Ellington wrote them out for her and hung them on a partition for her to read. "He wanted only one take," she told Lind at the time.

Some clues about the interaction of the musicians can be gleaned from the tapes. The beginning of the session reveals tentative playing from Ntshoko and Gertze; even Asmussen takes his lead from Ellington. Further into the tapes, there is a greater feeling of swing and cohesiveness in the supporting instruments. The contrast between the presence of Sathima's voice in the jazz fabric and Abdullah's at the piano, when he is the featured performer later in the session, is striking. It speaks clearly to a kind of gendering in jazz performance, certainly as it pertains to Sathima and Abdullah. Her voice has a delicate wistfulness; her instrument is the voice, and she sings songs of love, pain, and longing. While she intuitively grasps the complex harmonic language that underpins her jazz melodies, her voice conveys a vulnerability. It is hard not to read the words as autobiographical. When her recording was over and Abdullah took center stage, his wordless piano performance takes complete control of the event. He has developed a pianism of his own: the textures are rich, bold, and multivoiced.

There is no archival record of what happened before the musicians walked into the studio. Sathima remembers that they arrived about half an hour prior to the scheduled recording time, and Ellington, his partner, and Strayhorn soon thereafter. As she recalls the event, there was little preparation or rehearsal before the buzzer sounded and the engineer turned the dials. As a result, spontaneity has become Sathima's key guiding principle for all performance, inside the studio and in live venues. She prefers a single take, two at a stretch.[14] Spontaneity, nevertheless, has an underside in much jazz scholarship because of the manner in which it was often believed to caricature Africans in America—as nonliterate, unschooled, unplanned, or irrational.[15] But Sathima invokes the spontaneous to support rather than diminish the power of musical creativity among those who work with her.

While there may not have been much conversation about how the morning's session would proceed, there can be no doubt that Ellington had done some thinking about what might emerge from this gathering of musicians. Sathima's deference to her partner and Dollar Brand's musical output may have prodded Ellington to give her a chance to place herself. It was, after all, Sathima who began the recording session. It was her voice, powerfully articulating a womanly subjectivity with the word "I," that one hears before anything else on the unpublished copy. Ellington stops her. "Once more," he asks. "*I should care*," she sings. He stops her again, this time to suggest to Ntshoko better ways to support her words on the bass.

To showcase Sathima's voice, Ellington urges the musicians to create a lean instrumental texture, first bowed, then plucked violin playing, with a spare bass line. They leave considerable space within the instrumental frame for the singer to project her own style and to tuck the words into musical phrases that demonstrate a particular approach to pitch, modulation, and timing. This is the kind of freedom she relishes. The musicians, all men, are clearly listening to what she does and responding to her musical calls, often with extraordinarily delicate and beautiful melodic and harmonic materials. The music supports or overlaps with the richness of tone quality and timbral possibility in her own voice.

In these unpublished tracks one senses an instant empathy between Strayhorn's piano playing and the singer;[16] Abdullah is similarly supportive, as are Asmussen's endlessly inventive pizzicato melodies. There is no indication from the pianists who play for Sathima in the published version—Strayhorn, Ibrahim, and Ellington—of any need to use their instruments to dominate her voice. Rather, Benjamin's performance is framed by each of these men in supportive and sensitive ways. Such musical engagement stood in stark contrast to the gendering of social interaction Sathima learned from her grandmother in South Africa, where women always acted in subservience to male needs, and to some of her experiences with male musicians in Cape Town. In this context, it was Ellington who set the standard of professional engagement, helping Sathima to know what she might expect from American musicians when she started her own label in 1979 and formed her own trios from the 1980s on.

The songs Sathima sang in this recording session are largely the popular songs of the era, written by Ellington and Strayhorn. All deal with the idea of love in some fashion, and it is the subject of love and the loss of love which is central to Sathima's repertory to this day. In the 1980s she would discover while traveling in Europe, where the anti-apartheid movement was active, that romantic love was not considered sufficiently political—even though from the perspective of many women, like Winnie Mandela, whose husbands and partners were political prisoners, such memories of love may well have driven their survival in the darkest moments of the struggle. And if one thinks of the story of jazz migration, of the years of constant travel between cities, countries, and continents, a song like "In My Solitude" becomes so much more than the words of a girl pining for her man. It resonates with the isolation characteristic of living in the diaspora. Sathima, Abdullah, Johnny, and Makhaya were coming to realize this loneliness in 1963.[17]

Missing in this session are three elements that become hallmark qualities of Benjamin's voice in jazz. First, there is little independence of line or function for the bassist. Once she starts to compose her own materials, often a bass line comes first, before the other musical materials. And bass players are given enormous latitude to be playful and wickedly creative, often "singing" their own countermelodies to Sathima's voice. While the bass player becomes much more than the mere shape of harmonic progression, there is no inkling of that dimension of her performance in this earlier moment. Second, Sathima demands of her drummers a particular sound that is highly percussive; some call it a qualitatively African feel—they bring brushes, use their sticks to create a dry, woody timbre in the rhythmic outline of a piece, and often make the drums seem to speak. On occasion she requires the drummer to sound out the Cape Town rhythm, or *klopse* beat, to mark place through rhythmic articulation. Third, Sathima gives her trio considerable freedom to solo: to express themselves musically within an improvisational format.

I have already discussed Ellington's place in postwar South African jazz circles, but I have wondered and have asked Sathima several times what it was that drew her individually to the music of Ellington. She has responded that it was Ellington's sound, his melodies and harmonies, but she remains quite vague about the specifics. Better guides are three specifically musical responses from Sathima: listening to the CD *A Morning in Paris*, which is available for purchase; reflecting on the song she wrote in homage to Ellington; and hearing the hard-to-find album of his music entitled *Sathima Sings Ellington*, which she recorded after settling in New York City in 1979, as well as numerous Ellington songs she has subsequently recorded.

Sathima recounted to the writer Ken Franckling of *Downbeat* that when she first encountered Ellington in the studio she was totally in awe: "I felt enchanted, as if a spell were placed over me. Duke made you feel that you could do anything. It was his gift. He had this wonderful way of bringing out treasures that you didn't even know were inside you."[18] Sathima pays tribute to Ellington in her "Gift of Love—Song for Duke," recorded in 1987 on her *Lovelight* album in words that, despite her apprehensiveness about paying adequate musical tribute to Ellington, a man of such extraordinary presence and productivity, convey her profound sense of his magnificence:

> Regal he was, and oh so grand
> Like the title, "Duke," implies.
> Elegant, and gracious and ever so wise,
> Ambassador of peace and love,
> The memory of him never dies.
> Wonderful glorious music for all the world to hear;
> His music, his music is a gift of love, gift of love;
> His music, his music is a gift of love.[19]

In many ways her portrait of Ellington resonates with the feeling of presence established in *Cabin in the Sky* (see chapter 3). There, Ellington transcends the rest in terms of personal character, the richness of his musical output, and the genuine love for the music and its makers, a love many musicians recall when they reflect on their encounters with Ellington in his lifetime. And he was not only an ambassador of peace and love. Ellington also spent a decade traveling on State Department Jazz Tours, performances the federal government hoped would spread a positive message of American democracy and an image of racial equality, a mission many of the musicians recognized did not reflect racial realities in the United States in the postwar period.[20] What may set Sathima's perspective apart from that of others is the line about remembering Duke — "the memory of him never dies" — and the manner in which she keeps her personal relationship with him alive more than two decades after his death (see below).

Despite the fact that Sathima's recording was not released, this transnational gathering of musicians in Paris was fortuitous not only because the studio session was a thrilling event for the South Africans, but also because of the European jazz connections fostered, particularly with Asmussen and by way of Ellington's own networks.

Europe in the 1960s

These moments of encounter between the transnational community of jazz musicians opened new doors for Abdullah, and he often included Sathima in his live performance schedule through the mid-1970s. Such transnational music making would characterize the kinds of jazz ensembles and performances that South Africans participated in and constituted in the 1960s and 1970s, especially in their travels around the Europe. In fact, this is how several of the South Africans would define themselves in the European jazz scene: on nonracial, nonethnic, and nonnational terms. When asked by journalists if they wouldn't prefer to play with musicians from home, the reply would often be that while they missed home very much and longed to jam with musicians from there, Europe offered the possibility of a far wider musical palette. In contrast to the increasing divisiveness of the apartheid regime in South Africa, jazz musicians in the 1960s sought national and racial unity through performance — to prove apartheid was misguided. They did so by self-consciously harmonizing musical and national differences in the very fabric of jazz performance itself.

Nonetheless, Europe was not an easy place for South Africans, accustomed as they were to the warmth of the sun, the sound of English and Afrikaans and indeed of the Xhosa, Zulu, Pedi, Tswana, and other languages, and the presence of strong, vibrant communities of people. Growing up in South Africa, Sathima had come to hold Europe and its culture in high esteem, imagining it as something of a mystical space. But the everyday reality of the place was something quite different. Language itself sounded alien and, outside of the musicians they met, ordinary people seemed cold and uncaring. Furthermore, few Europeans had any idea that people of color from South Africa could be performing jazz in its sophisticated inflections. Africa, its people, its pace of life, its customary friendliness, and its color and energy seemed a long, long way away.

Switzerland and France

Two significant events occurred during the time Sathima and Abdullah spent in Switzerland and France: the first was the recording with Ellington, initiated in Switzerland, completed in Paris, and followed by an appearance at the Antibes Jazz Festival in Juan-les-Pins, France, by Sathima and the Dollar Brand Trio in 1963. The second event was the arrival of the South African Blue Notes with Chris McGregor in 1964.

An invitation to perform at the Antibes Festival in 1964, a year after Sathima and Abdullah had played there, was the motivation for the Blue Notes to leave South Africa. They flew to Paris via Lourenço Marques (now Maputo), Mozambique. The drummer Louis Moholo recalls what it felt like to travel to Paris and Antibes and to encounter American musicians in these places.[21] "We went to Antibes," he said, "and we saw Bud Powell and we saw Jimmy Griffin. We were knocked out! It was a fantastic period to be in Paris. Paris was the Mecca of music. We were lucky to be there at the right time. We heard Lionel Hampton playing. It was amazing. We saw Ella Fitzgerald right in front of our eyes! We were spoiled with the amount of musicians who were there. Dizzy Gillespie was there, can you imagine? Horace Silver was there too. That encouraged us to go on, of course."[22]

Despite their high hopes of making connections with the European and American jazz scene at the festival, the Blue Notes found themselves stranded on the beach at the end of the event. They called Abdullah and Sathima, who arranged for the group to stay in the basement of their student house in Zurich. The Blue Notes arrived, and the musicians did some playing together, but a few months later the Blue Notes moved to London. Soon after the Dollar Brand Trio and Sathima followed them there. Moholo recalled the time in Switzerland: "We felt a little uncomfortable: your heart will always be where you are born. We were stars back there; here we were unknown, so we became a bit frustrated. We were still young, we missed our families, it was cold, and the audiences were not like the African audiences we knew, loud and appreciating."

If it was so difficult, why didn't the musicians just go home? why keep moving forward? Moholo continues: "When there were crises and we wanted to go home, we would sit down and discuss it and come to an agreement. The more we stayed, the more we got used to it, and apartheid was going on in South Africa and we didn't want to go back to that. We didn't want to go back to South Africa. We saw what they were doing to our kin. It was a very dirty time. They were shooting to kill! We had to go out of South Africa to save the music. Otherwise we would have died, just like everybody else. We had to leave, to save the heritage of South Africa."

Some of the Blue Notes "were just kids, and Sathima took care of them," Abdullah reminisced a few years ago. "This horrendous situation we had experienced in South Africa, in one sense it was good to get away from it, but in another sense it was very hard to be away from home and family. The thing that was driving us was the music. At least it gave us some kind of serenity. And there was another dilemma they faced: I was one of the few persons who had at least a high school education, most of them didn't even finish primary school, so the only thing that stood between them and starvation was the instrument. They had no chance to follow up on their education, because they didn't have basic skills."[23] While the South Africans were grateful for their start in Zurich and would go back on occasion to perform, once the contract with Club Africana expired, they never returned permanently to the place.

Copenhagen

"I think we met everyone [that is, all the Americans] in Copenhagen," Sathima commented recently. The first time was just three months after the historic recordings with Ellington, Strayhorn, and Asmussen in Paris. In the time between performances at the Club Africana Sathima and the Dollar Brand Trio traveled to Jazzhus Montmartre, a club that was the hub of live and progressive jazz performance in Copenhagen.[24] The

Danish critic and historian Eric Wiedeman described the restaurant and its significance to jazz:

> From 1959 to 1976 the Montmartre restaurant occupied a central position in the jazz life of Copenhagen, and Denmark. It arranged visits to Denmark by many of the leading American musicians, often lasting several weeks, something previously unknown [in Denmark].
>
> Many of these musicians also visited other parts of the country, and the existence of the restaurant was instrumental in causing quite a few of them to choose Copenhagen as their residence and base of operations in Europe. Among the most important may be mentioned tenor saxophonists Stan Getz, Dexter Gordon and Ben Webster, pianist Kenny Drew and bassist Oscar Pettiford. During some years in the early sixties, a number of avant-garde musicians also had better working conditions here than in the USA, for instance, Cecil Taylor, tenor saxophonists Albert Ayler and Archie Shepp, and trumpeter Don Cherry. Through accompanying American musicians, several Danish musicians also received optimal jazz schooling. The Montmartre was clearly the most important single factor in shaping professional jazz in Denmark since 1960."[25]

Denmark had a quota system in the 1960s, which required that Danish musicians be given a certain amount of the total performance time. The venues met the quota by having the Danes play the late-night shift (1–4 A.M.) on most nights or anytime on Mondays, a slow time in the week for jazz, and they usually worked as accompanists and sidemen for American musicians. While other musicians traveled to Denmark, Wiedemann singles out Dollar Brand, who "first showed up with his trio in May 1963, the first foreign show to play the nightshift (1.30–4.30 A.M.)." Because she was just the singer, Benjamin is not mentioned anywhere by Wiedemann.

Despite Ibrahim's late-night engagement, the discographer Lars Rasmussen lists two recordings that came out of that evening's performance: *Round Midnight at the Café Montmartre* and *Anatomy of a South African Village*. These are live recordings and are still commercially available. On *Round Midnight* the noise of restaurant clientele and the kitchen are audible, something Abdullah quickly worked to eliminate in live and recorded performances.[26] A year later, in March and April 1964, by which time the trio was better known in European jazz circuits, Ibrahim returned to the Montmartre. This time he had been invited to perform in the early evening, the slot usually reserved for American musicians. In January 1965 he was assigned the same slot, until the American musician Ben Webster arrived to make his debut in Copenhagen and Ibrahim was summarily moved to the later time.

In July 1965 and again in April 1966 the Blue Notes also performed at the Café Montmartre. Key Blue Note musicians at the time included Chris McGregor as pianist and arranger, Johnny Dyani on bass, and Louis Moholo on drums. Moholo recalled that first encounter: "We went to Copenhagen in 1965, that was another magic place, and how we were welcomed. Mongezi Feza on trumpet, can you imagine, he just blew their minds! They loved us in Denmark. And there were musicians like Don Cherry, Kenny Drew, Dexter Gordon, and Ben Webster (who adopted Mongezi Feza)."[27] The Montmartre was also a key site for South Africans as they moved into the experimental or avant-garde music now called free jazz. They joined an illustrious corps of American free musicians, including Albert Ayler (performed there in 1964), Archie Shepp (performed in 1963), Dexter Gordon (performed there in July 1964), Cecil Taylor (1962), Bud Powell (performed there 1962), Sunny Murray (performed with Taylor in 1962), and the Danish-born John Tchicai, all of whom played at the Montmartre, some with extended stays in Copenhagen in the early to mid-1960s.

Ibrahim returned twice more to Copenhagen between 1962 and 1972: for three weeks in September–October 1969 with Ntshoko, who by then had been playing in the Montmartre's house rhythm section, and again in 1972, when the pianist Ibrahim spent the summer in Copenhagen performing solo and in duos with Cherry. According to Wiedemann, Ibrahim's music inspired Danish musicians, in particular the saxophonist Jan Kaspersen. In the spring of 1970 there were plans for Kaspersen's group, Blue Sun, to collaborate on a project with Ibrahim, but it withdrew after a conflict over payment arose.[28] In contrast to Ibrahim, Ellington traveled frequently to Denmark over several decades (seventeen times between 1939 and 1973), though he doesn't appear to have ever performed at the Montmartre. Nevertheless, in January 1965 he was in Denmark at the same time as Sathima and Abdullah, playing the concert halls in Copenhagen, Tivoli, and other Danish towns. Ellington invited Sathima to sing his "In My Solitude" with him at the Folkener Teatret.

London

Moholo remembers that when the Blue Notes arrived in London, "the British liked us. We knocked them out, musically, we were really flying. . . . We just smoothed ourselves into the scene and we were welcome, so we were lucky in that way. We injected some fire into the scene. They helped us practically: we helped them musically. We were living in Baker Street." Without doubt London is a key center, one through which most South African musicians passed in the 1960s and 1970s.[29] This was the point of entry for those who came with the African jazz opera *King Kong,* and the city that many of the cast members decided to remain in when the tour was over.[30] The Golden City Dixies and members of Spinono may also have traveled through London. The only talent agency that did business with performers of color, from Africa and the Caribbean specifically, was the Edric Connor agency, run by Edric and Pearl Connor until Edric's death. Pearl subsequently married Joe Mogotsi, the founder of the vocal group the Manhattan Brothers, and the two of them carried on that work for many years.[31] But these musicians and artists were concerned with the theater and did not derive from a more specifically jazz lineage.

Once the three-year contract with Club Africana expired, Sathima and Abdullah decided to move to London, and Abdullah was briefly appointed artistic director of the Transcription Center. They lived in an apartment in London owned by someone called Aminu. In April 1965 the former BBC employee Dennis Duerden organized a party at the Institute for Contemporary Art in London to celebrate the music of Abdullah, Sathima, and the Blue Notes. At that point they were all in London and being managed by the Transcription Center, the most significant site for South African musicians, artists, and writers, housed from February 1962 until 1969 on Dover Street.[32] Established as a kind of home away from home for African and Caribbean musicians, writers, and artists and run by Duerden, the Transcription Centre opened in February 1962, the same month Abdullah and Sathima left South Africa. Gerald Moore, who frequented the center in the 1960s, succinctly describes the venue:

> It was funded by the Paris-based Congress for Cultural Freedom (itself a CIA front), and its official brief was to record interviews with African or Caribbean writers, artists, and intellectuals, in London and elsewhere. Recordings or transcripts of these interviews were to be made available to

radio stations in Africa, the Caribbean, or anywhere else where interest in them was expressed. . . . In practice however its activities under its director, Dennis Duerden, proved to be much wider than this: branching out into the making of television films, radio plays, and music recordings, or the sponsorship of art exhibitions, concerts, stage productions, and wide-ranging discussions of many contemporary topics. It became something of an informal club for all black artists visiting London and a powerhouse for many of their activities.[33]

Duerden was critical to Sathima's and Abdullah's survival in London and, for a time, in New York City as well.

In June 1965 Sathima and Abdullah visited Oxford University and performed at the African Music Society on campus; that same month Duerden arranged a concert for them at the English-Speaking Union in London. At this time also Ellington secured a place for Abdullah to perform at the Newport Jazz Festival, with assurances that Ellington would accompany Sathima at the festival. Abdullah wrote to Duerden to ask for assistance in sorting out the immigration paperwork to obtain a work visa for the United States. Duerden asked Jack Thompson at the Farfield Foundation (a CIA-funded organization in New York City parallel to the Transcription Center in London) to assist with the visa request; Thompson assured Duerden that if the South Africans' paperwork was in order they should have no trouble getting a visa. The challenge was getting their passports renewed by the South African government for another three years—perhaps pressure from the CIA centers helped get these documents in order.

Besides the Transcription Center, South African jazz musicians recall the supportiveness of Ronnie Scott's jazz club, the Old Place in particular, where they were often able to play several nights in a row.[34] And many musicians, including those in the Blue Notes and in the subsequent big band Brotherhood of Breath, have warm memories of the white South African jazz musician and expatriate Harry Miller and his wife, Hazel. The Millers formed Ogun Records, their independent record label in London in the 1960s, a label that Hazel continues to run. Harry was a bass player who performed with a wide range of jazz musicians in the British free scene, and he also appears on many of the recordings on which Blue Notes musicians perform.

Another venue for African artists, intellectuals, and musicians in Lon-

don was the Africa Center, founded in the early 1960s. This was an institution that worked alongside independent African political leaders and
government representatives, and while some South Africans were associated with the center, especially in the 1970s through the 1990s, I have
not heard Sathima talk about it as a site of musical engagement in the
early to mid-1960s. It is clearly the Transcription Center that provided
the feeling of a home away from home for Sathima, Abdullah, Chris
McGregor and his wife, Maxine, and the musicians they performed with
in London in the 1960s.

The United States in the 1960s

Sathima and Abdullah left London in May 1965 for the Newport Jazz
Festival in the United States. Invited by Ellington their travel was arranged by Duerden, who told Thompson that the Transcription Center
would take 15 percent of Sathima's and Abdullah's earnings at Newport
as a commission. They traveled first to New York City. Sathima recalled
her first encounter with the city: "I remember upon arriving in New York
on a hot summer's day about a week before the Newport [Jazz] Festival
in 1965 that it felt wonderful to me — the energy, the flow, the sight of
its many diverse peoples. I was amazed that I did not feel intimidated at
all. The excitement swooped me up and it felt good to be here. The same
day we arrived we went to meet and hear Duke Ellington at a concert in
Harlem. It was all happening so fast — at times it seemed like a dream. We
stayed for awhile on Bleecker Street with a friend of Dennis Duerden, a
wonderful Nigerian man, Adamu Mohammed, who represented Nigeria
at the United Nations. He had a huge apartment and was very kind to us."
    Sathima's recollections of performing with Ellington in Newport re-
iterate her memory of the contingency of the moment, the spontaneity,
the unexpected, but also the overwhelming sense of personal capacity
Duke conveyed to her in that period. She told jazz writer Sally Placksin,
"Sometimes you felt Duke wasn't of this world. He could see so deep inside you the things you didn't even know you had. Perhaps you call that
clairvoyance. When he said you would do something, even if you didn't
know the words, somehow you would find the words."[35]
    Sathima's emotionally powerful rendition of "In My Solitude" left the

audience calling for an encore. There had been no discussion about what song would be used in that eventuality. Sathima continued, "I remember that because at Newport he said, 'Do you know, "In a Mellotone?"' I vaguely knew it, even though I had never sung it in my life. I was positive of the melody, even though I didn't have all the words together. And he said, 'Of course you know, let's go.' And the band started playing, and I stood there. I repeated the words of the verse twice, and no one knew the difference. The band was playing behind me. There was Duke at the piano. I just had to sing, and this band—Cootie Williams, Cat Anderson—it was so beautiful, you just sang!"[36]

Ellington urged Abdullah and Sathima to stay in the city, and it was he who really made it possible for the two South Africans to begin to establish themselves there. He called them his African family. He helped the couple secure the necessary Musicians' Union and Cabaret cards enabling them to work in New York City. Sathima remembered that "Duke introduced us to his dear sister—Ruth—and we were sort of handed over into her care. She helped us to get settled, found us an apartment on 56th Street, overlooking Central Park, and later, upon Duke's advice, we decided to apply for the 'green card' and settle in New York City."[37] They played other dates with Ellington around that time. According to Sathima, "We did several East Coast performances with Ellington. One was at Wolftrap, and another at Cotillion in Baltimore.

Thompson and Duerden put Abdullah in touch with the Juilliard composer and arranger Hal Overton (who did some arranging for the pianist Thelonious Monk), and once the visa was straightened out they connected him with the Rockefeller Foundation, which awarded him a grant to study composition and arranging with Overton for a year. In August 1965 the South African writer Richard Rive wrote to Duerden that Abdullah and Sathima had had their debut performance in Carnegie Hall. Ron Carter was on bass, Sonny Brown on drums, Eddie Diehl on guitar (specially for Sathima), and the South African pennywhistle and saxophonist Morris Goldberg joined the group as well. Voice of America recorded the concert for broadcast on African radio stations. In December 1965 Abdullah wrote in a letter that he had had a successful recording session with Columbia Records.[38]

Despite the support of the Farfield Foundation, Sathima and Abdullah struggled to make ends meet, so Ruth Ellington hired Sathima to work as her personal assistant at Tempo Music, one of the Ellingtons' publishing houses. Sathima answered the telephone and ran personal errands for Ruth. She was happy to do the work, that is, until she was sent to collect long blonde wigs for Ruth. That she could not do. Why wear wigs and not just your own natural hair color, Sathima wondered? At that point she decided she couldn't work for the Ellington company any longer. But Ellington also introduced Sathima and Abdullah to a true friend of jazz musicians, the Reverend John Gensel of St. Peters Lutheran Church, and on occasion the couple would perform in church sanctuaries: in a letter Abdullah mentions a piece titled "Lamentations" and a performance on solo piano, and accompanying Sathima's singing at a biblical seminary in October 1965.

The couple had moments of real joy but also of utter despair. Boots, a dog Abdullah and Sathima adopted, brought pleasure and companionship, although the letters suggest Boots was given away when they left New York City in 1968. The couple used to socialize with other South African musicians living in New York City, some of whom they had met on earlier trips. They included Mamsie and Jonas Gwangwa and Masekela. In January 1966 Abdullah substituted for Ellington at a performance, and Sathima sang as well; they managed a second Carnegie Hall concert that same year.[39] But the New York jazz scene was dismal, the club circuit especially bad in the mid-1960s. There was some talk of a tour in South Africa in August 1966, as Ian Bernhardt, of the Union of South African Artists, arrived in London from Johannesburg. The political situation in South Africa was deteriorating by the day, however. Bernhardt reported he had been allowed into the black townships on only two occasions in 1965, making it impossible to do any innovative, interracial musical programming in the country. He came to the Transcription Center in London to explore the possibility of establishing a Dorkay House for African musicians and theater people in London. There was an ongoing conversation in the Transcription Center archive letters between New York and London about a collaborative piece called *A Walk in the Night*, to be co-created with South African writers and Abdullah's music. Abdullah wrote incidental music for a theater piece by Rive.

Duerden describes in a letter to Frank Platt at the Farfield Foundation the successful South African jazz event he organized at the Hampstead Theater Club in London in June 1966. Abdullah started to travel with the

17. Sathima singing, with Abdullah Ibrahim on piano.
Collection of Sathima Bea Benjamin.

American Elvin Jones, and they made a recording together. The association didn't last, however, because there was a misunderstanding between the two musicians over the poor organization of accommodation and performance conditions.

Ibrahim did a recording for Atlantic Records in 1966 and had a gig at the Museum of Modern Art. In September 1966 the architect of apartheid, President Hendrick Verwoerd was assassinated in South Africa, creating turmoil back home. That same month Duerden wrote to Platt urging him to discourage Abdullah and Sathima from returning to South Africa because of the worsening political conditions in the country at the time. They would have to wait another two years before their dream of returning home would materialize. Abdullah talked again of opening a school of music in Africa, and Sathima started to teach at the La Guardia Preschool on 104th Street in Harlem. In his letters to Duerden, Abdullah expressed deep anxiety about his and Sathima's capacity to ever reenter their home country. One letter captures something of the fear that South

Africans had about the vicissitudes of the apartheid regime: "I am a little scared, what if they grab our passports?" he asks Duerden. "Can you help us with our papers?" he pleads.

In 1967 life seemed more filled with hope. Once again there is little sense of Sathima in the archival record but presumably she traveled with Abdullah, singing where she was able. For this reason, I map out his travels. Abdullah was back in Copenhagen in March to perform at the Montmartre, while Duerden organized a concert for him at the Institute for Contemporary Art in London and Joe Boyd managed a performance at the University of York. He returned to New York for a highly acclaimed concert with Goldberg, and on 30 August 1967 Abdullah wrote to Duerden to tell him their American permanent residence had been finalized. "That means we don't need to wander the face of the earth anymore," Abdullah commented. Both Ellington and Langston Hughes were instrumental in making this happen for the couple. Sathima and Abdullah would also move away from the Central Park area into an apartment on 153rd Street located for them by a fellow South African and Pan Africanist Congress member Sathima only remembers as someone named Nga.[40]

Back to Europe and South Africa

After traveling extensively in Europe, Abdullah and Sathima spent about ten days in London early in July 1968, but by the end of the month they had returned to South Africa. There are two separate addresses in the letters written by Abdullah and Sathima in South Africa. Sathima has talked with me about living on the beach in Strandfontein, where they met the South African artist Trevor Stone. Returning to South Africa was thrilling at the beginning—letters suggest that the couple's homecoming was celebrated with festivities and parties. Plans were put in place for a nationwide tour in August or September of 1968 under the direction of Bernhardt. Abdullah was commissioned to write a weekly column for the *Cape Herald* newspaper and already had several of his poems published (Langston Hughes was solicited by Duerden to assist in the process).[41] In addition, he signed a two-year recording contract with Teal/ RCA records.

The couple began their South African tour in October 1968 with a performance at the Hotel Planet in Fordsburg, a suburb of Johannesburg. A week later an article titled "Focus on Dollar Brand, Return of a Jazz Ambassador" appeared in the left-leaning *News Check* magazine.[42] The piece summarizes Abdullah's life and works to that point, along lines similar to those reconstructed here. And it pays tribute to Sathima for what they call "Dollar's transformation"—that is, by this time he had given up alcohol and become less aggressive: "It was Bea [Sathima] (who quite independently made a name for herself overseas with her understated, perfectly phrased bittersweet jazz singing) who went out and coaxed Duke Ellington to listen to Dollar's group. . . . It was the break they needed."

This piece captures, on one hand, a taste of Abdullah's brilliance and, on the other, his increasing distance from his local community, mostly because it did not appreciate his desire to incorporate local sounds and the expressive freedom he had encountered abroad into his music. Sathima had a similar experience in South Africa when she sang her composition "Africa." Two South Africans struggling to survive on their music and to address the stresses of living in the diaspora ultimately found it necessary to move in and out of the country. Having spent years on the move around the world, Sathima and Abdullah had had time to reflect on the musical richness of South Africa, a richness that few in the country would fully value for some time to come. Sophisticated musical intellectuals and artists, Abdullah and Sathima felt the gap between what they were striving to achieve musically—to incorporate the richness of musical language, diversity, and sound so pervasive in South Africa in the improvisational language of jazz—and what their audiences wanted to hear.

It appears that Abdullah was in Cape Town when he converted to Islam sometime in 1968. This was the moment when he changed his name from Dollar Brand to Abdullah Ibrahim. Abdullah has said that he converted to Islam because of the stress upon unity over division articulated in Islamic belief, but also because of the strong presence of Sufism in Cape Town in his youth. Sathima would adopt Islam to a point, and in fact in the 1980s her record covers acknowledge Allah, but eventually being a woman of Islam proved to be a straitjacket. She would be more selective about her expressions of faith and spirituality. "Jazz is my religion," she has told me on more than one occasion.

Abdullah traveled back to Switzerland in mid-May 1969. Sathima, who had had surgery in South Africa, arrived in Zurich sometime later. Soon after that Stone joined them for awhile and then moved on to an artist colony somewhere in Europe, where he spent time developing his style. Stone later joined the rest of his family, who were active with the ANC, in Australia. His parents had left South Africa just after the Sharpeville Massacre. In the 1980s Stone's sister Cheryl stayed with Sathima in New York City, where she danced with the Alvin Ailey Dance troupe, met the musician and singer Stevie Wonder, and had a child, Kwame, with him.

Abdullah and Sathima traveled to Copenhagen again in September and October 1969, then passed through London en route to New York City, where they had to appear at least once a year in order to retain their green cards and permanent resident status. Sometime during 1969 Dyani visited Abdullah and Sathima in their basement apartment in Brooklyn. Johnny was unhappy in his marriage to an English woman at the time, and he was longing to return to South Africa. "We used to talk into the night," Sathima remembered. "I later received a letter from him saying that he was getting a divorce and perhaps moving to Denmark. He also wrote to thank me for always giving him an ear, and being there to listen, and said from that moment on he would call me Sathima, a name from his people which means 'someone with a kind heart.' I told Abdullah about this name, which sounded very musical to me, and decided to add it to Bea Benjamin. So, thanks to Johnny Dyani, I now have this name. I love it."[43]

From here on, the narrative becomes less specific because Duerden was forced to move the Transcription Center from Dover Street to Warwick Avenue, the funding essentially dries up, and he ultimately shuts down in the early 1970s. A letter written from New York on 28 January 1970 by one Emily Hoyt of the African-American Labor Center in New York City to someone named Peggy reads as follows:[44] "Dollar and Bea are fine. They are having a party Saturday and charging—it is really a fund-raising gimmick for the Marimba School of Music in Swaziland that Dollar hopes to start. He may be going back to Europe next month as he has some work there, and from there he may go to Swaziland. Have tried to reach him but he hasn't a phone here, so will have to wait until he responds to a recent postcard asking him to call me. He did a record in Europe—prob. a Danish co.—try to find it. It came out in December there—we are still waiting here for it to appear."[45]

Giving Birth in Swaziland

Travel to Swaziland via Europe is exactly what Sathima and Abdullah did in 1970, and there Sathima gave birth to their first child, Tsakwe Adamu Ibrahim, in November 1970. Sathima was determined that her children would be born on African soil, and so she persuaded Abdullah to return to South Africa a few months before Tsakwe's birth. She recalls the experience:

> We were poor at the time. Abdullah would go to do concerts, he had a little Volkswagen bug, and he would drive to Johannesburg, do a concert, and come back. There wasn't much work there. The reason we were there in southern Africa was because we were in Europe at the time of the Soweto uprising, and I said I don't want my children to be born in Europe, I want them to be born at home. When we got to Johannesburg, Abdullah had family who lived there, the Pop family, and we went to stay with them for a while. That was part of his mother's side. They lived in Kliptown, a Coloured township in Johannesburg. We were there a few months before Tsakwe was born. So we were trying to make it to Cape Town, but by the time I got to Johannesburg I was in pain.
>
> On the way back to South Africa I had met this Swazi man, Simon (I forget his last name), he was one of the ministers in the Swazi government. I told him my husband would like to start a school in Swaziland, the Marimba School of Music. I think he knew who Abdullah was. He gave me his card and said, "Whenever you need something let me know." Abdullah really wanted to do something, to start a school, and Swaziland was not that far from Jo'burg. He could ride to Jo'burg; do some shows; speak to Rashid Vallee of Sun Records about all his recording connections. He could see a way because we really didn't know where we were going to stay in Cape Town. It was the same old story of my family not accepting Abdullah.
>
> So we got on a plane and went to Swaziland and found a house in Mbabane, a big empty house with three bedrooms. We managed to get a bed at some second-hand place, because there was nothing in the house. You had to have money to get furniture and things, there wasn't even a stove and fridge: there was nothing in there. I was very, very pregnant and I needed help. What I couldn't stand about this place is you step out into

your yard and there were big lizards, and in the garden part of it, there were obviously snakes. I was so terrified!

Tsakwe was born in Mbabane, Swaziland, high up on the mountain there. He was premature, he didn't go to full term because he was pressing against my sciatic nerve and causing tremendous pain. I was about eight months pregnant when the doctor told me to go home, get in a very warm bath, and take some castor oil. He said it would bring on the birth of my child. I was a little scared to do it, but I couldn't walk. I couldn't do a thing. And we had a young African woman to help me. Her name was also Beatrice. She came to help me in the house.

It was so beautiful. Abdullah insisted he must be there at the birth, so we went up to St. Michaels Hospital. The doctor, who was called Dr. Treadway, said to Abdullah, "Since you are here, put the gloves on, you can take the little one out." Then Abdullah stood there and he took Tsakwe out. Abdullah was very much Muslim by then. He said the *adhan*, the prayers, as he was taking Tsakwe out. Just before he prayed, he looked at me. "Are you sure you want to name him Tsakwe? Life will be hard for him in school, a Coloured boy with an African name." Abdullah queried the wisdom of the name. But, I had been calling my baby by that name for several months already, how could he be any other name?

Tsakwe is indeed almost a unique name, even in South Africa. Sathima told me that Tsakwe was the name of a hunter who assisted some Canadians when they went to record Khoisan music in the Kalahari, music that was published on the Folkways label. Someone gave Sathima and Abdullah a copy of the recording, and she started to study the Khoisan and to read the romanticized books of Laurens Van Der Post about the Kalahari Bushmen. She became interested in the nomadic habits, the deep spirituality, and the way the Kalahari Khoisan cared for women and their children. She loved the sound of laughter she heard on the recording, jovial women and children in the background as men played their instruments. And she was particularly drawn to the trance dance as a form of spiritual healing. "There is no crime, no greed, and they laugh all the time," Sathima told me:

The hunter was named Tsakwe, my son was due to be born in the month of the hunter, the man with the bow and arrow, the Sagittarius, and so I named him Tsakwe. I think there are some members of Parliament in South Africa who have that name too, but they never use it publicly.

From the very beginning Tsakwe was a screamer! And he would drink. I wanted to breast-feed, but he would drink so fast, like you are supposed to take twenty minutes this side, in a few minutes he was finished, then you put him here, then he would throw everything up. We ended up having to see a doctor and he said, 'This is a very nervous child, and when he is two he is going to be like he is five, and when he is five he will be like he is nine. He's a very nervous child. I suggest you go back to Cape Town and get some help. You will never make it here."

So we went back to Cape Town and stayed with my mom. She said to us, "Don't worry, I have had so many babies, I will manage this. You are making a big fuss about nothing." She tried to handle Tsakwe, but eventually she said, "No, you can go and stay with Joan. Find another place because I can't handle this one." Tsakwe cried all the time, he screamed, then we saw my friend Dunier—she died—she told us to see a white doctor in Sea Point. We did and he just smiled and said, "Has anyone told you this is a brilliant baby? Ok, he's going to be so advanced and I am telling you now so you can enjoy him." He asked me what I do, and I said I was a schoolteacher. He said, "You can enjoy him, and I advise you, tell your husband what will stop him crying: put him in a bath as much as possible, rock him, and drive in the car because motion helps." I am telling you it was true because when we would stop at a traffic light, it was fine, take him out he was screaming, he was a difficult baby. But his responses were true to what the doctor said.

By the time Tsakwe was one and a half or two he was reading books to me, the same with our daughter, Tsidi. Because I was a schoolteacher I knew how to teach them from that old South African style. You teach reading with the sounds and things. I don't remember it now, but I did then, my children were reading to me when they were two years old. Tsidi read *Little Women*, she was six years old and we were going to Senegal, she finished it between New York and Senegal. She read *Little Women* when she was six and comprehended it. I know I have extraordinary and brilliant children.

Sathima and Abdullah left South Africa with Tsakwe, their young son, in 1971 or 1972. Sathima remembers seeing Dyani in Copenhagen in 1972, when Abdullah, Johnny, Sathima, and Cherry formed an ensemble called Universal Silence and took it on the road in Europe.[46] In 1972 Sathima sang "Come Sunday" at one of the first Jazz Vespers at St. Peter's in New

18. Sathima's and
Abdullah's son,
Tsakwe. *Collection
of Sathima Bea
Benjamin.*

York City with Ellington.[47] He just called her up and asked her to sing
with him later in the day. In January 1973 Emily Hoyt of the African-
American Labor Center wrote to Duerden in London about Abdullah
and Sathima:

> Bea Brand is back in town, with Dollar apparently back in Swaziland fol-
> lowing a pilgrimage to Mecca. I guess they expect to meet in Europe in
> the not too distant future. She gave a concert here last weekend (I, un-
> fortunately, was out of town) and got a very good and lengthy review for
> this type of thing from the [New York] Times' principal jazz critic. It is
> enclosed. She was of course delighted with the review but not with the
> house; she had been counting on earning some sustenance from it and it
> brought almost nothing in. Bea spoke of it having been a long time since
> she and Dollar had been in London and was musing about the time being
> perhaps good for a concert there. You knew, didn't you, that they have a
> little boy who is now about two and a half?[48]

Bet-Car Records

During this visit to New York City in 1973 Sathima came to a highly significant realization, namely, that she could produce her own records. She
tells the story as follows:

In the early 1970s I came to New York City with Tsakwe. Abdullah was going to Mecca, and Tsakwe was one or two, and Abdullah said I should go to South Africa. I thought that that was too far. So I said I would go to New York while Abdullah was in Mecca. I used to stay with Italian jazz trumpeter Enrico Rava and his wife, Gracielle. She has died now. Argentinian jazz saxophonist Gato Barbieri and the Ravas were friends. When we came here in the 1960s Abdullah did something with Gato, what was that recording called?[49] I don't know how we got connected, but whenever we were coming to NYC, we would contact them, and if they were going to be away, we would take over their apartment for a month or so. So while I was here, Enrico was still here, I went to get the keys to his place from him. He was going to play somewhere downtown with jazz cornetist Don Cherry. Come to think of it it's amazing the role that Don Cherry plays in my life without us being like really involved. He led me to one place: he led me to another. It's strange.

Anyway, Enrico said, "If you want to come with me, I am going to a friend, and then going to hear Don Cherry." I said, "Oh, that will be nice." I had met Don Cherry before in Europe. I didn't want to be alone there, and the friend he was going to pick up was Barbara, who would become and remains my good friend Barbara. That's how I met her. So then we went to hear Don Cherry.

Barbara used to be a dance teacher, she went to Merce Cunningham. And she was a schoolteacher but she has given that up now. She is retired. She used to teach dance. She doesn't go for dancing anymore. She did that for years. She never married, but she loves children. She's a single person: that's a totally different lifestyle. She had a sister who died of cancer, she has two nephews, she has a brother Charles, and he always comes to my shows. I always call him my gentleman from the South. Barbara is from Alabama.

When I met her, she gave me her number because I was living on Claremont Avenue, and she was living on 95th Street, not far from me. I would walk with Tsakwe to her place. When I met Barbara she had a recording of the *Misa Luba*, and when Tsakwe heard it, he broke into a dance. Then she played Thelonious Monk, and he went crazy about Monk. So when I visited her, she would play this music. She had a garden. She lost that because now she lives on 101st between Broadway and Riverside, in a totally different place. She lived in a house that had a whole floor and back garden. She just fell in love with Tsakwe and he with her, that's the story. They are such old friends, and I think because she didn't have children, and he is so creative and highly intelligent, they had a good thing going there.

She played Thelonious Monk and the *Misa Lubba* for Tsakwe. Anyway, while I was there I picked up a record and it was one by Betty Carter. I had heard of Betty Carter, but I didn't really know too much about how she sang, I had just heard a lot about her. So that sparked my interest. At the bottom of the record cover I saw it was her *own* record. And it said "Bet-Car." That was her *own* label. Like me, she had problems too with nobody wanting to record her, I don't know what happened in later years, but this was in 1972. This was 1971 that I picked up the recording, the recording could have been from the late 1960s. Barbara had the one with Ray Charles. That's how people got to know her, through Ray Charles, and then she started her own label.

Later on when no one was interested in me and I needed to record myself, I remembered she had started a label herself. Bet-Car. It was just inspirational, I heard her. She wrote her own stuff, she put the whole thing together herself. Her independence told me I could be independent. But I never met her: it was her independent spirit I remembered, and I thought what a great thing, she has her own label.

Sathima would hold onto this knowledge until she came to live more permanently in New York City in 1977 and began her own label with Abdullah.

Further Travels

Sathima and Abdullah did a live recording at the Alte Kirche, a church in Boswil, Switzerland, on 28 April 1973, after which he left for Australia, initially for six weeks, though he stayed for almost six months.[50] Sathima remained in Switzerland with her young son, living with friends she had made in South Africa, Rene Kuhne and his wife and Meyer and his wife. Abdullah was back recording in New York City in November of that year and also in Germany a month or so later.

Sathima was in South Africa on the day Ellington died in 1974. She was completely devastated for a very long time. The death of Ellington, the recent birth of Tsakwe, the struggle to survive in a marriage with a musician who was so humanly overwhelming and who traveled so frequently — travel was becoming more and more difficult for her because of Tsakwe — caused a deep crisis for Sathima in 1974. This was the period in which the first of her own songs came to her: first was the emotionally evocative and spiritually powerful "Windsong," the song most akin to the spirit of free jazz of all her compositions. In 1975, stirred by a visit to Mozambique for that country's independence celebrations, she wrote "Nations in Me, New Nation A'Comin'." In 1976, back in South Africa, in response to the Soweto uprising of 16 June 1976 she wrote "Children of Soweto." Sathima recalls the trip that inspired "Nations in Me":

> We were working for the ANC in the mid-1970s.[51] That just happened because they had their offices here in New York City. Abdullah and I decided because we couldn't do anything in South Africa, and Europe was just like hunting ground, a place to work. Well, there was the Transcription Center in London, that was also sort of political, but when we came to settle here the ANC had their offices, and we decided that we would now involve ourselves as cultural workers. I decided wherever I could I would contribute to the cause. They had us singing all over the place.
>
> For a moment there, it was a bit puzzling to me because the story like went around that this white person going up there to sing like liberation songs! I had a lot to overcome to be included in the liberation movement. We had to explain in stories, we had to have the ANC endorse me. Nevertheless, when Mozambique had their liberation day, the ANC sent us as a family, they paid for everybody to go, Tsakwe was five or six. I think Albie Sachs was going to be there. We went via Paris to Mozambique. And Samora Machel was president at that time. The idea was to perform there. So we did.
>
> We were sent by the ANC. We stopped over in Paris for a day, and we had to connect, what a trip! When we arrived there was a big dinner. It was so beautiful because I sat down, that really impacted on me at that dinner. I saw all these people, they looked just like Cape Tonians, but the language — Portuguese — was different. But you know it was people of all spectrums, all colors. And they were all there and this was their Independence. And I told myself, "My God, if only we could come to this in South Africa." And on the way back, on the airplane, that song "Nations in Me, New Nation A'Comin'," that's where that whole song came to me, on the airplane back. When I got here I contacted Onaje Allen Gumbs and I said, "I have a song here," and he was the one who sat with me. He had a lot of patience. I think we had to meet twice. We made a chart (chord progressions and symbols used by jazz musicians) for "Nations in me, new nation a'coming." Because it was my vision for, I was just anticipating, wanting, I

19. Abdullah and Sathima meet President Samora
Machel of Mozambique and his then-wife, Graça.
Collection of Sathima Bea Benjamin.

was aspiring to a new South Africa. I mean we weren't there yet at all. I had
something to sing with these liberation concerts that made more sense
to me.[52]

Sojourning in Vienna in June 1976, Sathima watched reports of the
Soweto riots on television. Sathima was determined: they had to go back
to South Africa. Pregnant with her second child, she was determined that
Tsidi would also be born on African soil. Like many other women of her
generation who were in jazz, she had to choose between child rearing and
a career. She recalls that period:

Oh my goodness, at the Somerset Hospital in Cape Town there were those
nurses, when they found out that I lived in New York City, they said to
me, "Why don't you go back to New York?" They were talking in their
upcountry voices because I said that I wanted my husband there and I
wanted my doctor there. They were not used to that, a Coloured woman
making demands. You go to the hospital and you push a baby out and

that's it! I wanted special treatment and I said, "Call my husband." I had one of the best doctors there, Dr. Aziz Sami, actually I was having a problem: it's so strange to tell you that story. Tsidi was about to be born, she was pushing and pushing, she was about to be born I thought I was going to die, I told the nurses you have to call my husband!

Naming their daughter Tsidi was an extraordinary choice at the time. Those in the Coloured community never used African names for their children. Not so the Ibrahims. Sathima recalls that the name came to her in a dream, just before Tsidi was born. They were living in a house in Belgravia Estate in Cape Town:

I woke up one morning, and I said to Abdullah, "Is there such a name as Tsidi? I saw it in a dream." "Tsidi?" he asked, "Well, it's part of a name, it's seSotho. I will make some calls to find out." So Abdullah called his friend Monde Sekutshwa, who was living in Port Elizabeth. Monde told Abdullah "Tsidi" came from the name Matsidiso, which translates into 'Consolation.' What is interesting is that Abdullah's father was seSotho—he was murdered when Abdullah was only four or five years old by the Coloured people. Maybe the name came from him in my dreams. Anyway, I knew the baby was a girl, though I had no tests, because the pregnancy was so different from with Tsakwe. And I woke up in the morning with the name, Tsidi, a girl's name on my tongue. That's where Tsidi got her name. They are both African names, Tsakwe and Tsidi, and because Abdullah is Muslim, we gave them Muslim middle names, Adamu for Tsakwe and Azida for Tsidi. Azida also came in a dream. Azida is not a Muslim name, but the imam broke it into parts and said it meant someone with a very strong will.

Conclusion

In contrast to the narratives about Cape jazz, which circulated around a specific geographic location and historical moment, my discussion here of a period of jazz migrancy has fluctuated between place, country, and community, and it has moved in and out of a range of histories and political contexts. Sathima and Abdullah Ibrahim seem to be the only constant elements in the narration of this story, though even their names changed in this period. As I wrote the chapter, I was repeatedly struck by the sensation of continual, overwhelming disorientation. I often wondered how Sathima and Abdullah retained any feeling of centeredness through these years, and how Tsakwe lived through the first few years of his life, on the move and in and out of places, often saying goodbye to his father for extended periods of time.

Despite the migratory routes in search of work in jazz, several themes have emerged that are pertinent to the larger narrative of South African jazz in exile between the Sharpeville Massacre (1960) and the Soweto uprising (1976). The first pertains to jazz as made by South Africans abroad, what they remembered from their home communities, what they longed for, and the ways in which they sought to play with musicians in Europe and the United States. These musicians began in either an Ellington mode inflected by South African styles or the hard bop jazz style, quickly moved into the free jazz scene, and gradually harnessed the freedom that the free movement allowed to incorporate the sounds and sensibilities of music from home in South Africa. Several musicians insisted that while they sympathized with African American struggles, which were often racially defined because African Americans were a minority in the United States, they tended toward creating ensembles with a wider community of musicians, from Turkish, Argentinian, and Italian to Caribbean. And linked to this transnationalism in jazz ensembles, several European, not American, cities, including Copenhagen, Zurich, London, and, to a lesser extent, Paris, occupy a central place in shaping this community and its history. The European part of South African exile differs in character from the experience of Makeba and Masekela in the United States, as outlined in their biographies.

During this period of migrancy, Sathima resonates with an aesthetic of the nomadic by harnessing and studying the folkways of Kalahari Khoisan, more popularly known abroad as the Bushmen. In another transnational gesture, someone had given her a recording of the Kalahari Khoisan recorded by Canadians, released on the American label Folkways and consumed by the South Africans in New York City. They traveled a long way to hear the music of the Kalahari. And they expanded their listening by reading the work of the romantic adventurer Van Der Post, whose books, whatever their weaknesses, seemed to have made a significant impact on international communities interested in these desert peoples from southern Africa. The Khoisan imaginary accompanies both

Abdullah and Sathima in their travels around the world and continues to be a motivating force for Sathima, who is drawn to the absence of material goods, the abundance of spiritual wealth, and human goodness she believes can be found in the Kalahari communities.

In strong contrast to the sentimentality surrounding Khoisan folkways is the rather more sinister presence of what has now been revealed to be the CIA-funded centers in this story: the Transcription Center, the Congress for Cultural Freedom, and the Farfield Foundation. These centers documented, supported, and also observed the actions of African artists, writers, and musicians who came to metropolitan areas from the 1950s onward. Although these organizations promoted an anticommunist, free market approach to everyday life and at times acted in sympathetic ways toward African artists and musicians, there is nonetheless something disquieting about their lurking presence in this story. Duerden appears to have been a disarming character: he truly cared about the welfare of the artists and musicians. On the one hand, the behind-the-scenes letter writing hangs as a heavy shadow over the otherwise supportive environment Duerden created for African artists in London in the 1960s and the help he gave them when they traveled to Paris and New York. On the other hand, the Transcription Center archive is the only source of information I have had at my disposal to reconstitute this period in Sathima's life.

Most jazz biography rarely includes family life as a significant part of the musical dimensions of a musician's story, but we have included discussion of Sathima's children for several reasons. Sathima wanted to become a mother and to be available to her children as they grew up. This meant she could no longer travel to perform. Instead, her life became focused on the needs of her home and family in a strange land. As scholars reflect on her impact on the world of jazz singing, we have to factor in the years she spent out of the public eye because of those demands. Second, her decision not to return to postapartheid South Africa was one she made because of the life she formed around her children in New York City. And third, giving birth to children coincided with the birth of her own repertory of songs: (her discourse on song composition below in the response to chapter 5 reflects the two processes as overlapping experiences).

Finally, one cannot forget the generous, wonderful presence and assistance of Ellington in Sathima's and Abdullah's lives in this period. As I have written this chapter, I have come to realize it is quite possible that in the absence of Ellington and of Hughes's letter writing and, perhaps ironically, of the active engagement of the personnel of the Farfield Foundation and Transcription Center, Abdullah and Sathima would have a very different story to tell about their musical and personal lives in Europe and the United States in this period. Ellington's intervention raises the question of diasporic connections between South Africans moving out of the apartheid regime and American, particularly African American, musicians, first in Europe and then in the United States. Having already found a place for her music making through the life story and sound of Holiday as consumed in South Africa, Sathima experiences a brief moment of discovery and identification with the path of the American jazz singer and record producer Betty Carter.

INTERLUDE

Sathima's Spirit of Africanness

In 1998 I asked Sathima to talk about the spirit of Africanness in her singing to graduate students at the University of Pennsylvania who were taking a seminar titled "Reading Women in Jazz." She wrote a short piece on the subject, which she read to the class:

First, I must say that Dr. Muller, in inviting me to have this talk with you, prompted me to think consciously of the spirit of Africanness in my jazz singing. I say consciously because, simply put, I respond naturally to my passion and impulse to sing or compose a song. I have no intent whatsoever within my spirit (i.e., the time of performing or receiving the inspirational and divine gift of composing) of deliberately imposing on my song or delivery, an effect of Africanness in my jazz singing.

The way I get to know a song is not by singing it or practicing it over and over: I sing it within, I live it within, I imagine it, and let it grow and take shape within. I do this anywhere, at anytime. Of course, I will have to look at the lyrics and commit them to memory so it flows. I'm quick with melody, so that's an easy process. Then inspiration and imagination come into play and I begin to vibrate with the very essence of creating. Then it's time to call a fellow musician and impart my "spirit of Africanness." This can be a bit difficult sometimes, but there is no way to do the song other than the way I hear it. Because they are jazz musicians, their spirits are connected and open to my sense of Cape Town timing. I've heard it said that I sing on the "upbeat."

All of this musical jazz creative process is very spiritual: it's not just about playing with words and singing the notes for myself. I have been in tears when the musicians haven't been tuned into my spirit because even in rehearsal we need to capture spontaneity — a very necessary and magical ingredient. Our empathy with each other should make us feel as one, for the collective sound to vibrate and move participating musicians to a higher self. Only then do we fully understand and experience true African spirit liberation. We become responsible for our freedom in these moments. Past, present, and future sounds become available to us. And all the time we're involved in this process, we realize how sacred this music really is, from Africa. I've never stopped listening inside: I've kept my heart open and vulnerable.

I heard all this music growing up in Cape Town. How blessed I am because Africa to me is one big spirit of jazz. This music is so old, yet always so fresh and forward looking and growing off the basic traditional music forms. African music is at once simple and complex: the complex rhythms, the shades of sounds, the repetitive chords, and the passion given to making the music. It can soothe; it can excite; it can put you into a trance, it celebrates the moment; it casts a spell.

When working with jazz music I never consider myself as a singer out front with three musicians accompanying me. Rather, it's an attempt to bring together; to create a communal sound, a working together, taking the theme in unison, each one getting a chance to make a statement, celebrating the song in a very African way together using rhythms, sounds, colors, and lyrics.

Duke Ellington once said to me, "You are blessed with knowing from whence you come, and your imagination will keep you resilient and strong." I realize how fortunate I have been in meeting this great man of music. So universal is his appeal, and his music has the magic formula, the Spirit of Africanness in its sound, rhythm, harmonies, and colors. The other great musician I love and admire for the very same qualities is my husband, Abdullah Ibrahim, internationally renowned, world famous South African, Cape Town born and raised, like myself!

Sathima Bea Benjamin, 1998
New York City.

In 1974 Sathima wrote the words to a song entitled "Africa," the chorus of which reads as follows:

I've been gone much too long,
And I'm glad to say that I'm home,
I'm home to stay.
Africa, Africa.
I've come home; I've come home.
To feel my people's warmth,
To shelter 'neath your trees,
To catch the summer breeze;
Africa, Africa.[53]

And in 1990 Sathima explained the ties between jazz and the old and new African diasporas:

> My gut feeling is that jazz came out of the feeling of being ripped away from your continent, unwillingly, and your culture being taken away from you. That is why I say jazz from South Africa is similar, but not exactly the same as from the US.[54]

RESPONSE

A New African Diaspora

Reconstructing a New African Diaspora

Narrating Sathima's experience in the diaspora from the time she left South Africa in 1962 through the late 1970s, when she settled in New York City, has been extraordinarily challenging for a variety of reasons. First, she just cannot talk in much detail about that period in her life because it was truly a moment of exile and struggle, and the continual movement from one country and continent to the next in search of work makes recall difficult. Second, there are few tangible objects serving as reminders of that part of her life. While our project is helped by Abdullah's recording history, it is not always clear where Sathima was in all this activity. Third, with the exception of the recently discovered tapes of the recording in Paris and a couple of other recordings, there is very little musical archive dedicated to her—she is more typically the occasional vocalist on Abdullah's recordings. Finally, these years were also a time when many of the South African musicians were drinking heavily and going through phases of using recreational drugs, which translated into some very difficult experiences, some so painful it was easier to forget what happened than to continually relive the memories.

While the struggle to remember has posed methodological and logistical challenges, we have been helped enormously by the new research and writing about this era at home and abroad in the postapartheid years. Key to this body of work is the extraordinary contribution of Lars Rasmussen, the Danish secondhand book dealer and proud fan of South African jazz. Rasmussen published several substantial volumes on South African jazz, including works on Abdullah, Sathima, Joe Mogotsi, Johnny Dyani, and the Cape Town jazz scene of the late 1950s and 1960s, all of which have given new impetus to our project. What has become quite clear to me in reading the Rasmussen archive is the extent to which Sathima's verbal exposition is consistent with the ideas of others in the world of jazz, particularly the South Africans with whom she traveled and performed in the 1960s and early 1970s.[55]

Similarly, the archival recordings that have been put back into circulation have been useful in reconstituting this past. Since the early 1990s there has been a concerted effort to reissue the recordings of South African musicians living in exile that are on independent labels and are hard to find. Maxine McGregor published the biography *Chris McGregor and the Brotherhood of Breath* in 1996, and she has been responsible for getting several recordings reissued and making them available to mainstream distributional channels. South African students and scholars have also engaged in the oral history and archival research needed to trace this period.

My written narrative of the years of diaspora and migrancy was composed at the end of this project because there simply was no material available to me until I discovered the archive of the CIA-funded Transcription Center at the University of Texas. My book has been formed largely through the archive of the Transcription Center. The Transcription Center in London, the Congress for Cultural Freedom in Paris, and the Farfield Foundation in New York City all worked in close cooperation and under the watchful eye of the CIA. South African musicians and artists were commonly associated in some way with each of these organizations. These three centers ran in parallel to the so-called democracy tours set up by the U.S. State Department in the cold war period.[56] Sathima and Abdullah were closely affiliated with only the London and New York offices and their personnel.[57]

One feels deep ambivalence toward that material because the center was a CIA operation. For obvious reasons Sathima is not enthusiastic about highlighting this part of the story, though she has agreed to everything that has been included here because the archive represents the only path to reconstructing the European years in her biography. Sathima first spoke of the Farfield Foundation at an event we were attending that was held in her honor in April 2001 at the National Humanities Center in North Carolina. We were waiting for dinner to start when she came over to me and told me she recognized one of the women that evening. She had met her briefly in New York in the 1960s, through the Farfield Foundation — and she dropped the idea that it was a CIA front organization to observe African artists in New York City. There had been rumors at the time of CIA funding, but because she didn't know whether they were true we did not pursue this avenue any further that evening. I had no luck at the time tracking down further information on either the Transcription Center or the Farfield Foundation.[58] A further search for the Transcription Center in 2008, this time through the Google search engine revealed that the written archive of the Transcription Center was housed at the University of Texas, Austin.

The contents of the Transcription Center archive cover a wide range of people and artistic and creative materials. There are files pertaining to both Bea Benjamin and Dollar Brand/Abdullah Ibrahim. For the most part these consist of letters exchanged between Dennis Duerden and Abdullah and Sathima as well as with the personnel of the Farfield Foundation in New York City. There is also some material about South African jazz and apartheid embedded in the files. The archival content doesn't help much with the details of Sathima's and Abdullah's sojourn in London. It is more useful in delineating their movement outside the city as they travel between the United Kingdom, Europe, New York, and South Africa from 1964 until 1973, the most significant materials stemming from the mid-1960s.[59] One gets the sense from this archive of a lively, if poorly funded, hub of artistic and creative activity and interaction between South Africans, some Americans, but also other African and Caribbean artists and musicians, all in conversation with each other at the Transcription Center.

The archive contains commentary about the anti-apartheid movement and about the impact of apartheid on South African jazz, and letters written in support of the playwright and poet Wole Soyinka when he was imprisoned in Nigeria. Duerden was a passionate, committed director,

concerned for the plight of struggling African artists and creative musicians. At one time both Abdullah Ibrahim and Maxine McGregor were
employed by the center in London. Sathima recently remembered that
while she was in London she did a recording with Chris McGregor at the
Charles Fox studio, which was never released.[60] Abdullah mentions this
recording in correspondence with Duerden. How that studio was tied to
the Transcription Center is unclear, except that both Duerden and Fox
had worked for the BBC. Abdullah asks Duerden about the recording in
one of his letters. There is no documented response.

It was mostly the letters in the Transcription Center archive that enabled me to map out Sathima's and Abdullah's activities in the period
1965–69. There are only two or three letters in Sathima (Bea's) hand, the
rest having been written by Abdullah; most are concerned with his performing and recording arrangements, though in this period much of his
performance schedule included her on the program. While this book is
not primarily about Ibrahim, one can construct an account of Sathima's
travels only through his writings and recordings. The archive divulges
some information about the jazz scene in Germany in 1964, while Abdullah and Sathima were moving between Zurich, Britain, and other parts
of Europe. Duerden engages in correspondence with Henry Dunlap of
Voice of America (VOA) radio, about the translation of programs into
African vernacular languages for radio distribution, though VOA would
also record Abdullah's performances; the Blue Notes' arrival in Switzerland was noted as an outcome of Ibrahim's earlier successes. The British
record producer Alan Bates, who would subsequently produce several
albums for Abdullah, wrote to him about the challenges of establishing a
record label and creating distribution channels in Europe. Finally, there
is extensive legal documentation of Ibrahim's divorce from Sarah, his
first wife and childhood sweetheart, late in 1964 and of his marriage to
Sathima in London, which took place at 2:15 P.M. on 26 February 1965 at
the Register's Office in the City of Westminster.

Scholarly Reflections on the New African Diaspora

As an intellectual who has also moved between South Africa and the
United States, I have long thought about the relationships, musical and
otherwise, between the two places and its peoples. Musically, I have vivid

20. Sathima on the day she married Abdullah Ibrahim in London, 26 February 1965. *Collection of Sathima Bea Benjamin.*

memories of hearing Sathima Bea Benjamin and Abdullah Ibrahim in two live performances in the United States. The first occasion was the JVC Jazz Festival in New York City sometime around 1990. Abdullah performed a solo piano concert in the Weill Recital Room at Carnegie Hall. The second was a performance by Sathima in the "Women in Jazz" series at the Kennedy Center in Washington more than a decade later. Neither occasion was the first or only time I heard the couple perform. Nevertheless, these two events stand out in my memory for the profound way in which the sounds emanating from the grand piano and those carried by the human voice evoked a full-bodied, multisensory response in me. In the first moment, it seemed like I could see, smell, feel, and hear the Bo-Kaap district of central Cape Town. The second moment elicited a deep sense of longing, an aching in my body for the space called Africa that Sathima sang about. These utterances were musical echoes in diaspora, and probably I had been away from South Africa far too long.

In retrospect, what I heard in those moments were not memories of sounds and places I had experienced earlier in my life in South Africa. Rather, these were poetic invocations expressed out of a longing to return home that resonated for me in the music itself. In each performance the voice and instrumental sounds made contact with me as an audience member, acoustically generating images of faraway places for a fellow South African in America. While Ibrahim is not from the Bo-Kaap, a heritage site that has come to represent the history of Islam in Cape Town, this was the place of my imagining, the place I had visited a few years earlier in search of understanding Cape Muslim history; [61] and certainly, as I have written elsewhere and the words of her song suggest, "Sathima's 'Africa' is itself a space of longing. It evokes diasporic images of home, warmth, earthy smells, the innocent laughter of children, and [the sounds] of trees and summer breezes" (Muller 2001, 147). Recorded in the 1970s, after more than a decade of traveling outside of South Africa, Sathima's "Africa" is an early articulation of the new (South) African diasporic desire for a place where she imagines beauty, innocence, and certain kinds of freedom. And it is a song written in response to the deep feelings of alienation that accompanied living in Europe in the 1960s and 1970s.

It is in this context that the twentieth-century South African diasporic narrative presented in this book engages interrogatively with the ideas of what is increasingly known as the old African diaspora, by suggesting that there is now a new African diaspora. While it is clear that many of the South Africans who went into exile and came to live in the United States actively sought a place for themselves in the African American community by invoking notions of musical kinship and lineage, they also had a desire to tell their own stories, to speak a more nuanced, geographically dispersed language of African diasporic experiences. This new African diaspora speaks to a way of being in the world that is shaped by the forces of modernity, post-colonialism, and contemporary political conditions. Typically the new diasporic subject inhabits two or more places simultaneously: the first is the physical environment inhabited in the present, and the other references vivid memories of places they have lived in or passed through in their lifetime. In some instances, members of the old and new African diasporas have found points of commonality, but often, these two diasporic communities exist in tension with each other. What united South Africans with the African American community of musicians in the 1960s and 1970s was a longing to express a living relationship to Africa from their places in America and a vibrant recognition of the impact of racism and colonialism in their lives, yet South Africans also strove to articulate the specificity of their own living experiences of diaspora. They began to experiment with the memories of contemporary Africa and its diversity of languages and music inside the international language of jazz composition and performance.

Over the last two decades there has been an increased focus on the condition of diaspora as an outcome of what Appadurai calls "modernity at large" and the forces of globalization in the contemporary world. And there has been a growth in writings about the often discrepant connections between old and new African diasporas and their musical iterations. Paul Gilroy's (1993) notion of the "Black Atlantic" set the stage for reimagining the idea of *the* African diaspora, not least by discussing twentieth-century forms of diasporic music making in Britain. Ingrid Monson's (2000) edited volume on the musical perspectives of the African diaspora drew on Gilroy to examine manifestations of African music in places touched by the Atlantic. It references contemporary ethnomusicological work in the Caribbean and West Africa, includes a short piece on the global in jazz, and then moves primarily back to jazz ethnography in the United States. Robin Kelley (2002) reflects on the African diaspora as one of several failed social and political movements that, he argues, despite their failures should keep the dream of transformation alive. Penny Von Eschen has also deepened understanding of the African diaspora as an international political movement in the early to mid-twentieth century. Von Eschen (1997) constitutes her first narrative by using the African American press of the 1930s and 1940s. And then she extends her work (2004) into the specifically jazz and gospel dimensions of this story, writing about how the State Department sponsored musical tours of several jazz and gospel musicians to a variety of places suspected of engaging in communist activity and of fostering a communist ideology: parts of Africa, the former Soviet Union, Eastern Europe, and Japan. I published my first thoughts on the new African diaspora in 2003. Brent Edwards (2003) wrote a parallel narrative about black internationalism in literature, work that expands its reach into African and African American individuals and gatherings in Europe, and in Paris specifically, starting with a speech made by W. E. B. Du Bois in 1900. Edwards's work is the literary parallel to the growing body of scholarship on jazz in twentieth-century France, which features Josephine Baker in the 1930s and an increasing number of African American musicians, particularly in the era after the Second World War. Ingrid Monson's work (2007) on jazz and politics during the civil rights movement and the midcentury period of African independence reignites reflections on the ties between contemporary Africa and jazz, but it keeps the old diaspora territory intact. In 2009 two edited volumes on extending the black experience and the new African diaspora were published, supporting the arguments I make here (and have published elsewhere) about two forms of African diaspora, though neither volume deals specifically with musicians or people who have come from South Africa.

Finally, recent writing about the black diaspora in Britain, and specifically the position of Caribbean immigrants, similarly poses new kinds of questions about recent diasporas from African and African-derived communities currently living in the United Kingdom. The history of British jazz as a narrative distinct from the American story has at least in part been authenticated through Britain's own black diaspora, including musicians like Joe Harriot, Courtney Pine, and the group the Jazz Warriors from the 1980s, all of whom arrived in the United Kingdom from the Caribbean (see Moore 2007). These are the intellectual steppingstones I have followed as the foundation for rethinking African diasporic experience revealed in Sathima's story and in my work more generally.

Diaspora One: Musical Surrogacy

As evidenced by Howard Lawrence's review from 1959 (cited in chapter 3), when Sathima performed in South Africa in the late 1950s she made a deep emotional connection with her audiences. To quote him again: "What she did to the audience at Post's show, 'Just Jazz Meets the Ballet' was wow. I got it bad when she sang 'I Got It Bad.' Everybody else got it bad too and they kept shouting for more of that *feeling*."[62] Billie Holiday had had the same effect on audiences abroad. In the postwar period in Cape Town Sathima's voice made contact with Cape audiences through the emotional echoes resounding in the clearly articulated words and melodies, even though they did so in a foreign, but familiar, musical form: American jazz. While it was the sound of her voice and the bodily presence, both vessels of feeling and human connection were conveyed live by a local singer, the words of the song also communicated a universal message about the pains of love, making Sathima's rendition a powerful medium for connecting musically to the world at large. In this sense Ellington's composition rendered the local part of a wider transnational musical community in the minds of the South African audience.

In chapter 2 I described an extraordinary passion for twentieth-century music among Cape Town consumers in the postwar period, music that was mass mediated locally through radio, imported films, and sound recordings. The question left unanswered there is, Why did South Africans embrace imported genres like jazz in this period? There are several possible explanations. First, many local musicians had had experience during the war performing in the entertainment corps on the side of the Allies, particularly in North Africa. They brought the training, experience, and repertories back into local Cape culture. And yet, despite their service in the military corps, South Africans of color were increasingly excluded, during these years when apartheid was being legislated in South Africa, from all forms of urban public life on the basis of their racial classification. Not surprisingly, they began to look elsewhere for cultures of inclusion, and American jazz and popular music were often believed to operate inclusively.

Second, although very few American musicians traveled to South Africa in the 1950s, recordings by Americans were available in the country, as were films that featured American jazz musicians. Some of the live and mediated music came via American sailors whom South Africans met in the ports of Cape Town, Durban, and Port Elizabeth; recordings were purchased in local stores, and films were shown in city theaters. In Sathima's case, she also began to read books and other publications made available through public libraries by enlightened librarians. These were not pure commodities as such—rather they were viewed as the authentic sounds of the real musicians. They worked locally through the narratives constructed around them, as if they were the real thing: as objects with biographies.[63]

In other words, the music was heard locally in dialogue with the personal and collective histories of their makers and a growing awareness of the ties between the civil rights struggles of African Americans and those of people in similar social positions elsewhere in the world. The sounds and writings evoked feelings of intimacy, immediacy, and personal presence because of the parallel social and political places occupied by Africans and people of color in America and South Africa.[64] This sense of connection is beautifully illustrated in a story told by the trumpeter Hugh Masekela, who recalled that the day he heard Clifford Brown had died in an accident he wept uncontrollably, as one would mourn for someone known to them for a very long time. Masekela had never met Brown in person, though he felt he knew the man through the music he heard on record in Johannesburg. And finally, it was specifically as *music*, as a structure of deeply felt sentiment, that these commodities or renditions worked as surrogates for their human performers.

Although it was produced elsewhere by complete strangers, American music broadcast locally on radio in South Africa enabled an intimate identification between consumers and audiences and their geographically distant but acoustically real and present, temporally immediate, and emotionally centripetal musical cohorts. Put slightly differently, I am suggesting here that American jazz constituted a new kind of African diaspora through its worldwide distribution as musical commodity. These recordings and radio broadcasts of the music operated as surrogates in the birth and growth of jazz communities abroad.[65]

I borrow the idea of surrogacy from medical and legal discourses in which the surrogate is defined as one who serves as a substitute for or takes the place of another.[66] In regard to the music industry, one might think of the sound recording as the substitute that stands in for the musician. The sound recording is the designated carrier of a musician's performance: the human medium is replaced by the recorded medium, just as one woman might bear the offspring of another. From the musician's perspective, the recording is the one appointed "as a replacement for oneself." From the consumer's perspective, the recording is "the [one] appointed to represent or act [travel, perform] on behalf of others." The recording or the broadcast medium brings the music to new communities in the absence of the original musicians themselves, and it does so as a musical surrogate.

There is a specifically modern feel to this kind of process from the perspective of South Africans consuming American music because the continuities of intergenerational musical transmission, typically conveyed through face to face communication, is halted. The recording came to stand in as a medium of transmission that created a rupture in face-to-face transmission once new directions in local traditions began to be created through the intervention of sounds not of one's own extended family but from those of the same race living elsewhere. For these South African consumers of the American music conveyed in the sound recording or local broadcast of music, the surrogate might also be defined as "a person or animal who functions as a stand-in for another in a family or social role." The surrogate has the capacity to "receive or provide nurturing or parental care even though it is not related by blood or legal ties."[67] (The reference to blood ties resonates with my earlier reflection on musical lineage.)

Not every instance of American music that traveled from its recording centers in the United States outward to the margins of the global economy engendered a diasporic sphere. What distinguished a generalized global circulation of musical commodities from a diasporic one was the way in which musical objects were humanized or heard as musical echoes of parallel experiences by their consumers or audiences in their place of destination.[68] By means of the music made by Africans in America, South Africans of color resonated with the sounds of a modern African self, a self shaped by everyday experiences of racial discrimination, on one hand, and, on the other, by an individual and collective subjectivity that rehearsed the principles of freedom through the improvisational possibilities in American originating jazz, translated and transformed in postwar South Africa.

Diaspora Two: Jazz Migrancy

The pressure to continually move from place to place, language to language, and culture to culture in search of work forged an excruciating longing for home in both Sathima and Abdullah. Sathima recalls that the farther north she traveled, the greater was her sense of alienation and dislocation and the deeper she turned inside. At the core of her longing was the struggle to articulate how the story of place and nation might be told. A woman of unfamiliar racial mixture, her identity as a South African seemed to confuse rather than clarify. Sathima was confronted so often with the same set of questions and lack of recognition among audiences, reporters, and ordinary citizens regarding where she came from, whom she represented, and where she belonged in terms of her music and politics. The burden of not belonging weighed heavily on her. Could she legitimately tell the story of apartheid South Africa? Who was willing to hear her version?[69] These were the questions she asked when addressing Americans and Europeans.[70]

As Sathima traveled back and forth to South Africa, the apartheid regime was simultaneously making the country and its peoples unrecognizable locally. Earlier the black press regularly reported on South African musicians and artists living abroad, thereby closing the gap between home and elsewhere for South Africans. From the mid-1960s, the state increasingly placed banning orders on the creative work of South Africans living elsewhere. Much of the press was silenced; the news was stifled, and knowledge of South Africans living abroad disappeared from the local news channels. In such circumstances who would be able to comprehend the complex layering and folding of one place and experience into another that characterized this period of migration? Who in South Africa would bear witness to or begin to comprehend and sympathize with the lack of rootedness? The more they traveled, the deeper became the longing to be welcomed home, accepted into a group, or just to feel well placed.

At the same time South Africans who traveled abroad were keen to meet the musicians who had made the music they had listened to and admired so much before they left South Africa. Sometimes there was a close affinity established, while at other times the encounters were awkward, often frustrating. Dyani told Kenneth Ansell, writing for the British magazine *Impetus*, that when they arrived in London in the early 1960s they really livened up the scene, and when they played in France they had a particular identity as "those Africans." Some of the Americans, however, were dismissive: "Like Miles Davis used to call us 'bongo,' he thought Africa was just like playing bongos! But we surprised a lot of people. I guess we were very hip, we just didn't know it. But we did know what we were doing, we just had to keep going in our direction."[71] The South Africans developed lively friendships in Copenhagen and London, for example, with John Tchicai, Roswell Rudd, Don Cherry, Wes Montgomery, Horace Silver, and Albert Ayler and his brother Don. They associated with the British free musicians Derek Bailey and Steve Lacy, and with the South Americans Gato Barbieri and Enrico Rava.[72] These musicians would spend many hours playing, talking, listening to, and on occasion traveling together.

The period of continuous movement, of a daily feeling of not belonging except through the sound of the music South Africans were making together, increased the desire to hear and express the sounds of home in their music making. They wanted to sound less like American copies and more like South African originals. Sathima eventually composed the song "Africa" as an outcome of her sense of isolation, and in many ways her narrative of the "home within" was generated out of the constant sense of nonrecognition she experienced as a woman of mixed race who sang jazz. The question in this period became how to constitute a feeling of home in the music itself.

For Abdullah and the South Africans he performed with, the response was articulated in terms of black South African traditional musicians. In the mid-1970s Abdullah and Dyani experimented with incorporating the sounds of home inside their improvised music. "Ntsikana's Bell" published on Abdullah Ibrahim's *Good News From Africa* (1973) album, is one of the most powerful representations of the deep history of South African displacement in this period: of Eastern Cape music, mission Christianity, Islamic belief, and European migrancy.

Ntsikana's Bell Described

A voice cascades down like the force of water falling from rock to deep pool below. The voice is unaccompanied and singing in Xhosa, a language without reference and community in Europe and New York City in the middle of 1970s. Someone gently shakes a bell and taps a triangle. The man continues. A single bass note on the piano places the utterance tonally. We are comforted perhaps by the familiarity of harmonic language that starts to pour out from the piano. A second voice enters, thick with overtone. From here on, two male voices will build musical and emotional intensity through a tender call and response: one in the Xhosa language, the other in Arabic. Singing the story of Ntsikana in Xhosa recalls Eastern Cape mission history on the frontiers of the colonial project — Ntsikana is widely regarded as the first black South African Christian prophet; the other invokes the possibilities of recreated selves through conversion to Islam, and the larger story of Cape Muslim history.

*Both voices ultimately break out longingly into the high register cries of women
from home, sounding the echoing memories of the joyful ululation of sisters,
mothers, daughters, aunties, and grandmothers, all left behind.*

The Ibrahim-Dyani rendition of "Ntsikana's Bell" evokes the soulful rendering of South African religious and colonial history in the very fiber of
jazz performance. The overwhelming sense of homelessness experienced
in their continual movement between Europe and the United States
pressed Ibrahim and Dyani to capture the feeling of belonging and remembrance in the sounds created that invoked the sense of place and
home. In this frame, stories like Ntsikana's Bell and other local heroes,
told by those in the twentieth-century South African diaspora extend the
old narrative of the African diaspora induced through the transatlantic
slave trade, well beyond the borders of the United States. The southern
African diasporic accounts bear no real connection to the West African
routes of the seventeenth-century slave trade or its twentieth-century
jazz manifestations in the United States.[73]

"Ntsikana's Bell" engages interrogatively with many of the commonly
held beliefs about jazz and its history. For example, the diasporic integration of the sounds of what musicologist Sam Floyd calls an "African cultural memory" that Ibrahim and Dyani experimented with in the 1970s
produced a distinctive palate of sound, language, and voice. It was not
specifically about drumming or West African slavery. Instead, the evocative jazz rendering of "Ntsikana's Bell" speaks to an African diasporic
memory generated from the southern reaches of the African continent
in which the human voice, with all its timbral and emotive possibilities,
is the privileged vehicle of musical utterance. And it was composed as
Sathima and Abdullah wandered from European city to New York and
back again.[74]

South Africans in diaspora did not focus exclusively on performing with
musicians from home. In the course of finding a place for themselves in
the landscape of American-centered jazz performance in both Europe
and the United States, many South Africans would insist on a range of
possibilities for musical collaboration and experimentation that reached
out to include musicians from a wide range of places. We have already
seen that the postwar jazz community in Cape Town and Johannesburg
was both interracial and international — there were several visitors from

Europe in particular who shared their recordings, supported local musicians, and then left the country in the early 1960s. As a result, when South Africans performed in Europe their jazz could not be reduced to a single racial identity; rather, it was a musical language that opened itself to a worldwide set of possible performers, dialects, and local translations and transformations. (In this vein, South African jazz cannot simply be reduced to a single language, culture, racial group, or community.) While New York City was difficult terrain for all jazz in the 1960s and early 1970s, these were certainly not lean years for the music in several European cities: Copenhagen, London, and Paris regularly hosted African Americans and South Africans in their jazz clubs and concert halls.

Diaspora Three: In Exile

The postapartheid recognition of musicians in exile during the apartheid years is complex and conflicted. Most of the musicians who are remembered as having been in exile, like Sathima and Abdullah, are those who left in the late 1950s and early 1960s.[75] When they departed from South Africa they did so voluntarily, in performance groups like the Manhattan Brothers with the *King Kong* theater group, the Golden City Dixies, Spinono, and Chris McGregor and the Blue Notes. In other words, they left not because they were necessarily forbidden to play inside South Africa but because of the opportunities to perform elsewhere. *King Kong* and the Golden City Dixies had both had successful South African tours prior to their departure.

Sathima and Abdullah moved to Europe because they were urged by friends to do so, and they were frustrated with and afraid of the increasing repressiveness of the apartheid regime at home. Makeba went to Europe for the first time with the American filmmaker Lionel Rogosin to promote *Come Back Africa*, a film made secretly in South Africa in which she was the lead actor. As noted, Harry Belafonte took her under his wing and a year or so later traveled with her to the United States and introduced her to a wide network of powerful men and women in the American entertainment industry. Masekela begged the British priest and activist Trevor Huddleston to help him get musical training in England or the United States.[76] He ended up at the Manhattan School of Music in New

York City studying with the principal trumpeter of the New York Philharmonic.

Perhaps in contrast to the young South African political activists who left the country to join the ANC elsewhere in Africa, in Cuba, or in the former Soviet Union and to fight for liberation from abroad, the musicians' routes of travel seem more like musical opportunism than the condition of exile. Musicians appear to have left because of musical, not political, choices, and, retrospectively, many seemed to have benefited from the visibility South Africans gained from the international press about an increasingly repressive apartheid regime back home and the greater capacity to record their music.

Nevertheless, even if strictly speaking they had not been banned by the state and were not eluding the law or being branded as criminals at the time of their departure, there is a consensus that in the post-Sharpeville era playing their music in South Africa was becoming increasingly difficult. This was particularly true for a genre like jazz, which intentionally crossed over in terms of race, class, and gender. There were interracial groups performing, interracial audiences, and musicians were crossing the color bar in their personal relationships. In its constitution as a nonracial free space, jazz made in South Africa was a threat to the growing power of the apartheid regime in the early 1960s. After Sharpeville there was no turning back. As Sathima and Abdullah recall, it became impossible to do anything, and they felt that if they didn't leave they would cease to exist as musicians. We have already cited the Cape Town–born drummer Louis Moholo, who recalled that the couple left South Africa in order to preserve a piece of its musical heritage.[77]

Little is to be gained by arguing about who benefited more or who suffered the most in this period of political and cultural exile from South Africa. I am going to presume the condition of exile is a given for those who left South Africa as musicians in the post-Sharpeville period, and I do so for the following reasons. While musicians may well have departed because they were motivated by the prospects of musical opportunity elsewhere in the world, the majority of South Africans who went away were ultimately unable to return in any permanent kind of way to their families and communities until the early 1990s — if they lived that long — and by that time a whole new generation of South African children had been born and raised abroad. Returning could divide families in the same way apartheid itself had. Furthermore, those who left often did so having endured regular police harassment for contravening the many laws of apartheid — the Separate Amenities Act, the Immorality Act, the Group Areas Act — and because the venues were increasingly under security branch surveillance or simply shut down.

Once musicians began living abroad, conditions for black South Africans remaining in the country deteriorated as family members were visited by the security branch, and so life back home was increasingly seen as an urgent political issue, one that musicians could alert the world to: they could tell their story to a wider audience.[78]

The question is, on the one hand, whether the musicians could return without getting arrested and being harassed by security forces and, on the other, whether they couldn't be more effective spokespeople for the anti-apartheid cause outside rather than inside the country. Being away for so long, without having planned it that way and lacking the benefit of cheap, accessible forms of global communication, was extremely difficult. Telephone calls were almost impossible; letters were usually censored, not delivered, and hardly ever replied to. There is no doubt that for many South Africans who left voluntarily everyday existence abroad became a kind of life in exile. For South Africans living in exile, the ANC would often become a kind of surrogate site for new forms of postapartheid national identification.

The ANC opened offices in a range of cities in Europe and the United States, including Paris, London, and New York City. A new nation was being forged in exile, a nation whose "citizens" often included the younger generation of exiles. There was, of course, the silenced and censored older generation of political prisoners, including Nelson Mandela, Govan Mbeki, and Walter Sizulu, who were imprisoned in South Africa; and the exiled ANC leader Oliver Tambo lived in London for a time. A newer generation of exiles who joined the armed wing of the ANC was dispersed in a range of places that were more communist or socialist in ideology, places like Zambia, Tanzania, Cuba, Brazil, and the former Soviet Union.

*Diaspora Four: A Southern Touch Aesthetic
or the (Diasporic) Spirit of Africanness*

While visiting South Africa in 1974, Sathima had a dream vision. She says
in it, "I heard this glorious music, and saw these silver sands, they were
endless. And I saw all the peoples of the world, holding hands, and I guess
the people were singing, but I couldn't really hear what they were singing. I don't believe it was chanting, they were singing, but I don't know
what exactly. And there was this wonderful feeling of peace. I woke up,
and then the light came into my room and lit up the whole room. All I
could do was put my head on the ground. I was totally overwhelmed, not
afraid, but I felt more than awe."[79]

Sathima wrote a piece about it, but, she says, "I'm really very shy about
it. I'm afraid people will think I'm nuts." So the song remains unrecorded,
but the dream inspired the title of her projected fifth Ekapa record, *Lovelight*, which she recorded in September 1987 with the pianist Larry Willis,
the bassist Buster Williams, and the drummer Billy Higgins. The experience has also guided her career and put previous events in perspective
for her. She realizes that "Ellington gave this to me [the Lovelight] and
Winnie Mandela has it. And my musicians, I've been led to them because of this Lovelight. It makes energy, it makes harmony, and it makes
this glorious sound. I'm not really doing this, you see, I'm just another
light."[80]

In April 1997 Sathima reminded me of a story she had told before. It
was of an experience she had in Europe while traveling with her trio,
Ben Riley, Buster Williams, and Kenny Barron, during the anti-apartheid
struggle. A Dutchman had come up to Sathima after her performance
and demanded why she had dared to sing "You Don't Know What Love
Is." "How can you sing American standards, aren't you from Cape Town,
South Africa? Why don't you sing liberation songs?" he had wanted to
know. Sathima recalled she was a little taken aback by his aggressive questioning but was relieved when Riley intervened. "She is not from Cape
Town," he told the man. "Didn't you just hear us play? She is from Atlanta,
Georgia." The singer recalls being so grateful to Riley. He was also the musician, she recalled, who would say to her, "'Abdullah has the organization
called Loving Family, but you, Sathima, *you* are the loving family.' That's
what started me thinking about the *Southern Touch*," she remarked.

Though Sathima has never traveled in the southern United States, *Southern Touch* is the name of the album she recorded with Barron, Williams, and Higgins in December 1989 and released in 1990. "Southern touch" is the phrase she uses to describe her personal aesthetic in jazz singing, and it is the path she follows to achieving a unity between old and new African diasporas. She uses the term when she talks about the connections she imagines between her ways of being in the world, something she knows comes out of the South African experience, and the American South. These are the experiences articulated in the expressive and emotional freedom she hears in gospel music aired on television, but, even more so, in the parallel histories of those who perform jazz. Sathima's attraction to jazz, she told me in April 1990,

> happened at a time when I was thinking about my own identity, . . . 1957 — the 1960s. That was a very fervent time at home, and things were happening politically. And I was at such an age when it hit me. I said, "I am not going to take this." . . . What am I doing to do? I didn't write my own music then. That's the time I drifted to Duke Ellington's music. All I can say is that jazz came out of a very painful experience. It started with black people being ripped away, and then innately trying to go back. . . . They were denied so many things and were repressed. And the music comes out of that. And that we [South Africans] were drawn to it, it just seems natural to me. OK, we weren't ripped away from our continent, but our continent was ripped away from us.

In its most conventional use, the southern touch is a reference to individual character—the kind of person you are in relation to other people in the present, which is formed out of the substance of your individual past from a combination of genetic inheritance and childhood experience. Personal character matters to Sathima: I have sat with her after live performances in which she has taken note of whom she might like to work with in the future: her choices depend on the personal and musical demeanor of a musician on and off the stage.

Southern touch has an acoustical dimension. Here the touch is concerned with the manner in which the musicians, herself included, approach the music, with reverence and care, caressing melodies with subtlety and nuance, honoring the wishes of the lyricist, and retaining a respect for the composer's intentions while impressing on the music something of their own personal sound. Such qualities are found among musicians who have, in her words, "paid their dues" in life and consequently know how to work cooperatively without always seeking the spotlight. These are musicians who easily perform in a more democratic musical environment: a space of mutual reciprocity and cocreation between singer and instrumentalists. There is a utopian quality to this touch, especially as it circumscribes the space of music in the singer's life, experience, and belief system. In song composition, Sathima creates a connection between the southern touch and the physical environment.

At times a southern touch is thought of as anachronistic belief in the power and values of spiritual presence in dreams and visions. As indicated above, Sathima invokes the presence of the nonmaterial—those who have died—in her dreams. These dreams often reveal significant musicians and family members, particularly when she is about to perform live or undertake a recording project. Both Ellington and her biological mother regularly "come to her" as she starts a live performance in a club or church in New York. For a long time Sathima would begin her performances with an unaccompanied vocal rendition of the old spiritual "Sometimes I Feel Like a Motherless Child." Because she would go out onto the stage without a pianist, she would rely on the visionary presence of Duke Ellington to give her the right key to sing in, a process that required her to surrender completely to forces outside of herself. On other occasions, when she has been about to embark on a recording project, she will find reminders of Ellington all around her, serving to reassure her that he remains a musical force in her life. Recently, she told me that once, a couple of days before she was scheduled to perform at Sweet Rhythm in New York, she unexpectedly heard his speaking voice on radio, in one of those rare moments when someone had recorded him talking rather than conducting his band or playing.

Finally, in this reading of the southern touch there is often a close connection between memories of long-forgotten tunes and new technologies which make available past repertories, like the replaying of old show and movie tunes on the channels of digital television in the last decade and the reissue of popular tunes in new media. Fragments of these tunes and their times emerge, quite suddenly, into conscious awareness. Some come bearing the inflections of the voices of people she remembers singing those tunes—they were the signature tunes of childhood friends. Others retain a more general place in her memory. In Sathima's experience, the "spirit within you" parallels the voices heard streaming out of the radio: in the 1940s and 1950s in South Africa, the radio was the archive out of which flowed the melodies that Sathima now reinvents as specifically jazz tunes, straight melodies reinterpreted through temporal displacement.

These technologies fundamentally shape how particular repertories are received in certain communities and often the ways in which one repertory has come to be defined. For example, because radio was the primary medium through which Sathima recalls absorbing the repertory she now sings, there is a remarkable correspondence between her individual memories of prior radio-listening experiences and the ways in which she defines jazz. Unlike repeated listening to the records one owned, a process in which one decides what, when, and how much to listen to, what one heard on radio (other than request shows) was far less likely to be something the listener could control; it was the disc jockey and increasingly formatted playlists that determined what, when, and on which station. Consequently, the singer stresses the spontaneity and unpredictability of jazz performance over other qualities of the genre.

Summing up a New African Diaspora

Sathima's story requires that one create a rhetorical space for the possibility of a new African musical diaspora, consciousness, subjectivity, and cultural memory, generated out of more recent colonial and postcolonial experiences of displacement and suffering by people of African descent. This new diaspora tells stories about the streams of twentieth-century African immigrants and exiles whose diasporic narratives diverge significantly from those of the older, more familiar histories of the African diaspora that brought African slaves from the west and central parts of the continent into the New World. The new African diaspora articulates a more recent, often modern, urbanized, cosmopolitan African past that is continually animated in the present, rather than the less specific forms of "cultural memory" or signs of precolonial musical style valued as sacred in some contemporary African American communities and scholarship.[81] Such an African diaspora speaks of a less stable definition of Africanness, of who is included in the category of African. It incorporates a range of immigrants, passersby, refugees, and colonists of European, African, Asian, and mixed heritage. And it includes the routes of those who have traveled from Africa to other English-speaking parts of the world, including the Caribbean, the United Kingdom, the Indian subcontinent, and those who came from South Africa. In this way of being in the world, the human body is constituted as a kind of archive of personal and musical memories and of transnational connections that, in this case, [South] African musicians like Benjamin, Ibrahim, Makeba, and others who have lived or continue to live in the new diaspora regularly reference and draw upon as they have performed jazz differently in Europe, Asia, Africa, and the United States. All are fundamentally informed by new media and technologies, which further shape diasporic consciousness and subjectivity. These media have enabled new forms of community belonging or musical habitus, innovative ways of remembering multiple pasts in Africa, and envisioning a range of futures for the continent and its peoples.[82]

5

A New York Embrace

Coming to the City

"New York, New York. A place so wonderful they named it twice,"
Sathima repeated the commonly cited comment as we began to talk
in December 2000 about how she views her relationship to New York
City. Over the years we have come to see that Sathima's move to the city
in the mid-1970s was a shift toward achieving a greater sense of herself
as a woman, toward self-invention, and toward political commitment.
This was a period of enormous personal and creative growth for her as a
woman, musician, mother, and activist, growth Sathima attributes to the
freedom to be that the city gives to her and to the place created in the
anti-apartheid struggle of the 1970s and 1980s.

I met Sathima midway through her New York story. Because of her
retreat into the domestic sphere and because much of our conversation
was recorded in writing or in audio files, there is a stylistic shift in this
chapter into the particularity of Sathima's narration of the story. Even
though I have shaped her words to suit the needs of the book, there is
a greater sense of her pace, style, and turn of phrase in the words themselves. The response unfolds a gendered poetics of the jazz-self created
in Sathima's own words and ideas. It is there we capture the texture and
feel of Sathima's own creative process, musicality, and aesthetic sensibility. The shift in voice and the ongoing discussion of her music making
generate a tension in the writing between the past and the continuities
of experience and approach into the present. These ideas place her as a
woman in jazz: a singer, a bandleader, a studio musician, live performer,
and composer, and they invoke ideas of love, beauty, spontaneity, intuition, and spirituality as core elements of that self.

Mother

While in South Africa in the mid-1970s I decided I had to live in New York City because I had this thing I wanted to be the best mom in the world and I wanted to raise my children at home. When I had Tsakwe I was still going on the road. But when Tsidi came I said, "Oh no, I can't go now with the little one. I have to give this up, I have a little baby girl." That is when I said to Abdullah, "I need to go back to New York City." I didn't want Tsakwe to go to school in South Africa with all the racism. When I had Tsidi, I said I didn't want to raise her there either. Abdullah reluctantly agreed. He had to come ahead and look for a place for us to live. We had lived uptown most of the time we had been in New York City, but this time he had no luck finding a place that would work for us all. He was walking around in the Chelsea area when he bumped into Don Cherry. Again. Remember we had worked with him in Europe, and I told you that I met Barbara on Claremont Ave when we went to a concert of Don Cherry's?

Abdullah told Don Cherry we were looking for a place. "Look no more," he said to Abdullah and brought him to the Chelsea. That was in February — Tsidi was two to three months old by the time we arrived here. Don Cherry introduced Abdullah to Stanley Bard, who ran the Hotel Chelsea. Stanley started this hotel for artists, he wasn't asking for all these other securities or your employment history. We did need a recommendation, so we called Ruth Ellington and she sent a letter. Remember, for immigration we got something from Langston Hughes and Duke Ellington. That's how we got citizenship: we had these influential people in our lives. But it was Don Cherry that introduced Abdullah to Stanley Bard, and Abdullah said, "I found a place, not uptown, but downtown."

Sathima was reluctant to move downtown: "The Chelsea area was rundown, it was quite derelict. It wasn't the way it looks today, nobody really wanted to live here. We didn't have all these stores and things. It was quite desolate." The reluctance disappeared after she had a dream in which the ancestors gave her the authority to inhabit the space: "I will never forget. In my dream I was in a big canyon, but it was cone-shaped. And I was at the bottom. I felt very frightened. I heard a sound. It sounded like the wind, and all of a sudden I was spiraled up. I came up. All the different tribes of Native Americans, they were making that sound. They were making that sound, and the sound spiraled me up and out of that hole. I just knew then that it was okay for me to be here. It was an *okay* for me.

That was it."[1] Sathima's dream world takes on an almost Jungian notion of a collective unconscious—where it is the first peoples of the Americas who grant her permission to find her place in the most modern of all cities. Years later, when Sathima was reading about the Hotel Chelsea, she discovered that 23rd Street had once been a trail for Native Americans traveling from the waterfront, along Broadway, to Brooklyn. She has frequently told me that her mother said she had some Native American blood in her lineage and has on several occasions been stopped on the street and asked if she is Native American.

Motivated to come to New York City largely because she didn't want her children growing up or being schooled in apartheid South Africa, Sathima recalled that once they settled in the city her priority was to find the right school for Tsakwe:

When it came time to send Tsakwe to school, I knew he would need a stimulating environment because he was so intelligent. I had heard about the United Nations school and tried to enroll him there, but it was just too expensive. Someone then told me about PS 3, one of those progressive and open schools. He was put straight into second grade because he could read fluently. PS 3 was just a wonderful school, with the most thoughtful and loving teachers. It was located on 8th Avenue at the corner of Grove Street in the Village. Since PS 3 only went to fifth grade, Tsakwe then went to the Chelsea Art and Design school for a couple of years.

I would often walk back home and used that time to think about songs I wanted to sing. Sometimes I would just practice singing my songs as I walked. When Tsidi was about three years old, she was driving me to distraction with her mischievous ways. I asked her if she wanted to go to school. She couldn't go to PS 3 because she wasn't old enough. I found a Montessori school on 17th Street for her, I paid a fee, but it didn't really work out so well. She did nothing but pick up all the childhood illnesses—measles, chickenpox, even though she had been vaccinated. And it seemed as soon as I dropped her off I had to go and collect her again. So I waited until she turned four and then made a special application to the Board of Education for her to attend PS 3 where Tsakwe was. She went because she wanted to be with her brother. Tsidi was young but did very well there. When Tsakwe turned seventeen he went to the School of Visual Arts, where he studied for four or five years. He spent the last year of his degree studying at SUNY Purchase. He got his Bachelor of Fine Arts degree and was chosen as one of the three best students to have an exhibition downtown at their art gallery. It was a real honor.

I enrolled Tsidi at the La Guardia School of the Arts. She had done some danc-

21. School picture of Sathima's daughter, Tsidi. *Collection of Sathima Bea Benjamin.*

ing with the Alvin Ailey School, and she sang beautifully too. She was not happy there, so we enrolled her at the New York University School of Business and Management, which she said she couldn't handle because there were only males in the class. So that didn't work out. It was at about that time that she started doing some performing with some other young folk. This was a difficult time, we didn't relate well to each other. She was doing her own thing and in a way declaring her independent spirit as she still does to this day. I remember at the time she had quite a few young male admirers, one of them came knocking on the door with flowers for her every so often. Tsidi moved to Brooklyn when she was about eighteen. She also spent about a year in Cape Town working with Abdullah's M7 School. But eventually she came back to the Chelsea.

Tsidi has so many talents and is always figuring out how to use them. I am glad that she is strong, determined and, yes, a survivor. Being a Sagittarian, she has to be a survivor, with a strong sense of self and adventure. And she is like me, when she is down she will simply "pick herself up, and dust herself off" and start all over again. Tsidi is a professional hip-hop artist and her performance name is Jean Grae, a name taken from the X-Men comic book. Jean Grae, the one who flies about doing great things!

In 2007 Jean Grae wrote a dedication to Sathima on MySpace. Sathima wanted it in the book. A moving tribute from daughter to mother, it reads as follows:

My Mama, the AMAZING. . . . Sathima Bea Benjamin

I'm taking this week to introduce to those of you who do not know, the beautiful spirit and song of Sathima Bea Benjamin. Thankfully to the universe, it was decided that I was born to this amazing woman.

Beyond being the greatest, coolest, most understanding, FUNNY AS ALL HELL, learned, vulnerable, inspiring, sensitive, spiritual, potty-mouthed, dependable, independent, brave, innocent, determined and ONE in the world MOM . . . she is the most creative and musically inspiring spirit through the gentle vibrato of her honest notes.

I hate hearing people play cd 101.9 and thinking that Najee is jazz.

Or having to grow up watching her being over-looked; under-appreciated; and mis-categorized.

Critically acclaimed and Grammy nominated.

Understood and praised by jazz purists and scholars, those of us who believe in honest and beautiful music and weep at the moment a note pulls at our heartstrings.

This woman is a force and the reason I do what I do. Even when I want to stop, the only reason I exist and the music that I make exists.

I understand her struggle and her ambition because I have made it mine because she is such a warrior and fighter for things that are honest and true to her being and love and family.

She is a hopeless romantic and an inexplicable grace in being.

I am only a mirror of everything I have learned from her.

She has not quit or given up, so if the small recognition that I have fought for like she taught me to can allow anyone else to glimpse and experience her fight for life . . . it is all worth it.

I am keeping up and adding pictures, photos and music all week.

She has always believed in me, unconditionally, . . . as a daughter and as an artist. Given me the utmost respect and love.

I would now like to return the favor.

Please purchase a CD, spread the word, add her into your top, Google her, search for her, request her in your record stores.

My friends and I all have her current re-issue in heavy rotation: not because she's my mom, but because she is Sathima and she is amazing!

My life has and does mimic hers in so many ways. As its amazing to be getting some due after 15 years, she has been doing it for 40 plus and has yet to receive a real and true acceptance from the jazz and music commu-

22. Sathima's son, Tsakwe, in the early 1990s. *Collection of Sathima Bea Benjamin.*

nity as a living legend and the one and only true jazz singer from Cape Town, South Africa. . . . In addition to owning her own label and releasing her music independently.

Ride with us, Support honest music
www.sathimabeabenjamin.com

Sathima said,

Tsakwe lives permanently with me now at the Chelsea. He is currently working on perfecting a self-produced CD that he hopes to put out when the time is right. When he was about twenty-two or twenty-three he was diagnosed with a schizo-affective disorder, though he is on medication and functions quite well every day. A few years ago we returned to Cape Town and lived there for awhile, close to the clinic where he was receiving treatment and medication. Abdullah bought me a small apartment two blocks from the clinic. Ultimately, we decided to come back to New York City, because of the musicians who were here. That is when I really began to record myself on Ekapa Records, putting on a few of my own concerts at Carnegie Recital Hall and recording with the famous Rudy Van Gelder in Engle-wood Cliffs, New Jersey.

I had a very bad fall a few years ago, breaking both my feet, and was bedridden for six months. I then went in a wheelchair and onto crutches. Tsakwe took care of me, he was such a blessing, he did the shopping and the cooking. I had some other help from the housekeeper at the Chelsea, but Tsakwe was the one who cared for

*me on a daily basis. I don't know what he will do when I go back to South Africa—
I think he would like to live in Europe. He is talking to his Dad about that possibility. Tsakwe is making changes, and I believe he will be successful!*

Activist

On leaving South Africa in 1977, Sathima and Abdullah decided to openly
declare their support for the liberation movement abroad. As early as
1963 the South African singer Miriam Makeba, as noted, had testified before the United Nations about the vicissitudes of apartheid. In the late
1970s Johnny Makatini, a close colleague of the president-in-exile of the
African National Congress (ANC), Oliver Tambo, led the movement in
New York City.[2] Sathima recalls,

*I knew that I would be a better human being if I got out of South Africa and com-
mitted myself to the anti-apartheid struggle as an artist and tried to write music
about the struggle. I could sing about it for the world at large. Comrade Johnny
Makatini would come by the Chelsea when Abdullah was in town.[3] Tsidi was
about a year and a half or two at the time, and I remember how he absolutely
adored her. He called her his "sweetheart, little baby girl." When he found out that
I too was a performer, he suggested that I be the one to do a concert at the United
Nations to protest Frank Sinatra's trip to South Africa. Sinatra had agreed to tour
South Africa and to play before racially segregated audiences. You know it is interesting to me that Duke Ellington had also been approached for a South African
tour and he had turned it down. Ellington said that if he wouldn't tour the South
here in the United States because he would have to play to separate audiences, why
would he go to South Africa to do that there?*

*After doing the United Nations concert for the African National Congress,
Johnny told me I needed to keep doing work of this nature for the ANC. I founded
the Sechaba Pioneers, a group of young members of the ANC. We met each Saturday afternoon to sing freedom songs and discuss the political situation in South
Africa. I sang at three Women's Day events and began to give talks and performances at the United Nations, through the Artists United Against Apartheid
group, and other venues. Then Dulcie September was murdered in Paris.[4] Comrade Makatini sent me there to perform at her funeral. I remember being met at
the airport in Paris by an ANC representative. We were chased by car obviously
by someone from the apartheid regime.[5] It was a high-speed car chase that lasted*

about an hour until we reached Dulcie September's graveyard. We were there for the ceremony, and when I got back in the car, there was another chase all the way back to the airport. I was absolutely terrified that I would die and never see my children again. Fortunately, I got back to New York safely.

Later that year I was sent to São Paulo in Brazil to speak at a rally. After sitting at the São Paulo airport for about eight hours, I was finally met by two young women from Grenada, who were again trying to divert the apartheid forces who knew someone was coming to speak at this huge outdoor ANC rally. I was taken to a tiny hotel and hidden in the basement until I was picked up just in time to appear at the anti-apartheid rally. I only realized later that on both occasions I could have been killed by those apartheid regime folks.

In this period Sathima also volunteered in the ANC offices in New York City:

I worked in the office, addressing letters, mailing letters, and the children would go with me. I would call people to tell them there was going to be a show. Just in the office, several hours a day, for maybe two years. The kids were small and so I would take them with me. Through this work I met many African Americans who were sympathetic to the anti-apartheid struggle, though I don't really remember everyone's names.[6] These were good, creative years musically because you felt you were part of something larger. We did benefit concerts for everybody, wherever the ANC asked us to perform—in Europe, in New York City. Sometimes I performed with Abdullah and his trio, sometimes just with my own trio. The African American musicians I worked with were so supportive and often performed for the liberation movement without pay. I do believe they could identify with our cause because of the racial similarities here for them in the South.

There was growing pressure in this context for Sathima to sing explicitly political songs. Though Comrade Makatini had told her that she sounded like his favorite singer, Billie Holiday, she never actually sang Holiday's most famous political song, "Strange Fruit." Rather, Sathima began to write political songs relevant to the South African liberation struggle. She created her "Liberation Suite" by combining three of her own originals: "Africa," "Children of Soweto," and "Nations in Me, New Nation A'Comin'." The idea of combining the three into a suite resonated with the *Freedom Now Suite* composed by Max Roach and performed by Roach and Abbey Lincoln in 1960. The Roach and Lincoln suite outlined a musical overview of black liberation history in the United States, in the spirit of Ellington's *Black, Brown and Beige* and similar compositions from the 1930s to the 1960s. *The Freedom Now Suite*, discussed by Ingrid Monson (2007), is tied directly to South Africa, but in ways not specifically outlined by Monson. It was recorded the same year that Roach and Lincoln met Hugh Masekela. Masekela (2004) reports that he and Makeba were invited to dinner with Roach and Lincoln soon after he arrived in New York City.

Each of Sathima's songs invoked a place for South Africans in a newer African diasporic lineage as well. As I noted earlier, the song "Africa" expresses a longing for the African continent, its peoples, and a particular way of being in the world; "Children of Soweto" paid tribute to the courage of the children and to the significance of the uprising of 16 June 1976 in South African political history; and "Nations in Me, New Nation A'Comin'" reiterated a theme common to African American racial and musical struggles, as outlined by Graham Lock (1999): the insistence on the memory of an African and African American past and the utopian visions of a future society. Lock discusses at some length Ellington's use of music as a kind of poetic utterance of his people's history — *Black, Brown and Beige* is the obvious example, but so too is the lesser-known composition "New World A'Coming," based on the book of the same name (1943) by Roi Ottley. That composition spoke to African American history, while Sathima's rendition in "New Nation A'Comin'" related to the South African struggle. Significantly, "Nations in Me" also forged a rhetorical space for discussion of what it meant to be called Coloured or of mixed racial heritage or to have, as Sathima puts it, "many nations in you." Sathima's "Nations in Me, New Nation A'Comin'" fits into Lock's blutopian trope: examining the past in a new light and imagining a radically different future. As such, Sathima's music works as what Robin Kelley (2003) would call a "Freedom Dream," that is, a vision for political transformation that connected radical political movements around the world in the mid-twentieth century.

Jazz Singer

It was not only as a South African woman of color that Sathima performed: first and foremost, in her mind, was her identity as a jazz musician. Prior to coming to New York in 1977, she remembers, she always had to insist that she be allowed to perform in Abdullah's bands; or she waited for a call from Ellington. So shortly after arriving in the city Sathima decided to present a live performance of Ellingtoniana to pay tribute to the man who had occupied such an important place in her life and music. Sathima had presumed that Abdullah would play with her on piano. But she was in for a surprise. When she told him about the rehearsal and performance schedule, he responded by saying that he would no longer work with her, that she was in New York where all the musicians are and should go and find her own people to work alongside her. All Sathima can remember is how stunned and filled with fear she became:

In that moment I felt totally thrown away. I remember going outside and walking in the streets. I was devastated. I had no idea this was going to happen. It took me completely by surprise. To this day, he says that he did me a favor. In contrast, I felt like he threw me away that day, he just threw me away. Maybe he's right. It's just that I wasn't expecting that response. It is possible he could have sat me down and talked about it, and maybe I would have cried and not accepted it.

Anyway, it was late afternoon and I called my friend Melba, she is no longer alive. She was an African American woman who was married to the South African poet Willie Kgositsile.[7] At the time, Melba lived uptown, but she came down to the Chelsea and walked with me. She said to me, "Now listen, this is what you do when these kind of things happen." She really empowered me that day. She said to me, "You have to do exactly what Abdullah says. You are in New York City: you already handle all of Abdullah's schedules and musicians. So start with one musician and ask him to refer you to another musician until you have a trio in place." I was afraid, and said to her, "But they don't know who I am. They don't know that I really sing." And she said to me, "You just go home and try what I am suggesting." So I went home and called Cecil McBee, the bass player. He had been working with Abdullah at that point. He said to me, "Wow, I didn't know that you sang." And I said to him, "I am not asking that you work with me." I told Cecil McBee that I needed a pianist. He replied that he would give it some thought and call me back. That's when he gave me Onaje Allan Gumbs' number.

So I called Onaje Allan Gumbs, and I said, "Onaje, I am giving a concert up at Duke Ellington's place." Duke and his sister owned a house, Tempo Music, up on Riverside Drive, at 106th Street somewhere there. I had called Ruth, and she said I could have the ballroom, and the piano that Ellington and Strayhorn used to play. There was a white piano, and she said I could just use the place because I didn't have any money. Onaje agreed to meet with me. After we had talked a little

I thought I could work with him. I remember trying to teach him the song "Mood Indigo." He was giving me a really hard time. While I was there I told Onaje I needed a bass player and a drummer. And he said to me, "OK," and he called bass player, Buster Williams. While we were struggling with Ellington's "Mood Indigo"—it has three verses and a bridge and I was nearly going out of my mind because I really wanted to sing it at Duke Ellington's place. We just were not getting it together: I was standing there, and suddenly I heard this beautiful bass.

I turned around and this guy is saying to Onaje, "What are you playing? Why don't you play it like this?" It was Buster Williams and Onaje introduced me to him. Then I didn't have a drummer, but I think Onaje called Little Niles, Randy Weston's son. He had congas, even though I had originally wanted a regular drummer. Anyway, he was the one who broke Buster's bass that day. The congas fell over on Buster's bass and made a big hole in it. Buster always jokes that the hole will be there for the rest of his life. He says to me that he will take me with him always, the hole in his instrument means he will never forget me! I thought Buster was going to walk out, but he didn't. He continued to practice. He took the broken bass somewhere, had it fixed and we did the show. John Wilson, the critic from the New York Times *came, and he gave us such a great review.[8] That's when I started to do duets. I had two songs that I did, it was just so hard teaching Onaje everything but Buster knows everything. He knows almost every song on the planet. I did two duets with him. When John Wilson reviewed that performance he said, "I know these people have never played together and yet it seems as if they have played together for years." That's when I knew this is the bass player for me. And he is, even though I am not always able to get him for a performance or recording.*

Ekapa Records

In 1979 Sathima and Abdullah announced at a series of New York City performances that they would launch their own record label, Ekapa. Ekapa translates as "at or from the Cape," reinforcing the idea of their music as a reflection of their South African home. Recording was Sathima's primary mechanism for reinventing herself as a jazz musician and constituting a feeling of home in the music itself. Sathima tells the story of her decision to produce her own recordings: "It occurred to me that I could make a record. I really didn't know anything about it. I decided to do an album of Ellington songs because I figured, well, they don't know me here. Let me do something that is familiar. I was very unsteady with my own compositions, and I was very shy about them." With Ekapa established, Sathima could, in her words, let her records "do a little traveling" for her, in much the same way that American musicians had sent their music to South Africa starting in the 1920s.

Financially supported by Abdullah in exchange for managing his travels, Sathima made her first self-produced LP record at Downtown Studios in New York. The album, titled *Sathima Sings Ellington*, contains seven Ellington standards: "In a Mellow Tone," "Prelude to a Kiss," "Sophisticated Lady," "Mood Indigo," "Lush Life," "I Let a Song Go Out of My Heart," and "Solitude." Gumbs is on piano, Vishnu Wood on bass, John Betsch on drums, and Claude Latief on congas. She described making the record:

The recording session, which started around midnight and ended up in the early hours of the morning, was extremely relaxed and enjoyable. Please do not think me presumptuous when I say that there were moments during the session when I felt "HIS" [i.e., Ellington's] spirit very strongly — and that was beautiful.[9]

I did it, I went into the studio and I did it, [Sathima commented to me]. You know, Abdullah would say to me, I remember him saying this to me long ago, that I didn't realize the gold within myself. He said that a long time ago. The problem was that in my mind he was the overwhelming force, it took me a long time to come out from under, actually he will take credit that he established me as a jazz singer when we arrived here in New York City. And he is proud of that fact. But, you know, Carol, while I learnt much from Abdullah, each of the recordings I have made has been my own concept and project.

Once the studio session was complete and the tapes edited into an album, Sathima recalls,

I sat there with a couple thousand LP's and I said, "What am I going to do with all this?" So I had to get the courage and say, now who are all the critics in this jazz music business? I am going to write a little note, package it, and send it to them. They can either look at it, or throw it in the bin. Then I waited six months. I got feedback. I almost fell off my feet. It was so positive! I couldn't believe it.[10] *Then a distributor approached me. Everybody said this is an artist-owned independent company: this is what this woman has done. If you want to know anything more about this woman, here is the contact information. So this small company called me. That was how I found out I needed a distributor! It was just trial and error. I was actually very naïve, they came to me. That is how the stuff got out there. And that success inspired me to do my second album,* Dedications, *which I recorded in New York in January 1982.*[11]

Dedications is composed of two of Sathima's compositions, "Music" and "Africa," a song by Cole Porter and one by Eubie Blake and Andy Razaf, the remainder consisting of a mix of old Hollywood film favorites, operetta, and British music hall tunes sung in a jazz style. She explained her use of the earlier repertory of popular song almost as if it were a living archive or human reissue:

I bring the old songs back, I love doing that. I enjoy researching very, very old songs that nobody is singing any more. I think about how I can present this, how I can do it differently without offending the composer? There is a very old song that has recently come to me. It is called "Prisoner of Love," I don't even know who sang it, but it must have been some vocal group from long, long ago. These are songs from like 1945. I do these things because I actually heard them broadcast on the BBC. *There were singers like Vera Lynn. They had very good diction. That said, you can't live in the past, to be extraordinary you have to live for the moment and think about tomorrow. There isn't any yesterday. You can reflect and have memories, but they must be used to project something new. That is what I like to do with the music, I take something old and make it new.*[12]

Sathima talked with me about "Music" and "Africa" in 1989:

I don't know when "Music" started, but it was probably a long time ago. It surfaced in 1974 when I was on a visit home to South Africa. Maybe it was being back on the African soil, being with family, and looking at my life from another perspective. Having been there, gone away, and gone back. I was also going through a lot of personal difficulty, keeping a marriage together, having a four-year-old son, and not being able to sing. I think that was the third song that came after I realized I could write songs, though I kept it inside me for a long time. When I decided to record it in 1985, I gave it to the musicians and they just dived into it. We hardly rehearsed. We just went into the studio. They are real pros. They know more about this stuff than I do. As for "Africa": that song expresses how I imagined we would feel when we did finally go back home — as it became possible to do in the 1990s. I once tried to sing that in Cape Town, in the 1970s. Somebody wrote a review and said, "Well we don't know exactly what Africa she's singing about." And I said to Abdullah, "Now I know one thing, it is time to leave. It is definitely time to leave."

But I would sing it here in the United States and people would understand. It's funny how things work out.

Soon after recording Dedications, *I was in Europe and I came home to find a letter that said, "You are being considered for a Grammy nomination." I told Abdullah that I thought they had the wrong person. They said that you have to send eight copies of your record to the Academy of Recorded Sound immediately. Of course, it was a foregone conclusion that someone with a small label and only their second recording wasn't going to get the award. But I was happy that I was being considered seriously by the critics. That nomination inspired me to do another album I called* Memories and Dreams, *which has my "Liberation Suite." I was stunned because it just took off.*

The success of *Memories and Dreams* inspired Sathima to do *Windsong*. This is the album in which Sathima claims she found herself musically, but it is clear she begins to self-consciously assert herself as a woman as well. She recalled,

I start off the album with the old African American spiritual "Sometimes I Feel Like a Motherless Child." For twenty-five years I used to start all my shows with that old song. This was while my mother was alive even though she was away from me. It was as if I was singing the song to her, telling her how much I missed her as a child. But now she is no longer alive I can't sing that song anymore. I also used to sing it at funerals a lot. But it's not coming from that faraway place that it used to. It's over now.

"Windsong" is the song and the name of the group I used to take with me when I occasionally traveled. That song is my space capsule: it is what I am really all about. It is about keeping your heart in tune and atuned to what is really happening. And I believe there is a song that blows on the wind. You will only hear it if your heart is open. It is subtle and nuanced, and it carries tenderness and compassion in its sound. I am really old-fashioned, you know, because I believe that women and mothers have to catch tenderness and compassion and give it to their children, both boys and girls. These qualities are lacking in the world, but I have to believe that the Creator lets compassion blow on the wind. You can see that it is gone here in the United States, but in Africa you still can find it. Africa is always a little bit behind, but I have one foot here and one foot there. I dedicated that album to the struggles of women and children in South Africa. And I used the photographs of Tsidi and myself for the cover to represent all women and children in the struggle.

"Windsong," and "Music" came at about the same time. First came a bass line,

then the rhythm, and then the words. Much later the melody came too. I didn't have a melody: I just walked around with this bass line and words for a long time. But the musicians all love going into that music: there's so much space in "Wind-song." It leaves so much space for everybody. There is a structure, but it's also very open. You have to listen to each other: we cannot just ignore each other. They have to listen to me. I have to listen to them. Because the musicians I perform with have worked with themselves, they know how to listen to each other. And we have fun, we swing a little, I let everyone play a part, and then I take it out again. Everything is very spiritual because I can't write anything down. When the musicians are like this I know they are ready for "Windsong," musically and spiritually, and they embrace it.

Lovelight was the next album, recorded in 1987 and distributed by Enja Records in 1988. South Africans in exile in Europe in the 1960s and 1970s were known for the tributes they paid to other American and South African musicians through the music they wrote. Three tribute songs came to Sathima, one for Duke, one for Holiday, and a suite-like song for the now-fallen political hero Winnie Madikizela Mandela, the ex-wife of the then-political prisoner Nelson Rolihlahla Mandela. She also paid tribute to family and friends through songs composed by others but rendered in her particular style.

When the controversial piece she wrote in the mid-1980s for Winnie Mandela came to Sathima, Winnie Mandela was under house arrest, and there were no signs that Nelson Mandela would be released from prison anytime soon. Winnie Mandela, who relentlessly opposed the apartheid regime, had just published her autobiography *Part of My Soul Went With Him* in which she is portrayed heroically.[13] Another side to the woman would emerge in 1989 — when her bodyguards were accused of abducting and later killing a young soccer player Stompie Moeketsi. Sathima's tribute to Winnie Mandela should be read in light of the political context of the mid-1980s in South Africa:

There was all this controversy around Winnie Mandela just as I was about to re-lease Lovelight, *which has her song on it. I was told not to release the* CD. *But it's a good sign for me if something is going to be problematic, because I am used to having to survive against the odds. I did a lot of interviews about that song, and have always asked why can't we look at her track record of good things and not just her errors? What about the impact of solitary confinement on her personality?*

She could have chosen to do different things with her life, but for twenty-seven years she put her life on the line for Mandela. She survived a long separation with Nelson in prison and raised her children alone. She is human, and anyway, most of the time, we are just pawns in this big game.

That is why it is important to find out who you are, and what you want to do. I have always believed that given different circumstances we would have seen her as a wonderful woman, a survivor, a social worker who is very compassionate. But she has also been very vulnerable, without anyone to really protect her. Her husband was in prison. She couldn't talk to him on the telephone, or write personal letters. In apartheid South Africa, you had to keep your wits about you, I mean they were going to get you sooner or later. So I put out that song and continued to sing it despite the controversies around Winnie Mandela, because she spearheaded a movement for women. It took a lot of sacrifice. I am glad I wrote that song for Winnie.

Compositionally, the "Song for Winnie" just arrested me. It woke me up from my sleep and I had to call Don Sickler, the jazz arranger and trumpeter, and say, "Please write this down." Then I had to get Buster. I just had this song for Winnie. I didn't have the first part, the Nomzamo (Winnie's Xhosa name meaning one who endures difficult times) thing, so I went and did that other part. I had Buster Williams write it down. Recently he said to me, "I wrote that song" and I said, "Are you crazy, Buster? Sing it to me." And he couldn't. I said, "You didn't write it, but you did help me. You wrote it down, Buster." It was an extremely difficult song. We wrote it and then I came home and when I was making the children's supper, the Nomzamo part came. So I had to call him again. And I said, "This is the bass line."

That's another thing, Carol. Why is it that I write bass lines? So so many of my songs, "Music," "Africa," "Song for Winnie," start with bass lines. And so many pay tribute—the Song for Duke and Lady Day, these are portrait songs. It's amazing how I can't write a song for Abdullah. He's too magnificent, maybe one day I will think about whether I can write a song for him. I did write a poem called "Ahuri" many, many years ago and it's in a book somewhere. I don't even know how it goes. But I did. Maybe I could put that to music.

Anyway, it took a long while to write the song for Winnie Mandela because it came in three sections. I put an appeal out to God, or the Higher Spirit, or Creator. I wanted to write this song for Winnie, because I absolutely identified with her. I could feel her pain. I wanted to write this song, but it was the most difficult song I have written. It came in bits and pieces, so it is a complicated piece, like a mini-suite. It has different sections because women have different sides to their person-

alities. You could have three husbands and still they wouldn't know all about you. We are very mysterious—how could we expect our husbands to understand us? Someone is going to kill me for this, I am sure! I could see many sides to Winnie Mandela, her connection with Nelson—what a wonderful love to survive all that. I could see her political views: I could see her as an African woman representing womanhood across Africa.

I just remembered the pieces as they came. As I washed the dishes it would go through my mind. I have a very tiny kitchen, but at least when I am in there, running the water, I can't hear anyone else. I use that time to sing without actually singing, to sing inside. I wash dishes a lot. I use that place, it's a private place in a large apartment where there are no other private places for me. It makes me feel comfortable, and relaxed. I am never just washing dishes, I think a lot as I work. And running water is very soothing.

Southern Touch, Sathima's sixth album, was written in response to the trip she made to Europe during which she was asked why she always sang love songs if she was from South Africa. In conversation with students at Marymount College in Tarrytown, New York, in November 1990, Sathima talked about *Southern Touch*:

I am calling it Southern Touch *because I realize that through all of this there isn't anyone from South Africa doing jazz music. Jazz originated here in this country in the deep South with African Americans. It didn't come from anywhere else, and African Americans came from Africa. It wasn't jazz as we know it, it was a cry, it was pain, the pain is the same in South Africa and the traumas have been similar, if slightly different. And the connection is there music-wise. That's how it unfolded for me. And the music actually should be spontaneous. You have to have your stuff together and you have to come through what I have to get there. I couldn't have started with jazz: I had to grow into it. It's a process. You have to be patient with yourself, and it's the friends and people who are on the path with you, with the music, who will nurture you, guide and help you. It's in the sentence they say, or a look they give you that lets you know everything is ok.*

Sathima's next recording, released in 1997, was *A Morning in Paris*, the CD she produced out of the session in Paris in 1963 with Ellington, Strayhorn, Svend Asmussen, and the Dollar Brand Trio (see chap. 4 for discussion). Her recording *Cape Town Love*, from 1999, is the focus of chapter 6, and the song and recording entitled *Musical Echoes*, from 2002, frames the discussion in chapter 7. Sathima has also released two compilation recordings, *The Best of Sathima and Friends* (2001) and *Song Spirit* (2006), a compilation celebrating her seventieth birthday that includes all the pianists she has worked with over the years. She elaborated on her experiences with her record company:

Each little success—every record got me 4 or 4 ½ stars with Downbeat. *That's the story of how I ran Ekapa Records—one thing led to another. And it continues to do so. When I started doing Ekapa in 1979, the only other woman I knew running her own label in New York City was Betty Carter.*[14] *She's the other jazz singer who couldn't get the industry to take notice. So she decided she had to have her own label. She took her trio and consistently did her own stuff. Verve Records finally bought her over, they bought her whole catalog, and she could spend her time reissuing. She got that deal, so nothing belonged to her anymore, but her work paid off in the end.*

I would like the same thing to happen for me, but they would have to pay me. Because making that music was real blood, sweat, and tears—it's like giving your babies away. It would have to be for a price. Then I could use that money to create new projects. In retrospect I realize that I set up Ekapa because I didn't want to lose my freedom—if you go with the big companies you are going to be controlled. I have a lot of freedom with Ekapa. I choose my musicians, my title, my songs, my engineer. And when I am finished producing the recording, I get a larger company to distribute for me. I always say I have this little record company. I'm the President; I'm the musician; I'm the messenger; I go to the post office; I pay the taxes. I do absolutely everything.

Jazz Critics

For more than four decades it is the critics, those who know the lineage into which Sathima has inserted herself, who have been the staunchest supporters of her work. Despite the fact that Sathima's music is produced on her own label, several critics respectfully review each new recording. I have selected a handful of these reviews from the early years up to the present that illustrate their take on her place in the world of jazz. John S. Wilson of the *New York Times* reviewed Sathima's first performance in New York City. In the review, published on 1 March 1976, Wilson wrote that Sathima rendered the Ellington repertory in a "fresh and imaginative light." He described her voice as "vibrant and dark toned, with instrumental inflections paralleling Johnny Hodges; with a lot saxophone in 'In a Sentimental Mood.'" Wilson stresses her individual style in the ways in which she placed her voice "in provocative duets with Buster Williams." He describes the rest of the program in positive terms, ending with the following comment, a true tribute to Sathima's originality of voice and style: "But despite the firm, controlled sense of direction that Miss Benjamin brought to her interpretations, her trio — with Onaje Allan Gumbs, piano, and Azzedin Weston, congas — was so spirited and sensitive that the concert after seemed as much the instrumentalists' as it was Miss Benjamin's."

In *Downbeat* (1982), the critic Fred Bouchard wrote glowingly of a live performance at Carnegie Recital Hall. Bouchard relished the individuality of Benjamin's style, while referencing the vocal timbre of Holiday: "Sathima's concert in the dim, cosy [Carnegie] recital hall was sheer autobiography in song. She began her smooth unhurried way by exhorting the music with free associative poetry: 'Sing naturally, like a bird. . . .' She soared through two more orienting originals, 'Music' and 'Africa,' backed nicely by a quartet led by pianist Onaje Allan Gumbs. Her [South] African grandmother reared her on pop ballads not jazz, so she sang oldies like 'Just a Song at Twilight' and 'When We Were Very Young,' with tinges of Holiday tone and intensity and a beautifully relaxed phrasing all her own. Teenage nightclub days had her dust off 'Embraceable You,' 'You Do Something To Me,' and 'Someone to Watch Over Me' (with a fine Gumbs chorus) that she built strong as pyramids, and creamy as kefir. Sathima developed the set with more standards, capped with a unique version of 'Say It Isn't So' (in a Cape Town rhythm, a hair's breadth from calypso, where she squeezed out languorous quarter tones) and 'A Nightingale Sang in Berkeley Square,' decidedly un-British with parts of phrases repeated with great warmth and feeling."

Similarly, in a review of an early New York recital in 1983 the critic Jon Pareles wrote, "That voice is throaty and ethereal with just a hint of smokiness. Ms. Benjamin glides into a song, turning a melody into a series of smooth arcs and gracefully tapering off the ends of phrases. She favors slow tempos and even when her arrangements used a Latin or African groove — like the ingenious version of 'I Let a Song Go Out of My Heart,' her vocal lines took their time. She and the trio move in and out of time while maintaining a subliminal pulse, she could make a word cry out with just a flicker of vibrato."[15]

A fourth review from the jazz critics Bruce Crowther and Ed Anderson pays tribute to her style: "When it comes to the moment of performance, an overriding quality comes into effect. Every song that she sings, from Victorian ballads to Ellington, the songs from the great musicals to her own musings upon life, is performed with impeccable taste. She treats each individual lyric with respect and with regard to the sentiment intended by the writer and in some cases finds therein more than perhaps the writer intended."[16]

Jim Santella on the website *All About Jazz.com* writes of the song "Musical Echoes" on her recording of 2006 of the same title,

> Benjamin and Stephen Scott wrote "Musical Echoes" for her return to Cape Town. The tender ballad provides a reflection of her illustrious career, reminding us of her heartfelt love for country, along with a contagious passion for jazz. Benjamin and her musical partners provide a personal take on what makes the world turn. Moses' expressive bass solos add considerable warmth, and the singer is able to convey her feelings intuitively. Her unique interpretations leave musical echoes that transcend politics and settle comfortably in a world of aesthetic beauty.
>
> Benjamin uses her veteran ears to experiment with pitch, and her accompanists follow suit. Bassist Basil Moses slides gently through "Caravan," for example, bringing its exotic sheen out into the daylight. Pianist Stephen Scott provides dense harmony, drummer Lulu Gontsana adds unique rhythmic syncopation, and Benjamin has the freedom to interpret each song with her own approach. She's on her own, with the freedom to interpret as she wishes. The result is a unique performance that echoes her true spirit.

Life from the 1990s On

In the preface to this book I invoked the pivotal moment in February 1990 when President F. W. de Klerk declared he would lift the ban on the organizations of the liberation movement and just a short time thereafter stated that he would release Nelson Mandela and other political prisoners. Because of the pressure on the U.S. Congress in the late 1980s to impose economic sanctions on South Africa, the decades-long cultural boycott against South Africa, the prominence of the organization Artists

United Against Apartheid in the United States and Britain, and the support given to the South African fight against apartheid abroad by African Americans, de Klerk's pronouncements and the subsequent release of a range of political prisoners, including Nelson Mandela and Walter Sizulu, induced in South Africans living in places like New York City, London, and Berlin a feeling of the surreal.

Did de Klerk's declaration mean that those who had been in exile for so long could really return to South Africa?[17] Could those long silenced by the apartheid regime have their music aired on national radio and television? Could their voices now be heard in interviews and their words published in newspapers and books? For the better-known musicians like Makeba, Masekela, and Ibrahim, there was little doubt that going back to South Africa was the next step. But for lesser-known musicians, those like Sathima who were raising families and who had created deep connections to other places and communities and a feeling of home for themselves in the music, the possibilities of returning to South Africa were perhaps more complicated. Sathima was clear from the outset that she wanted to return, not just as a South African citizen, though that was important to her, but as a musician in her own right, one who would be welcomed back. She wanted the recognition of her quite extraordinary accomplishments—her participation in the anti-apartheid struggle, her fight as a woman, a mother, and, most of all, as a singer of jazz. She would quickly discover that reincorporation was a complicated process.

Nevertheless, in postapartheid South Africa the infrastructural support of jazz has grown considerably since 1990, with numerous festivals and educational initiatives in the field of jazz. In 1995 Sathima was invited to perform at the JVC Jazz Festival in Johannesburg. She headlined at the North Sea Jazz Festival in Cape Town in 2002 with the same trio she used in recording *Musical Echoes* (2002). In the same year she was invited to perform at the prestigious "Women in Jazz" series at the Kennedy Center in Washington. Her extraordinary passion and significant contribution to South African cultural history and to the place of women in that history have been acknowledged in the last few years. In 2002 she received the "South African Women for Women" award in Toronto. In March 2005 Pen and Brush, an arts group based in New York, presented her with a "Certificate of Achievement" as a performer, musician, composer, and activist in the human rights struggle against apartheid.

The definitive sign of return came when President Thabo Mbeki of
South Africa presented Sathima with the "Order of Ikhamanga," an award
for excellence in the arts, culture, literature, music, journalism, and sport.
Sathima was honored at a gala ceremony in the Union Buildings in Pretoria on 29 October 2004. The award cited her for her "contribution as a
jazz artist in the development of music in South Africa and abroad" and
for her contribution to the "struggle against apartheid." She was invited
to travel to South Africa with Tsakwe to receive the award. It was a moment she will cherish for the rest of her life.

About 2006 a young graduate of Columbia University, Seton Hawkins,
contacted Sathima, and since then he has worked for her on a part-time
basis, helping her to release recordings in the United States and increase
access to her catalog with distribution on the World Wide Web and in
other venues.[18] Over the last decade or so, recently with the assistance
of Hawkins, Sathima has organized a regular gig at Sweet Rhythm, a jazz
club in in the East Village in New York previously known as Sweet Basil.
At least twice a year, sometimes more, she gathers a trio of her favorite
African American musicians together. Well into South Africa's second
decade of freedom, it is quite extraordinary to witness the gathering of all
manner of South Africans, including many categorized as white, around
the music of the South African–born woman.

These moments bring the story told in this book full circle. From the
passionate and racially diverse community of jazz musicians and fans of
the late 1950s to the silencing of the music, to the exit by death or escape
of so many South African musicians in the years of grand apartheid, to a
transnational, completely non-racialized community that meets to celebrate the love, the voice, and the sound of this eminent artist from South
Africa.

On 23 January 2008 Sathima organized a live performance at Sweet
Rhythm, and it was announced that Tsidi, now in her thirties, would
perform alongside her. At the performance, Tsidi sat in the shadows on
the side of the stage for much of the first set and then walked onto the
platform with a huge bouquet of flowers for Sathima. She embraced her
mother, and the two launched into a moving call and response. The event
marked a beautiful moment of intergenerational musical transmission of
the old and new African diasporic genres, jazz and hip-hop. In April 2009
Sathima performed again at Sweet Rhythm to honor what would have
been Duke Ellington's 102d birthday.

23. Sathima singing at
Sweet Rhythm.

24. Sathima's favorite bass player,
Buster Williams.

Both photos by Carol Ann Muller.

25. The bass player Buster Williams and the drummer George Grey play at Sathima's seventieth birthday at Sweet Rhythm.

26. Sathima singing at Sweet Rhythm, with Stephen Scott on piano.

Both photos by Carol Ann Muller.

27. Sathima with her daughter, the hip-hop artist Tsidi Ibrahim, aka Jean Grae, at Sweet Rhythm.

28. Sathima's sister Joan Franciscus at Sweet Rhythm.

Both photos by Carol Ann Muller.

New York City: Meditating in Motion

Sathima is passionate about living in New York City, but how does she conceptualize that relationship? She calls it the New York embrace, a reciprocal relationship of embracing and being embraced by the utter humanness of the city and its peoples. "Europe was good for honing my craft," she said, "because I really couldn't connect to anyone there. New York is very different. You need the vitality here, all the musicians are here: you feel the energy here. I have a love-hate relationship with New York, who doesn't? You can never get complacent about where you are or what you are doing. There is something that the city gives you that no other city gives you. It is a kind of vibrancy that is in the air — polluted air, for God's sake. I mean I have lived here for so many years and the city is MY beloved New York now."

To Sathima New York represents the ultimate in opportunity and community for an artist, especially a jazz musician. It provides a sense of home, of being well placed, of feeling you can function. Home, for Sathima, is a place where you can be yourself without having to conform. In New York's neighborhoods people may get to know you, or you might wish to remain anonymous. The city nurtures jazz as a quintessentially urban rhetorical and musical practice. Jazz performance is the musical parallel to the experience of inhabiting the city as a walker, what Michel de Certeau (1988) calls "walking in the city." Both jazz and the city are spaces filled with surprises, requiring improvisatory skills to survive. Jazz works as a discourse of musical travel: every individual on her or his own path, sometimes connecting, at other times just going it alone, but operating always within the larger map of the city and the performance.

Like de Certeau's walker, Sathima embraces the city through a process she calls meditation in motion. The meditation part is thinking about life itself, practicing selflessness in the presence of those around her. But there is also a spiritual dimension: "It's about me talking to God. Sometimes I actually talk to God, I walk in the street and I just talk to God. And it's okay because everyone in New York talks to themselves. It doesn't matter. People don't think you are nuts. I mean, really, people are talking to themselves all the time."

Being always on the move is a lesson learned from Ma Benjamin in her childhood. She never allowed anyone to just sit and, for example, listen to the radio. If she were caught sitting and listening, her grandmother would reprimand her: "Why don't you just get right inside that thing, the big old radio?" Sathima said, "Basically I am very happy when I am keeping busy and moving. And that really means walking: I walk and I walk. I wouldn't go to church, I wouldn't feel right: I would feel fenced in, in a box, so I prefer to go to church walking in the street with everybody. There are lots of distractions on your walk, sometimes they are good and sometimes they are bad. That's the real way to meditate. You have to see and experience everything. I mean I can't be a Buddha; I can't sit on a mat and meditate."

More specifically, Sathima's sense of the city is inextricably tied to her memories of Ellington: "I have a love for New York City I can't quite explain. It allowed me to be, to do my thing. And I have been somewhat embraced. I couldn't have been in Zurich, and it is very easy to get lost in London. So I think I am fortunate and I have to thank Duke Ellington, who is magic to me. He's mysterious and magical. It started a long time ago, there's a connection there. These are mysterious things. I met Abdullah through Ellington's music, and we didn't know several years later we were going to leave and then we'd meet Ellington. And then he'd bring us here. And I can't think of anyone finer in the jazz world. I always say I rode on his wings, and I'm still on his wings."

Ellington's continued presence is regularly experienced by her through visions, dreams, in bookstores, on television, and, of course, on recordings of his music aired on jazz radio stations and through the replays of old jazz standards on the audio channels of digital television. These sounds without images evoke the intimacy and warmth projected by radio broadcasts of English and American music in Sathima's childhood home in Cape Town. This virtual relationship with Ellington is not that different in the early twenty-first century from when she was a young woman living in Cape Town in the 1940s and 1950s. As if coming from nowhere, his voice suddenly sounds in Sathima's head or she sees his image on television, in a bookstore, or in a commercial. Sathima's sense of the presence of Ellington extended into our research process. Just before she met me in May 2005 to talk about Holiday, she suddenly heard his voice on the radio—it is only rarely one hears Ellington's voice anywhere. "You see," she told me, "he knew I had to come and talk to you today, so I know he is with me." Assuming almost religious proportions, the master of jazz, a musician beyond category for so many, retains his presence in Sathima's life and imagination in a variety of media, and he makes his presence known in unexpected but, it seems, always timely moments.

Sathima's embrace expands beyond ancestral presence and comes from the jazz community itself: "I don't ever see the musicians, we don't socialize together. They are very busy. We try to rehearse, but if not, we have to leave it to chance. I know they love me and I love them, and we love the music." This community of what Sathima and others call true jazz artists in New York is like an extended family.[19] There is an uneasy relationship with the family, everyone competing for work, everyone struggling to survive. And as Sathima and Abdullah quickly learned, in contrast to their Cape Town experience, if you want to perform with these guys, they have to be paid. Nothing is done for nothing—except during the years of struggle. But you come together for specific ritual occasions, such as with the family to celebrate the holidays and in jazz to creatively fashion familial reunion in the very structures of improvised performance.

New York City works almost as a country unto itself for Sathima. After the launch of Lars Rasmussen's volume *Sathima Bea Benjamin: Embracing Jazz* at the South African consulate in New York in December 2000, Sathima talked about her sense of the city in exactly that way. She never thought in terms of the United States as a whole, seeing herself as a member of one of the five boroughs of the city. She is not alone in this sense of habitation or identification with the city as state. In an address to the European Parliament of Writers, Jacques Derrida talks of places like Paris and London that have similarly constituted themselves as "cities of refuge" for many who have come seeking sanctuary from repressive regimes. Such cities, Derrida writes, necessarily consider themselves relatively independent of the state, a view that feeds into the conversation about defining what one means when one talks about American music and how it is defined beyond the borders of the United States.[20] Ultimately, the history of the extended jazz family is an integral dimension of New York City's own history: Holiday, Ellington, Strayhorn, Vaughan, the grand ancestors of the tradition, all honed their craft and made their mark in New York. Sathima feels a deep sense of identification with the city's jazz community, even if it is only as a distant cousin.

Conclusion

I have outlined the biographical and musical details of Sathima's move to New York City, a move that in many ways made a place for Sathima to be a woman in a very conventional way: as a mother and wife. Yet she was forced by political circumstance to step out of the safety of her role as mother into the public eye as a political activist, voicing her opposition to apartheid through her music, a stand that cost her her South African citizenship. Because she has long felt the call of music as a force in her life, she did what few other jazz musicians have done: create an independent record label as a means of documenting her music in the studio and ensuring a place for herself in the annals of jazz history. With each recording she tells a part of her life story and renders a narrative about South Africa's place in the reception and creation of jazz repertory and style.

RESPONSE

Women Thinking in Jazz, or the Poetics of a Musical Self

Ellington said when he brought me here, "You have the greatest gift of all that God can give anybody, that's the gift of imagination because if you can imagine things, the sky is the limit in jazz and in life itself."
— Sathima Bea Benjamin, 16 March 1990

Paul Berliner's *Thinking in Jazz: The Infinite Art of Improvisation* (1993) was a monumental intervention in ethnomusicology and jazz studies for the breadth of information it provided about what happens when jazz musicians improvise or spin out complex musical utterances in the absence of music written as a template. The book was important to ethnomusicology equally for its use of the voices of musicians themselves — the ethnographic as a means of data collection; and for the ways in which it spelled out in concrete terms just how musicians think in the moment of performance. I have returned to Berliner's work many times over the years as I have grappled with the challenge of creating a rhetorical space in jazz studies for Sathima as a singer of jazz not born in the United States. Contrasting with the lack of recognition Sathima has experienced as a singer from South Africa, there are numerous instances of overlap between how Sathima talks about jazz composition and performance and the discourses of Berliner's interlocutors. Some of the musicians he interviewed, like Kenny Barron and Buster Williams, for example, have performed with Sathima. Further, Berliner refers repeatedly to what it was like to work with Betty Carter, a singer whom Sathima never met but whose artistic independence she has long admired. Sathima clearly fits the discursive dimensions of jazz thinking. And she has much to add as a South African–born woman in jazz.

My purpose here is to extend ideas about "thinking in jazz" beyond the focus on improvisation and the mostly male musicians Berliner interviewed. I want to ask what the contours of thinking in jazz might look like in a more intentionally women-centered account. The inserting of women into the canonical narratives of male-centered jazz history and articulating the gendering of jazz itself are developments of the last two decades or so, emerging from the work of journalists and scholars like Sally Placksin (1982), Elaine Hayes (2004), Hazel Carby (1998), Sherrie Tucker (2000), Farah Griffin (2001), Stuart Nicholson (1995), Angela Davis (1998), and others. While this field of scholarship has made important strides, it remains rich with possibility for exploring not only American women in jazz, but also the many women in other parts of the world, women like Sathima, who have adopted jazz as a vehicle for personal expression, musical exploration, and individual freedom.

The first challenge is to situate Sathima's music, biography, and ways of thinking about jazz into a more general discourse on women in jazz. To this end I draw on Margery Wolf's *A Thrice-Told Tale* (1992) as a model for placing Benjamin in a larger lineage of jazzwomen by harnessing three textual forms. My discussion begins with a summary of themes in the life stories of jazzwomen contained in a collection gathered by Wayne Enstice and Janice Stockhouse (2004) entitled *Jazzwomen: Conversations with Twenty-One Musicians*. The interviews are intentionally gendered in terms of the questions posed by the interviewers, and the responses of the jazzwomen overlap significantly with Sathima's life experiences in jazz, with some exceptions pertaining to her life story. My purpose is to locate Sathima's narrative in a body of experiences held in common by a wide range of women jazz musicians. Turning to the biographical, I examine the formation of Sathima's "jazz self" in several distinct phases of her life, which requires selectively revisiting key points in her life story discussed earlier in the book. In contrast to the generalizing impulse of the first discussion, the biographical stresses the particular and idiosyncratic. Third, Sathima speaks in her own words to tell how she has shaped the discourse of jazz to her own purposes, thereby placing herself firmly into its community of performers and composers. I reflect on how Sathima has imagined herself as a woman in jazz by drawing on Nadia Serematakis's ideas (2006) about the poetics of the everyday and a self-reflexive femininity. I position her femininity in contrast to the forms of masculinity that, according to Carby, writing about Miles Davis, jazz instills for many male musicians.

Women Thinking in Jazz

The collection *Jazzwomen* is composed of interviews with twenty-one jazzwomen, mostly instrumentalists but also some singers and mostly from North America. Enstice conceived of the volume in response to a question posed by a woman jazz musician: was she in the earlier volume of interviews with jazz musicians he had compiled? He realized, to his dismay, that his and Paul Rubin's earlier book of interviews, *Jazz Spoken Here* (1992, 1994), focused exclusively on male musicians. Enstice resolved to remedy the startlingly poor representation of jazzwomen in books by producing *Jazzwomen* in collaboration with Stockhouse. Because of the pressure Enstice felt to get the work published, the book provides transcribed segments of much longer interviews conducted with these women. Though readers are not told how the excerpts were selected, each piece is interesting as a free-standing interview. There is, nevertheless, an inconsistency in the kinds of questions posed and biographical materials provided, making it hard to generalize about themes common to all the women. As a result, there is no synthesis of the relationship between gender, jazz performance, and the stories told by these women in the book. The volume is nevertheless quite useful from the perspective of South African women thinking in jazz precisely because so many of the experiences, ideas, and practices shared by the women in the interviews overlap with Sathima's perspective. In this sense, much of what these jazzwomen have to say is not specifically American in character.

Like Sathima, many of these jazzwomen learned the jazz repertory by listening closely to the radio and to recordings played in the home and often by transgressing parental authority in order to hear the music live; several of the older generation expressed an ambivalence about institutional musical training — college and university jazz programs — and sometimes were reluctant to learn to write music; a few of these older women claimed with pride and a sense of authenticity that they had never had a single formal lesson in their lives.

Many of the women valued jazz as a musical means of self-expression, others for its storytelling capacity. Some took up jazz because of its more generically masculine attributes, that is, performance that demanded they take risks, assume a particular kind of freedom, and embrace the chance to live and perform on the edge. One or two women talked about jazz as a vehicle for defying the odds, on one hand, but also as being a fairly solitary path, on the other. Some relished the lifestyle, even though it usually negated possibilities of personal accumulation of economic prosperity.

Jazzwomen's relationships to male musicians were frequently expressed in a positive or neutral light, except for the moments when they were pressured to exchange sex for opportunity. Several of the women saw the world of jazz opened to them as performers through male intervention — they were transformed by a recording of John Coltrane, for example, or by a male musician who made a critical invitation or introduction that opened professional doors. There was minimal discussion about being married to or sexually involved with other jazz musicians. A few of the women mentioned giving up portions of their careers in order to raise their children, a part of the story one simply never reads about where male musicians are concerned.[21]

Consistently these women talked about the lack of female role models in the profession; there were very few women in the industry, and almost none working as critics. Finding a manager seemed to be a perennial challenge to the women. Few women in jazz, those in this book or generally, risked forming their own label, as Sathima did (with Abdullah's help initially); some were lucky to be signed by a commercial label — Enja Records, for example — while others performed almost exclusively live.

Billie Holiday occupied a key position in the call to jazz for several women, thereby creating a female-centered musical lineage. More than a few traced their musical heritage to the sound and place of Holiday in jazz and blues history. One woman's childhood experiences included the loss of her mother and some abuse, experiences that both Holiday and Sathima had undergone. Like Sathima, that woman harnessed the music not to articulate her victimization, as many think Holiday did, but to transcend the pain and humiliation of those early years. As it was for Holiday, race was a factor in shaping the experiences of several of these women in jazz and the world at large, though there is not much expansion on any political involvement that may have enhanced or detracted from their career paths.

Finally, a handful of women talked in ways that parallel Sathima's imaginative response to jazz. They mused about the larger psychic and spiritual dimensions of jazz performance and creation, and some recalled dream experiences that had proved to be pivotal interventions in their journeys into the music. Several focused on jazz and its capacity to nurture, nourish, sustain, and, indeed, to heal emotionally and psychologically. Many of the singers focused on the interpretation of love songs as their core repertory. Some talked about compositional process and preparation for live and studio recordings.

Sathima's Life Story

When you sing for instance you are not just using your voice, you are using your whole reaction to life itself, and jazz allows you to do that. — Sathima Bea Benjamin, 16 March 1990

While I have outlined the significant overlaps in biographical themes and details between Sathima and these jazzwomen, the fundamental difference pertains to the fact that Sathima was born a woman of mixed race in South Africa, and she lived through the transition to apartheid and its demise. To survive as a jazz musician she was forced to leave South Africa and endure years of incessant travel in search of work in unfamiliar countries and amidst communities who simply didn't recognize her as a jazz singer coming from Africa. Her formative and migratory years profoundly shaped her sense of self as a woman, her output as a singer, and the strategies she has harnessed to articulate a place for herself in jazz.

Decades of continuous movement have impeded her capacity to position herself as a jazz musician in a single city or country, to build a loyal audience base, or even to secure a contract with a major label for her lifework, as Betty Carter, Shirley Horn, and Abbey Lincoln were able to do. Furthermore, Sathima projects herself as a particular kind of woman, one who prioritized being a mother available to her children as they grew up in New York City; she was thrust into addressing the political issues that apartheid imposed upon people of color, particularly those in exile; she desired to be a supportive wife to Abdullah, though few jazz musicians survive as couples for extended periods of time; and by her own admission, she is traditional, even old-fashioned in her values and beliefs. Strong and passionate, her values and beliefs are intense and uncompromisingly articulated in her life and music.

Biography is a useful analytical tool for thinking about many women in jazz for two reasons. First, the life story provides a comprehensive picture of the formative years, specific moments of transformation, and the long-term development as an artist. This picture of the *longue durée* is necessary if one is to understand women for whom jazz is just one of many activities that occupy their time and also because developing a distinctive voice in jazz takes years, even for those who pursue their careers full time. In contrast, for example, to Abdullah, who has dedicated his life to the pursuit of jazz, Sathima's days, with the birth of her second child, have been filled with the mundane: caring for the family, supporting Abdullah, paying bills, sorting out the taxes. Sathima's musical career has had to be squeezed into the routine demands of everyday life, extending out of what she was already doing for Abdullah. It is really only in the last decade or so that Sathima has begun to carve out her own place in jazz, while Abdullah has been regularly recording since the 1960s. Second, the life story of many jazzwomen (particularly the older generation of living musicians) requires that our analysis be focused on the poetics of everyday life, on finding a balance intellectually between the forgetfulness and demands produced by the mundane and the joyful remembering that creating and performing jazz instills in its makers, listeners, and scholars.

Phase One: Formative Years

Sathima's earliest memory of her own music making was that it was inserted into the crevice or secret spaces of everyday life. The first source of such activity was her grandmother's radio and the popular songs that streamed out of the box daily while she did chores in the kitchen, cooking, cleaning, and ironing clothes. These songs were intended to function as background music, but Sathima remembers being deeply moved by the words and melodies and wanting to sing them herself. She secretly created a repertory that she sang in competitions held during intermission at the movies. The point here is that listening and gathering songs was a forbidden pleasure — Sathima's grandmother did not know the girl was singing these songs in public from about the age of eleven, and it had to be kept secret — but this music transformed the daily schedule of cooking, ironing, and cleaning from the mundane into the memorable and musical.

At the time, Sathima's repertory included songs like "Somewhere over the Rainbow," performed by white women from England and America. "You began by copying, by sounding just the same as Joni James or Ella Fitzgerald," Sathima recalled, "but eventually you had to move away from that. Eventually you had to sound like yourself. No two singers are the same." Sathima stopped singing those songs when she became more aware of the politics of race and coloured identity, but they were the first signs of the possibilities of travel through music, and they were first heard in the kitchen, a place in which Sathima would spend much of her time when she settled in New York City to raise her children.

This body of vocal material was supplemented with the dance hall melodies originally played by several saxophones in dance bands in Cape Town; Sathima assumed the line of the saxophone in remaking the music and then found the words in sheet music stores in New York. Finally, she would add to her repertory the music she gleaned from the recordings of Holiday and Ellington that traveled to South Africa in the postwar period. This music has been reconstituted in many moments of stillness through years of diasporic movement and after she settled in New York. In restoring a repertory of songs from her childhood through the language of jazz "an entire past sensory landscape was translated into a present act" of musical remembrance and celebration (Serematakis 1996, 16).

Phase Two: Revolutions of the Heart

The British social psychologist Wendy Langford (1999) argues that falling in love produces in women the feeling that they have the capacity
for deep emotional connection, strong feelings of intimacy, attachment,
and the freedom to be themselves. Falling in love means finding companionship; it fulfills a desire for a sense of security and enables women
to move out of the controlled environment of being children in a patriarchal household into a space where the couple — and Langford's focus
is the heterosexual man and woman in love — is autonomous and free to
make decisions about their lives without interference.

Langford proposes two heterosexual models for falling in love in the
contemporary Western world: the romantic and the democratic love
models. In the romantic love model a woman falls in love as outlined
above. There is in this model, nevertheless, a point of counterrevolution
when disillusionment and disappointment in the male partner often sets
in for a woman. At this point they fall back into the wife as mother figure
in their relationship, rationalizing the incompleteness and weaknesses, as
a mother would where her child was concerned. The man in the relationship will then begin to view his spouse as either a good mommy, one who is
always forgiving and filled with unconditional love; or a bad mummy, one
who tricks or teases him and and makes demands he cannot hope to sat-
isfy. In this model men ultimately begin to exert demoralizing control over
their spouses, and women try to figure out what makes their partners tick.
The alternative model is the more democratic practice based on reason. In
this model, individual women and men both know what they want, what is
good for them, and how to negotiate an equitable place for themselves in
the relationship. Despite the ideals of equality and freedom that a democratic model would appear to embody, Langford argues that this model
produces similar outcomes to the romantic love process. She concludes
her book by suggesting that love remains a dubious ideal for most of us
in the contemporary world as we elevate it to the level of the spiritual and
mysterious. Despite our best desires, love remains a form of dystopia.

The two models of romantic and democratic relationship, articulated
as a kind of "revolution of the heart," are useful for framing what I suggest are the two moments of falling in love in Sathima's early life. The
first was when she chose to form a lasting relationship with Abdullah and

not to pursue marriage with her then-fiancé Sam Isaacs; and the second was her move into, her sense of falling in love, with the music. There is no doubt that the two processes were intertwined because, as Sathima often recalls, it was the music of Ellington and particularly the song "I Got It Bad and That Ain't Good" that brought her and Abdullah together. These were two individuals who were truly in love with the music: it was through their passion for jazz that they formed a long-term relationship. As much as their move into jazz, their romantic relationship was a rebellion. Love for the music, like love for each other, instilled feelings of freedom, intimacy, the capacity to be true to themselves, to take risks, and to move from one social status to another. While theirs was a largely romantic revolution of the heart, much later in life Sathima would begin to move toward the more democratic model, particularly in her relationship to jazz performance. This is outlined in her discourse on jazz composition, performance, and recording (see below).

Phase Three: Diasporic Reflection

Leaving home in 1962 and then living with Abdullah as a musical migrant was hard on Sathima. Europe offered occasional work but very little sense of home and familiarity. In this period she became far more introspective, reflecting on her heritage as a woman of mixed race and many origins. The memory of home and community sustained Sathima in these years: she began to look inside herself for inner strength, to remember past repertories, and to read on a wide range of subjects, all in search of a place in the world for a woman like herself. Personally and professionally these were challenging years.

Much of Sathima's time in Europe was spent taking care of the South African musicians she traveled with. The pain of exile led to severe bouts of substance abuse among the male musicians; she kept free from addiction but in the process had to take care of the men. This was the period in which she was named Sathima, the one who listens. She also spent her time on the road woodshedding and honing her vocal craft. During this time her first compositions were given to her, and she began to formulate a set of ideas that would link her to the larger African diaspora and its community of jazz performers. Sathima recorded several times, but there is little commercially available beyond the recording *A Morning in Paris*.

Phase Four: On Becoming a Woman in Jazz

Coming to New York City meant that Sathima had to begin to consolidate the range of musical, racial, political, and cultural experiences she had had and to make them work for her as a woman in jazz on her own terms. One of the primary challenges was to find a way to do all the things she had to do as wife, mother, and political activist, while still finding time to make music, either alone in her kitchen, in the recording studio, or in public. She couldn't be on the road very often; she wasn't able to perform live and thereby earn her keep or regularly rehearse with her trio. In other words, because she refused to give up on the music, she had to devise alternative means of creating, performing, and distributing her music, so she could remain at home; and she had to rely on Abdullah to fund her occasional projects in the recording studio. These were the compromises she made in order to fulfill her desire to be the best possible mother to her children.

In the domestic sphere, in the midst of the ebb and flow of everyday life Sathima pulled out the old repertories she remembered from her childhood and then gave them to her musicians. Collectively they breathed new life into the old repertory in the language of jazz; or she composed new songs given to her, she says, as gifts "from God." She has created a distinctive songbook by reintroducing songs from a past long forgotten by the trio but restored to their country of origin and newly made in performance into rare, beautiful things: beautiful in themselves but equally poignant in the face of a history of injustice, oppression, gendered struggle, and forgetfulness.[22]

Imaginatively harnessing the principles of jazz performance, Sathima has also constituted what Serematakis (1996) calls "moments of stillness," or what women often experience as "resting moments." "Stillness," writes Serematakis, "is the moment when the buried, the discarded, and the forgotten escape to the social surface of awareness like life-supporting oxygen."[23] Certain smells, practices, photographs, reissues played on radio or digital television triggered the depths of childhood memory, bringing into being melodies and texts Sathima had sung and danced to in her Cape Town days. These tunes opened up the possibility of remembering, an imaginative return to a particular place, event, or group of friends. Remembering in word and sound in a moment of stillness reconstituted a very old body of songs as something new, even biographical, for the South African singer in New York City.

Going Home

Going home involves returning to South Africa, musically and personally. She has gone back for several performance events, though Sathima strongly desires to return home musically as well. Ideally, this would mean being invited to teach young people about life and the world of jazz singing.

Mother of Song

Music is the spirit within you, within you. Deep within you, deep within you, deep within you is music, music, music. Find your sound, then let it flow, free and easy and out. — Sathima Bea Benjamin, "Music" (1988)

Sathima built a place for herself as a jazz singer, band leader, composer, and recording artist by extending the possibilities of jazz history into a distinctively female domain. There can be no doubt that Sathima's thinking in jazz is shaped by the specificity of her life experiences as a woman, a mother, a wife, and an artist born in South Africa.

In 1999, on a return trip to South Africa, Sathima expressed her sense of the early history of jazz. "Jazz," she commented, "is a cry. It is a survival skill for the spirit. I think it must have started with a woman who just let out a wail. Then came the accompaniment."[24] In other words, in Sathima's mind and imagination the earliest sounds of what is now called jazz were the unaccompanied utterances of a woman crying out, a woman longing for healing and wholeness, a woman yearning to be free. When Sathima sings, her voice constitutes a momentary acoustical tie to or echo of those original moments. Through song she carves out a utopian place formed of what she believes to be the ideal qualities of jazz music and its makers: spontaneity, love, respect, intuition, emotionality, subtlety, nuance, personal space, and human freedom. Music that reflects these qualities constitutes the poetic and emotional labor that Sathima produces in song performance.

Why jazz? For Sathima, jazz is a personal music, a vehicle to express one's very existence, to state what one feels about life. "My message here is be true to yourself," she told students in a class I taught at Marymount College in Tarrytown, New York, in 1990:

Listen to my song "Music" because the most important thing is to find your own sound. And when you do, everything gets easy. I wrote "Music" because we must all find our own individual sound. We all went through listening to other singers, you want to sound a little bit like them, or you just start in a vacuum. Do you remember I told you we had the local bands, and this Cape Town sound of the saxophone stretching the lines? I sing those old songs from the 1920s. When I teach these songs to American musicians they say, "Where did you find this, what is it?" They don't even know the music and it is actually from here. It went to Cape Town, and I am bringing it back to musicians in New York City. We give the song jazz changes, really hip changes underneath the melody, and I swing it. And then it sounds like I wrote it, but I didn't. It's just my memories of Cape Town that come back to me in New York City. All these musicians have this "fake" book. And they go through it and choose a song. I don't have a fake book. I don't even own one. Whatever I'm singing is in my repertory because I have heard it before and then it comes to mind again. There's a reason it comes to mind, and then you have to sing it.

The reason I am doing jazz is it affords you a certain amount of freedom of thought, freedom to be different and unique. And it dares you: it lets you pull out whatever courage you have. You have to take risks. That's the whole thing. I could have inherited this courage, I think even things like that come through in the genes. My mother had to take risks. Just growing up in South Africa not being white, you learnt how to survive and take risks. My grandmother taught me to be careful and stay out of trouble, but eventually I rebelled against that, that whole rebellion thing led me to jazz, I saw that as music of rebellion: maybe it wasn't but I think it really was.

The music doesn't speak to my head, it speaks to my heart, and I listen only to that. I have never been able to listen to what my head tells me. If I had, my whole life would have been different. This is where the music resides: within my heart. In my head I remember it all, but the music is all in my heart. They all say it must come from the heart. I think all jazz musicians, if they are jazz musicians, this is how we operate, and that is why it is such a dear music. What did Abdullah say? I wish I had said it, but Abdullah says that jazz is the most advanced music in the world: advanced because you dare to expose your heart. You leave yourself so open, so vulnerable. Your heart is an open book that you leave for everyone to read. Even

Buster [Williams] will say, "Sathima, you just put your whole heart out there." I say that you cannot be afraid to be vulnerable. People need to hear that, and that is what will draw your audience to you and you will get drawn to the audience.

When I asked her recently how she sees herself in the American-centered jazz singers' lineage, she responded by saying in addition to Billie Holiday, she sits between Betty Carter, who inspired her to form her own record label, and Abbey Lincoln. Why Abbey, I wondered?

First of all I was a really big fan of hers because basically I think there's this bond. Well, she doesn't know this because she doesn't know me. One time when I went to hear her, Abdullah said I should introduce myself to her. I told her I was Abdullah Ibrahim's wife and that I was also a jazz singer. Her only response was, "Oh, I know Abdullah Ibrahim." She didn't acknowledge that I'm a jazz singer. So I just shook her hand and said I was a great admirer. I live in New York City and when she sang I would come to listen.

What I like about Abbey is that she is just honest and forthright. But she has a very different approach from mine. When she sings she just goes on to the stage, and she's Abbey! It's like her audience is there, but you get the feeling, "Listen, this is me here, I don't care if you don't like what I am singing because this is my show." She takes total control. Maybe it's because for a while she was under, she was also married to Max Roach. They had a fiery relationship, and well in the end it worked for awhile but it didn't work forever. He loved her and he presented her to the world with the "Freedom Now Suite." I have heard it said he unleashed a lot of her inner power.

Ultimately, however, the "caged bird" as Abbey Lincoln describes her early life, set herself free by escaping the ambivalent relationship with Roach.[25]

It is curious, nevertheless, that while Sathima inserts a woman at the start of history—and we know it was Holiday's voice that provided a feeling of place for the Cape Town girl, she never performs with other women because she sees her performance as a kind of musical unity formed between the heart of the female singer and her male trio, who in turn communicate with the hearts of their listeners:

What I know it that I love performing with men, combining the yin and the yang. You see I am an old-fashioned romantic. That is why I don't perform with other women—the struggles for women are too great—it is better to relax inside the music with male performers. I am always amazed at what happens when men blend their musicality with mine in performance. To do so they have to be spiritually inclined, have worked with their spirits, and not allow their egos to get in the way of the music.

This is why the music is healing for me. My grandmother drummed into me that I had to be submissive to men: I had to fight hard to overcome that. I've changed, but it took a very long time. I was raised to believe that men are the most important, and that I have to serve them. I love to serve all people—though a woman serving others is looked down upon in America. There is submission to each other in the music—we are a completely democratic unit.

While Sathima doesn't perform or interact much with other women in jazz, her approach to jazz is patently as a woman. In this regard, she embraces the ideas traditionally associated with the otherness of women— the spontaneous, intuitive, spiritual, and loving—and claims them as a core part of her personal strength, her voice in jazz, and her place in the world at large. It is a way of being that often brings her into conflict with those who seek out a more systematic and rational approach to life. As she said to me,

I am a complete romantic, jazz rules my life, and I live intuitively. It doesn't make for a planned life, knowing exactly what you have to do, doing what you supposedly like for someone like my husband, Abdullah, it's hard sometimes. It's very hard for a husband to understand a wife who says, no, I am still here in New York City and not in South Africa because I live intuitively. Well, that's true. I am still supposed to be here, I know it's almost over but it's not over till it's over. I will know it and I will recognize it and say, "That's it, I am ready to go." Like I do with everything in my life. Am I waiting for my daughter to get married, am I waiting for a grandchild? Am I waiting for a record deal? I certainly know that New York City is not a place to die, and since nobody knows when he or she is going to die, I hope to live a long life. I run on a kind of energy that rejuvenates. I don't exercise or do any of these healthy things to stay young or regenerate myself, but I do music all the time, and I always have a song on my mind. It's never out of my mind, I wake up with it and I go to bed with it.

Some might think it shouldn't be hard for Abdullah to understand my intuitive side because he's an artist. But he's also a man, and he comes from South Africa and you know South Africa is still a man's country, that whole continent of Africa is. We [women] always have to continuously sneak our things in, and if you get too forceful they just put you away. They say, "You are crazy, I can't live with you, I can't deal with you!" As a woman I do force a place for myself, and I insist that I have my own mind and that there are always two sides to a question and answer. Black is black and white is white, and you can come to an agreement somewhere. But if the male is too forceful there is nothing else for a woman to do but separate, otherwise she will go under completely. If I collapsed just because I am a woman, then what would happen to me with the music? This is a whole survival thing and why, in the end, I am not with Abdullah. I was with him for forty something years, raising the children. I wanted my kids to have some kind of normal if you can call it normal lives. Of course, I have this friend who she says it's very different for children who have both parents into jazz. "You might call it normal, Sathima, but it's not. It's jazz," she said to me the other day.

I have often thought about the other part of my life; those years working with Abdullah and you know helping him with his career, because I did that for many years. While Abdullah was the breadwinner he could put a roof over our heads: nothing that I did was going to make any money. I don't know why it is so, and I don't know whether it's going to change or not, but thank goodness I don't do the music to make money. That is a blessing in itself because it leaves me artistically free to express myself and do only what I hear within. Abdullah and I separated a few years ago, and I had to get over that, you know. Basically the separation has to do with where I wanted to live and raise my kids and where I want to be for now.

The older I get and the more I care about integrity, the more resonance I hear in my voice. I have turned into an artist. I am not just a singer. There are times when there is a lot of suffering going on in my soul, and I am not singing. I have to take care of the things with my family that you couldn't pay anyone for because no one would do it for money. It seems like such a life of self-sacrifice sometimes. I suppose every experience is thrown at you and you are supposed to run through that, and you get your heart squeezed. The next time I sing it will sound different. If I get squeezed too much, though, that will be the end of my art. But these are the times that I want to bring something musically new again. And it doesn't mean standing in front of an audience, it just means spending a couple of hours in a studio with me. That is the happiest. Those are the times I don't feel like being visible as a physical person, because they are not going to see my soul. I am an unconditional lover.[26] The music has never let me down. What I get out of this is I get love back.

Remember, I am an interpretive singer. I love working with sound, its subtleties and nuances. I have a natural gift much like Billie Holiday's approach, I urge musicians to feel free within a format. There is so much freedom and space within the music: you have to weave your voice in and out. Listen to what is happening and breathe your own thing into it. I heard Abdullah tell someone once that I am a renaissance woman. The jazz musicians will say, well, you know, Sathima you have got to pay your dues. This jazz music that you do with your whole self, it is about total surrender to yourself. This is what it's about, total surrender to the beauty inside so that you can bring it out. Ben Riley once said that you can't have too many people loving jazz because it's a very improvised way of looking at things, it makes you think for yourself, to be very free. If people aren't ready, you can have all the freedom in the world, but you have to be able to handle it. You have to listen with your heart, if your heart's open everything will tingle, that's why you hear the resonance in my voice. Some people will never hear it.

In Sathima's view, three key elements define her compositional and musical processes: intuition, spontaneity, and inspiration (that is, coming from the heart, in the moment, and without the mediation of music writing):

I am just an inspirational composer, I don't sit down at a piano and say, I am going to write a piece. It just comes, and sometimes it doesn't come for a long time. I don't write down my own music. When I have a song, I have to ask somebody to write that down and you go through that whole process. But I think if I learnt to write, I would be interfering with my antennae and I don't want to do that. I gravitate to musicians like drummer Billy Higgins because he can hear subtleties and nuances, and he can help you punctuate them. It's wonderful to have someone like that in your orbit. And he's paid his dues.

When do I compose? I find that when I am walking through the streets and it's crowded, I get a lot of things because people impact on you. I don't have to walk down a lonely country road. It works for me to take long walks, even a subway ride. When I am standing on the platform waiting for a train, nobody can hear me singing. If I want to try something out, I try it out there and nobody hears it. Remember, Carol, when my children were young I used to take them to school—for almost ten years I did this every day during the school year. I had to go by subway or by bus, but always chose the subways to take them there, and then I would walk back at least a mile and a half each day, early in the morning. There were never many people about, so you are fresh, and then lots of things come to you.

In conversation with the website All About Jazz's Maxwell Campbell, Sathima expanded on the notion of inspiration by talking about how she prepares her songs. She thinks about them as stories that have been given to her by God:

It's a very sacred gift from God. I believe in God. How else do you get your talent? It was given to me by the Angels. They just work out when a song has to be written; they decide, "I think she is ready for that song." I don't really write songs down, it can come at any time. I don't have any control over this. Parts of the thing can come as a poem, or I can hear a melody and no words, and things come . . . then one day I say wait a minute these words go with this melody. Or I can get the whole thing.

Only three songs came like this, and all three are about people. "Lady Day" came at midnight, the shortest song I have ever written, I couldn't sleep, I couldn't write anything down. I called Don Sickler, I could get any musicians at that time. So I called Don Sickler in the morning, and said I just need to sing this to you and then I want you to put it on paper.

Usually the lyrics and not the music come first. In the beginning, lyrics came as poems, and I remember saying to myself, "Poems? Am I writing poems?" And then a few months later, melodies start floating around, I become aware of them, and then I realize that a melody works with the lyrics. That's the magic of it. It truly is very mysterious and magical. Nothing was ever written down. It if has to be written down, I will remember it. I've lost many things that come, in the supermarket, for example, and I say to myself as I walk home, "Oh, I hope I don't meet anyone along the way! But if it is meant to be, it will come back." My daughter has shown me countless times how to use a simple tape. But I am very bad with technical things. I am actually afraid of them. They gave me one as a present. I put something on it, and went in the bathroom because I was very shy about it. I wanted to hear it, and the next thing I realized, I had pushed the wrong buttons and erased it. I was really frustrated because there was no one who had heard me, and no way to recapture it. Sometimes things come back.

All my compositions start musically with the bass line. Then I go to Buster Williams or Onaje Allan Gumbs and he says, "Do you know how difficult it is to write these bass lines?" Because there are spaces in between and if they play it wrong, if someone doesn't write it down the way actually, they can look at that as a guide, but sometimes it confuses them. What they have to do is actually feel and learn the bass line. Like in "Africa," you know. [Sathima hums the line.] There is a space there. Some musicians just cannot accommodate that space in their minds. They have to stamp their feet in between there so they don't play in the wrong place. If you don't play it as written, it is pretty horrible. It's the space in between that gives it that whole feeling. This is in both "Africa" and "Windsong."

I haven't done "Windsong" for a long time because it's the same thing — the musicians don't get it. Maybe now I have Buster I can do it again. They just don't hear the space. I tell them it's like an extension, it's like the male and then the female takes over. I don't know how to explain it to these guys. But if they play it like that, exactly like I am singing it to you, it sounds very corny. I don't like to come down hard on the musicians. But they feel bad and they say what is she talking about? Its not about the notes, it's just a feeling. That's why I love Stephen Scott, he will say you need to listen. Buster will tell Onaje, "Just listen to what she is doing: just be quiet. Sathima says how it should be done." We have to do it that way, because if they don't oh, it's so horrible, I will start and can't wait to finish it.

My music is about essence and feeling. Betty Carter was very much like that too, I don't know about Abbey Lincoln. I can't write the feeling in the music down. The musicians, when they look at it, and they start dissecting it, and say, "Oh, my goodness!" Even my husband will say to me, "This is a really expensive song, Sathima." He means it is rhythmically complex and will take a long time for the musicians to learn how to play it correctly, and that costs. It's very difficult because I get impatient if I have to take someone on a gig when I can't get the real guys, and they can't play my music. And I say, "But it's so simple" and my husband says, "It's not so simple. Besides the feeling, what is required technically is not that simple."

Once Abdullah said I should go to school and learn how to write music because I always have to share the credits with others. I say that if I go to school and learn how to write down the music I am entering into another way of doing the music. I might not get the inspiration anymore. Inspiration is dear to me. This is what I rely upon, that God will send or he won't send a song to me. So I was scared to do it, I am still scared, and I won't do it. I don't mind giving the credits to the pianists who helped me write my music down, I really don't mind. Well, music doesn't belong to me anyway, or to them. I would say to the pianists, "How much do you want from me for writing my song down?" They say they don't want money they just want the credit, so there is obviously something in that.

I have sometimes wondered, you know, Onaje, Buster, Steven, all these guys I work with they are so outstanding, how come they are not composing? They just go to work, get a gig and go to work. I think if they would sit down, like Buster, he could compose. Maybe people are not interested in composing. I am the one who is spontaneous and takes risks: I am just jumping off cliffs all the time by writing my own songs. They do mostly safe things. They want to know how much money are you going to pay me, what time must I be there? They play, get their money, and go home. I have never had that approach. But I don't perform often because I can't afford it.

It's hard to explain how I write my music. The only way I can is to say that you have your antennae ready and they have to be clean. They have to be like laser beams so they attract—it's like what I call a lovelight. In the windsong, there's a lovelight. I don't have any control over this: I am just a channel of the music from the Creator. The antennae are actually inside. They have to be inside and then it comes. I think we are dealing with something that is very divine, that's not something that you can study. I don't know when a song will come. I just keep living my life until the Creator sends me something. So my heart must be clean.[27]

"How do you prepare for a performance, do you just go out there and sing?" a student at Marymount College asked Sathima in 1990. "I usually go out and sing by myself," Sathima responded. She continued:

The guys say, "Are you going to do that thing again where you just go out solo? Because we know the music, we can start with you." And I say, "Yes, I am going out alone because I have to draw the audience in to myself, and then you can come out and join me." The first three notes are crucial. I have a certain strength, and we are going to have a beautiful time together. You learn to stand on your own two feet, to harness your energy, and go out there and do it. That is my approach. Everything I do is about love.

People have ideas about singers, that they should be pretty and stand there looking great. That is an approach that people have come to expect, and I am not trying to be openly defiant, but I don't think it's necessary. I try to look less dramatic in the way I dress: I don't want people to come to see how I look. I really am very shy. Singing has helped me to overcome shyness. I don't know how I have made it so far, when I first began to sing my knees used to shake. I was just like a stone, unable to move. I can move now. I wear my dancing shoes and imagine myself dancing like I did growing up. The more I sing, the more the support comes from the audience, and the more you get from behind you in the trio. It's a beautiful package, you know.

People ask me about my sense of timing. The musicians ask about where in the measure they should come in. With me it is just between beat one and two, they count and so want to know exactly, but I can't tell them. Everything I do is completely intuitive. When I sing, I imagine myself dancing, and bass player Buster Williams, he knows just how to dance with me. The way you turn a corner in ballroom dancing—that is how his playing feels to me. I did a lot of ballroom dancing when I was young. I think that's got a lot to do with my sense of timing. Somewhere between one and two, before we get to that two I am going to be sliding in there.[27]

When I sing the words of a song, for me it's a story being told with the lyrics and the sound. It's a story you are telling. Everything has to make sense. I don't suddenly just sing a song. I will figure out what the story is here. That impacts on where I am going to put the accents and which word is more important in the line. Every song is a story. How on earth did you get this gift of storytelling in song? It comes to me when I am meditating in motion. I think about songs when I am walking in streets here amidst all kinds of people. I do not retire to some place and say, "OK, I am gonna write or sing a particular song." It's not about that. It's very divine and inspirational.

Sometimes rehearsals can be fun, it depends, someone like Stephen, Onaje will always say, "Oh, Sathima doesn't need to rehearse." I can only afford to rehearse the day before, most musicians they are rehearsing constantly, I don't have money for this, it's a question of funds. I have a two-to-three-hour rehearsal the day before so it's fresh in their minds and in mine. Then I just keep this whole forty-eight-hour thing going in my head. When I am preparing for a performance I do need somebody to help me. I call on my South African friend Julia who lives in Vancouver because first of all, you have got to get the piano chart. And you need a bass chart, and the drummer also looks at the chart, I didn't think the drummer needs one, but Victor Lewis and George Gray say they need one too. So we do the charts when we are rehearsing.

Like several of the South Africans and some of the American jazz musicians Sathima and Abdullah met in Europe in the 1960s and 1970s, Sathima relies on spontaneity, that is, on playing without the fake book and performing without being able to read, which produces a particular kind of musical aesthetic:

I have my antennae open to receive inspiration from God. I am an innate intuitive, I am not a technical person. I retain the freshness and spontaneity in performance by not reading or writing the music down. My advice is always to be natural and follow what is inside you, use your imagination, do your own thing. Jazz is about having courage, taking risks, and packing your bags and and saying I am leaving. In Europe, we didn't know most of the time where we were going to next, success is never instant, instead it is a journey.

I want my music to always feel spontaneous. Duke Ellington believed in only one take. That means the dials are set, you call the tune and you do it.[28] He said you only repeat yourself: you only do a second take if there is a technical hitch. I still do my recordings in that way. I learnt that from Duke Ellington. I prepare myself beforehand, and I go into the studio knowing exactly what I want to do and I do it. He said if you do it twice, it's already a bad thing, and if you do it three times you will sound like a bad imitation of yourself. I think he is right, absolutely right.

Jazz music should be extremely spontaneous—you have a plan ahead, but when it happens it is spontaneous.

I don't work a lot, but I try to work with the same people. They are very support-ive, even though they know my little idiosyncrasies. They make fun of me. But it's very tight, very beautiful, and very warm. I have had to survive many things: I am such a survivor. I even had to survive a very famous husband. You have to insist that you have your own career. Sometimes I have felt that things are a little unfair, perhaps I could be doing as well. But I chose to be the mother and to stay home and put that behind me. It was a good choice because the records traveled. It took ten years to establish a reputation but it's getting there. It's good because there is still a lot to do. It is not easy to have a wonderful musician like my husband. He can do anything. His music is wonderful. He can command, he can sit down, and write a piece. He's both inspirational and he has the technical know-how. I'm not jealous of him but I do wish I had more time to give to my own things.

That is the bond I naturally work towards. That is what I want to achieve. It's not that I am this fantastic musician; while I think it's true I have a great sound, that's not the most important thing. The most important thing is when I have my guys around me. They are males: I want to touch them in such a way, because I am sensual, but without a hint of sexuality. It's not about sex. I want to keep the purity. The point is I am working with three men, and I am letting them touch their fragile and feminine side, and they do it in spite of themselves. Men are just natu-rally macho, and I say I am the one who has to stand out in front, you are behind me, you are going to embrace this song just like I do. I think I achieve that.

The day after one of my shows recently, my daughter sent a bunch of flowers and this card, and she said she thought I was brilliant in that performance. She was so thrilled to have been there and been a part of it. She said, "You purified the room with that sound." I get goose bumps as I say it. That is what I try to do even if I don't succeed every moment and with each song. For most of the performance I am trying to draw something else out from these guys who work with me. That is what makes any performance I do powerful, because it's not only me, it becomes a very democratic unit. It's the yin and the yang, the male and female interact-ing, but never crossing the line. You have to keep the music quivering. There is the excitement, and you get caught up in that. It becomes all four of us. In some mo-ments, when I am there and I am listening, we hear it! We are so together. I don't know if the audience hears it, but some do if they are tuned into it, they do. And if they don't they can't disturb me, even if they try. We are really making the music at that moment.

That is why I also love the studio because when you are with the musicians, you *have selected the piece, and you can see it—they enjoy the piece right from the start. When I have the earphones on, and I am hearing them, then everything just comes out of me, they are pulling it out. It has nothing to do with ego, it's just a question of making the whole thing sound as beautiful as you can get it to sound. On stage you often have to fight too many things. The musicians come in, they can be on ego trips, and you have to dispel that. We do that, eventually, but it can take a few bars and I will say, "Wait a minute, we are making 'Windsong' here. You may be the best bass player in the world, you will get your moment, but right now you need to listen to me."*

The audience expectation has a lot to do with the ego thing. But when I am performing music I want to find the magical way, where making the music is a total embrace. This is where there is no longer the feeling of a stage and an audience looking at what you are wearing. I want them to listen to what I am saying through the music. So I often feel I need to close my eyes at the beginning of a live performance to center myself in relationship to the audience. That way I can draw them in. But you can't close your eyes the whole way. When I was young that is what I would do. Now I close my eyes when I feel there is too much eye contact because I can't do the music when there are too many egos out there. I need camaraderie around the music.

I need to feel the embrace and to embrace back. The music for me is about love and how it travels. There are so many different ways to love. Love is supposed to be merciful. The basis of everything I do, in life and in my music, is love, a little capsule of tenderness and compassion I am trying to put that into my sound. That is the most natural thing to me.

Toward a Gendered Poetics of Self in Jazz

There can be no doubt that this book tells a woman's story: Sathima represents herself in traditional ways: as mother, wife, and singer; but she expands her world to become manager, political activist, composer, producer, record label owner, and organic intellectual. The home she has created in the music she makes is similarly formed from traditionally feminine attributes: spontaneity, intuition, caring, respect, love, and beauty, though she doesn't restrict these attributes to women. These are the qualities she looks for in the male musicians she invites to perform with her. She creates space in the musical fabric for each to express himself by performing feminine qualities; she urges them to embrace the freedom she offers to find the softer sides of their musical selves and even to flirt a little in the moment of performance.

The depth of emotion Sathima feels toward the music parallels the passion evoked when a woman falls in love with a man. In her ensembles music making is sensual in the moment of performance but never spills over into after-hours sexual pleasure. Reaching the state of perfect union in the moment of performance is challenging: nothing comes easily; everything requires a level of struggle and the strength and courage to survive the difficulty. But once Sathima and her musicians have overcome the difficulties creating the charts for the sounds she hears; after she has convinced her musicians to listen closely to each other and to uncover the beauty inside themselves; and when they are in tune with each other musically and emotionally, they are able to make the most thrilling music together. At the end of an evening of live performance or a session in the studio, there is, in Sathima's mind, a feeling of having reached a climactic moment of pure joy, akin to the momentary ecstasy that many experience when they have fallen in love or felt the pangs of romance.

Sathima's stress upon the feminine dimensions she expects her musicians to embody is juxtaposed with the more masculine elements of risk taking that jazz improvisation and performance characteristically require. In this sense, Sathima sees jazz as constituting a place for exploring, even performing the gendered self—its masculine and feminine dimensions. She would argue that her kind of music making enables men to explore parts of themselves they would never dare to if they were in exclusively male ensembles. Her ensemble style thus provides a powerful counternarrative to the discourses of masculinity in jazz articulated in the autobiographies of some male musicians. Hazel Carby, for example, characterizes Davis's autobiography, *Miles*, in ways that both overlap with and diverge from Sathima's story. At eighteen Davis traveled to New York City from his home in Texas because, like Sathima, he believed New York to be the center of jazz performance in the United States. He arrived there to explore the freedom that a major urban area like New York provides.

Carby argues that Davis's "concept of freedom remains limited to the misogynistic world of jazz, and it manifests itself principally in the musical relations among the male instrumentalists with whom he worked"

(Carby 1998, 136). Davis's ideas of freedom include breaking loose from the confinement that women create for men, and he insists on the freedom to operate in a world defined by male creativity (ibid., 138). This is a world in which men, not mothers, are his mentors and nurturers, and his lineage in jazz is a patrilineal one. Carby goes so far as to suggest that Davis thought of women, including his mother, as obstacles to his growth as a musician. His relationships with his first wife and child and with his subsequent wives are all tinged with a taste of disgust. For Davis, when his life with women thrives, the music goes badly. When the music is good, the way with women is rough (Carby 1998, 141). Ultimately, Davis's biography reveals a man who becomes a pimp, exploiting these women with unlimited patriarchal power for sex but refusing to acknowledge his exploitation. Men are his resource for creativity, nurturance, and stimulation; women "exist to be exploited and to service his bodily needs" (Carby 1998, 143).

Davis hears in one of his first experiences of live jazz performances, in 1944, an intensity of emotion and passion that he likens to desire in a sexual relationship. While Sathima doesn't go quite this far in her description of the unity constituted out of performance with her trio, one easily reads that into the words she provides. Nevertheless, Sathima's goals in performance are sensual, possibly more maternal: she creates a musical space for her trio that she hopes will set them free, to find the vulnerable, even feminine, dimensions of their maleness. In return, she demands that they listen to her, enable her to perform her music by coming to understand her sense of timing and her intonation and, indeed, by coming to know something about her past, her history in a place that is worlds away from theirs. This is not a position achieved without risk, pain, and struggle, but it is a place that will ultimately produce real love, deep joy, and beautiful music.

Sathima's thinking in jazz is concerned with a woman who lives intuitively, with her heart, mind, and eyes open to new ways of doing old songs. The reiteration of songs from almost a century ago intervenes in the present, as living witnesses to a past that cannot be simply forgotten. Each new rendition of a tune from the late nineteenth-century British music hall, an early Hollywood musical, or a Strayhorn or Ellington composition serves to remind its listeners of the past in the present. Aligning herself with the words of her mentor, Duke Ellington, she has positioned herself inside the lineage of the finest jazz singers of the twentieth century, while her way of being in the world is in every sense beyond category. "Music isn't a style, it's an idea — I don't hear much of that anymore," commented the seventy-six-year-old Ornette Coleman in an interview with Ben Ratliff of the *New York Times*.[29] It is exactly Coleman's notion of idea over style that Sathima strives to create each time she takes a trio into the studio or on stage with her — southern touch, music as spirit inside you, as songspirit, as echo, or as home within — though the nature of the idea begins a long way away and in another time.

In return, it is Sathima's dream that one day jazz consumers in both of her home countries — the United States and South Africa — will finally find it in themselves to hear the emotive depth and beauty in her voice, to allow themselves to be decentered by the vocal presence nested inside the intricate lines of her trio, to come to know her story, and to relish the echoes of music of the old and new African diasporas, echoes that have crisscrossed the Atlantic Ocean many times in the twentieth century and the twenty-first. With this desire in mind, a sense of place in the New York–centered jazz world, and a clarity about South Africa's position in the global history of jazz, Sathima returned to South Africa for two more recording projects: *Cape Town Love* (1999) and *Musical Echoes* (2006).

6

Returning Home?

When I think about Cape Town relative to New York City, part of me wants to just sit and watch the waves come in, in the place where I am from. I long to feel the safeness of the mountain, to breathe another air, and to feel the magic in that air. — Sathima, in conversation with Carol Muller about *Cape Town Love*, 2000

CALL ▪▪▪▪▪▪▪▪▪▪▪▪▪▪▪▪▪▪▪▪▪▪▪▪▪▪▪▪▪▪▪▪▪▪▪▪▪

Cape Town Love / *An Archeology of Popular Song*

The contents of the *Cape Town Love* recording as laid out here can be listened to as streamed excerpts at www.africanmusicalechoes.org.

Cape Town Love Tracks
Singer: Sathima Bea Benjamin; Piano: Henry February;
Bass: Basil Moses; Drums: Vincent Pavitt

1. "When Day Is Done," written in 1926 by Buddy de Sylva and Robert Katscher

2. "I'll Be Seeing You," written in the 1940s by Irving Kahal and Sammy Fain

3. "If I Should Fall in Love Again," written in 1939 by the British songwriter Jack Popplewell

4. "If You Were the Only Boy in the World," written in 1916 by Nat Ayer and Clifford Grey

5. "You Go to My Head," written in 1938 as a Tin Pan Alley song by J. Fred Coots and Haven Gillespie

6. "I Only Have Eyes for You," written by Harry Warren and Al Dubin, first sung by Dick Powell in the film *Dames* (1934)

7. "I Wish I Knew," written by Harry Warren and Mack Gordon

8. "Body and Soul," written by John Green, Robert Sour, Edward Heyman, and Frank Eyton

When I first met Sathima in New York City, like many other South Africans who were part of the anti-apartheid movement abroad, she talked often of returning home to South Africa. There was nothing specific, just an overwhelming desire to be welcomed back by friends, family, and the nation exiled South Africans had imagined into being while away from the country. With the birth of a new democracy, the removal of old restrictions, bannings, and unjust laws, those who had been out of the country for decades began to confront the real possibilities of leaving their homes abroad. They wondered what it would be like to go back to the new South Africa, the "rainbow nation" miraculously transformed with the release of Nelson Mandela, Walter Sisulu, and a host of others who had been imprisoned, exiled, or simply left in difficult circumstances. Abdullah returned home—he admits he had never really felt part of the New York jazz scene—but for Sathima the choice was not that simple. She had raised her children in New York City, with the financial support of Abdullah, but often single-handedly.

Raising children roots one in ways that coming in and out rarely does. Parents have to adhere to daily routines, integrate into their community, and know who their friends are. The only home Tsidi had ever known was the Hotel Chelsea: she was the most Americanized of the four. Though he doesn't remember his first six years, during which he was traveling abroad, Tsakwe was also schooled and raised in the city. While they had heard much about South Africa and knew much about Cape Town, its natural beauty, the extraordinary music scene of the fifties, their extended family, and its traditional forms of social engagement, neither Tsakwe nor Tsidi could realistically be expected to just fit in there by simply stepping onto its soil. And Sathima has often wondered what life would be like for her, as a woman who had traveled so far, struggled so hard to achieve what she had, and relished the freedom that being away enabled, if she went back to Cape Town. And yet the longing to be embraced at home has continued to haunt her. In the late 1990s she had an idea, one triggered by a call from Abdullah who urged her to record her old mentor, Henry February. No professional recording had ever featured the gifted pianist. So Sathima decided to go ahead. She gathered together a trio, with February on piano, Cape bass player Basil Moses, and Vincent Pavitt on drums. The group recorded the old songs Sathima recalled from her youth in Cape Town. On the flight home she decided to call the record-

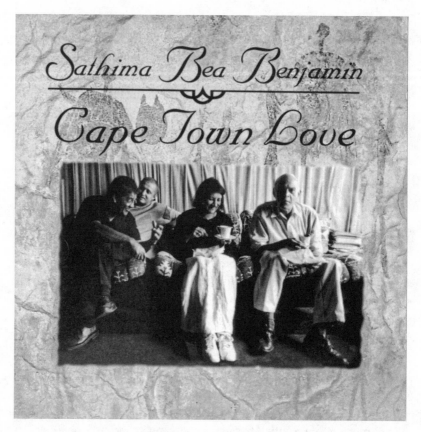

29. Cover of Sathima's CD *Cape Town Love*.

ing *Cape Town Love* to honor the musicians she had spent two days remi-
niscing musically with. This is the story of that historic recording.

   There is nothing like a good hot cup of tea to make people feel like they
have arrived home. And tea, cup after cup, is served between takes at the
Milestone Studios in Cape Town. Tea drinking, that old British tradition,
produces laughter and rich sociability among the Coloured musicians
and the white engineer, Murray Anderson. Take a good look at the cover
of Sathima Bea Benjamin's recording *Cape Town Love*. A black-and-white
photograph whimsically inserted into a larger frame of Khoisan rock
paintings from the Kagga Kamma reserve in the Cape shows Sathima
and her Cape Town trio comfortably sitting on a couch taking a break
from the recording session to drink some tea. The bass player Basil Moses
listens to what the drummer Vincent Pavitt has to say. Sathima has the

familiar white china cup and saucer in her hand. She smiles as she raises the steaming liquid to her parched lips. The pianist Henry February, the oldest and most intense of the musicians, is surprised by the flash of the camera. He stares ahead, thinking about the food in the wax wrapping nested in the palm of his hand. A longtime friend and artist, George Hallett, Sathima remembered from the old Kew Town library days, dropped by to capture these contingent moments in the photographic image.

Though Moses and Pavitt were younger, the recording sessions were just like old times for the singer and the pianist. Fifty years earlier they had performed together in Cape Town's white nightclubs. Unlike the weekly Coloured dance gigs, the white clubs allowed the musicians to explore the music more — as long as they sat in the kitchen or outside in back of the club during intermission. "I called those experiences my 'Night School,'" recalled Sathima. "I learnt so much and most of all I had a chance to sing what I wanted, how I wanted. The audience might be dancing or dining but that did not matter. The musicians and I used it to hone our craft. All the so-called jazz gems and standards were played, and we were all so in love with this music called JAZZ."[1] In those days it was February who mentored the young singer. In the 1999 recording it was her turn to give back. She invited February to inscribe his music on record with her. In just nine hours over two wonderful mornings nestled at the foot of Table Mountain they recorded songs they remembered playing in those early days. There was "so much love coming through our sound and approach to jazz," Sathima recalled after the event.

When one listens to the music on *Cape Town Love* and contemplates the black-and-white images, one can't help but think of Ry Cooder's Cuban project, the *Buena Vista Social Club*. Produced at about the same time, *Buena Vista Social Club* reinstates a musical repertory from a similar historical period, namely, the 1940s and 1950s, the years prior to the Cuban missile crisis and Fidel Castro's ascendance to power in Cuba. Focused on the genre of the Cuban *son*, the words of the Spanish-language songs are simple, unabashedly sensual, and romantic. The innocence, beauty, and deep emotion of a bygone era are reconstituted in the drawn-out tempos of vaguely remembered ballads. As one does to the storytelling capacity of Sathima and her trio in *Cape Town Love*, one can only listen in awe and with longing.

The fundamental difference between the projects of Sathima and Cooder, however, is that Sathima's is not a project about music resurrected by a powerful white American (or British) record producer who travels and accidentally happens upon the human representatives of a past tradition, musicians who, according to Cooder, no longer made the music of an almost-forgotten era, forgotten in Cuba because of political pressure, just as elsewhere the passing of a style is dictated by the marketplace. Rather, it is the story of the kind of agency that democracy as daily practice inspires: a woman producer returns home to pay tribute to those who nurtured her talent by providing them with the opportunity to record with her. In the absence of the powerful white male producer, the recording struggles to move through the networks of global distribution. Nevertheless, the lack of industry recognition enables a kind of intimacy between the listener and the project, its producer, and musicians. One can listen without being bombarded by the relentless repetition that market recognition brings on radio and television. And one should relish that gift.

Each recording project that Sathima produces has been carefully imagined, and each has a specific purpose. *Cape Town Love* is no exception. The project was triggered by a fax sent by Abdullah Ibrahim after he heard February (already, as noted, seventy in this recording) performing in the Cape. Despite a lifetime spent as a gifted professional pianist and teacher in Cape Town, February had never been recorded. Abdullah suggested to Sathima that she think about recording him. Her purpose quickly transmuted into more than mere documentation. *Cape Town Love* became the moment for Sathima to return home: to pull from deep within her the songs she remembered so vividly in exile, from her childhood and young adult life, but had never performed with American musicians. Now was the time to make visible, for the record, as it were, the home she had carried within her for so long. This was her chance to go back to the music that had been the vessel pushing her out of the movie theater at intermission and into the world of professional singing. February had been a key force behind that move.

For decades Sathima had carried these memories of Cape Town, her audiences, the musicians, and their sheer love and passion for the music inside. She remembered the sounds of the city, street hawkers, newspaper boys, flower sellers, all sounding out their wares and prices in song; and she had visceral recollections of the movement of wind through the city, the rhythm of the ocean, and the noise of the neighbors.[2] Without having to explain to her audiences (or so she hoped) what she remembered Cape Town to have been in her youth, here was a possibility of return, the capacity, when so many other musicians had already passed on, to resurrect the past with the pianist who, more than anybody before him, had drawn her into the world of jazz performance. I remember Sathima calling me from Cape Town: I could hear the sheer joy, even exuberance, in her voice because she was back home. "I am walking past my memories everyday!" she said laughingly.

These were not ordinary memories but the unquenchable longings for a feeling for place that diaspora and exile force upon individuals. Longing and desire had long pressed in against the perceived absence of such qualities in newfound habitats elsewhere in the world. Sathima recounted the nature of those memories in New York City, around the same period: "Cape Town, South Africa, my home for 23 years, nurtured my musicality from the moment I was born. . . . The magic, the mysticism of that wonderful city I have carried within my soul. I treasure all these gifts and when I sing I am transported in my 'spirit song' to all that I know and remember since birth—I remember songs, smells, sights, people, and it's all music to me. I know my sound, my sense of rhythm and time comes from there—and so it is that I endeavor through jazz singing to give that 'sound picture' 'to the listener.'"[3]

Cape Town Love was recorded on March 18 and 19, 1999. The published compact disc has eight songs, though two more were recorded when the musicians returned to the studio with a Cape filmmaker some months later. She was hoping to produce a documentary on Sathima Bea Benjamin. The musician who most vividly recalled the songs of the post–Second World War period was, of course, February, but it didn't take Moses long to recall the melodies. Pavitt was younger and did not necessarily remember the tunes, but he certainly could play with a Cape Town rhythmic feel. Likewise, readers and listeners may not remember the songs or feel pangs of nostalgia upon hearing them, in the ways Sathima and the people she sang with in the late 1950s do. In fact, Sathima puts such a fresh spin on these decades-old melodies that it is easy to imagine that the quaint romantic sentiment in the singer triggered her compositional spirit—one may even think she wrote these songs herself. She did not. Rather, these are her echoes of a repertory originating in the United States and Britain and sounding out from the southern part of Africa.

One might more appropriately think of these echoes of prior perfor-mances in terms of the visual images of the Khoisan rock paintings that cover the pages of the liner notes. Both the song repertory and paintings work as palimpsests: each mode of artistic expression bears audible (in the case of the songs) or visual traces of prior representations. Each relies on the aural memory, sound recordings, or visual residue of previous art-ists. This is not just about influence or mere imitation but about visible and audible evidence of the past that continues in the present. Premod-ernist (and now possibly postmodernist) in conception, the palimpsest insists on ancestral presence, layered into the sounds of the old newly made by a succession of new painters or singers. Like memory itself, while the palimpsest references the past, it only ever allows for a par-tial view of original substance, which is viewed or heard in the present through layers of prior utterances or inscriptions.

Here, I take *palimpsest* as articulating the complexity of popular song history quite literally. And I do so in two ways in the account that follows. First, I provide a brief media lineage for each song—the date of birth and surrogate medium in which the song lived—this being the English-language, global, popular culture narrative.[4] Second, through the ethno-graphic data I provide commentary on or recollections about the songs as accounted for by Sathima in two interviews, the first made soon after she went into the studio in 1999, and the second after the launch of the recording in Cape Town in 2000.

TRACK 1. "When Day Is Done" was written in 1926 by Buddy de Sylva and Robert Katscher. It was recorded by Paul Whiteman, though it was more popular in Britain than in the United States, specifically through the dance band performances led by Bert Ambrose.

In 1999 I asked Sathima if she had specific memories tied to the songs on *Cape Town Love*. She replied,

Let's take these two: "When Day Is Done" and "If I Should Fall in Love Again." I will definitely associate them with ballroom dancing. Joan and I would do that: we would go dancing without partners. That was a terrible thing, considered very unladylike—girls following the bands. We had our favorites, like the Philadelphia Rhythms, the Alf Wiley and the Willy Max bands, whenever they would play, we would go to hear them. I don't know how we got there, but we would go. We just wanted to dance. So these two songs, I don't really know the words, but I know the melodies. Those melodies, they did something to me, you know, there was magic in the melodies. After we would dance a square, well, there's a lot of dancing and it's a bit wild at times, so after the squares they would play a beautiful waltz, or a very slow piece to calm you down. These were two calming down songs.

I asked her if she remembered whether she was just sitting and listening to the music or actually dancing. She replied, "You are dancing but you are also taking in what you hear musically. My ears are always open. So I associate these two songs with the dancehalls." She said that when she asked Henry and Basil if they knew the songs they would say they didn't, at first. Eventually it would come back to them because they had played these songs in the dancehalls too: "I knew they would dance with me, Henry and Basil are not just playing with me, they are dancing with me. They are just doing a whole Cape Town thing, which I would not get, not that overall effect, that total memory, the collective thing, from American musicians. Just listen to 'If I Should Fall in Love Again,' you actually feel like taking a partner and doing that slow waltz. I don't know about you, but whenever I hear it, I say, 'Is there someone here that I can have a dance with?'"

"If I Should Fall in Love Again," it would seem, was a song that none of the *Cape Town Love* trio could immediately place in the collective memory of the postwar period. Sathima told me in February 2000, however, that this song became a mechanism for teaching the three men to learn to listen to her. This is how she described the interaction:

I knew we could do the recording if they would just listen, and that is how I got "When Day Is Done." I said that everybody had to be quiet, nobody should play, not even Henry. I said, "Don't play, just listen." Then I explained, "If you will just listen, you will get the song." Because they will say, first of all Basil Moses will say, "I don't know that song." Then I say, "No, when I sing it . . . you do know it Basil, you do, you just don't remember it yet." And I sang it absolutely by myself.

I can't explain the experience. I had these three guys from home that I didn't want to intimidate, but I was trying to get a point across. If they would just give themselves to me, just for that, maybe not even a minute and a half, and hear that song, kind of for the first time, we were going to do something. And they listened.

A little later, she reflected again on the process: "And I must say that immediately I went into it, Henry was the perfect accompanist for that song because he really did listen. He did know the song, and after that Basil said, 'Oh, I know that song.' The only one who didn't was the drummer, he was young. But he had been to university there, he had studied jazz, so he came with a very subtle dynamic. And we were passing something onto him, so precious, you know. And I was simply utilizing the skills I had acquired here."

TRACK 2. "I'll Be Seeing You," written in the 1940s by Irving Kahal and Sammy Fain, is still a part of the collective memory and nostalgia for those who lived through the 1940s in the United States (Crowther and Anderson in Rasmussen 2000). Sathima recalled,

"I'll Be Seeing You" is a song from wartime, you know after we did it in the studio, we just sat down. I couldn't remember where I learnt that song but I didn't have to look for the words of the song, so it means it must have been very popular on the radio. During the war, the people were singing that song, so I was very young. Henry said to me, "So, that was good, we're not going to do that song again." He said, "By the way," you know he smacks you, he hits you very hard, he says, "if you had sung that song before Vera Lynn, she would never have sung it." I thought that was a very nice way for him to compliment me because he is that way—it was such a great compliment coming from Henry. Then I realized that I probably had heard Vera Lynn sing it, though sometimes I can't directly remember. I am a singer and there are so many songs. But I realize 1946, 47, how old was I? I was ten, eleven, so okay, that was the time I was really beginning to sing, when I was beginning to love it. Because I was eleven when I entered the talent contest in the bioscope— remember I told you? You could win a prize, and the prize was eight free tickets to the movies (July 1999).

TRACK 3. "If I Should Fall in Love Again," written in 1939 by the British songwriter Jack Popplewell, this song was extremely popular in Britain and was recorded numerous times by a range of artists. (See discussion in track 1 above.)

TRACK 4. "If You Were the Only Boy in the World" was written by Nat Ayer and Clifford Grey in 1916 (during the First World War) as the ". . . the only *girl* in the world." Sathima changed the title and lyric content to *boy*. The song first appeared in the stage show "The Bing Boys Are Here."[5]

" 'If You Were the Only Boy in the World,' I heard that in the house with Ma Benjamin. It's old, from the 1920s," Sathima told me. Putting the song together with the *Cape Town Love* musicians was not straightforward, though it turned out to be a remarkable moment for Sathima, Moses, and February. None of them had ever heard it in any form other than its straight dance hall version, that is, there was no prior jazz archive of the song. It would require risk and imagination, and there was very little time to work it out prior to laying it down in the studio. February was reluctant. Moses was more inspired initially. Sathima recalls,

The melody was stored, they knew the melody and the harmonies, but they were straight harmonizations. I am asking them to put some jazz—like I started talking about a modal piano style. Henry didn't like that, he said, "I am not doing that. Don't start talking about McCoy Tyner or John Coltrane." I said, "Okay, fine. I am going to be fine with the rhythm section, I would like to do this with the bass player." Then Basil Moses just starts this with an African line, and I said, "That's it, I want an African waltz." Now, here we might find the racism thing [that is, they wanted nothing to be perceived as black African in a Coloured jazz recording].

Not Basil Moses, not with him. He wanted to lose his inhibitions, to jump in there, but not Henry. I said, "You can go and sit in the engineer's box, and listen. You can be free of this one." Because I knew what I wanted to do. . . . Then Basil Moses really started to get it when he sang that little African thing. We weren't recording. I thought, "Hey, what is he doing? I started to sing, 'Bebadabadabadoba.'" It was flowing from one thing—and that is the essence of this music—we had to take it into an African mode to get there. It pulled it out of us—my God, if we had more time, we could explore this more with more songs. Even I lost my inhibition, and I just dared to sing wordless. I have never sung wordless in my life. I caress the words. But what language was I singing in? I wouldn't know. And then Henry heard me—it went around like this, first the drummer was doing his thing, then Henry—that's where he opened up—he said, "Wait a minute, I am going to be left out here." He came in, slowly, and that's where he opened up. I am telling you he has never gone there. I have never been there either, in singing, but not wordless. Because you came from there you could do that. It came out of that string instrument, the Khoisan music, with the one string.

Once again tying her music to Khoisan origins, Sathima comments on the reception of the rendition of the song in *Cape Town Love*: "'If You Were the Only Boy in the World,' that took off in Johannesburg because there is an African flavor there, it just happened. How can you sing an old English song in this way? It is also very avant-garde, very modern at the same time, with my phrasing and the sensitivity I inject into the lyrics. Old-fashioned, almost corny lyrics, but you know it is simple and also very direct. So I am amazed that that song is taking off in Johannesburg, they just love it" (February 2000).

TRACK 5. "You Go to My Head," was written in 1938 as a Tin Pan Alley song by J. Fred Coots and Haven Gillespie.

Sathima recalled in 1999 that this was a song she remembers Holiday had sung. "A very difficult song," she commented, which she thought she should check against the Holiday version to see if she was singing in the same key. In fact, earlier in the day that I spoke to her she had been listening to the radio in her apartment, when she heard Holiday singing the version. Abdullah was watching a Holiday film on television at the same time and came through to see if it was Sathima doing "You Go to My Head."

Of the *Cape Town Love* rendition, Sathima told me that February had introduced her to that song, had told her to learn it when she was singing with his Nat "King" Cole trio in the late 1950s. He gave it to her one week, and "I did it with him the next week in the clubs." The *Cape Town Love* version is February's arrangement. "I told him we would do it as a ballad, how we had always done it. I dedicated that song to him because I associate it with him as my teacher," she commented.

TRACK 6. "I Only Have Eyes for You," a song frequently recycled in television commercials in the United States, was written by Harry Warren and Al Dubin and first sung by Dick Powell in 1934 in the film *Dames*. It was performed again in 1949 on the "Jolson Sings Again" soundtrack by Jolson and rendered again in the film *Young Man with a Horn* (1950), starring Doris Day. Day repeated the song the same year in *Tea for Two*. Day's repertory and style were important in Sathima's childhood — Sathima was sometimes called Cape Town's own Doris Day or Joni James, though she does not sound anything like Day anymore. Sinatra sang a version of the song, as did many others in the 1950s.

Of the actual recording of the song on *Cape Town Love*, Sathima remembered the final stressful moments of the session: "I told the guys, because there were about eight or twelve minutes left and we needed another song, I said, 'Well, you know, I spoke about doing "I Only Have Eyes for You." We ran through it the other day. But do you think we can do that because now I don't know what else . . . we do have a chart and we do have a key. So can we just do this now?' And Murray just put the dials on. 'We're going to do it. Who's going to take choruses dah dah dah? That's how come those two songs [are on the CD].' Sathima told me that she learned "I Only Have Eyes for You" at home too, that it was very popular in Cape Town. People loved the song. "Cape Town is a melodic city, and there is something in the air there that makes everyone able to sing and everyone able to hear songs and everyone want to sing," she recalled.

TRACK 7. "I Wish I Knew," written by Harry Warren and Mack Gordon, was sung in many Hollywood films. Betty Grable sang it in *Billy Rose's Diamond Horseshoe* in 1945; it was heard in 1952 in *By the Light of the Silvery Moon*" and again in 1957, in *The Helen Morgan Story*. Sathima recalled,

I've always wanted to do that song but never had the opportunity. I don't know where I learnt that song, but I found out it is from the movie the Diamond Horseshoe *with Dick Haimes. As we were doing the song in the studio Henry reminded me that Dick Haimes used to sing it. But, he says, "Haimes was a crooner, you are not a crooner."*

This is how it came: We had twenty minutes in the studio, it was going to close, Murray was out of his mind. He said, "I have no more, ok, I will give you twenty minutes." I was nearly in tears. I said to the guys, "We have wasted our time arguing about I don't know what, and now we only have twenty minutes. So I must go back to New York and come back another time and finish the CD." And Henry said, "Don't give up, don't give up. What is it you want to sing?" "I Wish I Knew." And he said, "Let's find the key," and he found the key, I am telling you, he found the key. We just did it. We didn't rehearse it.

TRACK 8. "Body and Soul" was written by John Green, Robert Sour, Edward Heyman, and Frank Eyton, was first recorded by Coleman Hawkins in 1940s, and was made popular in numerous versions by Holiday, Nina Simone, and other singers. There is no ethnographic comment on this song from Sathima.[6]

Unreleased Tracks

The *Cape Town Love* ensemble recorded four additional songs, none of which is on the final CD. These were "Because You Are Mine," a song with a beautiful melody by Sammy Khan and sung by the very popular Mario Lanza; "I Wished Upon the Moon," with words by Dorothy Parker, the melody of which February had whistled for Sathima, and she recalled hearing Holiday sing; "Take Me to Your Heart Again," the old song sung by Edith Piaf; and, finally, "Falling in Love Is Wonderful," in a Cape Town rhythm or *klopse* beat. Sathima told me that "Basil worked with the drummer (this time it was Denver Furnace), with the Cape Town beat. It's so beautiful. Oh, this drummer is wonderful, our fast Cape Town klopse. I said, 'Henry, do me a favor, just go into the jazz upbeat'; I wanted to prove a point: Henry is going to blow their mind. They will see now the connections, the swing. There are all kinds of Cape Town beats. I played it for Sally Placksin, and she said, 'How do you do this? It's very difficult.' I can take any song and put it on top of a Cape Town rhythm, but I think you must come from there. I don't think you could write it down."

The *Cape Town Love* collection consisted of the songs Sathima had wanted to record for a long time but knew wouldn't work with American musicians. She needed the vitality of a collective memory of the music and of the occasions of live performances in the Cape Town community—in the dance halls and clubs, specifically. Of the last song, "They Say That Falling in Love Is Wonderful," Sathima reminisced in July 1999, "Henry was fooling around on the piano, and I said, 'That sounded like "They Say That Falling in Love Is Wonderful." You know what, I really want to do this.' The words just came to me. We didn't have time to write it down. The bass player played such a beautiful solo. The filming guys said, 'You should be taking the world by storm with this.' It worked because it was a ballad without a bridge. We were laid back as only Cape Tonians can be. It's about the love of the music, and the sincerity which matches mine. Sometimes I think I have been blessed because I have never been paid, because it is done totally for the love of the music. Thank God I can still sing. I think it's got better, but there have been long silences."

"*Cape Town Love* is a part of my home within," she mused. "My home is in the music. Even critic Lee Jeske, he calls me the jazz world's best-kept secret, and I thought, let me go to him with *Cape Town Love*. Lee Jeske said I went to the best home of all: I went to jazz. That word means so much more, it's that place, that healing place. Yes, it's the freedom: that liberated place. So it's not really any country. But I would say how South Africa shaped that way for me."

Embedded in the pieces of conversation cut and pasted above is a story about a woman who returns. More than merely Sathima's reentering South Africa, *Cape Town Love* was about returning to the musical home that had nurtured her passion for singing from as far back as she could remember. She was not just the "singer out front" but also the lead musician with a clear acoustical vision of what she needed her trio to accomplish. It was all about pulling the old songs out of collective memory and dressing them in a new, contemporary, liberating style. "Let me tell you," Sathima said, "*Cape Town Love*, words cannot explain what it did for my musical soul. I just have felt so good since then; it was a healing experience for me."

The recording was not mere repetition of an older repertory, but temporal and physical displacement and the freedom of expression that transcending place and community enables and that she found in jazz as musical echo and as a diasporic musical vocabulary. These Cape Town musicians were to recreate the repertory in a way that no one had heard before—no record produced in America could guide them. This was their moment to take the risks that creative performance required, to weave a rich harmonic and rhythmic fabric out of known but rarely performed words and music. A repertory composed through the First and Second World Wars and used in nightclub singing and dance band performance in the postwar era was given a Cape Town jazz sensibility in postapartheid South Africa. To reach that musical destination, old and new modes of engagement tussled with one another; men joked while the woman insisted they focus and listen so she could sound out the melodic path. Struggle, submission, silence. Finally, they surrendered to the singer's guidance.

And *Cape Town Love* was the result: an expression of total love for the music. "On the plane going home to New York City," Sathima told me in July 1999, "all I could think of was the wonderful, wonderful moments of joy in the music. It was so loving. All I could feel was love, and so I called the recording *Cape Town Love*." In an interview with me in December

1999, even February, an institution in the jazz history of Cape Town, admitted being transformed by the process. Making *Cape Town Love* was something he knew went beyond anything he had done before, through the spontaneity the singer demanded: he had allowed himself to be possessed by the musical moment, to play those old tunes in ways he had never before imagined possible.

The Musical Means of Returning Home

What exactly does it mean to a musician born in South Africa to return home musically? What are the differences between performing jazz in New York or Paris or even London rather than in Cape Town or Johannesburg? In other words, how does one make sense of the significance of where it was done? There are several paths to arriving at an answer to that question (not all necessarily contained in *Cape Town Love*), and I shall touch only briefly on each. First, there is the distinctive sound of South African saxophone playing in large groups that are sometimes described as a wailing sound; the Cape Town, or klopse, rhythm evoking the Cape Town Carnival beat; the cyclical *marabi* harmonic pattern of 1930s South African jazz; and the sense of timing that speaks of the ties in jazz to ballroom and langarm dance. Second, Sathima places the music and its makers in a parallel but different strand of African diasporic history than the conventional jazz narrative centered on the African American diaspora formed out of the slave experience. She creates real and imagined links in a peculiarly South African diasporic lineage, forging a far more complex and racially inclusive history that links several elements: the Khoisan; Cape Sufism and the musical writings of the Indian mystic Imrat Khan; the free jazz movements led in South Africa by Abdullah Ibrahim and particularly Chris McGregor in the late 1950s, with its wider resonances in Europe and the United States in the 1960s; the familiar repertories and musicians, including the music of Ellington, Holiday, Nat "King" Cole, and others; and the popular music hall repertory transmitted from England via the Atlantic island of St. Helena. Third, I take a closer look at the mixed reception of *Cape Town Love* in South Africa through the writing of a series of better- and lesser-informed music critics. Finally, one reminds oneself, there is no purely *musical* home, in that returning home is always a political issue in South Africa and for South

Africans, that is, return is as much about political recognition as it is about the music itself.

Expanded Lineages

The musical lessons of *Cape Town Love* went well beyond the sounds produced in the studio those two days in March 1999. What the recording suggests, in the visual image of the Khoisan rock paintings and in the ways in which Sathima encouraged the musicians to work musically, is also a painful opening up of the silenced history of what it means in South Africa to be categorized as Cape Coloured. Not for all, but certainly for some. *Boesman* (bushman) was the derogatory term applied to those Cape Coloureds who were small in stature and had tight, curly hair and whose ancestors had mixed freely or in bondage with European settlers, Chinese and Indian indentured laborers, and freed or bonded Africans from the Eastern Cape, Angola, and Mozambique. These *basters* (bastards) with their curly hair are the ones whose art and beliefs are inscribed into the pages of the *Cape Town Love* liner notes, redefining the supposedly shameful past of the boesman as something that should be closely examined for its extraordinary qualities.

Sathima invoked that lineage in the studio when Basil Moses, the bass player, began to play with the idea of an African waltz in "If You Were the Only Boy in the World," and Sathima found the courage to sing "wordless." When the two musicians surrendered to the music and allowed for a more local feel in rendering the song, Sathima remembered the Khoisan connection. She reminded me in our later conversation of those strands of musical history in the Cape: the string playing of the Khoisan peoples, and of *tariek* (trance), the form of trance one needs to enter if one is to creatively transform the old into something new. *Tariek* is a word that emerged out of Cape Muslim history, a history of Sufi musical and spiritual practices that came to the port with the first Indonesian exiles sent to the Cape of Good Hope in the eighteenth century. But it is also an idea embedded in Khoisan healing practices and medicinal rituals. Here, trance, generated out of long strands of fragmented cultural memory, is constituted as a form of diasporic connection, bringing continuity and wholeness for the South African–born singer returning home.

Cape Muslim history, focused on Sufism and Islamic practices from

Indonesia rather than from the Middle East, reveals a similarly complex musical language and belief system in the Cape. Sathima was raised Anglican, although she would later convert to Islam along with Ibrahim. Her newly adopted name, Sathima, is not actually Muslim (Fathima would be) but, as noted, was given to her by the South African jazz musician Johnny Dyani in Europe. While she no longer adheres to Islamic law, particularly because of the restrictions it places on women, I can't help but hear the sound of the muezzin in the ways in which Sathima plays with the nuances of pitch and in the microtonal inflection in her singing. Her respect for the words of a song is equal to the respect shown for the words of the Qu'ran in recitation. And with the sound of the words, her tender caressing of each syllable, Sathima makes her place in the world of jazz, much like the muezzin articulates the particularity of his own style and voice by means of minute timbral contrasts in the Adhan and recitation of the Qu'ran.[7]

Local Reviews

For the most part, South African jazz critics welcomed *Cape Town Love*, reading it along the fault lines of musical memory and the emotional depth and love instilled in the listener. For those whose childhood memories or past personal experiences are stirred by the music—the critic Gary van Dyk, for example, recalls the Gracie Fields version of "If You Were the Only Boy in the World" played on a "scratched 78 in our household"—*Cape Town Love* is recognized as a piece of living history ("Tonight," in the *Cape Argus*, 26 July 1999). The music and the musicians represent prior eras of jazz performance that continue to resonate with listeners through the freshness and creativity of the musical interpretations. As the music of Ellington was valued for its references to material abundance, upward social mobility, and signs of social prestige in the 1940s, so Sathima's voice is likened to the upper echelons of social class: "Voice like chocolate cream liqueur in a crystal glass" (de Villiers, *The Citizen*, 24 June 1999); and, invoking the refined taste required to recognize the high quality of a red wine or the authenticity of provenience of a priceless piece of antique furniture, Tebogo Alexander calls it "a definite collector's piece for connoisseurs."[8]

The musical renditions might evoke the local, but it is the emotional intensity, the warmth, romance, and even love that reviewers read into the recording, which mark a greater sense of the universality of jazz as human expression. Being open to the emotive ties that bind listeners of a range of class, gender, and racial categories together in their attachment to the *Cape Town Love* recording is also historically and politically situated. In the anti-apartheid struggle one was considered a sellout if one used the emotive qualities or words of love songs: there had to be a clear political agenda reflected in the performance and its interpretation. In the apartheid era, a white Afrikaans man like Kobus Burger, the critic for *Die Burger*, is unlikely to have told the singer in an interview when she asked him why he liked her music that it was the warmth and the emotion he responded to. And Sathima would never have had the freedom to reply, as Burger reported her to have done: "Ons is almal emosionele mense, baie warm mense. (We are all emotional people, very warm people)" (*Die Burger*, 29 June 1999).

Finally, Sathima performs both a curatorial and creative role in *Cape Town Love*, by both opening up the archive and showcasing the living representatives of a musical tradition, namely, Coloured langarm, or ballroom, dance. She pays tribute to these musicians and the music they perform by providing a musical space for them to explore the full extent of their creative capacity, accompanied by round after round of hot tea and also of full-bodied laughter, not because life is funny but because laughing is often the only way to transcend its absurd character and often painful legacy.

Ultimate Contribution

I have already suggested that there are no easy ways to return home, whether after three decades in exile or after having been away for just a while. And this is certainly the case for those seeking to reconnect in postapartheid South Africa. But the gift that great leaders like Mandela and thousands of other less famous South Africans — politicians, economists, singers, dancers, actors, painters — have given to South Africans in the twentieth-century diaspora is the capacity to reenter, if not completely return to, the land of their birth. This is a fundamental difference between the contemporary experiences of Africans whose ancestors were sent to America as slaves, and who may have struggled to go back to the sites of exit (into slavery) several hundred years ago. There is no clear way for members of the old diaspora to reconstitute the missing links, to fill the gaps in history, culture, religion, and, indeed, the complete loss of language (Henry Louis Gates is arguing that DNA may provide a solution to these forms of loss, but only time will tell how useful this mode of analysis is).

The story has been a fundamentally different one for South Africans like Sathima and Abdullah, who, when life in South Africa became unlivable, found a way to constitute a home away from home through the music, both local and imported. It was the music, again, that enabled survival when these musicians moved abroad. And it is ultimately as musicians and through musical means that each struggles to carve out a path of return, to open themselves to the local once again, and to begin to share with those who remained behind something of what they have learned outside South Africa.

RESPONSE

Jazz History as Living History

Racism messes history up. Its victims get separated from their past and are condemned to dwell in a permanent present. . . . There should be no surprise that the struggle against racism involves a tussle over what will count as history. As it unfolds, we discover that the line between the past and the present is not fixed. It can be moved around. Where the threshold falls determines when and how history can appear, what its shape will be, and the extent of its claims upon those who inherit it. — Gilroy, liner notes to *London Is the Place* recording

Living history is the idea expressed when those from the old and new African diasporas play and record jazz together. This capacity to perform together, and to archive such performances through recording, extends the story of jazz from a linear geographical progression to one that circulates back and forth between Africa and America. When musicians from

30. Sathima's African diasporic lineage in jazz, from an early Benjamin record cover. *Left to right*: Rudy Van Gelder, Abdullah Ibrahim, Billy Higgins, Onaje Allan Gumbs, Buster Williams, Sathima Bea Benjamin, Ben Riley, Carlos Ward. *Photograph by George Hallett.*

the new Africa diaspora perform with those of the older diaspora, the music itself becomes the material evidence of routes and layers of African musical history over the past several hundred years right up to the present. The joint performances urge one to look with fresh eyes at the parallel and overlaid chronologies of African and American musical pasts as well as at their points of intersection.

The notion of living history also extends narrations of the past to include ordinary citizens who otherwise remain without historical representation. What separates this kind of historicism from the more conventional forms is that it is the participants—the groups and individuals—who recognize the historical significance of the moment and their part in the making of history while they are alive, not years after they have passed on. It is a kind of historical inscription from the bottom up. Such recognition of significant events in the present that are making history is typically fueled by the mass media in its local, regional, and, often, global messages. Claims to a place in history are not necessarily carved out in terms of their individual contributions to human knowledge or the betterment of the human condition, but often are earned through the individual and collective suffering caused by oppressive regimes. It is as members of a community, whether religious, national, or political; as witnesses to unprecedented social transformation at a particular place and moment in time; and often as survivors that individuals constitute a space for themselves as agents of history. This is democratic historiography.

To participate in the present is to lay the foundations of future representations of the past, of histories that will be written in the future. Ordinary citizens living in extraordinary times inscribe the ordinary self into the annals of greatness. "To see oneself on the scale of History, this action is recent," writes Roland Barthes. He attributes such consciousness to the development of new mediums of self-inscription, specifically, the photograph: "The Photograph is the advent of myself as other, a cunning dissociation of consciousness from identity."[9] So, too, the phonograph and the video camera have become media of dual markers of the self.

There are those, for example, who viewed the construction and then the fall of the wall that separated East from West Berlin; those who survived concentration camps or oppressive regimes; and those who witnessed the departure of colonial regimes in Africa. Americans were largely excluded from such experiences in their home territory until the terror attacks of 11 September 2001 and, more recently, the historic election of the first African American president, Barack Obama. Similarly, South Africans who lived through the transition from apartheid to the newly formed nonracial democracy carry with them an exuberant sense of having become living participants in and witnesses to the makings of history. To have stood in line in the first democratic elections was to know and to feel in that moment what it is like to have done something that would go down in history. It was to leave one's mark in a small but personally, nationally, even globally significant way. Similarly, to have voted in the election of 2008 in the United States when Barack Obama became the first black president was to have been a part of what everyone knew was historically significant. American citizens were living the moment children would learn about as history in succeeding generations.

Living history conveys the will to animate the past in the present using new technologies: all three examples explored below involve accessing and thickening one's memory of the past through contemporary media and technologies. Each accomplishes what might have seemed impossible in earlier times. Each breathes life or liveliness into the frailty of human memory. One thinks, for example, of the desire that grips the mourner as she lovingly gazes at the photograph of a cherished family member, now gone, but more alive in one's memory through the life of the image. Similarly, one captures the feeling of living history upon hearing the voice of someone who has died resurrected through recorded sound, as in "Unforgettable," the digitally generated duet sung by Nat "King" Cole and his daughter Natalie. Third, in an emotionally less fraught but equally mediated example, I am reminded of my marriage in Durban, South Africa, in 1987. There were three forms of visual documentation: the black-and-white art photos, the more conventional pictures in color, and the video camera. I hadn't thought of the three forms as being connected prior to that day. Within hours of the event we sat down to watch the video my uncle had shot of the day's events. A week or so later we mulled over the color photographs. An odd sensation came over me: as I looked at the still images, fragments of the video created a kind of soundtrack in my mind to the otherwise lifeless images in color or black and white. Quite unexpectedly, while the color photographer was taking more or less posed portraits of the family and bridal party, the videographer was standing close at hand. These "memories" of the day, captured on video, viewed earlier, replayed in my mind as we looked again at the still photos, filling out the details with what would otherwise have been forgotten—the silly comments and offhand laughter. Rather than slipping into the recesses of contingency and the forgotten details of life as it passes by, these moments were resurrected, even *reinvented*, through the running commentary inserted in my head via the audiovisual format of the videotape. These layers of image making of a single event function much like the aural palimpsest of popular song articulated in Sathima's *Cape Town Love* project.

Living history can also convey a desire *not* to animate the past in the present, but rather to remain completely removed from the power it can exert over one. The capacity to silence the echoes of the past, to purge oneself of its memory is what those who have lived through traumatic times often wish for. The rupture between past and present, the satisfaction that the past they lived through and survived was over, once and for all, and the sense of possibility that the present and future offered were manifestly articulated for me in the interviews I conducted with Sathima's extended family in 1996. Just two years after Mandela had been democratically voted into power as state president, Basil Rich and John Samuels drew the line several times as we spoke between the pre-Mandela days and the years of his governance in the mid-1990s. They were visibly (and audibly) relieved that they would never again have to live under the repressive ways of the past. In contrast to this gesture, Colin Miller at the District Six Museum in Cape Town told me of the ways in which regime change seemed to free people in the Coloured community to reminisce about the past, to tell their stories freely, without fear of harassment or retribution. No one had any desire to return to those days, and, freed from the fear of their return, they could now tell their side of the nation's history. "The restoration of narrative" is how Njabulo Ndebele talked of the significance of the Truth and Reconciliation Commission and of the larger project of nation building in the mid-1990s.

Postapartheid policymakers have privileged those who have "lived history" to stand in as witness to past brutality. Like others overseeing public institutions and sites of remembrance elsewhere in the world, South Africans have incorporated political prisoners under the apartheid regime as tour guides in the places of their incarceration on Robben Island and dispossession in District Six, Cape Town. The World Trade Center in New York has followed suit: those who lost family members at ground zero in September 2001 have been trained as tour guides. In South Africa, those who testified before the Truth and Reconciliation Commission, pathologized as unpatriotic in the apartheid era, were reclassified as human witnesses to the devastating effects of apartheid on friends and family members. They qualified because they bore the burden of torture and incarceration. Human voices testified, sometimes uncertain voices, tripped up by frail memories, often halted by irrepressible pain. "Truth has become woman," wrote Antje Krog in *Country of My Skull*, the partly poetic, partly truthful account of her experience as a journalist covering the commission. And in becoming woman, history as we knew it could never again be so sure of its method. In the process historians have gained a far more textured knowledge of their subjects.

Finally, living history is useful in thinking about the past in jazz, a phrase I prefer over jazz history. These are currently two conventional ways of

thinking about jazz: the first privileges the immediacy and ephemeral-
ness of the present moment in the "infinite art of improvisation," that is,
the newly made in each performance;[10] the second constitutes a durable
past for itself through the immutable material object, the sound recording. The dialectic between the mutability of live performance and the immutable sound recording has largely been naturalized in jazz historiography — performers carry inside themselves archives of prior performances
that bear the traces of other performances, much like a palimpsest, while
jazz historians constitute a historical narrative through the analysis of a
series of sound recordings grouped into self-contained eras or stylistic
periods. I play with this dialectic in reflecting on new paths for thinking
about the past in jazz, invoking the idea of living history as one such possibility.

In introducing the idea of living history to jazz (and popular music)
studies, I will address below the conventions and practices of jazz historians with a key dialectic in jazz performance and history. The dialectic encompasses the lack of congruency between permanence and eva-
nescence that jazz engenders among its performers and generates for its
consumers, critics, and historians. I suggest that the contradictory demands provide clues to innovative ways of rethinking jazz historiography,
from the evolutionary paradigm of musical periodization that marks the
"march of musical progress" into the future — which individual recordings of past performances sustain — to a more visceral or "spirited" connection between past and present.[11] I want to think of the past in three
dimensions: as a palimpsest as well as a chronology, and viewed in its
verticality at least as much as in its horizontal movement from point A
to point B; the third dimension stems from the idea of living history, the
spirit of the past carried forth in human memory. This depth of perception should provide a mechanism to reinvigorate jazz history by making
it into a narrative shaped by a freshly conceived diasporic sensibility, a
sensibility that continually inserts other times and places into present
moments and spaces.

To illustrate my point, I return to the relationship between jazz performance and the city, introduced in my earlier discussion of Sathima's
relationship to New York City and to Cape Town, the place of her childhood. I ask you, the reader, to picture in your mind a series of images of
a city skyline.[12] First, think of yourself as being at a considerable distance

from the skyline, positioned on the other side of a river, for example. With the image clear in your mind's eye, move the eye slowly from left to right across the skyline — and as you do so, imagine that each building represents an era in jazz history, or at least a different moment in the chronological mapping of jazz history as you know it. Imagine now what you might be able to deduce about the building or historical moment from what you are able to make out from your place across the river. What you see on the outside might be as much as there is to know from where you are standing. Perhaps, if you have some knowledge of architectural history, you can identify the name of the architect by the size, shape, and character of the construction of the building, but it is unlikely, from your position, that you will be able to glean much more knowledge than the surface information projected by the building to the outside world. One certainly cannot capture the sound of each place at such a distance or any sense of the people who inhabit the city. This is a two-dimensional perspective of the past in jazz, identical to its representation in the written narrative — it lacks a sense of hearing.

Now, get a slightly different feel for the city by positioning yourself inside its skyline and at the top of one of its buildings. To help you arrive at this imagined space, read de Certeau's description of what it is like to view the Manhattan skyline from the perspective of Windows on the World, the restaurant that was at the top of the North Tower of the World Trade Center. He writes, "Seeing Manhattan from the 110th floor of the World Trade Center. Beneath the haze stirred up by the winds, the urban island, a sea in the middle of the sea, lifts up the skyscrapers over Wall Street, sinks down at Greenwich, then rises again to the crests of Midtown, quietly passes over Central Park and finally undulates off into the distance beyond Harlem. A wave of verticals. . . . To be lifted to the summit of the World Trade Center is to be lifted out of the city's grasp. One's body is no longer clasped by the streets . . . nor is it possessed . . . by the rumble of so many differences and by the nervousness of New York traffic."[13]

Elegiac in the wake of the attacks of 11 September on the United States, this excerpt is particularly powerful in the image it produces of the topography of verticality that characterized this view of New York City. De Certeau refers to the godlike sense one gained from being at the top of the building. It invoked the city as stationary, a fixed but welcoming set of landmarks easily recognized from a celestial vantage point. As one reads the description and calls to mind prior experiences of viewing the city from the Twin Towers or from a similar place, like the midtown perspective of the Empire State Building, the mind's eye moves over the changing contours of the city's skyline. Positioned within the boundaries of the city, one nevertheless remains beyond the "liveness" generated by the sounds and experiences of the city — one has a sense only of what it looks like from above. By way of analogy, this is the view one has of the past in jazz as one surveys the progression of style through the medium of sound recordings and jazz history books in the twenty-first century. The listener can understand the historical progression and garner some knowledge of the past neatly packaged into specific periods, but one remains aloof, never really feeling humanly connected. Each period of the past in jazz remains sealed off from the next, each is a building unto itself, even if the total spectacle coheres as a single entity: a skyline or history.

Now, imagine taking the elevator down from the buildings and reintegrate yourself into the life of the city on the ground, through the words, again, of de Certeau but also of Jean Baudrillard. De Certeau describes those on the street as walkers, creating a grounded citizenry defined by movement through the city: The ordinary practitioners of the city live "down below. They walk, an elementary form of this experience of the city; they are walkers."[14]

From Baudrillard one captures a greater sense of the city as performative; he conveys the drama of the city for ordinary walkers and, finally, what it sounds like: "Nothing could be more intense, electrifying, turbulent, and vital than the streets of New York. They are filled with crowds, bustle, and advertisements, each by turn aggressive or casual. There are millions of people in the streets, wandering, carefree, violent, as if they had nothing better to do . . . than produce the continuous scenario of the city. There is music everywhere."[15]

In de Certeau's analysis, those who walk in the city are always moving, passing by without ever seeming to arrive. The contrast between the first image — of the two-dimensional skyline; and the second — of the three-dimensional panoptic view; and the third — the embodied sense of being in time and on the streets — is striking, almost unnerving. The first is clearly mapped, stationary, without human connection; the second brings one a little closer to the action but retains a panoptic power and a distance; but the third, the more humanly engaged, is always in process. All are ways of knowing the city and, to extend the metaphor to jazz, ways of knowing the past and present in jazz, that is, from the distant, objective narrative of the past to the liveliness of new performance in the present. There is a fourth and final vantage point: this is the perspective that brings one into much closer contact with the city walkers and the relationship they imagine with the built environment of the city, which invokes in one a desire to connect to the past through the built environment or jazz performance. From a perspective far less exaggerated and more personal than Baudrillard's, Sathima's description of her relationship to New York City reads as follows: "New York affords you much. . . . I actually use the busy streets as a place to ponder and reflect. I call it 'meditation in motion.' Being amongst its diverse peoples every day, I feel at home."[16]

A similar but more historically self-conscious position is described by the Haitian historian Michel-Rolph Trouillot in his writing on silences in historical accounts of the Haitian Revolution. His visit to the Palace of Sans Souci, the burial place of "Christophe — Henry I, the King of Haiti," prompts him to write, "I walked in silence between the old walls, trying to guess at the stories they would never dare tell. I had been in the fort since daybreak. I had lost my companions on purpose: I wanted to tiptoe through the remains of history. Here and there, I touched a stone, a piece of iron hanging from the mortar, overlooked or left by unknown hands for unknown reasons. . . . I stepped across my dreams up to the pile of concrete . . . I knew the man. I had read about him in my history books as do all Haitian schoolchildren; but that was not why I felt close to him. I wanted to be closer. More than a hero, he was a friend of the family. My father and uncle talked about him by the hours when I was still a child."[17]

"Tiptoe[ing] through the remains of history" is a delightful metaphor for what both the historian and the singer struggle to achieve in their engagement with remnants of the past. Trouillot's narrative works in parallel to the ways in which I have argued Sathima has engaged the past in jazz as a medium for contemporary renditions in the present and the future. Jazz performance embodies for Sathima a relationship similar to the past that Sans Souci does for Trouillot: both strive to connect by animating memories of earlier times in the present; not to the past as shut off from the present in closed containers of historical periods that are over and done, but to the past as open and receptive to the present as it is woven into the larger historical narrative. The singer and the historian engage in a continuous process of reevaluating, respectively, the life of jazz and the life of history in the future by thinking of its past as an archive of living history that musicians and historians, in their presentations and representations, are continually recuperating, reinterpreting, and envisioning new possibilities for. In this vein, jazz performance and historiography shift from being narratives of innovation and rupture to ones in which there is greater continuity in transformations from one form or period to another and a far stronger connection between living people and their pasts. In this more spirited and certainly more poetic mode of being in the world of jazz, jazz history is not solely a thing of the past, objectified and fixed as a series of great, but forever lost, moments; rather, it is shaped out of a past always newly imagined and recreated in live performance, instilling a certain agency into those still living.

I am positing a fundamentally different way of thinking about one's relationship to the past and to notions of jazz history in ethnomusicology. This new way of thinking is, I believe, a distinctive contribution ethnomusicologists can make to larger questions about the relationship between anthropology and history because it addresses the differences between a written and an oral and aural past and their connection to human memory. Sound matters to human memory, and the medium of transmission shapes its message. This is perhaps best illustrated in a pattern I have noticed in the telling of the past in jazz in the United States on public radio and in written texts. On radio, particularly public stations broadcast from historically black universities and colleges, program content relies heavily on the memories of particular musicians and on oral testimony, while official written narratives of jazz history draw far less on the perspectives of cultural insiders themselves, focusing instead on seminal moments contained in sound recordings and the authority of the critic or scholar. There are notable exceptions to this notion, but in general radio is a superior medium for giving life to the narratives of musicians than the written word.

Such a perspective on the past in jazz is quintessentially a way of imagining oneself present in an ever-expanding sense of a living history: a history of absent voices invigorated and enlivened through the presence of voices themselves from other times and places. If scholars think about the expanding sense of living history in the context of the new African diaspora we begin to incorporate new vocabularies for older models to allow for new sounds and standards of judgment. Not only are music scholars to rethink our assumptions about *the* African diaspora, but as ethnomusicologists we should lead the way in opening the boundaries of jazz performance to a worldwide palette of musical possibilities. We need to insist on the possibility of multiple narrations in the writing of official histories and invite multiple sources of origin, forms of memory, and musical overlay.

7

Musical Echoes

Musical echoes shine like the mirrors of my soul;
Reflecting all the joy and pain and the love that makes me whole.
Transcending all the blues; my tender spirit pays its dues.
And all the while, in a jazz-tinged style,
Those musical echoes heal my broken heart.
—Sathima Bea Benjamin, "Musical Echoes,"
from the CD *Musical Echoes* (2004)

CALL

Sathima's Musical Echo

In 2002, several years after receiving the words and melody of "Musical Echoes" in a dream, Sathima traveled from New York City to Cape Town to record the song and produce a CD of the same name. Her trio included the American Stephen Scott on piano and the South Africans Lulu Gontsana on drums and Basil Moses on bass. I have borrowed Sathima's notion of the musical echo for the name of this book, but also for reflecting on the possibilities the echo offers to music scholars for thinking about jazz and popular music as globally distributed forms in the twenty-first century.

My point of entry is the cover of the CD *Musical Echoes*, which shows a color photograph of Sathima at home, alone at the edge of the Atlantic Ocean in Cape Town as the sun begins to rise. Sathima's name and the disc title are italicized silver lines in the clouds. Her trio has no visual counterpart, but their names are inscribed on the right side of the image. Sathima stands to the left of the frame, facing right, staring out into the expansiveness of the ocean, an ocean that connects her to the Americas, her other home. Her hands are clasped at her breast, layers of white chiffon envelop her small frame, and an opaque shawl hugs her upper torso. She is barefoot on freshly washed white sand.

A profound feeling of solitude, of deep reflection at the dawn of a new

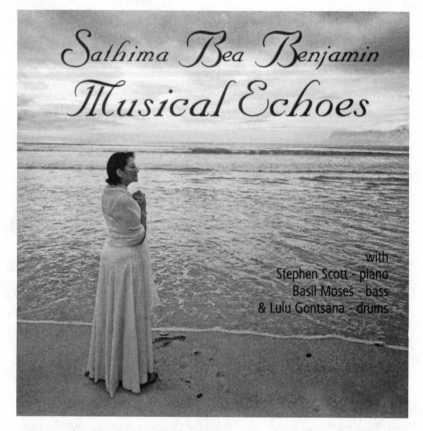

31. Cover of Sathima's *Musical Echoes*.

day pervades the image. The tide is low: long, languid waves gently ebb and flow. Though the water is tinged with blue, there are no other signs of turmoil, pain, or struggle. The echoes of the ocean caress the ears, the wisps of an early morning breeze touch lightly without disturbing the peace. She knows where she is, but the usual topographical or tourist markers do not appear in the image. There is no close-up of the level top of Table Mountain, with Devil's Peak on the right, the cableway lining the mountain slope; no view from Blaauwberg Strand, the Table Bay view, or the sight of the Twelve Apostles. In Sathima's photograph there is a feeling that the scene could be of any coastline in the world. Ambiguity prevails. Here the local and personally significant merge with the universally familiar. So too does Sathima's voice elide into the globally constituted world of jazz.

In fact, her standing at the edge of the ocean reminds one of Sathima's approach to jazz and to life itself: she is the romantic, the woman who privileges the natural and the unprocessed but subtle, in her sound. The viewer has no inkling of the intrusion of the noises of modernity, the bustle of the city, or the emotional stresses of everyday life. Rather, the solitariness of the moment gives her the space to let her heart and mind roam freely: to imagine, remember, dream, envision, and return to the sounds of her childhood — family visits to the beach, the movies, the sounds of radio and record, live and mediated, copies and originals, on stage and in the streets. As she revisits the echoes of sound she has carried inside for so long, the real and the remembered merge: it is this singularity, captured in the photographic moment, a coming full circle, uniting past and present, home and elsewhere, which ultimately heals.

The absence of the noises of modernity and mass-mediated music stands in stark contrast to the observation I have made over and over in this book, that the first echoes of the British and American originating music Sathima embraced as her own came out of her grandmother's radio and from audio recordings, the soundtracks of Hollywood film, and especially the musicals that were so popular in Cape Town during her childhood. Such technologies brought the music that shaped new communities locally; they certainly stimulated individual imaginings of a host of musical forms and constituencies, indigenous and imported, and sometimes enabled those who moved away to retain memories. South African jazz and popular music and Sathima's place in the history of that music are two manifestations of that process. We have already seen how Sathima coined a variety of terms to articulate a place for herself in jazz history, as an American, a South African, and, indeed, in a new narrative of the African diaspora. The musical echo is the most recent of the metaphors she has used to create a place for herself as a subject of contemporary African diaspora and the idea most pertinent to this book.

RESPONSE

Reflections on Echo

What does Sathima allude to when she invokes the musical echo? What makes the idea of the *musical* echo a resonant metaphor in Sathima's story about South African jazz, both at home and abroad? I define the echo as an acoustical rather than a specifically musical phenomenon, that is, as sound that travels through space rather than as culturally situated performance. I propose that the practice of echolocation is crucial to a project like *Musical Echoes* because it allows for temporal and spatial displacement i.e., diaspora, and for the possibility of a response to the original sound. I examine the recurring figure of Echo in classical mythology, and the perhaps surprising ways in which the story of the mythical character Echo continues to resonate transhistorically: it contributes to my purposes here and parallels Sathima's story. Drawing on Elaine Scarry's essays that argue the value of beauty lies in the creative responses it evokes in its viewers, I suggest that jazz has operated in similar ways for its consumers and listeners both in the United States and much farther away. In Sathima's mind, the musical echo involves call and response as an ongoing process between communities dispersed around the world. It was, after all, the echoes of the music that traveled to South Africa from the United States in the postwar period that gave birth to a whole new community of musicians, who in turn shared their sounds with others as they traveled.

The Echo Defined

Acoustically, an echo is simply defined as the repetition or imitation of a sound emanating from a source. Visually, one represents this phenomenon as an acoustical signal in the center of ever-widening circles or waves of repeating sound. The image is useful for representing the idea that a source sound in a resonant space can echo back, but it is less helpful for communicating ways in which an original sound, or the resonances of the original, might be transformed at any point on the resonating waves. In other words, in relation to the original sound the echo is conventionally viewed as something hollow or fading; it abides by a currency of diminishing returns and is dismissed as mere repetition or imitation.[1] In the canonical history of jazz, it is Walter Benjamin's aura of the *original* sound in the age of mechanical reproduction, and not the echo or copy of the original, which has been valued by American musicians and historians. There has been little recognition that the replica could generate new possibilities of any real value elsewhere in the world.

In a limited manner, this perspective began to shift when the original—live or recorded live—moments of jazz were distributed by the music industry worldwide. In this context, the echo or copy of the original moment accrued value as a commodity. Copies were mass produced as musical objects and globally distributed for profit, a process that contributed to the global hegemony of the original moments of jazz and to the canonical histories written about those moments for Americans and the world market. While the owners of music industries relished the spread of jazz for the profits they reaped, until recently jazz historians and consumers in the United States tended to remain closed to the effect that traveling commodities might have had on local communities.

Sathima's story suggests, however, that by tracing how these commodities travel the world one gains a capacity to see the echo or copy of the original sound from a new perspective. This idea is illustrated in the commonly used dictionary definition of the echo: the "persistence of a sound after its source has stopped," which introduces the idea of a time lag, of temporal displacement, but also perhaps of fashion and its consequences or, indeed, of the capitalist notion of uneven development in the so-called Third World.[2] In this reading, each repetition of the initial sound makes contact with an ever-widening circle of possibility. Imagine, for example, how complex the story of Duke Ellington's *Black, Brown and Beige* would become if we tracked the routes traveled by several copies of the recording simultaneously. One goes to London, one to Tokyo, another to Brisbane, a fourth to Moscow, one to Venice, one to Hamburg, and the last goes all the way to Cape Town, South Africa. Assuming each record is bought at each of these places, one quickly realizes that the original takes on a life of its own once it leaves the shores of the United States. Each gains what Arjun Appadurai called a "social life," and the lifespan of the echo would extend from being a single, transient moment in time and place to occurring over a period of time and encompassing a certain distance. And, in the hands of musicians in local communities, the recorded echo would soon begin to generate its own sounds. While there might have been some audible connection to the original sounds local musicians once heard and copied, translated locally over time their origins would become unrecognizable.

Echolocation embodies this principle. It is defined as a sensory system found among animals, including bats and dolphins, in which high-pitched sounds are sent out so that their echoes can be used to determine the direction and distance of objects. In other words, the reverberation of the acoustical echo maps distance via a sonic signal. With its return comes the capacity to measure proximity. In this sense, echolocation signals the pressure to constantly evaluate the relationship between parts in space and time and displaces the hegemony of the original sound at the center.

Setting the echo in motion, as I am suggesting scholars need to do, opens up the rhetorical space for those who heard American originating jazz and popular music as it traveled the airwaves and embraced and transformed it to fit local sensibilities. For many living beyond the United States, the music that echoed out from the United States generated points of contact and realized new relationships at a variety of places on the acoustical landscape. Through the echoes of sound produced elsewhere and translated locally as exact recorded repetition, entire communities absorbed, reenacted, and mastered foreign repertory and style. In other words, I believe that at its core the echo conveys the qualities of and bears strong resemblance to the diasporic subject. The echo articulates spatial, temporal, and cultural displacement, which is frequently accompanied by a discourse of loss and suffering. The echo may also reference individuals and communities on the move in search of upward social mobility, people who nevertheless inhabit two or more spaces simultaneously: living in one place, they continually exist in reference to vivid memories of and imaginings of continuing relationships with another. This is how I have defined new or contemporary forms of African diaspora.

The Bengali historian Dipesh Chakrabarty has derived the notion of the two histories of capital, which provides a theoretical nest for the relationship between the sound of jazz and its echoes in the world at large that I propose here. Chakrabarty's "History One" is the universal narrative of the universally accepted singular history of capital.[3] That history originates in Europe and catches up elsewhere in the world through a discourse of "uneven development." In the history of jazz and popular music, History One is the universalizing narrative of the production, circulation, and distribution of musical commodities that begin in the United States and subsequently spread elsewhere. This narrative is conventionally categorized as the canonical history of jazz and popular music. There are several versions of the narrative of jazz and popular music, and they are continually updated with the emergence of new technologies, new modes of distribution and consumption, and the merging and acquisition of transnational entertainment corporations. It is a history that is both celebratory in its demonstration of the powers of the free market economy to spread to the farthest corners of the earth and characterized by anxiety, as the global entertainment industry is read as a central mechanism of twentieth-century cultural imperialism and homogenization.[4] In other words, Chakrabarty's History Two, while indelibly tied to History One, is not merely the dialectical other (2000, 66). History Two is a category "charged with the function of constantly interrupting the totalizing thrusts of History One."[5] Chakrabarty's History Two is the affective history that allows for narratives of human belonging and diversity that the totalizing narrative of History One sublates. In the application of Chakrabarty's two histories to music, History Two becomes the affective history of the consumption of American jazz and popular music in commodity form.

I have found Chakrabarty's notion of two histories to be particularly useful as I have struggled over the years to constitute a rhetorical space for writing about South African jazz so that it strikes up a conversation with the American canon, rather than existing in a regional studies cocoon, as if there was no point of contact between the two places and their musical pasts. Furthermore, while I am concerned about an inherent feminization in Chakrabarty's characterization of History Two, that is, as disruptive and affective relative to the rational, established master narrative presumed by History One, I continue to find it a useful point of departure for conceptualizing a worldwide history of jazz and popular music.

The Echo in Greek Mythology

In Greek mythology, "Echo was the name of a nymph whose unrequited love for Narcissus caused her to pine away until nothing but her voice remained."[6] A second definition provides more detail and greater violence. "Echo: . . . a nymph deprived of speech by Hera in order to stop her chatter, and left able only to repeat what others had said. On being repulsed by Narcissus she wasted away with grief until there was nothing left of her but her voice." In a third account Echo was loved in vain by the god Pan, who finally caused some shepherds to go mad and tear her to pieces; Earth hid the fragments, which could, nevertheless, still imitate other sounds.[7] A further telling of the myth suggests that the punishment inflicted on the nymph was double-edged. Renamed Echo, she would never again be permitted a place as primary utterance, as, on one hand, "second sex" speech was futile and lacking real value;[8] but on the other, hers would always be the final articulation: she was given the last word.

Several readings of the myth are relevant to "Musical Echoes," each of which is defined by a feeling of resonance between what is heard coming from the outside and what is produced locally. First, the idea of a resonating echo ties the history of the first African diaspora—a diaspora forged out of slavery, the sale of Africans into bondage from the seventeenth century through the nineteenth—to that of the new African diaspora through similarities in the social, political, cultural, bodily, and musical experiences of Africans. In a second reading of the myth, the figure of Echo foreshadows sound recording technology in the contemporary world, where the body is absent, the whole person is compressed and conveyed in the sound of the voice alone or in its supplement, the musical instrument. The voice or its supplement, not the living human being, transmits remnants of distant places, experiences, and sounds to far-flung people. It is the objectified voice or its supplement that makes contact. Via a third, more dramatic reading of the echo, one might explain jazz under apartheid in South Africa. There, the story of Echo foretells the horrible acts of violence inflicted by the state on South Africans: silenced voices, dismembered bodies, grieving women—tearing, shredding, narcissism, driven to madness. As such the ancient myth resonates transhistorically with the experiences of many South Africans and, more specifically, with dozens of musicians, jazz and otherwise, in the era of grand apartheid: the state and its keepers (as Narcissus or Pan) against the people (as the feminized character Echo).[9] There is a fourth and final level of value in the mythical account: when I related the story of the wasting away of Echo because of her unrequited love for Narcissus, Sathima commented wryly that the story of Echo was indeed her own, opening the way for the echo and autobiography, as does the song written by Sathima (cited above). Sathima has frequently said her recordings are all her children will inherit when she dies; and certainly her struggle as a singer of jazz has been a battle against the common view of the futility of female chatter in jazz performance.

The Echoes of Jazz and the Reinstatement of Beauty

At the heart of Sathima's struggle as a jazz singer has been, on the one hand, the lack of recognition by some that South Africans could be jazz musicians and creators of their own improvised music; and, on the other, the perceived problem that she didn't look or sound African enough in her body or articulation of musical style.[10] This was particularly the case in the anti-apartheid struggle abroad. Duke Ellington did much to welcome her into the jazz fold and to set her up in New York City. But he died in the early 1970s, and not everyone in the world of jazz has had Ellington's breadth of vision and understanding of the ties between the old and new African diasporas or of the global spread of jazz (and of his music in particular) from the earliest moments of its recording. Many have asked, how could Sathima and other South Africans have embraced this musical language in the ways they have if they were not born in the United States?

In response, my final reflections on the appropriateness of the musical echo for articulating Sathima's story come from an unlikely place: the writings of the literary scholar Elaine Scarry on the work of beauty as a project of social justice contained in her two essays included in the book *On Beauty and Being Just* (1999). Underlying Scarry's argument for restoring a central aesthetic place to beauty is the idea that beauty calls out to her readers, drawing them into her space and inspiring them to constitute similar acts and forms of beauty, to seek out unconventional figures, and to protect other beautiful things from harm and destruction. Reading

Scarry several years ago, I was struck by how aptly she seemed to describe the call of jazz for Sathima.

"Beauty," Scarry writes, "brings copies of itself into being. It makes us draw it, take photographs of it [and perform it and record it], or describe it to other people. Sometimes it gives rise to exact replication and other times to resemblances and still other times to things whose connection to the original site of inspiration is unrecognizable. . . . The generation is unceasing."[11] A similar sense of possibility was conveyed in the echoes of American-made music and jazz specifically when they resonated outward from the United States to South Africa in the middle decades of the twentieth century, creating what Scarry, in a similar context, calls a "shared field of attention." Such a shared field is created when "beautiful persons and things incite the desire to create" so that there is the possibility of more than one beautiful object available to the viewer. "You began by copying, by sounding just the same as Joni James or Ella Fitzgerald," Sathima recalled, "but eventually you had to move away from that. Eventually you had to sound like yourself. No two singers are the same." Sounding like James or Fitzgerald, creating the copy, constituted a "shared field of attention" between South Africa and England or the United States.

In this frame, Scarry's writing about beauty constitutes an important intervention in restoring the work of beauty as the goal of aesthetic pleasure and a gesture of social justice in human experience. Her purpose, she writes, is to reinstate the value of beauty in a world in which beauty has become unhinged from notions about the sacred and the transcendent, and where staring at beautiful things and people in particular has come to be defined as action that violates the object of the gaze. She interrogates the current premises of such belief, reminding readers that the idea that the viewer holds power over the object, and not the beautiful object over the viewer, has emerged only relatively recently. Instead of harming the object, Scarry proposes that allowing beauty to transform the viewer may incite in that viewer the urge to protect or to act on behalf of an object of beauty. Further, she argues, beauty exerts pressure on the distributional, that is, the viewer begins not only to care for the extraordinary and singular, but also to value objects of lesser beauty within her field of vision.

For Scarry beauty is a calling. As one responds to beauty's invocation, one is decentered: a "transformation then takes place at the very roots of our sensibility."[12] Beautiful things "act like small tears in the surface of the world that pull us through to some vaster space; or they form 'ladders reaching toward the beauty of the world,' or they lift us . . . letting the ground rotate beneath us several inches."[13] When those called to beauty come back down to earth they discover their perspective has changed, and they exist in a new relationship to the world around them. In the face of beauty, we "willingly cede our ground to the thing that stands before us."[14] In other words, beauty provides an occasion for unself-ing, a process in which our consciousness is changed from a focus on the self toward a desire for goodness. As such beauty is read as a lifesaving mechanism.[15] An extreme form of pleasure accompanies the moments of decentering, moments that enrich the life of the viewer. "The absence of beauty," Scarry concludes, "is a profound form of deprivation."[16]

Scarry's invocation to reconsider beauty parallels ways in which Sathima and others perceived the power of American jazz in their lives and community in South Africa after the Second World War, on one hand, and the kind of alternative habitus constituted out of the sounds of the music and principles of jazz performance, on the other. "Even when beauty and justice are both in the world," writes Scarry, "beauty performs a special service because it is available to sensory perception in a way that justice . . . normally is not.[17] In postwar South Africa there was very little feeling of a just society for people of color, and it was almost impossible to defy the apartheid regime because of the threat of imprisonment, death, or exile. In this context, jazz became a means of imagining a path to freedom. Jazz conveyed the capacity to practice alternative ways of being in the world that were by definition built on principles of freedom of articulation, individual expression in a context of group support, and improvisation.

Particularly once she settled in New York City, Sathima found that jazz became a vehicle for performing the work of beauty that Scarry invokes. As a mother, wife, political activist, and increasingly as a manager, composer, producer, and bandleader, Sathima has created one shared field of attention after another, tenderly opening up acoustical spaces for herself and her male musicians. In each of these spaces she is driven to protect, to act on behalf of, and to require of herself and her musical companions to be decentered by the power of the sound and aesthetic sensibilities of jazz improvisation. In her mind, these sensibilities include spontaneity, love, tenderness, compassion, subtlety, nuance, and the revelation of the sounds of inner human beauty. Her work began not in the corridors of institutions of high art but in the safe corners of her home at the Chelsea and in the anonymity and motion of the streets. Here, she made her music, by spinning "moments of stillness" in the midst of daily routines of childcare, cleaning, cooking, and serving. It was at these moments she insisted on keeping the music and the memory of its source and travel alive in her heart and imagination. These are the moments Serematakis describes as points of self-reflexive femininity.

Performing and recording jazz renditions of old melodies with African American musicians, Sathima has long constituted a field of attention with transatlantic potential. At these moments the histories of the old and the new African diasporas and other transcontinental connections between England, South Africa, St. Helena, and the United States become irrevocably intertwined. As she reintroduces songs from a past long forgotten by the trio but restored to their country of origin and newly made in this venue, such performances create rare, beautiful things: beautiful in themselves but equally poignant in the face of a history of injustice, oppression, gendered struggle, and forgetfulness.

These were and continue to be radical and controversial ways of being for women of color. Nevertheless, these processes have a long history in Sathima's life. When she heard Billie Holiday's voice in song, she knew she had found a musical place for herself in American jazz with a voice that was distinctively her own in every way—from the peculiarity of her South African life experiences to the ways in which she played with melody and timbre, the naturalness of its production, and the depth of feeling she poured into every note she uttered. This resonance heard and rearticulated by Sathima Bea Benjamin has opened up the possibilities for telling a new kind of story about music that travels in the twentieth century and the twenty first.

8

Outcomes—Jazz in the World

While *Musical Echoes: South African Women Thinking in Jazz* has focused
on the specifics of Sathima's life story, and the scholarly reflections that
emerge from that particular story, it begs the question: can a series of
pasts be composed for communities of jazz performance constituted out
of the resonating echoes of music originating elsewhere in the world? If
the answer is yes, then the story of the musical echo fundamentally challenges the contours of ownership, categorization, and place held by the
United States in jazz and popular music history. Instead of imagining history inside the geopolitical borders of America, one must necessarily set
the sounds of jazz in motion well beyond the closed confines of jazz clubs
and concert halls in the United States, imagining them traveling quite
literally across the globe. And it returns scholars once again to the dialectical tension in jazz, a subject raised earlier in the book, between the
unrepeatability of live jazz performance and the fixity and repeatability of
the text in jazz as commodity. I will illustrate this core tension in current
jazz historiography, that is, the tension between the live performance that
cannot travel and the recorded one that does, by asking readers to imagine two different scenarios.

In the first scenario I will illustrate the character of jazz as American
music by asking you, the reader, to take a moment to reflect on the images
conjured in the mind's eye by the words *American nation*. Do they convey a sense of something bounded, geographically bordered, contained,
centered, stable? Or, in this post–9-11 world, is there an increasing unease
about the permeability of a space previously thought to be safe, secure,
and even impenetrable? In a similar vein, consider for a moment what
words or images are evoked when you think about the term *American
music*. How do you respond to the category? And where do you imagine that that music may be located? Is American music contained inside
a dimly lit, intimate club in Los Angeles with a jazz trio and a singer, a
better-lit pub in the Twin Cities with an Elvis impersonator, a karaoke bar
in Chinatown in San Francisco, a concert by the New York Philharmonic
Orchestra, or a bluegrass music festival in the Appalachian Mountains?
Was the image live and communal, associated with people you know? Or

was it with strangers? Do you have a particular place of performance in mind? Perhaps you even recall a multitude of memories tied to repeated listening to a particular song heard on your Walkman or iPod in a variety of places? It is possible you simply drew a blank, even briefly, when you focused on the category. Did you hesitate because suddenly you wondered, what *is* American about the music I consume? Is there a difference between the category of "American" music, i.e., music made in America largely by the "folk," and the more generalized "popular music," made by Americans but intended for global consumption? Perhaps more fundamentally you ask just where is American music located and what exactly do we mean by the category in a world characterized by displacement, diaspora, and deterritorialization?

The second scenario involves the traveling character of jazz as musical echo. Close your eyes and insert into the mind's eye a large dot on a page representing the original site of the sound or style. As the sound is heard it sends out sound waves. Each wave repeats what has just been heard in an ever-widening pattern of concentric circles. In this acoustical image of the echo, one conventionally presumes the space into which the waves are set in motion to be the air around her or him. It is not a place-specific model. In contrast to this, now transfer the acoustical image of the single dot and its resonances onto a surface that is specific as to place, like a world map. Insert the dot representing the sound in a recording studio in New York City, for example. Let it sound once and then allow the waves to ripple outward, making sure that at least portions of the concentric circles of sound reach out to the southernmost tip of Africa. Begin to name the regions, cities, and towns in other continents situated on the rim of the waves generated by the original acoustical event. Put a date on that image; then repeat the process with a new date, perhaps a few days later with either the same musicians or another constellation of stars in your studio in New York City, Chicago, Philadelphia, or Los Angeles. Finally, imagine that you began your acoustical imaging on sheets of transparent or at least translucent paper. Now place one sheet on top of another, and you will capture a glimpse of the new paradigm for thinking about jazz in global perspective through the trope of the musical echo. It is both widely distributed and densely sedimented.

What does this layering of time, place, and acoustical event say about the potential for jazz history to become a multisited, even global, musical phenomenon? At the very least, unlike conventional jazz historiography it is no longer a single narrative that moves from one place on the American map to another, following a linear chronology of significant musical events, personalities, and emergence of new styles every decade or so. While it is clear that particular performances and recordings heard and reenacted have set the sound of jazz in motion, both inside and well beyond the geopolitical borders of the United States, this newer picture of the past in jazz is dense, multilayered, and three-dimensional. It works more as a palimpsest than as an evolutionary chronicle of musical progress that characterizes much writing about jazz history. And it certainly presents a wider palette of musical possibilities for incorporation into its archive.

Final Reflections

By what means do scholars move toward a global, comparative jazz epistemology? E. Taylor Atkins's book *Jazz Planet* (2003) sets the conversation in motion by recognizing the global spread of jazz in the twentieth century from the earliest moments of the history of the entertainment industry.[1] He puts a range of places and a part of their local jazz histories in a single viewing area: the edited volume. In many cases folk idioms indigenize the transnational language of improvisation, chord substitution, and rhythmic displacement that characterizes much performance called jazz. The folkloric is constituted as a mode for local experimentation and distinctive national display in the curatorial manner so familiar to world music traditions of the late twentieth century. Readers witness the difference in jazz between places, an opportunity the edited volume generically provides. Geared toward an English-speaking audience, *Jazz Planet* turns its readers into believers — a global narrative of jazz in the world at large is possible and necessary. And all of this is good.

On further reflection, however, I wonder if putting all these places and their stories into a single book adequately recognizes the challenges endemic to the study and writing about the past in jazz outside of the United States? Other than creating an academic panopticon, how does Atkins's volume differ from simply putting the relatively small, but not insignificant volumes on jazz in Japan, Australia, England, Germany, Cuba, South

Africa, and France on a single shelf in an academic library? Is undertaking research, constructing a narrative, and writing about jazz in other places really the same process as doing such work in the United States? What about methods of investigation? Surely, one has to ask, what is the nature of the extant or possible archive in each place? Are there not fundamental differences in the archival potential between places with supportive and active recording facilities, for example, and those without? What about the relationship between repressive political regimes and those that were more tolerant? And where are the women, where, even, the singers in Atkins's collection of articles? Why does jazz historiography remain so resolutely male regardless of where it is performed or written about?

Another problem in constituting histories of jazz beyond the United States is that all such performance persists in being evaluated by privileging the American center and dismissing music that is purportedly derivative or has been perceived as being influenced by its originals in the United States.[2] In the rare instances that a non-American musician travels to the United States and gains recognition, he (usually it is a male instrumentalist) is subsumed into the supposed history of jazz as if he were born in America. This is particularly problematic for instrumentalists, who rarely speak when they play and thus do not reveal a place of origin by means of accent or terminology. Musically speaking, he ruptures the ties to his non-American past.[3] Or, worse still, musicians from somewhere other than the United States are simply shut out of the American scene by a denial that jazz exists in other places. It has been said so many times: jazz is American music. While this is certainly true in terms of sites of original production and distribution, the commodity history of American-originating jazz tells quite a different story.

Until recently scholars have been reluctant to acknowledge these other pasts: the repertories and performances generated elsewhere in the world have effectively been silenced. South Africans in exile, upon meeting American and European musicians and audiences, quickly discovered that musicians and consumers alike have refused to acknowledge that music made in and by Americans has traveled to *and* sometimes come back from other places. In jazz historiography the challenge to greater inclusiveness is not in the least intended to displace the central place of African Americans as stylistic innovators and pivotal cultural producers. Rather, I would hope that in setting other places and pasts in dialogue with the American version, scholars would more fully recognize the significant worldwide contribution of African American creativity. Such a process is what has taken place in American studies generally, as the real contribution of African American cultural practices — in sport, music, and literature — to American culture has been reevaluated in the post–civil rights era. Now is the time to extend the reevaluation in jazz studies to other parts of the world to create a more equitable and just paradigm on global terms. The question is, how to proceed toward that goal?

One possibility for circumventing the presence of the master narrative is to embrace recent writing about new forms of and ideas about diaspora, discrepant and patriotic forms of cosmopolitanism, and the call for an insertion of "the transnational" into American studies on the other.[4] These are ideas used in a range of other contexts to talk about processes of global cultural travel, and each word is often redefined in specific contexts. While Atkins prefers to frame the "jazz planet" in terms of the globalization of jazz, I have not found global talk a helpful intellectual location for jazz specifically. Globalization certainly speaks to a process of worldwide distribution through corporate structures; but that is only one strand in the story because jazz moves inside and between communities through a range of noncentralized, often noncapitalist ways. There are other equally important sites of alternative distribution, including independent labels, unrecorded histories, human memories, live renditions, and even bootleg copies of performances and studio recordings.

One has also to be aware of the implications of jazz in global circulation. When the marketplace intervenes, chronologies of style in a variety of places become messy: calendrical sequencing is replaced by marketplace rationalizations — the first to arrive in a place is not always the first to have been recorded, and in some instances parallel musical initiatives in two separate places are not necessarily recorded or given the same kind of media attention.[5] Such temporal disjuncture and mass-mediated communication alter the way in which communities around the world conceive of musical styles and their histories and tend to reflect how the plethora of styles and pasts in music coexist in the contemporary marketplace.

This is not strictly a jazz problem but will also increasingly be endemic to representing any kinds of past in the United States. The invention of the Internet, the World Wide Web, and computer file sharing have rendered a chronological narrative of the past, even the past itself, anachronistic. To some extent, pieces of the past are everywhere in the world, some more available than others at a particular moment in time. In theory, all things are now simultaneously available; some are legally and acquired, others not. For those willing to take the risk or pay the money, the music is available and often appears without any sense of a past attached to its sound.

Finally, to reflect further on the theory and method necessary to constituting a past in jazz for the world at large, I am not proposing a specific model but have instead culled an ensemble of keywords generated from the content of this book. These keywords seem appropriate for describing the different kind of historicism required in writing a history of jazz; jazz that derived from but also quickly departed from the models and stylistic categories generated in the United States by American musicians in the twentieth century and was sent out, largely though not exclusively, by the entertainment industry in the form of mass-mediated products and broadcast programming. Others working elsewhere will surely need to modify the keywords and the uses to which they are put in localized jazz communities as well as add to the list.

Keywords

To transmute the image of the musical echo into a usable and broadly representative narrative about the past in South African jazz presents enormous challenges to the music historian for a host of reasons, reasons that simply don't apply in the United States—though they may in places that have endured repressive regimes. First and foremost is the problem of *the archive*. The apartheid era drove South African music and musicians away from home, underground, apart from fellow musicians, or into the banalities of commercial music making. And there was no parallel kind of local *music industry* that could or would have created the recordings to support a coherent history of jazz. Under apartheid, those, like Sathima Bea Benjamin, who sang in English and rarely used foreign forms were recorded locally, either by the dominant commercial company, Gallo Records, or by the state-controlled South African Broadcast Corporation.[6] For several decades the state prohibited the broadcast over

South African airwaves of music by those who had gone into exile and declared their opposition to the apartheid government. Locally recorded music was hard to distribute because there was no access to mass mediation and because it was often banned or heavily *censored by the state* as soon as it was released. When exiled musicians did record their music, the fluctuating rate of exchange between the South African rand and the U.S. dollar, for example, increasingly made imported recordings prohibitively expensive. Much of the music made in exile was not available in South Africa, and many musicians died before they were able to go back to South Africa. And the attitude of some South Africans who remained behind and endured the apartheid regime has been less than welcoming to those who have returned. Adding insult to injury, when some South Africans began to think about writing the jazz history of South Africa, they found that the state had destroyed the archives—not deeming African jazz, for example, worthy of a remembered past. Each of these issues exacerbates the recuperation of a nationally unified cultural memory or even consensus on what should constitute a past in South African jazz.

As much as South Africans might all wish to move on from the impact of *racial difference* and the imposition of racial categories on South Africans under apartheid specifically, it is imperative that we continue to reflect on the implications of race in constituting a past for South African jazz. This is important internally, because jazz has both a racially divided past and a past that strove to achieve a nonracial musical community—and externally, because while many South Africans looked beyond the nation to find models of identity and forms of belonging in racial terms, some prefer to recall jazz as a musical discourse that transcended such division. Furthermore, the ways in which race plays itself out in the world vary according to where one is located. The word *Coloured*, for example, continued to be used in South Africa as an official category of the state well beyond its use in the United States. And to be part of a white numerical minority in South Africa meant something quite different from being white and part of a numerical and cultural majority in the United States in the same period.

Living history is a notion of the past that is more open-ended than the conventional chronology allows. It is a past shaped more in the manner in which jazz musicians quote and recycle materials from prior performances. It calls for a process that connects to the past by animating memories of earlier times in the present, by viewing the past not as being shut off from the present by incorporating personal pasts into a larger historical narrative. As living history, historiography and jazz performance shift from being narratives of innovation and rupture to narratives in which there is a far stronger connection between living people and their pasts.

The notion of living history also requires one to think about the past not as linear chronology, moving from one moment in time to the next and never returning to any of those pristine but forever finished moments. Rather, we imagine its capacity for representation as *palimpsest*, a *World Wide Web*, or even just a *web link* with its layers of prior performances embedded in the text. Each musical moment bears the traces of other performances, elsewhere and in another time. In the metaphor of the echo, each acoustical event has the capacity to generate new waves, that is, to locate that event in relationship to a host of resonances heard from other places. The idea of the palimpsest as a kind of layered topography of sound is particularly important, as illustrated in the discussion of *Cape Town Love* (see chapter 6). One might think of the palimpsest as a kind of visual counterpart to the idea of the resonating musical echo.

A living history has at its core the *human voice*, as a particular kind of utterance: an acoustical signature in its capacity to bear witness and in the particular way in which it combines words and music as a vehicle of deeply felt emotion. The focus on the voice places the human body and the heart back into narrations of the past. So if we think about the reception of jazz in South Africa, we have to reevaluate the workings of musical transmission and media. And we do so through the process of *musical surrogacy*—in which the media of *musical transmission* are constituted as vessels of a disembodied person-to-person musical transmission between far-flung communities of music-makers. Appointed as replacement for the self, the musical commodity or surrogate becomes the appointed carrier of musical sound, standing in for the musician, as a surrogate mother might convey the offspring of another inside her own body. Here the recording or radio broadcast brings new forms to communities in the absence of the original musicians themselves. The recording stands in for the musician: it intervenes in local transmission of traditions and fosters new musical families and kin groups, often created out of the sound of the music itself—its warmth, romantic sentiment, and also its capacity to fuel political consciousness through its stress upon freedom, improvisation, self-expression, and insistence on the right of an individual to articulate a voice in the collective fabric of the music and of society itself.

Living history suggests the notion of *imagined musical lineages* and requires a revision of prior ideas of the first *African musical diaspora*. The *new African diaspora* is a way of being in the world that inhabits two places simultaneously—the physical environment currently lived in, on one hand, and the vivid memories of places you have visited and perhaps imagine yourself traveling back to in the future, all creatively invoked through musical iteration live or in mediated form. Furthermore, there can be no doubt that defining a past for South African jazz has to be both about what had been made locally, in terms of vernacular languages (there are eleven official languages in South Africa) and culture, *local lineages*, and what was brought in from the outside. It is a problem of simultaneously inhabiting the here and the elsewhere, of living *interculturally* or "between two or more regimes of knowledge, or living as a minority in the still majority, white, Euro-American" world (Marks 2000, 1). The question has to be how we deal with the essentially hybrid, creolized, mixed, and certainly decentered character of these kinds of cultural formations and musical practices.

In this book I have invoked four possible ways of interpreting and performing jazz in the world: the *transnational, diasporic, cosmopolitan,* and the *exiled.* I have suggested that for many people jazz is more of a transnational and diasporic form than a cosmopolitan one because for the most part jazz has not been harnessed to empower the cultural mainstream in many societies. For example, among white South Africans in the postwar period, it is possible that jazz, largely translated through Britain, could be viewed as part of a *cosmopolitan worldview,* that is, part of metropolitan cultural mainstreams. But it seems that while the more commercial forms of jazz were represented in Hollywood, it was largely through sound recordings, through the sophisticated jazz of Ellington, and then the more progressive forms of jazz generated by bebop and free musicians that jazz worked more as an articulation of an *African diasporic consciousness* than as cosmopolitan form. And there are clearly *transnational communities* of jazz musicians as well, that is, those for whom jazz is an international language, even if it is not part of a musical and cultural mainstream in metropolitan centers. Free jazz would qualify as a transnational musical discourse.

For many South Africans from the mid-twentieth century to the present, *cultural and political exile* was a defining way of being in the world, producing sounds of excruciating longing and loneliness, but also urgent incorporation of the sounds of home into jazz made a very long way from the place in which they were born and raised. *Exile* forced a particular relationship to place: it was never just an abstract expression of stylistic innovation and difference in the transnational marketplace. What exile produced was also a particular *rhetoric of the political* and a *discourse of musical freedom* of a deeply political *loss and longing*.

We must be concerned with *restoration*, a process of folding into a single space in the present what was impossible to achieve in its time of lived experience: the coeval performances of jazz in the range of racially distinct residential areas that the Group Areas Act enforced in the apartheid era. In that era, Indians played jazz for the Indian community; Coloured dance bands performed weekly for their constituencies; white jazz musicians were moving between Durban, Johannesburg, Margate, and Cape Town; black South African swing bands played in the townships of Johannesburg; and the interracial groups of Chris McGregor (Blue Notes) and Abdullah Ibrahim (Jazz Epistles) insisted on progressive and experimental jazz as nonracial free spaces.

This narrative encapsulates what Sathima calls a *southern touch* in jazz performance and creation. The southern touch is the connection she imagines between the people of the U.S. South and those from South Africa who have suffered, whether because of slavery, racism in the United States, or apartheid in South Africa. I have suggested we might think about the ways in which Sathima talks about *jazz composition* in relation to Scarry's reflections on the *efficacy of beauty*. Both women invoke their subjects as something sacred, unprecedented, lifesaving, as an agent that quickens the heart, makes life more vivid, animated, and worth living. Both states of being — beauty and jazz — incite deliberation and thoughtfulness; they invoke a sense of conviction and a transcendent certainty in the viewer and listener and performer. Beauty and jazz fill the mind and heart while inviting the search for something beyond the self. As beauty and jazz enable such transformation, they decenter the subject. In this frame, jazz performance is constituted as what John Rawls calls a "just arrangement" that should be supported as a medium for bringing new kinds of beauty and music into being. The absence of jazz and beauty would result, Scarry argues, in profound deprivation. In contrast, allowing oneself to be immersed in audible beauty in jazz enables a kind of distributional fairness. We are open to its form, the freedoms therein; to its poetry, and ultimately its beauty. Jazz, beauty, and fairness, come to exist in symmetrical relationship to each other and extend out to those who bask in their presence.

Finally, and perhaps most important, this book has told the story of an extraordinary *woman in the world of jazz*. Through a woman's story we have opened up a new rhetorical space for writing about jazz as an expressive form, as a way of life, and as an arena for the dreamer, the visionary, and the spiritual soul. Jazz has been defined as a quintessentially natural musical utterance, that is, one that emerges out of lived experience, the formation of a powerful sense of womanly subjectivity and voice; it prizes the inspirational and spontaneous over song creation as writing and recording through multiple takes. We have written about jazz as a kind of calling for women, a calling akin to the process of falling in love, where jazz is perceived to be more loyal to the individual than a partner or spouse turns out to be. We have mentioned the priorities of women in the profession, and what has been lacking for them as artists — managers of any gender, women critics of any ethnicity, and support for them as primary caregivers of children and others who need them. These deficiencies have often taken women musicians out of circulation for extended periods of their professional lives. But we have also seen how a woman like Sathima has fought hard to find her place: to create mechanisms for composing and recording her music and to insert herself rightfully in the worldwide archive of twentieth- and twenty-first-century jazz.

Conclusion

Does the image of the echo enable a productive mechanism for thinking about music history more generally in the twentieth century, when the technologies of innovation made it possible to send out waves of musical sound to multiple sites simultaneously? How are we to represent and incorporate the responses, real and imagined, generated by these echoes, which created new lineages for individual songs and performances? How do we extend the archives of jazz and popular music history to incorporate these echoing responses from around the world?

It is clear we cannot simply write a linear narrative, one that starts in one place and basically travels in a circumscribed national or geopoliti-cal area. Rather, as the image of the acoustical echo illustrates, music is recorded in one place, recordings are sent out, each rearticulation sends out one echo after another—waves of sound that have consequences in the places of transmission. If we are to begin to define new space in American-centered jazz historiography for the compositional and per-formance histories of twentieth-century South African musicians like Sathima Bea Benjamin, we need to work critically inside of dominant narratives, while simultaneously creating new, emergent flights or lines of inquiry. We need to build a language that allows for the kinds of musi-cal experiences, values, histories, and performances created by those who strive to live concurrently inside of, and self-consciously beyond places, histories, and communities, who embody the state of in between-ness that jazz composition and living in diaspora and exile simultaneously in-voke and resolve. Such language emerges with a movement away from the profound colonization of consciousness that apartheid forced upon its people in South Africa, on one hand, but also urges us to examine the hegemony of American stories in the world at large on the other.

Ultimately, we are proposing that a key outcome of drawing on a con-cept like the musical echo in American music studies requires a radical refiguring of the ideas about and place of American and popular music, its scholars, and its scholarship in the contemporary world. I suggest we move from a binary, "never the twain shall meet" model of popular music that travels in a typically imperialistic manner and of American music—the seemingly *more* innocent, *less* mediated folk performances which stay home—to a truly comparative, more equitable paradigm that clears rhe-torical and intellectual space for all those who have been on the receiving end of music made in and by Americans in the twentieth century.

We need a lively engagement with the subject of America and its music as a worldwide phenomenon that has frequently, if not always inten-tionally, spawned new forms of musical community and music making far from their points of origin elsewhere. Some of these have erased "America" from memory in the process of re-articulation, others have remained true to their source. Whatever the individual lineage of each strand of twentieth century history, I argue we can no longer simply pre-sume a singular narrative in the musical pasts of soul, bluegrass, hip-hop and barbershop singing for example, and certainly not in the global travels of American jazz over the past hundred years or so. Rather, I argue that there is an ethical imperative to open up the intellectual and musical borders in the study of music made in and by Americans, to the rich polyphony of narratives to be told about the travel of this music to all parts of the globe in the twentieth century as we shape the structures of a more equitable global musical inquiry in the contemporary world.

Notes

1. Beginnings

1. The relationship between music and Islamic belief is a complex one — but one increasingly under scrutiny in marginal Muslim spaces, particularly in secular countries in parts of West Africa, South Africa, and the United States, where musicians more and more are integrating their music making with their faith and where starting in the 1960s several African American jazz musicians have converted to Islam. Students at the University of Pennsylvania have explored the relationship between music and Islam, particularly as it is manifest in popular culture, in our field methods classes. See the website http://www.sas.upenn.edu/music/westphillymusic/ for films made by graduate students about this subject.

2. When I first met Sathima she would talk about the Chelsea or the Chelsea Hotel, but a few years ago she told me the owner wanted it called the Hotel Chelsea. So we have changed our language accordingly.

3. Like Sathima, my parents were aware of the two worlds, but, like many white, English-speaking South Africans, they initially felt powerless to effect change. My father would begin to address issues of racial injustice through his place in the Presbyterian Church in KwaZulu Natal in the 1970s and 1980s. My mother has similarly addressed the inequalities in her work as an early childhood educator and author of training manuals for grass-roots women now published in numerous local languages. Our family was more the exception than the norm when we lived in Cape Town and later moved to Durban.

2. A Home Within

1. Ramsey's reflexivity and explanation (2003) parallels my own reflections on the relationship between lived experience and intellectual inquiry (1999, chap. 1).

2. For different but equally important accounts, see Layne (1995), Bruinders (2005), Nixon (1997).

3. Interview with Abdullah Ibrahim by WNCU jazz DJ Aasim Inshirah, in Senegal, ca. 2000/2001.

4. See discussion of internal dispossession in Field (2001).

5. The reputation for tolerance is largely owing to a series of ordinances put in place by the British in the early nineteenth century, one of which was the emancipation of slavery (1834, and realized in 1838); another allowed greater mobility

to the indigenous Khoi peoples. For further discussion of slavery, sexual relations, and race in the Cape, see, for example, Hendricks (2001).

6. See Bickford-Smith et al. (1999), Martin (1999), and Erasmus (2001), for
example.

7. Evelyn Green married twice, the first time to Edward Benjamin, with
whom she had three children, Beatty, Joan, and Maurice; her second marriage
was to Edward Green, with whom she had Edie, Noma, Christy, Henry, Irma
(who died at the age of seven), Elana, Maurice, and Errol. Sathima's stepsister
Ruth was from her father's third marriage to a woman named Ruth. His second
marriage was to Hettie van Vuuren, the wicked stepmother, who had a son, Alan,
with Edward Benjamin.

8. Information retrieved from www.livingstonehigh, 26 July 2010.

9. Adhikari (2009) provides a brief historical overview of Coloured political
movements of the twentieth century, most of which were tied to the Coloured
elite, among whom these teachers would have been counted.

10. Van Riebeeck was believed by white South Africans to have been the
founder of the Union of South Africa, but his presence was read quite differently
by those not of European descent in the country.

11. In postapartheid South Africa there has been a concerted effort to chronicle
the key role played by teachers' training colleges in educating Coloured people
under apartheid because there were few other sources of higher education, particularly for women. Battswood College has an intriguing history: it was founded
by a Cape woman who was the daughter of a slave but who married a British
aristocrat living in the Cape. When he died she donated money for the foundation of a school, which later became the Battswood Teachers' Training College
(http://media1.mweb.co.za/wellingtonmuseum/martha.html, retrieved 16 August 2008).

12. Notable exceptions are Jorritsma (2006), Coetzer (2005), Baines (1996).

13. See Coombes (2003).

14. In my reflections on Coloured removals in the response I list several
books written about life in District Six.

15. Abdullah has similar memories of his own mother's repertory of hymns,
which she played on the piano in his childhood home. She was the pianist for
the American-based African Methodist Episcopal community in Cape Town.

16. Interview with Joan Franciscus, September 1996.

17. A view that contrasts with Sathima's can be found at www.labyrinths
.co.za, retrieved 26 July 2010.

18. In my discussion of southern touch in the diasporas section, I return to
the issue of church music. While living in the diaspora, Sathima imagines a deep
sense of connectedness to the southern black experience through the emotional
vehicle of gospel music (see interview of July 1999, just after launch of *Cape
Town Love*).

19. Interview with Jimmy Adams, 26 May 1998, Cape Town.

20. I discuss the idea of the natural voice in the *Cape Town Love* section, and it surfaces in the reflections on Billie Holiday, though Griffin critiques the use of the category of natural when applied to mulatto women (2001, 31). For Sathima, a natural voice is one that has not had formal training; singing naturally means singing without reading the music, but from the heart and from memory.

21. Nixon (1997, 20).

22. Sathima could not recall James's last name.

23. Interview, September 1996.

24. Interview with Ruth Fife (and Joan Franciscus in the background), September 1996, Cape Town.

25. Nasson (1989, 302).

26. Nixon (1997).

27. Vincent Kolbe, interviewed by and cited in Nixon (1997).

28. See, for example, Abdullah Ibrahim's compositions "The Journey" and "Sister Rosie," both of which use the *klopse* rhythm. Sathima's trio plays a klopse rhythm on "If You Were the Only Boy in the World" on her recording *Cape Town Love.*

29. Radio broadcasts in South Africa in the early to mid-twentieth century offered South Africans additional forms of cosmopolitan identification, depending on race, language, and access to radio receivers. There were several options for broadcast radio programming at this time: the BBC, the Voice of America, and what was transmitted regionally in southern Africa, particularly in South Africa and Mozambique. For the most part, the broadcast world beyond South Africa that was available locally was an English-language domain. Locally produced radio programming in the early twentieth century began rather informally when the South African Railways in Johannesburg established a station in 1923. It ran out of money, and a year later was taken over by the Scientific and Technical Club in Johannesburg. A similar service financed with listener licensing fees started in Cape Town and Durban in the English language and was later controlled by a private corporation called the Schlezinger organization, which formed the African Broadcast Corporation in 1927. Finally, the South African government ordered an inquiry into radio broadcast that resulted in Act no. 22, the Broadcast Act of 1936, the year Sathima was born. This legislation mandated broadcasts in two languages, English and Afrikaans, and brought all radio programming under government control, as the South African Broadcast Corporation. The English Service became known as the A program and was modeled on the public broadcasting model of the BBC; Afrikaans language and culture were comprised in the B program.

30. Once television was introduced to the country in the mid-1970s, the popularity of Springbok Radio went into decline, and it closed in 1985.

31. Email communication, Chris Turner, May 6, 2006.

32. Tachhi (2003) cites the narratives of two people, one a woman who used radio to imagine herself into other racial spaces—Jamaican in this case—and

the other a woman who immigrated to the United Kingdom from India and listens to classic radio stations because she often hears, quite unexpectedly, songs she remembers from her childhood in India. This use of radio parallels examples cited by Tachhi among British residents in Bristol, England.

33. The social historian Thelma Gutsche (1972) discusses the origin of the term *bioscope* to refer to movie theaters. She suggests that the term was popular in the United States for a short time. In England people preferred to use *cinematograph*, shortened to cinema; and Europeans from the Continent used the word *kinematograph*, shortened to kino. *Bioscope* was commonly used until the 1960s in South Africa to refer to the cinema.

34. See, for example, the discussion by Roy Rosenzweig of audiences in Worcester, Massachusetts (1983) and British working class audiences (Richards 1984).

35. Nasson (1989, 286–87).

36. Interview with the actor John Kani by Peter Davis, Johannesburg, 1990, cited in Davis (1996, 23).

37. The derivations of the word *moffie*, meaning "cross-dresser," have a variety of sources. The word may refer to hermaphrodite (Joanne Meyerowitz, conversation with the author, National Humanities Center, October 1999). It could also be a local version of the eighteenth-century term *molly*, which was used to name cross-dressers (Jeffrey Kallberg, note to the author, Philadelphia, October 2000). In a recent volume on South African gay and lesbian history, there is more detailed historical description and analysis. See Shaun de Waal, "Etymological Note: On 'Moffie'" in *Defiant Desire: Gay and Lesbian Lives in South Africa*, edited by Mark Gevisser and Edwin Cameron (New York: Routledge, 1995), xiii. Three other chapters are important to this discussion: Dhianaraj Chetty, "A Drag at Madame Costello's: Cape Moffie Life and the Popular Press in the 1950s and 1960s," 115–27; Jack Lewis and Francois Loots, "'Moffies en Manvroue': Gay and Lesbian Life Histories in Contemporary Cape Town," 140–57; and Zackie Achmat, "My Childhood as an Adult Molester: A Salt River Moffie," 325–41. De Waal says that the "most plausible" etymology is that it comes from the word *mophrodite*, a variation of *hermaphrodite*. The word *mofrodiet* is also used in Dutch. A reference to mophrodites in Henry Fielding's novel *Joseph Andrews* (1742) seems to indicate opera-singing castrati, or to conflate the two terms. The word *mophy* is also recorded in *Sea Slang* of 1929 and by slang lexicographer Eric Partridge. It is "a term of contempt among seamen for delicate, well-groomed youngsters." Cape Town being a port city, this sea slang term might make sense. Other possible origins of *moffie* are Afrikaans *mof*, meaning a muff, sleeve, or socket, as well as a bastard, cross-breed, or undersized animal; or *moffie*, meaning a mitten. In these instances, semantic links are extremely tenuous. It has also been suggested that *moffie* comes from *mauve*, a color associated by some with homosexuals.

38. Nasson (1989, 301).

39. In the 1950s a handful of historically important, if ideologically slanted, locally produced South African films showcased black and Coloured South African talent. They were enormously popular because finally South Africans could see their own people on screen. Three in particular have recently been reissued by Villon Films in Canada: *Zonk!*, *African Jim*, and *Song of Africa*. *Zonk!* is discussed in some detail in chapter 3.

40. Interview with Sathima Bea Benjamin, 12 September 1996.

41. Sathima Bea Benjamin, personal communication, 9 April 1990.

42. Nuttall mentions the issue of DNA and entanglement, referencing the comedian Pieter Dirk-Uys's discovery that he had some African pieces in his DNA (Nuttall 2009, introduction).

43. Sathima's romanticized project of a nation free of talk of color and race resonates in striking ways with the manner in which those forcibly removed from racially integrated neighborhoods like Sophiatown and District Six remember their communities. These memories are often tinged with nostalgia for what South Africa could have been if apartheid had not destroyed these communities.

44. Coloured rejectionism became more contentious in 1992, when, as the leader of the ANC in South Africa, Nelson Mandela urged recognition of the Coloured community as the ANC prepared for the first democratic elections in 1994. They needed the Coloured vote in the Western Cape. Despite Mandela's move, to this day those called Cape Coloured have not voted the ANC into power in the Western Cape.

45. Adhikari (2009) reminisces about his position as a historian researching Cape Coloured history in the 1980s. He describes how people accused him of being a divisive scholar for separating Cape Coloured history from that of black South Africans more generally.

46. See Bickford-Smith et al. (1999, 43) and Adhikari (2009) for a discussion of early efforts of the Coloured elite to internalize European middle-class values.

47. Erasmus (2001, 19).

48. "Interstitial" is Bhabha's (2004) word. The South African writer Bessie Head was born in a mental hospital in Pietermaritzburg, South Africa, in 1937. Her white mother had been admitted because she had had a relationship with a black man. She was judged insane when her pregnancy was made public (Nixon 1994, 119).

49. Erasmus draws on the work of the Caribbeanist Edouard Glissant here. Black British cultural studies similarly looks to the work of Caribbean scholars in articulating a place for race theory in the United Kingdom. See Owusu (2000), for example. British mixed race studies have similarly engaged literature from both the United States and the Caribbean; see, for example, Ifekwunigwe (2004).

50. Erasmus (2001, 24).

51. Just what and who constitutes an African has become a very complicated

issue in postapartheid South Africa—presumably Erasmus references those who have historically spoken Bantu or Khoisan languages and adhered to specific cultural practices and beliefs.

52. Strictly speaking, not all those so classified by the apartheid regime were racially mixed; some were simply people of color from other parts of the world, like China and India. *Cape Coloured* and *Griqua* imply particular forms of racial mixing or "miscegenation." Even so, no racial categories like Coloured, black, African, and Bantu are never completely stable marks of identity. In the years of colonial segregation, terms of classification by the colonial government were often poorly defined and frequently changed meaning and application. This was particularly true for those classified as Coloured in the twentieth century. Who used the terms, who identified with them, who refused the terms varies with the political moment under discussion, how one is positioned in terms of class, race, and gender, and what there was to be gained from assimiliating or rejecting the categories. Generally speaking, *black, African,* and *Bantu* refer to people with dark brown skin color and curly hair who had inhabited the continent, if not its southernmost region, for several generations. *Coloured* refers to those who have mixed blood, including a wide range of people from many places in the world who converged on the Cape from the sixteenth century to the present. *White* describes people of European descent who had not been involved in racial mixing. But these categories are all problematic if taken as fixed, reified forms of identification.

53. Once again, the distinction between having African ancestry (as African Americans claim) versus being mixed is perhaps what has caused contemporary scholars of Coloured identity to look to the Caribbean rather than to African American theories of identity formation.

54. Information on Cape slave history is derived from Mountain (2004), Shell (1994), Da Costa and Davids (1994), and Mason (2003).

55. In the nineteenth century a community of mixed-race children also began to emerge in what is now KwaZulu Natal, once the British arrived in the region in the 1840s and began associating with Zulu- and Xhosa-speaking women in the eastern part of the country.

56. Adhikari (2009, xi).

57. There is ambivalence in the historical record about what constitutes a "native" person—black South Africans were initially categorized as "native," so the question was whether Khoisan, who mixed with Europeans, were "native" i.e., "Black"; or "Coloured," i.e., mixed with Europeans.

58. Magubane in Mattera (1987, xiii–xvi).

59. While the years of segregation were much harsher for African peoples than for Cape Coloureds in that the Land Act of 1913 took land away from black South Africans and the Immorality Act applied specifically to black South Africans, nevertheless, in 1936 Cape Coloureds were removed from the Common Voters' Roll and were unable to vote as full citizens until the democratic elections of 1994.

60. Brian Isaacs's commentary is taken from the Swedish documentary film *Musik in Eksil*, filmed in Sweden. I viewed a copy in the District Six Museum in Cape Town. The documentary tells the story of the Golden City Dixies, the first traveling show of black and Coloured South Africans to travel to Europe (see chapter 4).

61. Placksin (2000 [1984], 13).

62. Later, the Population Registration Act and its amendment created two basic race types: those who were white and those who were not. Those who were not visibly white were further divided into three large groups: Coloureds, Bantu, and Asiatic — those who had traveled from India as indentured laborers or free passengers, the apartheid regime believed, had no rights to claim land for themselves. Bantu people or natives were those who spoke a variety of Bantu languages — these were named specifically, and each language (and cultural) group was assigned a specific territory they would call home.

63. See Besten (2009) for further discussion of Khoisan classification and identities.

64. See the response on lineage in chapter 3 for the Benjamin family photograph.

65. These responses are anomalous in many ways, particularly because one of the earliest political organizations for Coloured people called itself the *African* Political Organization and founded the first newspaper aimed at a Coloured readership in May 1909. See Adhikari (1996, 1).

66. It is significant that neither Adhikari nor Erasmus addresses the St. Helenian strand in the Cape Coloured racial category. In many ways St. Helenians fit the requirements: they were mixed and tied to a history of slavery on the island itself but not to Cape Town's particular slave past. The Canadian literary critic Dan Yon, who was born in St. Helena, has produced a documentary film, *One Hundred Men*, which tells the story of one hundred St. Helenian married men who set off for England in the late 1940s with a two-year contract to work as agricultural workers. Some decided not to return to St. Helena at the end of the contract, and Yon interviews several of those who decided to stay. One captures in Yon's film a rich variety of heritages represented by these men from the Atlantic Ocean island. See also Yon (2007) for further discussion of the links between St. Helena and South Africa.

67. See Soudien (2001) on District Six and memory.

68. "Malays" — Muslims often are the Afrikaans speakers, they were praised by President Malan in the early twentieth century for their place in Afrikaans language, etc., see Jeppe (2001). Nevertheless, language was often an indicator of social class: those in the Coloured community who spoke "the Queen's English" were thought to be of a higher social standing than those who spoke Afrikaans. Adhikari remarks that in the early twentieth century, choice of English or Afrikaans was contested, as both were markers of ties to Europeanness.

69. The Promotion of Black Self-Government Act (1958) entrenched "separate development" by creating independent homelands for Bantu peoples,

puppet administrative structures peopled by Bantu representatives, and separate areas for those classified as Cape Coloured in the Cape. So Zulu-speaking people had to live in KwaZulu and were governed by Zulu-speaking administrators paid by the apartheid regime; so too for Xhosa-speaking people in Transkei; Tswana-speaking people in Bophutatswana, and so forth.

70. Trotter (2009, 49).

71. See, for example, Field (2001, 101–2), who talks about the impact of the Group Areas Act on the mixed community in Windermere in the Cape Flats, which originally included several racial groups of different classes living together. The community underwent mass removals and relocation into a Coloured community. Trotter (2009) addresses the impact of forced removals on Coloured identity in the Cape, arguing that the common experience of forced removal has created narrative communities. Individuals relate their common experiences of forced removal as a mechanism for coping with the trauma.

72. Each of these laws is discussed in Brian Barker et al., *The Reader's Digest Illustrated History of South Africa: The Real Story*, 3d edn. (Cape Town: Reader's Digest Association, 1992), 374–81.

73. *Black, Brown and Beige* is the title of an Ellington composition.

74. Conversation with Sally Placksin, reprinted in Rasmussen 2000, 13.

75. See Adhikari (2009) for a discussion of twentieth-century political movements among those identified as Coloured. Adhikari argues that these were mostly elite movements that had little real impact on their communities.

76. Sathima didn't come to this realization in Europe because she was warmly accepted there; rather, as I discuss in chapter 4, her deep sense of alienation from Europeans drove her to read widely and to come to terms with her personal history and to see it in a new and positive light.

77. Conversation with Sathima Bea Benjamin, 3 and 4 October 1996.

78. Nutall (2009, 2).

79. Ibid., 11.

80. See Farred (2006) for a thoughtful discussion on the dialectics of transcending race in postapartheid South Africa.

81. Erlmann, *Nightsong* (1996).

82. See, for example, Ifekwunigwe (2004) and (1996); Root (1992); Clarke and Thomas (2006).

3. Cape Jazz

1. See Ballantine (1993) and Coplan (2008) and various online sources for discussion of *marabi* and *mbaqanga* as African jazz. Whether Cape Town has become the place for jazz or whether it remains Johannesburg is debated in *Drum Magazine* between two journalists in May 1961. At the very least, by this time Miriam Makeba, Hugh Masekela, and others had left South Africa to perform

in England, Europe, and the United States, depleting what was an active but not very large jazz world.

2. Abdullah Ibrahim is known to the jazz world for a more comprehensive compositional and performance output than just the sounds of Cape jazz. See Rasmussen (2000a).

3. Abdullah Ibrahim was born Johannes Brand, nicknamed "Dollar" because of his exchanges with African American sailors in the Cape harbor. The sailors brought their instruments and jazz recordings when their ships docked in the Cape Town harbor in the 1940s and 1950s. He would change his name once more when he converted to Islam in the 1960s. The trumpeter Hugh Masekela told Gwen Ansell that he met several older South African women living in Brooklyn who had married sailors and immigrated to the United States in this period (Ansell 2004). Though some people in Cape Town stubbornly hold onto the more familiar name Dollar Brand, Abdullah Ibrahim is the name by which he is known internationally. Because I grew up in Cape Town, I had long presumed that the name Brand was an Afrikaans name, but Sathima told me (May 2006) that Abdullah's grandfather was Scottish, so Brand references the part of his heritage that is British, again pointing to the very complex nature of the racial category Coloured.

4. See Layne (1995) for a comprehensive discussion of this genre in Cape Town, and Coetzer (2006) for another account of *langarm* in the Grahamstown area.

5. Regan was also a cofounder of the first Coloured political organization, the African People's Organization in 1906.

6. Information on the bop parties is taken from interviews with Harold Jephtah and Jimmy Adams (1999) and Ruth Fife (1996).

7. Tem Hawker is an extraordinary figure in Cape jazz history, having traveled the world three times with the South African navy before settling down in Cape Town. Lars Rasmussen interviewed several of his family members, who give a glimpse into this legendary, if mostly forgotten, musician and innovator (see Rasmussen 2003a).

8. See Ballantine (1999) and Coplan (2009).

9. See Muller (2008) for further discussion of racial and musical crossovers.

10. See Allen (MMus diss.) and Coplan (2009) for discussion of *kwela* history.

11. See McClintock (1995) for negative stereotyping of the Irish.

12. Kolbe's comments were made to Michael Nixon and published in 1997.

13. Roller-skating rinks were introduced in South Africa in the 1890s. Gutsche (1972, 5) comments that the Vaudeville Theatre in Cape Town was converted to a skating rink but eventually lost its patronage to the more popular Sassin's skating rink. Skating rinks were kept "select" in the Cape, i.e., exclusive to the well-to-do. This meant racial and class exclusions.

14. Interview with the jazz writer Sally Placksin, see Placksin 1983 (reprint in Rasmussen 2000b).

15. Operatic training and performance experience was offered to Coloured people through the Eoan Opera group, a white initiative to culturally uplift people of mixed race in the Cape (and incidentally to keep them out of white opera). It became highly controversial in the 1950s when it was realized that the opera group was being supported and promoted by the apartheid regime to promote their policy of separate development (interview with Ruth Fife, September 1996). There is an article in the *New York Times* on Joey Gabriels's performance at the Metropolitan Opera in the 1960s (Porter). Hilda Roos, a graduate student, is currently working on the Eoan archive and presented a paper entitled "Complicity or Survival: The History of EOAN under Apartheid," at the South African Society for Research in Music Conference, held in Port Elizabeth, SA, 21–23 August 2008.

16. Ansell (2004). Gabriels was trained at the Wesley Training College in Salt River in Cape Town in the mid-1950s and "discovered" by Dr. Manca of the Eoan Opera Group, which he joined in 1957. Before leaving South Africa he hosted and performed with Jay Wilbour and the Firestone Strings on his radio show, the Firestone Show on Springbok Radio. Gabriels was the first South African to sing a major role at the Metropolitan Opera in New York City. He sang the lead role of Canio in Leoncavallo's *Pagliacci*. (This information is taken from a newspaper article about Gabriels that has no source or date cited but is contained in the music files at the District Six Museum, Cape Town, retrieved July 2009. It is probably from the mid-1960s and from the *Golden City Post*.)

17. South Africa was the Union of South Africa until 1961, when it became independent of British control and was renamed the Republic of South Africa.

18. Interview with Carol Muller, 12 September 1996.

19. Equally striking is the pervasive shadow of minstrelsy that characterizes the show. How does one interpret minstrelsy in the present? Minstrelsy and its impact on black South African performance culture is a complex historical and political issue. Locally called the Coon Carnival, Cape minstrelsy may feel uncomfortable to those outside of its culture, though Coon Carnival is in fact what those who perform in the New Year's festivities of working-class Coloured people proudly call their New Year celebrations. It is certainly challenging to watch performances that originate in one place and travel elsewhere, not to read the same messages and meanings into the texts. In defense of the continuing of the Coon tradition in the Cape, one of the current minstrels explained to a reporter "One culture's taboo is another's celebration." The question for cultural outsiders is how they renegotiate the label without dismissing the important history and pride attached to this festival by those who have relished and participated in its annual festivities and celebration with great pride.

20. Robeson visited South Africa in 1936 to star in the film *King Solomon's Mines* and had political ties to the South African Coloured and black elite (see Von Eschen, 1997).

21. The train has long been a powerful symbol, for good and bad, in the black South African experience. It was the vehicle that carried migrant workers to and

from the urbanized workplaces and their rural homes in the twentieth century. But it is also the vehicle that divided the country between rural and urban, migrant and country dweller. Hugh Masekela has commented on this issue in several contexts; see, for example, three films, Hirsch (2002), Powell (2000), and Singh (n.d.)

22. See Muller (2008).

23. For further information on Piper Laurie, see Gevisser and Cameron (1995).

24. The Bantu Men's Social Center (opened in 1924) and Dorkay House (important in the 1960s and 1970s) were two buildings at the end of Eloff Street in Johannesburg where black and Coloured South African musicians, writers, and artists gathered to listen to music, rehearse, debate, and watch movies. Dorkay House is now a residential building, while the Bantu Men's Social Center continues to function as a performance and educational site.

25. In the late 1980s Swedish television produced a two-part documentary on the Golden City Dixies' performances in Sweden in the early 1960s, and told the story, with Brian Isaacs as the central actor, of their decision to remain in Sweden rather than return to South Africa. The documentary is titled *Musik in Eksil*. A copy of the documentary is contained in the District Six Museum in Cape Town, South Africa. I am not sure of the dates of production.

26. See Molefe (1997).

27. Phahlane was a reporter for *Zonk! The African People's Magazine*.

28. See Makeba (1987) and Masekela (2004), both autobiographies.

29. Rag is an annual event in which university students build floats to parade through town in an effort to raise funds for a variety of charities.

30. This story was recorded in conversation between Michael Nixon and Vincent Kolbe, see Nixon (1997).

31. Q-Town, later Kew Town, was the prize project of the war years in South Africa, a symbol of well-planned segregation, on one hand, and of a façade of social uplift for Coloured people, on the other. "Wide boulevards and open spaces are characteristic of this new city on the Cape Flats, where slum life will be forgotten," announced the government in 1941. Q-Town was to be a self-contained planned city, a carefully conceived scheme for "rehabilitating that [slum] population and for developing among its present numbers and their successors the degree of 'social consciousness essential to good citizenship'" (Bickford-Smith et al., 1999, 148).

32. I keep the distinction in spelling, *Coloured* in the United Kingdom and South Africa and *Colored* in the United States, to maintain a sense of the historical differences between these communities.

33. Basil Rich, interview with the author, Cape Town, September 1996.

34. Masekela (2004, 77–78).

35. Ibid., 78.

36. See reviews of Sathima's performance (she is called Bea/Beatty) in *New York Retreat*.

37. Kolbe to Nixon (1997).

38. Jimmy Adams to Carol Muller, 12 September 1996, Cape Town.

39. Meyer's wife has the acetate copy of the original made by Sathima and a trio of Cape musicians.

40. This song can be found on several of Abdullah Ibrahim's commercial recordings, including *Blues for a Hip King*.

41. This is an intriguing reference to the Beat movement in Greenwich Village, New York. The relationship between the jazz avant-garde of African American musicians and the Beat movement in the Village is explored in Jon Panish (1997). This was one of numerous connections between South African musicians and those in the United States that some South African scholarship has begun to explore. See, for example, Ballantine (1993), Erlmann (1999, 1991), and Coplan (2008).

42. *Drum Magazine*, May 1961: 46, emphasis added.

43. Sathima Bea Benjamin, personal communication, April 1988.

44. Stockmann in Rasmussen (2001, 112–13), emphasis added. This notion of "anything in between" speaks again of the complex ambiguity about racial mixing, or miscegenation, even in the minds of those participating in the progressive jazz community.

45. The idea of jazz as home, of "home is where the jazz [heart] is," is one that many of the musicians active in this scene but who left South Africa in the 1960s carried with them into cultural and often political exile. So, for example, in this period (1960s through the early 1990s), Abdullah called his jazz ensemble Ekaya, which means "at or from home," and Sathima named hers "Windsong," a site of warmth and understanding she remembers feeling in the strong winds of Cape Town's southeaster. Similarly, in the late 1970s they established a record company based in New York City that they called Ekapa, meaning "at or from the Cape." *Ekapa* elicits memories of a particular place and kind of experience in the southern part of Africa that their brands of jazz performance continually reference and are derived from. More recently, Sathima has begun to talk about music as a "home within," alluding to a deeply diasporic notion of the human body as archive, to the central place of human memory in reconstituting the recent past, and, indeed, to the significance of her early musical life in South Africa.

46. Information from http://www.fpb.gov.za retrieved August 5, 2008.

47. Barthes (1982, 105).

48. This comes from the video *Africa I Remember*, see Balmer (1995).

49. Foucault (1972).

50. See Feld (2000).

51. See Taylor (1997, introduction).

52. Erlmann (1999).

53. See for example, the special issue of *American Quarterly* 57/1, 2005, that addresses the question of transnationalism in American Studies.

54. See Kelley (2003), Monson (2007), and Von Eschen (2004) for discussion of the relationship between African American political movements and jazz in the cold war era.

55. While I use the film from 1987 as my example, it is clear in 2006 that over time and wider exposure to new musical forms the discourse of musical belonging and familial resemblance shifts in focus and scope.

56. The loss of language to living descendents of those who were brought to the United States as slaves is a striking theme in this narrative, a point that emerges in a range of places in this book.

57. Students at the University of Pennsylvania have been involved in constructing a living history archive of gospel music in Philadelphia, see www.sas.upenn.edu for further information on these projects. The Mother Bethel church in South Philadelphia is a living religious community, and the AME church archives are housed right in the neighborhood of the University of Pennsylvania, at the corners of 38th and Market Streets. See ccat.sas.upenn.edu.

58. See Ballantine (1993).

59. Bing Lee, a University of Pennsylvania undergraduate, wrote a thoughtful, even intriguing, paper on Abdullah Ibrahim's conception of harmonic relationships in this familial structure for a seminar on Jazz as a Global Phenomenon I held at the University of Pennsylvania.

60. From transcript of interview for WNCU Radio, NCCU, Durham, North Carolina, 2000.

61. Those born of slaves in Cape Town were given the month of their birth as their last names, removing all responsibility for care from the European master and denying any real feeling of kith and kin to the so-called bastard child (Western 1997). This is part of what has long considered to be a shameful history of Cape Coloureds.

62. Sathima often talks about Duke Ellington's gift as a clairvoyant.

63. Conversation with Sathima Bea Benjamin, July 1999.

64. Both quotes here come from an interview with Sathima Bea Benjamin, August 2002.

65. Masekela (2004, 81–82).

66. See Okpewho and Nzegwu (2009).

67. Ibrahim in Capellari (2006).

68. Muller (2008), Meintjes (1990).

69. Coplan (2008).

70. Erlmann (1999).

71. Gabbard (1996, 98, 170–71).

72. Ibid., 181.

73. I found useful the commentary provided about the film by the USC film critics Todd Boyd and Drew Casper on the DVD release of Cabin in the Sky (2006).

74. For further examination of the impact of films on black South African

culture, see, for example, Coplan (2008), especially the chapter on Sophiatown; Ballantine (1993), Erlmann (1991), Nkosi (1983, especially "The Fabulous Decade: The Fifties"), Nixon (1994, 1997), Titlestad (2004).

75. Abdullah Ibrahim, for example, attributes his early musical exposure to the fact that his grandmother was a pianist for the AME church in District Six (see Austin, *Brother with Perfect Timing*), and Hugh Masekela writes about the power of the prayers and voices of the black church women through many of his childhood illnesses (2004, 17).

76. Gabbard (1996, 181).

77. See tracks 20–27 of *Cabin in the Sky*, on the 1999 DVD reissue of the film.

78. Ellington is reported to have said that jazz was music that was "beyond category."

79. Masekela (2004, 8–9).

80. Ibid.

81. Rathebe in "Ubuyile 2000" oral history project cited in Ansell (2004, 54).

82. This information was collated from information provided by Griffin (2001).

83. Side B has two lesser-known show tunes, the Victor Herbert melody for "Indian Summer" and "Song of Songs," written by Harold Vicars, Clarence Lucas, and Maurice Vaucaire, two chestnuts that bookend "Dreams," another of Sathima's compositions.

84. See also Shelemay (1988) and Waxer (2002) for similar sorts of ethnomusicological exploration.

85. See Griffin (2001) and Tucker (2000).

86. I had originally presumed when I began this project that the picture on the cover was the one on the book I owned, the reprint of 1992 of the edition from 1956. It is not clear, however, because in looking at the images in O'Meally (1991) I realized the first edition had a different photograph on the cover. I am not sure which image was on the book Sathima read. That said, one brings a certain retrospective vision to this reading in 2006. So it really is not that important which of the many faces of Billie Holiday was on that first cover; reading race and gender into the picture as the young Sathima Benjamin did is the process I strive to understand. Many of the Holiday–Benjamin images work in this way.

87. Robert O'Meally, in the beautiful photo essay with written commentary, *The Many Faces of Billie Holiday*, writes that no single camera could possibly capture the complex subject and "elusive essence" of Holiday. So many of the images that remain of the woman present quite distinct representations. A far smaller archive of Sathima's photographic images is extant from this period, but a similar claim might be made of those that do exist. Both are extremely complex personalities, musically, visually, and as women.

88. Conversation with Sathima Bea Benjamin, May 2005.

89. Mphahlele (1984) provides a beautiful rendering of jazz singers through the course of the chapter in which he recalls Denver in 1966–74 (see esp. 133–38).

90. Significant additional parallels can be read in retrospect, but I will keep the focus on what would have been more obvious to Sathima in the 1950s.

91. O'Meally (1991) and Griffin (2001).

92. Billie Holiday was presumably named after the filmstar Billie Dove, though she claims her father called her Bill because she was such a tomboy, a name she modified to Billie. In the autobiography Holiday recalls purchasing a glamorous bed like one she had seen in Dove's films.

93. Even though Sathima and Abdullah converted to Islam in the 1970s, Sathima is not an Arabic name.

94. O'Meally (1991, 197).

95. Chris Waterman (in Radano and Bohlman 2001) on being colored in the United States. Eileen Southern distinguishes between light- and dark-skinned African Americans, a difference tied to slave history: the lighter skinned had favored status inside the house versus field workers, who were dark skinned.

96. Griffin (2001) comments on the issue of skin color, expressing a certain frustration with the preference many black men in the jazz world have for light-toned black women.

97. See Griffin (2001, 31) for the problematic position of those categorized as mulatto as being individuals without lineage or history, as they always have to invent these narratives anew. This reference cited comes from Holiday (1956, 8).

98. Holiday (1956, 25).

99. See ibid., 77.

100. This view on the differences in racist attitudes in the northern and southern regions of the United States is paralleled later in the South African diaspora. I have often heard a similar kind of comparison, only this between the racism of apartheid South Africa, and that of the United States, which in the post–civil rights era, presented an image of having rid itself of the kind of racism that continued under the apartheid regime in South Africa. South African musicians who had lived in both places quickly realized that this simply was not an accurate representation.

101. Holiday (1956, 61).

102. Ibid.

103. Ibid., 81.

104. Ibid., 170.

105. Davis (1998).

106. Drawing this distinction between a kind of improvisation based largely on oral transmission versus one that has evolved with the increased archive of recordings, fakebooks, and written transcriptions of solos available to jazz musicians is a significant one in theorizing on improvisation as a process of thinking in jazz. This historical differentiation gives greater meaning to improvisation as the more rationalized, in every sense of the word — as objectified and thought through by writing and reading as well as by hearing — way of thinking in jazz over the improvisation that is more spontaneous. One should be careful, nonetheless, not to assume the evolutionary narrative — that the more spontaneous

is earlier historically and so also less complex and sophisticated. In Sathima's case, her desire for spontaneity continues in her recording sessions into the early twenty-first century.

107. Holiday (1956, 59–60).

108. Ibid., 62.

109. Ibid., 89–90.

110. Ibid., 59.

111. Ibid., 170.

112. See Solberg (1996) for further discussion of South African jazz saxophone sounds and practices.

113. Interview with Colin Miller in 1999.

114. Holiday (1956, 114–15).

115. Ibid., 120.

116. Ibid., 172.

117. Ibid., 175–76.

118. Ibid., 48.

119. Stewart (2002, 108).

120. I expand on the idea of an old African diaspora (the diaspora that brought slaves to the Americas) and the new African, i.e., the twentieth-century African diaspora, in the response in chapter 4.

121. The "Click Song," released on *Miriam Makeba*, has been reissued and released on a two-LP compilation, originally sold separately as *Miriam Makeba* and *The World of Miriam Makeba* in 2006, released on RCA 2276 and 2750.

122. Nkosi (1983).

123. Holiday (1956, 48).

124. For further discussion of the idea of individual nuance in the context of rehearsal and formal performance, see Jean-François Lyotard, "God and the Puppet," *The Inhuman: Reflections on Time*, trans. Geoffrey Bennington and Rachel Bowlby (Stanford: Stanford University Press), 153–64.

125. I have been moved by Elaine Scarry's book (2001), which reexamines the relationship between visual beauty and being socially just. I suspect a fruitful dialogue might be generated between her work on beauty and an archeology of jazz singing such as this brief excursion into the Holiday–Benjamin relationship suggests.

126. Scarry (2001).

4. Jazz Migrancy

1. Probably written by Paul Trewhela, the reference to *Drum Magazine* appears in an article in *News Check Magazine*, October 1968, found in the Transcription Center archive at the Ransome Center, University of Texas, Austin.

2. See Rasmussen (2003b).

3. Compiled from Hajdu (1997) and Placksin (1984)—reprinted in Rasmussen (2000b).

4. From Placksin (1984).

5. Interview with Sathima Bea Benjamin, April 1997.

6. Rasmussen (2000b).

7. See Asmussen, Grappelli, and Nance (1963). The Grappeli recording has been released as *Duke Ellington's Jazz Violin Session*.

8. All quotes from interview with Sathima Bea Benjamin, in April 1997.

9. Gerhard Lehner, Liner Notes, *A Morning in Paris*, 1997.

10. Sathima Bea Benjamin, personal communication, April 1997.

11. Dates taken from Von Eschen (2004).

12. The archival records of the Transcription Center, a place that hosted African artists and musicians in London and is discussed at length later in the chapter, give contact information for Reprise Records in a letter to Abdullah. It would seem that they were trying to help Abdullah and Sathima to track down the unreleased materials.

13. Thanks to Lewis Porter, who gave me copies of both Abdullah's and Sathima's sessions with Ellington, and to Lars Rasmussen who had a shorter version. Neither of these copies had the complete session, i.e., I have not been able to listen to the tape version of Sathima singing Ellington's "In My Solitude," which is on the CD Sathima produced.

14. At the start of the unreleased tape there is more than one take on a couple of occasions, though it would seem, this is attributable to the fact that it was the beginning of the session. It is not a trend that continues once the musicians, producer, and engineer find a place of equilibrium.

15. See Ballantine (1996) for a discussion of African composers, written in response to Berliner's (1994) discussion of compositional process.

16. There is a different order of songs in the unpublished and the published record of the event.

17. I will return to the idea of falling in love with men and music in the response to chapter 5.

18. *Downbeat* (June 1997).

19. Despite the overall richness of the trio on *Lovelight*, it is the gesture and the words which stand out in this rendition. This is not the track that conveys the feeling of rapport and creativity that characterizes much of her other output. Sathima Bea Benjamin, "Gift of Love," on *Lovelight*, Enja R2 79065, 1988, track 5.

20. Von Eschen (2004).

21. A growing body of scholarship on the African American presence in France from the early twentieth century on and on jazz in France specifically reveals that Paris was often considered the mecca of jazz outside of the United States. With the arrival of Josephine Baker in the 1930s, Paris began to be considered a kind of destination for African American jazz musicians, writers, dancers, and artists like Paul Robeson, Richard Wright, Ornette Coleman, and others. It

does not appear to have become home to the South Africans in quite the same way, at least as far as I can tell, although Paris is the city in which Richard Rive (1981) met Langston Hughes.

22. Rasmussen (2003b, 65).

23. Ibrahim in Rasmussen (2003b, 79).

24. This is not the place to outline the history of jazz performance in Denmark. Readers who are interested in the subject might look online and in Wiedemann (1991) and Holt (2002) for further discussion. Suffice to say that a dance restaurant called Montmartre had existed for several decades in Copenhagen before it changed to the Jazzhus Montmartre. In the late 1950s there were two late night jazz clubs in a single building, the Blue Note and Club Montmartre. Club Montmartre opened in 1959 with performances by the clarinetist George Lewis and his band. Late in 1961 a relatively unknown American musician living in Copenhagen suggested to Kerluf Kamp Larsen that he should purchase Club Montmartre, which he did. Jazzhus Montmartre opened in March 1963 and featured postwar musicians, swing soloists, and musicians from the New York avant-garde who had difficulty finding work in the United States at the time (Wiedemann 1991, 38–65).

25. Wiedemann (1991, 275).

26. Nevertheless, these recordings reveal something of the complexity of Ibrahim's self-presentation through his music at this time. He invokes his African—read "folk"—roots with the *Anatomy of a South African Village* suite; his diasporic connections paying tribute to Thelonious Monk's "Round Midnight"; his American songbook relationship in his play with the Jerome Kern song "Smoke Gets in Your Eyes"; while also providing something distinctively his own in sound and compositional voice. "Mama" pays a kind of universal tribute to the maternal figure.

27. Rasmussen (2003b, 70).

28. Wiedemann (1991, 288).

29. I have recently been told by Barak Schmool, an active jazz musician in the British scene, that the impact of South African musicians on British jazz has been enormous. He mentioned about twenty musicians with whom he has had contact or learned from, including British musicians who actively promote the South African styles in the contemporary jazz scene in the United Kingdom. But the details of that community await further research.

30. Though not all musicians did so—see the profiles of women in Molefe and Mzileni (1997).

31. Information drawn from Rasmussen (2002).

32. The Transcription Center has remained something of an anomaly to me until quite recently, when I came across a short article about it by Gerald Moore in the journal *Research in African Literatures*. I found that the written archive of the center is housed at the University of Texas, Austin and the sound archives at the British Library, with some pieces deposited in a variety of other institutions.

And there is recent writing about the relationship between the arts, culture, and the CIA in the cold war era. See, for example, Saunders (1999).

33. Moore (2002, 167).

34. See McGregor (1996) for a description of Ronnie Scot's Old Place.

35. Placksin (1984), reprinted in Rasmussen (2000).

36. Placksin (1984).

37. Benjamin in Rasmussen (2000b).

38. One captures in these letters a sense of the largesse of Abdullah's dreams for South African music and musicians in the draft of a proposal he writes for the Farfield Foundation. It ranges from establishing radio stations in Africa, booking agencies for African artists, travel for South Africans to Europe, and clubs for the music in London.

39. Abdullah had to battle just to practice with a poor piano, and like so many others at the time he drank excessively. The longing to return home became excruciating for both. In February he traveled to Copenhagen, Hamburg, Zurich, Lausanne, and Paris for individual performances. In March, the *Anatomy of a South African Village* recording made in Copenhagen was released (it was later banned by the South African government).

40. Inserted into Abdullah's letter is a list of titles of Abdullah's compositions—all copyrighted by Ellington's Tempo publications, underscoring again the key part played by Ellington in establishing Abdullah and Sathima in the United States. Ibrahim writes Duerden to see if the thirteen-part series on jazz for the BBC is still a possibility. On 30 November 1967 Abdullah played at the Lincoln Center Library and, a few days later, at the University of Toronto. His Rockefeller Grant expired in January 1968. At this time Jack Thompson wrote of the plans in place for Abdullah to work from February 1968 in Europe: in Denmark, Sweden, Germany, Italy, and Austria. Live performances as well as radio and television recordings were scheduled through April. Sathima would travel with him. Abdullah performed on Radio Hamburg with Makhaya Ntshoko, John Tchicai, Gato Barbieri, and Barre Phili. It is clear, nevertheless, from a letter Abdullah wrote that the stress of being so far from his people was wearing him down—he signed the letter: "1/2 Dollar Brand-Xahuri."

41. Langston Hughes was the only African American to write for *Drum Magazine* (personal communication, Gavin Steingo).

42. There is no author attribution, but it is likely the piece was written by Paul Trewhela, the son of the music journalist Ralph Trewhela, who worked closely with SABC and Gallo personnel. Trewhela's son was a member of the South African Communist Party and a writer for *News Check* at the time.

43. Johnny Dyani interviews with Lars Rasmussen (2003b, 82).

44. The African American Labor Center, located in New York City, was part of the larger AFL-CIO union movement; it too appears to have been part of the CIA's attempts to keep tabs on the South Africans. The AFL-CIO and African American Labor Center both were strongly anticommunist in this period,

which might explain their ties to the CIA. The ties, if they are verified, make their connections to the anti-apartheid movement, which was closely aligned with the South African Communist Party, quite sinister. The AFL-CIO did lend support to South African workers in this period.

45. Sathima thinks that this Peggy was Peggy De Laney, who worked for the mining magnate family the Oppenheimers in South Africa. Probably through a connection made by Ian Bernhardt, the Oppenheimers helped to fund Abdullah's Marimba School of Music in Swaziland.

46. This was about the same time as Johnny Dyani and Abdullah worked on the "African Space Program," a musical project in which they incorporated the aesthetic principles and musical sounds of Xhosa traditional music into their improvised and free jazz performances. Two exquisitely beautiful recordings emerged out of that collaboration, *African Space Program* and *Good News from Africa*. Ntsikana's Bell is described in the response below.

47. Ellington was so closely associated with this community that the church became the headquarters of the Ellington Society in New York City (allaboutjazz .com, retrieved 18 August 2006).

48. Information from box 14, Transcription Center Archive housed at UT, Austin.

49. It is a duet between Abdullah and Gato Barbieri titled *Confluences* (1968) and issued by the Black Lion Record Company in London. It has been reissued on CD as *Hamba Kahle!*, Fuel 2000 Records. See Rasmussen discography of Abdullah Ibrahim for further information (1998, 31).

50. Rasmussen (2000b).

51. This was also the period in which the anthemlike "Mannenberg" was created by Abdullah Ibrahim, Basil "Mannenberg" Coetzee, and others in a Cape Town studio.

52. Interview, 30 May 2008.

53. Extracted from "Africa," by Sathima Bea Benjamin 1974.

54. A sentiment expressed many times in conversations between Sathima and Carol.

55. The challenge of identifying the originator of a musical or verbalized idea is at the core of the controversy over who composed the tune "Mannenberg," which Abdullah Ibrahim has claimed as his own; and there is a similar question concerning Paul Simon's jam sessions in Johannesburg with South Africans who played their music, sounds that were laid down as tracks for the producer Simon to manipulate into a texture palatable to a mainstream pop sound.

56. The democracy tours featured many African American jazz musicians, including Ellington, Armstrong, Gillespie, and others who traveled for the State Department to Africa, Asia, the former USSR, and Europe. The tours were intended to suppress communist ideology by promoting democracy and the free market economy in emerging nations in the mid-twentieth century. In this context, jazz was defined as a quintessentially democratic musical medium, and its

African American musicians symbols of racial progress for the world at large (even if such progress was not always visible at home). Makeba married Stokely Carmichael, the civil rights activist, and was exiled from the United States back to West Africa. She never really returned to the United States to live permanently after that. America wasn't always a refuge for exiled South African musicians. The story of those who went into exile in Africa, Cuba, and the former Soviet Union has not been fully explored yet, but the literature on the ANC cultural tours in Zambia, Brazil, and Russia has begun to be explored.

57. The Congress for Cultural Freedom provided fellowships for Richard Rive and Peter Clark (box 5, Transcription Center archive). The Farfield Foundation provided a scholarship for the architect Julian Beinart, who has written several pieces and radio programs and has conducted interviews on South African jazz.

58. Maxine McGregor also writes about the Center in *Brotherhood of Breath* — she worked as Duerden's assistant there for a period of time in the 1960s. The South African literary critic and author Lewis Nkosi, who created an ongoing series of radio programs for the Transcription Center, wrote about Jack Thompson of the Farfield Foundation, who visited Johannesburg in the late 1950s — though it wasn't clear whom he represented at the time.

59. Several other South Africans who frequented the center in the 1960s were Lewis Nkosi, who hosted a weekly radio program, Frene Ginwala, Es'Kiah Mphahlele, Harold Jephthah, the saxophonist of the Golden City Dixies, and Julian Beinart. The ethnomusicologist Gerard Kubik is closely aligned with the center, as is Andrew Tracey.

60. I haven't found further information on this studio, though Charles Fox appears to have been a BBC radio reporter and producer.

61. Ibrahim grew up in the Kensington area of Cape Town, a place I don't recall ever having visited as a child growing up under the Group Areas Act.

62. *Golden City Post*, 25 January 1959.

63. See Appadurai (1986) and Hoskins (1998) for elaboration on the idea that, respectively, things have a social life and objects have biographies.

64. Baudrillard says that live music is always distant, while recorded music is elevated into an object (into pure materiality) as it is listened to and is thus much closer.

65. A similar circulation of repertory back to the United States at about this time was Solomon Linda's Mbube/Wimoweh song, which has mutated into literally hundreds of different songs, becoming a core part of American popular culture. See Muller (2008) and Malan (2001).

66. Wordnet, 2003, Princeton University, retrieved from dictionary.reference.com, 2 March 2005.

67. Ibid.

68. In Von Eschen's account of the State Department diplomacy tours made by African American musicians like Armstrong and Ellington in the postwar

period, the music was sometimes heard as a "universal language," as "national/ folk music," "transnational," or as the Armstrong example demonstrates, "diasporic."

69. Here one is reminded of the controversy of who should sing the U.S. national anthem, whether it can be translated into Spanish and still be thought of as American? Butler and Spivak (2007) address this in their conversation, *Who Sings the Nation-State? Language, Politics, Belonging*.

70. No political struggle can win with a complicated public message or image — examining the complexity of Coloured identity could not happen in the forum of the anti-apartheid movement's public discourse. This really could be addressed only in a postapartheid context.

71. Johnny Dyani, cited in Rasmussen (2003b, 210).

72. Johnny Dyani and Louis Moholo traveled to South America with Steve Lacy, Gato Barbieri, and Enrica Rava on what turned out to be a disastrous tour. Lacy doesn't really talk much about Dyani and Moholo in conversations he had with Jason Weiss contained in the recent book (2006), but he does talk about the formative moments in Italy with both Moholo and Dyani in the mid-1960s.

73. See Monson (2007) and a growing body of literature on African Americans in Paris.

74. A few years ago Ibrahim recalled how challenging it was to perform this music at the time: it was the "expansion of tradition, a full circle of experience, swing and bebop, and the African experience." The duo work, out of which the *Good News from Africa* recording and "Ntsikana's Bell" track emerged, Ibrahim comments "really opened up a whole lot of stuff because we could delve into the traditional sounds. And the idea of vocalizing the songs, like Ntsikana's Bell, in a sense, it was not only playing the music, but affirming history. We were actually ... consolidating our background experience, our history. And we found out that it was valid" (Rasmussen, 2003b).

75. There was also a wave of musicians who moved into exile in London with Ipi Tombi in the 1970s. Research on this will come later.

76. See Bernstein (1994) for insights into these experiences.

77. So many others died without making a recording, often after they had stopped playing. They certainly had not been recorded or recognized for their musical contribution inside the country.

78. In other words, these South Africans were never really free to just engage musically but increasingly were heard at least as much for their political as for their musical voices. There were more subtle forms of exclusions for those South Africans of color who didn't neatly fit the profile of a black South African: they were not sufficiently political in their sound or message or didn't look authentically African; they were singers, not instrumentalists; they were too traditional in the sounds or not traditional enough.

79. There is remarkable resonance between Sathima's dream description and the compositional dreaming of Joseph Shabalala of Ladysmith Black Mambazo (Ballantine 1996), of Isaiah Shembe and his followers (Muller 1999).

80. *Coda* (Canada) 216, October–November 1987, written by Ed Hazell.

81. Ramsey (2003).

82. At times the copresence of multiple worlds comes to haunt individuals—this is the terror of diasporic consciousness manifest in mental illness, something that has been a part of the South African experience in exile.

5. A New York Embrace

1. Personal communication, 8 December 2000.

2. I have not been able to find much published material on the ANC's work in New York City. There is more information available about their work in Europe, Africa, and the former Soviet Union (1960–70) than there is in the United States.

3. Makatini was a member of the ANC National Executive Committee. In 1966, he was appointed ANC Chief Representative in Algeria. In 1977, he was appointed head of the ANC Mission to the United Nations and later head of the ANC's Department of International Affairs." From http://www.thepresidency .gov.za/pebble.asp?relid=1263, retrieved 7 March 2011.

4. Dulcie September, the ANC representative in Paris, was murdered in 1988. The Dutch journalist Evelyn Groenink published a book in Dutch about September and others who, she claims, were involved or posing a threat to the apartheid regime's collusion with the French government in covert nuclear arms deals. (Translated, the title of the book reads: *Dulcie: A Woman Who Had to Keep Her Mouth Shut*, Amsterdam: Atlas, 2001.) In this book Groenink claims that September was assassinated by someone representing the two interest groups because she had stumbled upon evidence of these deals. Apparently she was shot in the back with a weapon that had a silencer on the morning of 29 March 1989. I have no additional evidence surrounding September's death, other than to say that Sathima's experience in France seems to suggest there was a larger conspiracy afoot—there were no other reasons for her to be chased around Paris as she was. Three men are possible suspects in the killing of September, though no one has ever been convicted. This information was taken from the Anti-Censorship Programme of the Freedom of Expression Institute entitled *Third Progress Report submitted to the Open Society Foundation for South Africa* in March 2004, pp. 7–8. Retrieved from www.ifj.org/.

The ANC web archive outlines her life and place in the struggle: see www.anc .org.za, retrieved 1 December 2008.

5. According to the Anti-Censorship Program's account Groenink speculates in her book that this was the Civil Cooperation Bureau (CCB), a state-sponsored hit squad sponsored by the apartheid regime, which chased her car.

6. In an interview in Senegal in 2000, Abdullah talks about how long it has taken him to get over the fear of security forces, not just in South Africa but abroad as well. The fear of surveillance and attack was very real in the 1970s

and 1980s. The death of February in Paris by letter bomb is a clear example of the ways the apartheid regime worked hand in hand with others to track down South Africans abroad who were believed to be working against the regime.

7. See, for example, "For Melba" (1970), "My Name Is Afrika" (1971), "When the Clouds Clear" (1990); "If I Could Sing: Selected Poems" (2002).

8. *New York Times* review, 29 January 1973.

9. Benjamin, liner notes, 1979.

10. Sathima Bea Benjamin, Marymount College, Tarrytown, N.Y., October 1990.

11. *Dedications* was reissued in 2005 on CD by Celeste Company (Japan).

12. Quote derived from interview by Maxwell Campbell in *All About Jazz*, April 2008, 13.

13. I recall reading the book and being completely taken by Winnie Mandela's story of courage and brutal struggle against the apartheid regime.

14. See Bauer (2003, 119–20) for a discussion of Betty Carter's label, Bet-Car records.

15. *New York Times*, 3 April 1983.

16. Rasmussen (2001b, 62).

17. There is a small but growing literature on the issue of exile and the possibilities of return pertaining to the 1990s for South Africans living around the world. One of the most powerful is Hilda Bernstein's (1994) collection of interviews with a range of South Africans.

18. Hawkins's parents had lived in South Africa and left before he was born, but his ties to the country were deep and strong.

19. The idea of a true jazz musician seems to be quite common among an older generation of musicians who sense the gap between musicians who played jazz as a vocation for the sake of the art or the common good in some spiritual and collective sense and the younger generation of musicians who strive for financial gain. At a memorial service for one of the older musicians at St. Peter's church in Manhattan in 2006, it was striking how the musicians paid tribute to similar qualities in the musician being honored.

20. This is taken from Derrida (2001: Part One). I am grateful to Gavin Steingo for giving me the Derrida book at just the moment I was thinking through these issues — serendipitous and most kind. Thank you.

21. Drawn from a conversation we had on 22 August 2006.

22. The idea of beauty is not new to African diasporic or jazz thinking. Here I am reminded of the reflections on beauty by Ornette Coleman in his Atlantic Records collection, *Beauty Is a Rare Thing*; Kofsky (1970) has a conversation with John Coltrane on beauty; see also Nutall (2007) and Nakedi (2006).

23. Serematakis (1996, 12–15).

24. Sathima Bea Benjamin, as reported on by Jill de Villiers, *The Citizen*, 24 June 1999, 33.

25. A similar release became necessary to Sathima's survival and capacity to

thrive as a musician in the 1990s. She and Abdullah decided they needed to live separately, though he continues to support her financially.

26. Quote derived from Muller with Benjamin, February 2000.

27. Derived from *All About Jazz* interview, April 2008, 6.

28. See Lock (1999) on Ellington and issue of spontaneity.

29. "Seeking the Mystical in Music," 22 September 2006, retrieved from nytimes.com.

6. Returning Home?

1. Liner notes, *Cape Town Love*.

2. Abdullah has similar memories. In an interview for the Canadian publication *Coda Magazine* in 1974, he told Ib Skovgaard Petersen, "[In South Africa] I was exposed to all kinds of music. In the community there lived Indian people, Chinese, Xhosa, Zulu, . . . and Western music, American jazz, European music, it was all there. It was very good schooling. . . . Basically it goes down to a whole way of life, not just the music, two entirely different worlds. . . . Like you said, in Africa we are exposed to all different kinds of music, and in many groups. It's not like when you're in Europe; when you're a musician you must either play classical music or play jazz, or now maybe rock. In Africa there are many different groups and ways of thinking." On his return to South Africa in 1991 he was interviewed by the South African Don Albert, who wrote, "Ibrahim says that when he was growing up he played in dance bands, traditional African bands, carnival bands and jazz groups, so that when he composes he draws on all the different experiences. 'When I compose, all these sounds are integrated into my compositions, then I need to find the musicians who are able to play in the particular idiom in which I have written.'" *The Star*, Johannesburg, 7 March 1991, 12.

3. Rasmussen (2000, 67).

4. All this information is drawn from Bruce Crowther's and Ed Anderson's piece "Song of Memories" in Rasmussen (2000, 57–63).

5. Changing pronouns in this way is one of the most common transformations in cover versions. See Dai Griffiths, "Cover Versions and the Sound of Identity in Motion," *Popular Music Studies*, edited by David Hesmondhalgh and Keith Negus (London: Arnold, 2002), 51–64.

6. "Body and Soul" is the most widely recorded tune in jazz history and functioned as an anthem in Harlem in the 1930s.

7. See Nelson (1985).

8. See www.williambowles.info, retrieved 11 September 2006.

9. Quotes from Barthes (1982, 9–11).

10. Berliner (1993).

11. De Veaux (1991).

12. I am not the first to posit a relationship between the New York City sky-

line and jazz performance. See, for example, Kouwenhouven's article, "What's 'American' about America?" written in 1954 and published in 1955 in the *Colorado Quarterly* but revised for O'Meally (1998, 125–28); and Wynton Marsalis's comments in his interview with O'Meally about the New York skyline, skyscrapers, and jazz and Ellington's music in O'Meally (1998, 145).

13. De Certeau (1984, 91).

14. Ibid., 91–93.

15. Baudrillard (1989:16).

16. Sathima Bea Benjamin in Rasmussen (2000b, 71).

17. Trouillot (1997, 31–32).

7. *Musical Echoes*

1. Jules Epstein, liner notes to *Musical Echoes* (2004).

2. See Chakrabarty (2003) for comment on the problem for the Third World in relationship to the European center: it is always just behind, never quite catching up, with European progress, chronology, and history.

3. Though I had read *Provincializing Europe* earlier, I am grateful to Tim Rommen for pointing me back to the notion of two histories, an idea I have found most productive in moving my thinking on this subject forward.

4. Feld (2000).

5. Chakrabarty (2003, 66–69).

6. All definitions of *echo* from the *American Heritage Dictionary* 2000, retrieved 22 June 2004 from http://dictionary.reference.com.

7. Ibid., referencing the *Oxford English Research Dictionary* (1996, 445).

8. Simone de Beauvoir (1965), an early critique of women as always being the secondary subject in society.

9. The Emmy award–winning documentary *Amandla! Revolution in Four-Part Harmony* (2002), directed by Lee Hirsch, constitutes a contemporary take on the Greek myth of Echo. Similarly, my own work (Muller [2008]) argues for the power of the human voice, individually and collectively, in articulating a strident medium of resistance, anger, but also reconciliation, in twentieth-century South African politics.

10. See Hayes (2004) for a discussion of the reading of gender and race through the sound of the voice in jazz, specifically, regarding Sarah Vaughan's voice.

11. Scarry (1999, 3–4).

12. Ibid., 111, citing Simone Weil.

13. Ibid., 112.

14. Ibid.

15. Ibid., 112–13.

16. Ibid., 118.

17. Ibid., 108.

8. Outcomes — Jazz in the World

1. Bohlman and Plastino have an edited volume, *Jazz Worlds/Worlds of Jazz* forthcoming from University of Chicago Press.

2. Atkins (2003, Introduction).

3. Moore (2007).

4. "New ideas about diaspora": Clifford 1998, 1997; Monson 2007; "forms of cosmopolitanism": Clifford 1998, Malcolmson 1998, Ong 1998, and Turino 2000; "the transnational": see Amy Kaplan's Presidential Address to the Society of American Studies, 2003, published in *American Quarterly* 56/1 (2004).

5. Moore (2007).

6. South Africa currently has eleven official languages and several others considered significant to the nation because they represent important constituencies of the population.

Selected References

Published Sources, Dissertations, and Theses

Adhikari, Mohammed. 1996. *Straatpratjes: Language, Politics, and Popular Culture in Cape Town, 1909–1922*. Cape Town: L. Van Schaik.

———, ed. 2009. *Burdened by Race: Coloured Identities in Southern Africa*. Cape Town: UCT Press.

———. 2005. *Not White Enough, Not Black Enough: Racial Identity in the South African Coloured Community*. Athens: Ohio University Press.

Allen, Lara. 1993. *Pennywhistle Kwela: a Musical, Historical and Sociopolitical Analysis*. M.A. thesis, University of Natal, Durban.

———. 2003. "Commerce, Politics, and Musical Hybridity: Vocalizing Urban Black South African Identity during the 1950s." *Ethnomusicology* 47/2, 228–49.

———. 2004. "Music, Film, and Gangsters in the Sophiatown Imaginary: Featuring Dolly Rathebe." *Scrutiny 2, Issues in English Studies in Southern Africa* 9/1, 19–38.

Andersson, Muff. 1981. *Music in the Mix: The Story of South African Popular Music*. Johannesburg: Ravan.

Ansell, Gwen. 2004. *Soweto Blues: Jazz, Popular Music, and Politics in South Africa*. New York: Continuum.

Appadurai, Arjun. 1986. *The Social Life of Things: Commodities in Cultural Perspective*. Cambridge: Cambridge University Press.

Atkins, E. T. 2001. *Blue Nippon: Authenticating Jazz in Japan*. Durham: Duke University Press.

———, ed. 2003. *Jazz Planet*. Oxford: University Press of Mississippi.

Baines, Gary 1996. "The Little Jazz Town: The Social History and Musical Styles of Black Grahamstown in the 1950s and 1960s." *Papers Presented at the Symposium on Ethnomusicology*, ed. A. Tracey, 14. Grahamstown: ILAM.

Ballantine, Christopher. 1993. *Marabi Nights: Early South African Jazz and Vaudeville*. Johannesburg: Ravan.

———. 1996. "Joseph Shabalala: Chronicles of an African Composer." *British Journal of Ethnomusicology* 5/2, 1–37.

Barthes, Roland. 1982. *Camera Lucida: Reflections on Photography*. Translated by Richard Howard. New York: Hill and Wang.

Baudrillard, Jean. 1989. *America*. New York: Verso.

Bauer, William. 2003. *Open the Door: The Life and Music of Betty Carter*. Ann Arbor: University of Michigan Press.

Behar, Ruth, and Deborah Gordon, eds. 1996. *Women Writing Culture*. Berkeley: University of California Press.

Berliner, Paul. 1994. *Thinking in Jazz: The Infinite Art of Improvisation.* Chicago: University of Chicago Press.

Bernstein, Hilda. 1994. *The Rift: The Exile Experience of South Africans.* New York: Random House.

Besten, Michael. 2009. "'We are the Original Inhabitants of this Land': Khoe-San Identity in Post-Apartheid South Africa." *Burdened by Race: Coloured Identities in Southern Africa,* ed. M. Adhikari, 134–55. Cape Town: UCT Press.

Bhabha, Homi. 2004. *The Location of Culture.* New York: Routledge.

Bickford-Smith, Vivian, et al., eds. 1999. *Cape Town in the Twentieth Century.* Cape Town: David Philip.

Bohlman, Phil, and Goffredo Plastino, eds. Forthcoming. *Jazz Worlds/Worlds of Jazz.* Chicago: University of Chicago Press.

Born, Georgina, and David Hesmondhalgh, eds. 2000. *Western Music and Its Others: Difference, Representation, and Appropriation in Music.* Berkeley: University of California Press.

Breakey, Basil. 1997. *Beyond the Blues: Township Jazz in the '60s and '70s.* Cape Town: David Philip.

Bruinders, Sylvia. 2006–7. "'This is our Sport!' Christmas Band Competitions and the Enactment of an Ideal Community." *South African Music Research* 26/27, 109–26.

———. 2005. "Performance of Place: How Musical Practices in Cape Town Recreate a Displaced Community." *Papers Presented at the Symposium on Ethnomusicology* 18, 17–20.

Bull, Michael, and Les Back, eds. 2003. *The Auditory Culture Reader.* Oxford: Berg.

Butler, Judith, and Gayatri Spivak. 2007. *Who Sings the Nation State? Language, Politics, Belonging.* London: Seagull.

Carby, Hazel. 1998. *Race Men.* Cambridge: Harvard University Press.

Carson, Charles. 2008. "'Bridging the Gap': Creed Taylor, Grover Washington Jr., and the Crossover Roots of Smooth Jazz." *Black Music Research* 28/1, 1–15.

Chakrabarty, Dipesh. 2003. *Provincializing Europe: Postcolonial Thought and Historical Difference.* Princeton: Princeton University Press.

Cheah, Pheng, and Bruce Robbins, eds. 1998. *Cosmopolitics: Thinking and Feeling beyond the Nation.* Minneapolis: University of Minnesota Press.

Clarke, Kamari, and Deborah Thomas, eds. 2006. *Globalization and Race: Transformation in the Cultural Production of Blackness.* Durham: Duke University Press.

Clifford, James. 1998. "Mixed Feelings." *Cosmopolitics: Thinking and Feeling beyond the Nation,* ed. Pheng Cheah and Bruce Robbins, 362–70. Minneapolis: University of Minnesota Press.

———. 1997. *Routes: Travel and Translation in the Late Twentieth Century.* Cambridge: Harvard University Press.

————, ed. 1986. *Writing Culture: The Poetics and Politics of Ethnography*. Berkeley: University of California Press.

Cockrell, Dale. 1987. "Of Gospel Hymns, Minstrel Songs, and Jubilee Singers: Towards Some Black South African Musics." *American Music* 5/4, 417–32.

Coetzer, Boudina. 2005. "Langarm in and around Grahamstown: The Dance, the Social History and the Music." *Journal of the Musical Arts of Africa* 2/1, 70–83.

Coombes, Annie. 2003. *History after Apartheid: Visual Culture and Public Memory in a Democratic South Africa*. Durham: Duke University Press.

Coplan, David. 2008 [1986]. *In Township Tonight! South Africa's Black City Music and Theater*. Chicago: University of Chicago Press.

Da Costa, Y., and A. Davids, eds. 1994. *Pages from Cape Muslim History*. Pietermaritzburg: Shuster and Schuster.

Davis, Angela. 1998. *Blues Women, Black Feminism*. New York: Pantheon.

Davis, Peter. 1996. *In Darkest Hollywood: Exploring the Jungles of South African's Cinema*. Athens: Ohio University Press.

Dawe, Kevin, ed. *Island Musics*. Oxford: Berg.

de Beauvoir, Simone. 1965. *The Second Sex*. New York: Bantam.

de Certeau, Michel. 1988 [1984]. *The Practice of Everyday Life*. Translated by Steven Randall. Berkeley: University of California Press.

Derrida, Jacques. 2001. *On Cosmopolitanism and Forgiveness*. Translated by Mark Dolley and Michael Hughes. Preface by Simon Critchley and Richard Kearney. New York: Routledge.

de Veaux, Scott. 1991. "Constructing the Jazz Tradition: Jazz Historiography." *Black American Literature Forum* 25/3, 525–60.

Douglas, Susan. 1999. *Listening In: Radio and the American Imagination*. New York: Random House.

Edwards, Brent. 2003. *The Practice of Diaspora: Literature, Translation, and the Rise of Black Internationalism*. Cambridge: Harvard University Press.

Ellington, Duke. 1976 [1973]. *Music Is My Mistress*. New York: Da Capo.

Enstice, Wayne, and Janice Stockhouse, eds. 2004. *Jazzwomen: Conversations with Twenty-One Musicians*. Bloomington: Indiana University Press.

Epstein, Jules. 2004. Liner notes to *Musical Echoes*. New York: Ekapa.

Erasmus, Zimitri, ed. 2001. *Coloured by History, Shaped by Place: New Perspectives on Coloured Identities in Cape Town*. Cape Town: Kwela.

Erlmann, Veit. 1991. *African Stars: Studies in Black South African Performance*. Chicago: University of Chicago Press.

————. 1996. *Nightsong: Performance, Power, and Practice in South Africa*. Chicago: University of Chicago Press.

————. 1999. *Music, Modernity, and the Global Imagination: South Africa and the West*. New York: Oxford University Press.

————, ed. 2004. *Hearing Cultures: Essays on Sound, Listening, and Modernity*. Oxford: Berg.

Farred, Grant. 2006. "'Shooting the White Girl First': Race in Post-Apartheid South Africa." *Globalization and Race: Transformations in the Cultural Production of Blackness*, ed. Kamari Clarke and Deborah Thomas, 226–48. Durham: Duke University Press.

Feld, Steven. 2000. "The Poetics and Politics of Pygmy Pop." *Western Music and Its Others: Difference, Representation and Appropriation in Music*, ed. Georgina Born and David Hesmondhalgh, 254–79. Berkeley: University of California Press.

Field, Sean. 2001. "Fragile Identities: Memory, Emotion, and Coloured Residents of Windemere." *Coloured by History, Shaped by Place: New Perspectives on Coloured Identities in Cape Town*, ed. Zimitri Erasmus, 97–113. Cape Town: Kwela.

Fortune, Linda. 1996. *The House in Tyne Street: Childhood Memories of District Six*. Cape Town: Kwela.

Foucault, Michel. 1972. *The Archeology of Knowledge and the Discourse on Language*. Translated by A. Sheridan Smith. New York: Pantheon.

Gabbard, Krin. 1996. *Jammin' at the Margins: Jazz and the American Cinema*. Durham: Duke University Press.

Gevisser, Mark, and Edwin Cameron, eds. 1995. *Defiant Desire: Gay and Lesbian Lives in South Africa*. Johannesburg: Ravan.

Gilroy, Paul. 1993. *The Black Atlantic: Modernity and Double Consciousness*. Cambridge: Harvard University Press.

Griffin, Farah. 2001. *If You Can't Be Free, Be a Mystery: In Search of Billie Holiday*. New York: Simon and Schuster.

Gutsche, Thelma 1972. *The History and Social Significance of Motion Pictures in South Africa 1895–1940*. Cape Town: Howard Timmins.

Hajdu, David. 1997. *Lushlife: A Biography of Billy Strayhorn*. New York: Farrar, Straus, and Giroux.

Hamm, Charles. 1995. *Putting Popular Music in Its Place*. Cambridge: Cambridge University Press.

Hayes, Elaine. 2004. "To Be Pop or to Bebop: Sarah Vaughan and the Politics of Crossover." Ph.D. diss., University of Pennsylvania.

Hendricks, Cheryl. 2001. "'Ominous' Liaisons: Tracing the Interface between 'Race' and Sex at the Cape." *Coloured by History, Shaped by Place: New Perspectives on Coloured Identities in Cape Town*, ed. Z. Erasmus, 29–44. Cape Town: Kwela.

Hine, Darlene, Tricia Danielle Keaton, and Stephen Small, eds. 2009. *Black Europe and the African Diaspora*. Urbana: University of Illinois Press.

Holiday, Billie. 1956. *Lady Sings the Blues: The Searing Autobiography of an American Musical Legend*. New York: Penguin.

Holt, Fabian. 2004. "Erik Wiedemann's Career and Works." *Annual Review of Jazz Studies* 12, 173–94.

Hoskins, Janet. 1998. *Biographical Objects: How Things Tell the Stories of People's Lives*. New York: Routledge.

Ifekwunigwe, Jayne, ed. 2004. *"Mixed Race" Studies: A Reader*. New York: Routledge.

————. 1999. *Scattered Be-Longings: Cultural Paradoxes of "Race," Nation and
Gender*. London: Routledge.

Jackson, Jeffrey. 2003. *Making Jazz French: Music and Modern Life in Interwar
Paris*. Durham: Duke University Press.

Jeppie, Shamiel. 2001. "Reclassifications: Coloured, Malay, Muslim." *Coloured by
History, Shaped by Place: New Perspectives on Coloured Identities in Cape Town*,
ed. Z. Erasmus, 29–44. Cape Town: Kwela.

————. 1990. "Aspects of Popular Culture and Class Expression in Inner Cape
Town from the Late 1940s to the Early 1960s." M.A. thesis, University of Cape
Town.

Jorritsma, Marie. 2006. "Sonic Spaces: Inscribing "Coloured" Voices in the
Karoo, South Africa." Ph.D. diss., University of Pennsylvania.

Kelley, Robin. 2003. *Freedom Dreams: The Black Radical Imagination*. Boston:
Beacon.

Kofsky, Frank. 1970. *Black Nationalism and the Revolution in Music*. New York:
Pathfinder.

Krog, Antje. 2000. *Country of My Skull: Guilt, Sorrow, and the Limits of Forgiveness
in the New South Africa*. New York: Three Rivers.

Langford, Wendy. 1999. *Revolutions of the Heart: Gender, Power, and the Delusions
of Love*. New York: Routledge.

Layne, Valmont. 1995. "A History of Dance and Jazz Band Performance in the
Western Cape in the Post-1945 Era." M.A. thesis, University of Cape Town.

Lewis, Desiree. 2001. "Writing Hybrid Selves: Richard Rive and Zoe Wicomb."
*Coloured by History, Shaped by Place: New Perspectives on Coloured Identities in
Cape Town*, ed. Z. Erasmus, 131–58. Cape Town: Kwela.

Lipsitz, George. 1997. *Dangerous Crossroads: Popular Music, Postmodernism, and
the Poetics of Place*. New York: Verso.

Lock, Graham. 1999. *Blutopia: Visions of the Future and Revisions of the Past in the
Work of Sun Ra, Duke Ellington, and Anthony Braxton*. Durham: Duke University Press.

Lucia, Christine. 2002. "Abdullah Ibrahim and the Uses of Memory." *British Journal of Ethnomusicology* 11/2, 125–43.

Makeba, Miriam, with James Hall. 1987. *Makeba: My Story*. New York: New
American Library.

Makwenda, Joyce. 2005. *Zimbabwe Township Music*. Harare: Storytime Productions.

Malan, Rian. 2001. "In the Jungle." *The Best Magazine Writing 2001*, ed. Harold
Evans, 51–83. New York: Public Affairs.

Malcolmson, Stuart. 1998. "The Varieties of Cosmopolitan Experience." *Cosmopolitics: Thinking and Feeling beyond the Nation*, ed. Pheng Cheah and Bruce
Robbins, 233–45. Minneapolis: University of Minnesota Press.

Margolick, David, and Hilton Als. 2001. *Strange Fruit: The Biography of a Song.* New York: Harper Perennial.

Marks, Laura. 2000. *The Skin of the Film: Intercultural Cinema, Embodiment, and the Senses.* Durham: Duke University Press.

Martin, Denis-Constant. 1999. *Coon Carnival: New Year in Cape Town, Past and Present.* Cape Town: David Philip.

Masekela, Hugh, with D. Cheers. 2004. *Still Grazing: The Musical Journey of Hugh Masekela.* New York: Crown.

Mason, John Edwin. 2003. *Social Death and Resurrection: Slavery and Emancipation in South Africa.* Charlottesville: University of Virginia Press.

Mattera, Don. 1987. *Sophiatown: Coming of Age in South Africa.* Boston: Beacon.

McClintock, Anne. 1995. *Imperial Leather: Race, Gender, and Sexuality in the Colonial Contest.* New York: Routledge.

McGregor, Maxine. 1996. *Chris McGregor and the Brotherhood of Breath.* Flint, Mich.: Bamberger.

McKay, George. 2005. *Circular Breathing: The Cultural Politics of Jazz in Britain.* Durham: Duke University Press.

Meintjes, Louise. 1990. "Paul Simon's *Graceland*: South Africa and the Mediation of Musical Meaning." *Ethnomusicology* 4, 37–73.

Miller, Colin. 2007. *"Julle kan ma New York toe gaan, ek bly in die Manenberg"*: An Oral History of Jazz in Cape Town from the mid-1950s to the mid-1970s. *Imagining the City: Memories and Cultures in Cape Town*, ed. Field, Meyer, and Swanson, 133–49. Pretoria: UNISA.

Min-Ha, Trinh T. 1989. *Women, Native, Other.* Bloomington: Indiana University Press.

Molefe, Z. B., and M. Mzileni. 1997. *A Common Hunger to Sing: A Tribute to South Africa's Black Women of Song, 1950–1990.* Cape Town: Kwela.

Monson, Ingrid, ed. 2003. *African Diaspora: A Musical Perspective.* New York: Routledge.

———. 2007. *Freedom Sounds: Civil Rights Call Out to Jazz and Africa.* New York: Oxford University Press.

Moore, Gerald. 2002. "The Transcription Center in the Sixties: Navigating in Narrow Seas." *Research in African Literatures* 33/3, 167–81.

Moore, Hilary. 2007. *Inside British Jazz: Crossing Borders of Race, Nation, and Class.* London: Ashgate.

Mountain, Alan. 2004. *An Unsung Heritage: Perspectives on Slavery.* Cape Town: David Philip.

Mphahlele, Es'Kia. 1984. *Afrika My Music: An Autobiography, 1957–1983.* Johannesburg: Ravan.

Muller, Carol. 1996. "Musical Creation, Exile, and the 'Southern Touch' in the Jazz Songs of Sathima Bea Benjamin." *African Languages and Culture* 9/2, 127–43.

———. 1999. *Rituals of Fertility and the Sacrifice of Desire: Nazarite Women's Performance in South Africa.* Chicago: University of Chicago Press.

————. 2002a. "Covers, Copies, and Colouredness in Postwar Cape Town." *Cultural Analysis* 3, online, no page numbers.

————. 2002b. "Archiving Africanness." *Ethnomusicology*.

————. 2007a. "South Africa and American Jazz: Towards a Polyphonic Historiography." *History Compass* 5, 1–16.

————. 2007b "Musical Echoes of American Jazz: Towards a Comparative Historiography." *Safundi* 24, 57–71.

————. 2008. "South African Music: The Lion Sleeps Tonight." *Focus: South African Music*. New York: Routledge.

Nakedi, Ribane. 2006. *Beauty: A Black Perspective*. Pietermaritzburg: UKZN.

Nasson, Bill. 1989. "'She Preferred Living in a Cave with Harry the Snake-Catcher': Toward an Oral History of Popular Leisure and Class Expression in District Six, Cape Town, ca. 1920–1960." *Holding Their Ground: Class, Locality, and Culture in 19th and 20th Century South Africa*, ed. Philip Bonner et al., 285–309. Johannesburg: Ravan.

Nelson, Kristina. 1985. *The Art of Reciting the Qur'an*. Austin: University of Texas Press.

Nettleback, Colin. 2004. *Dancing with de Beauvoir: Jazz and the French*. Melbourne: Melbourne University Press.

Ngcelwane, Nomvuyo. 2001. *Sala Kahle District Six: An African Woman's Perspective*. Cape Town: Kwela.

Nicholson, Stuart. 1995. *Billie Holiday*. Boston: Northeastern University Press.

Nixon, Michael. 1997. "The World of Jazz in Inner Cape Town, 1940–1960." *Papers Presented at the Symposium on Ethnomusicology* #13, ed. Andrew Tracey, 19–23. Grahamstown: International Library of African Music.

Nixon, Rob. 1994. *Homelands, Harlem and Hollywood: South African Culture and the World Beyond*. New York: Routledge.

Nkonyeni, Ncedisa. 2007. "*Da Struggle Kontinues* into the 21st Century: Two Decades of Nation-Conscious Rap in Cape Town." *Imagining the City: Memories and Cultures in Cape Town*, ed. Field, Meyer, and Swanson, 151–72. Pretoria: UNISA.

Nkosi, Lewis. 1965. *Home and Exile and Other Selections*. New York: Longmans.

Nussbaum, Martha. 2003. *Upheavals of Thought: The Intelligence of Emotions*. Cambridge: Cambridge University Press.

Nuttall, Sarah. 2009. *Entanglement: Literary and Cultural Reflections on Post–Apartheid*. Johannesburg: Wits University Press.

————, ed. 2007. *Beautiful/Ugly: African and Diaspora Aesthetics*. Durham: Duke University Press.

Obama, Barack. 1995. *Dreams from My Father: A Story of Race and Inheritance*. New York: Three Rivers.

Okpewho, Isidore, and Nkiru Nzegwu, eds. 2009. *The New African Diaspora*. Bloomington: Indiana University Press.

Olwage, Grant, ed. 2007. *Composing Apartheid*. Johannesburg: Wits University Press.

O'Meally, Robert. 2000. *Lady Day: The Many Faces of Billie Holiday*. New York: Da Capo.

———. 1999. *The Jazz Cadence of American Culture*. New York: Columbia University Press.

Ong, Aiwha. 1998. "Flexible Citizenship among Chinese Citizens." *Cosmopolitics: Thinking and Feeling beyond the Nation*, ed. Pheng Cheah and Bruce Robbins, 134–62. Minneapolis: University of Minnesota Press.

Owusu, Kwesi, ed. 2000. *Black British Culture and Society: A Text Reader*. New York: Routledge.

Panish, Jon. 1997. *The Color of Jazz: Race and Presentation in Postwar America*. Oxford: University Press of Mississippi.

Pillay, Shunnah. 2007. *Shadow People*. Cape Town: STE.

Placksin, Sally. 1982. *American Women in Jazz, 1990 to the Present*. New York: Putnam.

———. 1984. "Sathima: Music Is the Spirit within You." *Women and Performance: A Journal of Feminist Theory* 2/3, 21–31. Reprinted in Rasmussen 2000b.

Putnam, Robert. 2000. *Bowling Alone: The Collapse and Revival of American Community*. New York: Putnam.

Radano, Ronald. 2003. *Lyin' Up a Nation*. Chicago: University of Chicago Press.

Radano, Ronald, and Philip Bohlman, eds. 2001. *Music and the Racial Imagination*. Chicago: University of Chicago Press.

Ramsey, Guthrie. 2003. *Race Music: Black Cultures from Bebop to Hip-hop*. Berkeley: University of California Press.

Rasmussen, Lars. 2000a. *Abdullah Ibrahim: A Discography*. Copenhagen: Booktrader.

———. 2000b. *Sathima Bea Benjamin: Embracing Jazz*. Copenhagen: Booktrader.

———. 2001. *Cape Town Jazz, 1959–1963: The Photographs of Hardy Stockman*. Copenhagen: Booktrader.

———. 2003a. *Jazz People of Cape Town*. Copenhagen: The Booktrader.

———. 2003b. *Mbizo: A Book about Johnny Dyani*. Copenhagen: Booktrader.

Rasmussen, Lars, and J. Patterson. 2002. *Mantindane (He Who Survives): My Life with the Manhattan Brothers, Joe Mogotsi with Pearl Connor*. Copenhagen: Booktrader.

Reddy, Thiven. 2001. "The Politics of Naming: The Constitution of Coloured Subjects in South Africa." *Coloured by History, Shaped by Place: New Perspectives on Coloured Identities in Cape Town*, ed. Z. Erasmus, 62–79. Cape Town: Kwela.

Richards, Jeffrey. 1984. *The Age of the Dream Palace: Cinema and Society in Britain 1930–39*. London: Routledge and Kegan Paul.

Richmond, Yale. 2003. *Cultural Exchange and the Cold War: Raising the Iron Curtain*. University Park: Pennsylvania State University Press.

Rive, Richard. 1981. *Writing Black*. Cape Town: David Philip.

————. 1986. *Buckingham Palace, District Six: A Novel of Cape Town.* New York: Ballantine.

Root, Maria, ed. 1992. *Racially Mixed People in America: Within, Between, and Beyond Race.* New York: Sage.

Rosenzweig, Roy. 1983. *Eight Hours for What You Will: Workers and Leisure in an Industrial City (1870–1920).* New York: Cambridge University Press.

Said, Edward. 2000. *Out of Place: A Memoir.* New York: Vintage.

————. 2002. *Reflections on Exile and Other Essays.* Cambridge: Harvard University Press.

Samuelson, Meg. 2007. "Re-Imagining South Africa via a Passage to India: M. K. Jeffrey's Archive of the Indian Ocean World." *Social Dynamics* 33/2, 61–85.

Saunders, Frances Stonor. 1999. *The Cultural Cold War: The CIA and the World of Arts and Letters.* New York: New Press.

Scarry, Elaine. 2001. *On Beauty and Being Just.* Princeton: Princeton University Press.

Serematakis, Nadia. 1996. "The Memory of the Senses, Parts I and II." *The Senses Still: Perception and Memory as Material Culture in Modernity,* 1–44. Chicago: University of Chicago Press.

Shelemay, Kay. 1998. *Let Jasmine Rain Down: Song and Remembrance among Syrian Jews.* Chicago: University of Chicago Press.

Shell, Robert. 1994. *Children of Bondage: A Social History of the Slave Society at the Cape of Good Hope, 1652–1838.* Hanover: University Press of New England.

Solberg, Bjorn. 1996. "African Horns: Saxophone Players in the South African Jazz Tradition." M.Mus. thesis, Norwegian University of Science and Technology.

Soudien, Craig. 2001. "District Six and Its Uses in the Discussion about Non-Racialism." *Coloured by History, Shaped by Place: New Perspectives on Coloured Identities in Cape Town,* ed. Z. Erasmus, 114–30. Cape Town: Kwela.

Stewart, Susan. 2002. *Poetry and the Fate of the Senses.* Chicago: University of Chicago Press.

Szymczak, Colette. 2006–7. "Jonas Gwagwa: Musician and Cultural Activist." *South African Music Studies* 26/27, 47–70.

Tacchi, Joe. 2003. "Nostalgia and Radio Sound." *The Auditory Culture Reader,* ed. Michael Bull and Les Back, 303–10. Oxford: Berg.

Taylor, Timothy. 2007. *Beyond Exoticism: Western Music and the World.* Durham: Duke University Press.

————. 1997. *Global Pop: World Music, World Markets.* New York: Routledge.

Titlestad, Michael. 2004. *Making the Changes: Jazz in South African Literature and Reportage.* Pretoria: UNISA.

Trotter, Henry. 2009. "Trauma and Memory: The Impact of Apartheid-Era Forced Removals on Coloured Identity in Cape Town." *Burdened by Race: Coloured Identities in Southern Africa,* ed. M. Adhikari, 49–78. Cape Town: UCT Press.

Trouillot, Michel-Rolph. 1997. *Silencing the Past: Power and the Production of History*. Boston: Beacon.

Tucker, Sherrie. 2000. *Swing Shift: All-Girl Bands of the 1940s*. Durham: Duke University Press.

Turino, Thomas. 2000. *Nationalists, Cosmopolitans, and Popular Music in Zimbabwe*. Chicago: University of Chicago Press.

Viljoen, Shaun. 2007. "Proclamations and Silences: 'Race,' Self-Fashioning, and Sexuality in the Transatlantic Correspondence between Langston Hughes and Richard Rive." *Social Dynamics* 33/2, 105–22.

Von Eschen, Penny. 2006. *Satchmo Blows up the World: Jazz Ambassadors Play the Cold War*. Cambridge: Harvard University Press.

———. 1997. *Race against Empire: Black Americans and Anti-Colonialism 1937–1957*. Ithaca: Cornell University Press.

Watkins, Lee. 2001. "'*Simunye*, We Are Not One:' Ethnicity, Difference and the Hip-Hoppers of Cape Town." *Race and Class* 43/1, 29–44.

Waxer, Lise. 2002. *City of Musical Memory: Salsa, Record Grooves, and Popular Culture in Cali, Colombia*. Middletown, Conn.: Wesleyan University Press.

Weiss, Jason. 2006. *Steve Lacy: Conversations*. Durham: Duke University Press.

Western, John. 1997. *Outcast Cape Town*. Berkeley: University of California Press.

Wiedemann, Erik. 1991. "Duke Ellington the Composer." *Annual Review of Jazz Studies* 5, 37–64.

———. 1996. "The Montmartre, 1959–1976: Towards a History of a Copenhagen Jazz House." *Musik & Forskning: Mjusic in Copenhagen: Studies in the Musical Life of Copenhagen in the 19th and 20th Centuries*, 274–93. N.p.: n.pub.

Wolf, Margery. 1992. *A Thrice-Told Tale: Feminism, Post-Modernism, and Ethnographic Responsibility*. Stanford: Stanford University Press.

Yon, Daniel. 2007. "Race-Making/Race-Mixing: St. Helena and the South Atlantic World." *Social Dynamics* 33/2, 144–63.

Interviews, Informal Conversations, and E-mail Communications

Jimmy Adams, Cape Town, South Africa, September 1996.

"Auntie Beatty," Cape Town, South Africa, September 1996.

Sathima Bea Benjamin, some specific moments, as indicated in the book, but many informal conversations face to face in New York City, in Cape Town, and by telephone.

Zelda Benjamin with Colin Muller, District Six Museum, copy kindly given to me.

Ruth Fife, Cape Town, South Africa, September 1996.

Joan Franciscus, Cape Town, South Africa, September 1996.

Harold Jephthah and Jimmy Adams, Cape Town, South Africa, December 1999.

Jeffery Kallberg, Philadelphia, October 2000.

Vincent Kolbe, Cape Town, South Africa, September 1996.

Joanne Meyerowitz, Durham, North Carolina, October 1999.
Basil Rich, Cape Town, South Africa, September 1996.
John Samuels, Cape Town, South Africa, September 1996.
Chris Turner, by email, May 2006.

Recordings

Sathima Bea Benjamin

Sathima Bea Benjamin. N.d. *My Songs for You.* Not released.
————. 1979. *Sathima Sings Ellington.* New York: Ekapa (USA), Ekapa 001.
————. 1982. *Dedications.* New York: Ekapa (USA), Ekapa 002.
————. 1983. *Memories and Dreams.* New York: Ekapa (USA), Ekapa 003.
————. 1985. *Windsong.* New York: Ekapa (USA), Ekapa 002.
————. 1987. *Lovelight.* Munich: Enja Records, ENJ 6022 1.
————. 1989. *Southern Touch.* Munich: Enja Records, ENJ 7015 2.
————. 1997. *A Morning in Paris.* Munich: Enja Records, ENJ-9309 2.
————. 1999. *Cape Town Love.* Cape Town: Ekapa SA 001.
————. 2006. *Musical Echoes.* New York: Ekapa (USA), Ekapa 004.
————. 2006. *Songspirit.* New York: Ekapa (USA), Ekapa 003.
————. 2001. *The Best of Sathima Bea Benjamin.* Cape Town: EMI and ENJA CDSRIK WL 7861500.

Additional Recordings

Dollar Brand Trio. *Duke Ellington Presents the Dollar Brand Trio.* New York: Warner Brothers, 1997 [1963].
London Is the Place for Me 2: Caplyso & Kwela, Highlife and Jazz from Young Black London. London: Honest Jons Records, 2005. Paul Gilroy contributed to the liner notes.
Ornette Coleman. *Beauty Is a Rare Thing: The Complete Atlantic Recordings.* Boxed set. 1993.
Svend Asmussen, Stephan Grappelli, and Ray Nance. *Duke Ellington's Jazz Violin Session.* Paris: Reprise 1963.
Thelonious Monk. *Solo Monk.* Original recording remastered. New York: Sony 2003.
Various Artists. *Cape Jazz.* Cape Town: Mountain Records.

Selected Films

Austin, Chris (director). *Abdullah Ibrahim: Brother with Perfect Timing.* New York: Rhapsody Films, 1988. Reissued as DVD.

Balmer, Paul. *Africa I Remember: A Musical Synthesis of Two Cultures*. New York: Filmmakers Library, 1995.

Baush, Ike Brooks (director). *Zonk!* Vancouver: Villon Films. Reissued in VHS, 1996.

Capellari, Ciro (director). *Abdullah Ibrahim: Struggle for Love*. Berlin: Produktion 1, 2006.

Hirsch, Lee (director). *Amandla! Revolution in Four-Part Harmony*. Santa Monica: Artisan Entertainment, DVD 2002.

Minelli, Vincente (director). *Cabin in the Sky*. Originally released in 1943. Santa Monica: MGM/UA Home Video, 1999.

Powell, Aubrey (director). *Gumboots! An Explosion of Spirit and Song*. Chatsworth, Calif.: Image Entertainment, 2000 (DVD).

Seig, Matthew (director). *Lady Day: The Many Faces of Billie Holiday*. Turner Classic Movies, 1993.

Singh, Anant (director). *Sarafina!* With Whoopi Goldberg. Burbank, Calif.: Hollywood Pictures Home Videos, n.d. VHS.

Stevenson, Robert (director). *King Solomon's Mines*. Original release date 1937, release as DVD 2001, Santa Monica: MGM/UA.

Stone, Andrew (director). *Stormy Weather*. Original release in 1943. Beverly Hills: Fox Home Entertainment, 2005.

Yon, Daniel (director). *Sathima's Windsong*. Toronto: South Atlantic Productions, 2009.

Index

Adams, Jimmy, 24, 32, 55, 78, 85; SABC contract of, 60; theft of arrangements of, 61

Adhikari, Mohammed, 35, 37–38

"Africa," 166–67, 172, 179, 197, 201, 233

Africa Center, 147

African American Labor Center, 153, 157, 315n44

African American music, xviii, 11, 109

African American musicians, 55, 76, 102, 165, 174, 196, 210, 282

African diaspora, xvii, xxi, 103, 111, 225, 273; consciousness of, 188, 291; contemporary, 103; in exile, 181–83; Gilroy and, 173; legitimate membership of, 10; musical diaspora and, 99; musical surrogacy and, 98, 174–77, 290; new, 167–88, 241, 260, 261, 270, 276, 278–79, 282, 291; old (first or West), xvii, 111, 126, 172, 174, 256, 278; reconstructing, 167–70; South, 126, 173, 179–80, 259, 260; southern touch aesthetic and, 184–87, 205, 241, 292. *See also* black diaspora; jazz migrancy

African Jazz and Variety (African Follies), 55–56, 72–74

African musical diaspora, 187, 291

African National Congress (ANC), 1, 71, 183, 195; Culture Desk, 3; freedom charter, 34; New York office of, 83

African People's Organization (APO), 60

Afrikaner nationalism, 40

"Ah! Sweet Mystery of Life," 23, 67

Ambassadors, The, 86, 89, 91–93

American music, xv–xvi, xviii, 3, 11, 283–85, 109, 176–77, 215–16

American musicians, 3, 55, 76, 100, 102, 108, 138, 141, 143–44, 175, 200, 228, 246, 249, 254, 261, 275, 282–84, 286, 288, 294

American nation, 283

Anderson, Murray, 244, 253

anti-apartheid, 138, 169, 183–84, 189, 195–96, 217, 243, 259; activists for, 102, 209; musical events for, 35

Antibes Jazz Festival, 141

apartheid, 41, 60, 88, 104, 119, 124, 131, 142, 150, 169, 191, 204, 221–22, 262, 288, 292, 294; critique of, 51; fieldwork under, 50; forgetting of, 31; legacy of, 101; legislation, 45, 80, 175, 183; life under, 102, 181, 278; nightclubs under, 65; post-, 37, 46–49, 52–53, 60, 164, 168, 181, 183, 255, 259, 264; racial groups and, 45; story of, 178; struggle against, 184, 189, 195–96, 209–10, 259, 279

apartheid regime, 5–6, 12–13, 20–22, 28, 35–38, 40–44, 48–49, 54, 56, 71, 77, 82, 88–90, 94–95, 117, 128, 140, 151, 165, 178, 181–83, 195–96, 209, 264, 281, 289; opposition to, 34

archival recordings, 168

archive, xiv, xviii, 11, 12, 33, 49, 64, 119, 149, 164, 167–69, 187–88, 201, 251, 259–60, 265, 269, 285–86, 288–89, 293

Artists United Against Apartheid, 195, 209

Asmussen, Svend, xiv, 131, 205; records of, with Stephan Grappeli, 130

Athlone, 15, 17, 20, 43–44, 66–67, 85–86; Glemore Town Hall, 77–78

Ayler, Albert, 143–44, 178

Ballantine, Christopher, 1, 70

ban, 1, 44, 71, 82, 114, 178, 182, 208, 243, 289

Bantustan, 6
Barclay Studios, xiv, 130–31
Barron, Kenny, 110, 184, 218
Battswood Teachers' Training College, 20, 58, 65
beauty, 6, 13, 127, 243, 245, 280–81, 320n22; efficacy and value of, 274, 279, 292–93; poetics of, xxi, 238; Sathima and, xxxi, 131, 172, 189, 208, 232, 239, 241; social justice and, xviii, xxi, 280–81
"Because You Are Mine," 254
Belafonte, Harry, 64, 76, 102, 181
Benjamin, Edward, 14–15
Benjamin, Eva Thwaites. See Benjamin, Ma
Benjamin, Joan, 15, 17–25, 31, 54, 58, 66–67, 87, 91, 156, 248
Benjamin, Ma, 6, 14, 17–22, 25, 28–29, 31, 43, 54, 214, 250; songs from youth of, 23
Benjamin, Maurice, 15
Benjamin, Sathima Bea: Ahuri poem for Abdullah by, 204; Jimmy Adams and, 72–73; audiences of, 30–32, 45, 51, 53, 67, 120, 127, 131, 142, 152, 174, 176–77, 182, 195, 246–47, 286; awards of, 209; birth of, 14; books read by, 54, 80, 114, 155, 163, 175; Dollar Brand and, 54, 84, 86–89; childhood of, 12, 14–33; choir at Battswood and, 65–66; classified as "Cape Coloured," 43–45; compositional process of, 160–61, 165–67, 202–6, 228–38; considered for Grammy, 201; Billie Daniels and, 90; Downbeat rankings of, 206; dreams of, 10, 162, 184–85, 215, 268; Ekapa Records and, 199–206; Duke Ellington and, 89, 138–40; family history of, 14–21; family musical practices and, 22–27; Henry February as mentor of, 83, 243; as female Nat King Cole, 83; freedom and, 206, 228–32, 239, 243, 255, 259; Billie Holiday and, 80, 82, 85–86; Sam Isaacs and, 32, 65; jazz and, 46, 83, 109, 184, 216, 227, 228–29; at Kennedy Center, 171, 209; life story of, 221–27; longing of, for mother, 17, 116, 164; memories of, 20, 29, 47, 321n2; methodological challenges to studying life of, 168, 264, 286; as mother, 43, 66, 67–68, 77, 80, 85–87, 190–95; Mozambique experience of, 160–61; musical training of, 24; New York City and, 189, 195–99, 208–27; New York performances of, 149, 157, 198–213; Order of Ikhamanga and, 210; personal aesthetic of, 166, 185; political songs of, 34, 121, 138, 196; radio and, 12, 19, 25, 27–28, 33; record company of, xvi, xxi, 124, 129, 200–201, 206; recording projects of, 199, 200, 206, 210, 236, 279; recordings heard by, 80, 215, 220–21, 223, 273; repertory of, 9, 11, 23, 25, 28, 33, 120, 126–27, 131, 138, 164, 187, 201, 206, 217, 220–21, 223, 226, 228, 247–48, 252, 255–56; reviews of music of, 82–83, 85, 206–8, 258–59; South African songbook of, 9; style of, 11, 58, 64–66, 82–83, 121, 136, 138, 208; voice of, xxi, xxxiii, 9–10, 15, 24, 64, 189, 206–7, 209–10, 221–22, 227, 229–32, 241, 247, 258, 273. See also Adams, Jimmy; Battswood Teachers' Training College; Brand, Dollar; Ekapa record company and label; Holiday, Billie; Hotel Chelsea; Ibrahim, Abdullah; Isaacs, Sam; women thinking in jazz
Benjamin family, 6, 91; English cultural practices and, 22; gambling by, 19; household of, 19, 21–22; movies and, 29–30; musical practices of, 23, 25, 27; phonograph and, 23; radio and, 26–28; St. Helena and, 42–44
Benny Goodman Story, The, 32

Berliner, Paul, 217–18
Best of Sathima and Friends, The, 206
Bet-Car Records, 157–59
black diaspora, 52, 174
black press, 76, 178. See also *Drum Magazine; Golden City Post; Zonk! The African People's Magazine*
Bloom, Harold, 74
Blue Notes with Chris McGregor, 55, 104, 141–42, 144–47, 168, 170, 181, 256, 292
bob bops, 58
"Body and Soul," 242, 253
Bosman, Gerry, 60
Brand, Dollar, xiv, 1, 54, 86, 102, 131–32, 137, 169, 305n3; Ambassadors and, 89–94; *Anatomy of a South African Village,* 143; Atlantic Records debut of, 148; childhood sweetheart of, 170; Columbia Records recording of, 148; Communist Party woman and, 91; Dollar Brand School of Music and, 89; Dollar Brand Trio and, 118, 129, 141–42, 205; Juilliard Conservatory and, 148; *Round Midnight at the Café Montmartre,* 143; South African tour of (1968), 151–52; "Tintinyana," 90; *Voice of America* recording of, 148; weekly column of, for *Cape Herald,* 151. See also Ibrahim, Abdullah
Brooks, Lt. Ike, 69
Buena Vista Social Club, 245–46

call and response, xx, xxxiii, 179, 210, 274
Calloway, Cab, 30, 105, 108
Cape Coloured, xx, 31; as buffer zone, 39, 46; classification of, xxvii, 3, 11, 20, 34–35, 40–41, 45, 48, 85, 118, 257; education and, 19, 20; forced removals of, 21, 44, 49; history of, 37, 40, 52; Khoisan past and, 100, 155, 163, 164, 244, 248, 251, 256–57; marginality of, 3, 37; music of, 54–55, 61,

62, 65, 67–68, 76–77, 124, 244; politics of, 35, 37; rejectionism and, 34; slave past and, 14, 35, 38–39, 42; St. Helenians as, 22, 42–43
Cape Flats, 21, 44
Cape jazz, 55–95; Abdullah Ibrahim and, 54; as marketing category, 53
Cape Town: apartheid and, 20–21, 23, 45, 52, 54, 58, 60; beauty of, 6, 13; Carol and, 5, 8, 171; colonial history of, 14, 172; Coloured history in, 22, 25, 28, 30, 43–44, 48, 55–56, 61, 63, 68–69; liberal tradition of, 14; as Mother City, 45; as musical space, xiii, xv, 2, 11, 13, 26, 32, 33, 45, 53–54, 56, 60–63, 66, 72, 76–77, 80, 83–85, 100, 109; Sathima and, xv, 5–7, 12, 14, 17, 24, 33, 42, 55, 65, 73, 82, 90, 93–94, 155, 156, 161–62, 174; slavery in, 38. See also Cape jazz; *Cape Town Love;* Cape Town rhythm; dance bands; Holiday, Billie
Cape Town Love, xxi, 33, 80, 84, 101, 205, 241–42, 244–49, 251–52, 254–59, 263, 290
Cape Town rhythm (*ghoema* or *klopse* rhythm), 26, 138, 207, 247, 254, 256
Carnegie Hall, xiii, 132, 148–49, 171
Carter, Betty, 159, 165, 206, 218, 222, 229, 234
Catholic Church, 24; Holy Cross (District Six), 77, 88
censorship, 94, 289
Chakrabarty, Dipesh, xvii, xviii, 276–77
Cherry, Don, 143–44, 158, 178, 190
"Children of Soweto," 10, 160, 196–97
Christmas choirs, 25, 38, 46, 158
"Church's One Foundation, The," 23
CIA (Central Intelligence Agency), 145, 168
city and jazz performance, 265–68
cinema. See movies
Claremont, 15, 17, 19–23, 29, 42
club, clubs, 66, 77–78, 80, 82–83, 85–86,

club, clubs (*continued*)
106–9, 128, 181, 186, 210, 283; Africana Club, 129–31, 142; Circuit Club, 149; in Cape Town, 67, 72, 78, 207, 245, 252, 254–55; jazz, 88–95; Jazzhus Montmartre, 142–44, 151, 314n24; Paris, 132; Ronnie Scott's, 146; youth, 62

Cole, Nat "King," 25, 32, 62, 83, 109, 252, 256, 263

collaborative scholarship, 7

Color Bar Act, 6

Coloureds, 28; black identity and, 36; Chinese as, 42; classification of, 6, 22, 43, 45–46; as community, 21; as cornered community, 36–37; dance bands of, 56–65; defining of, 42; in District Six, 22; elite vs. working class, 55–56; forced removals of, 12, 21, 24, 44, 304n71; hair moments of, 42; history of, 31–42; Japanese and, 42; Khoisan, 42; leisure time of, 30, 57; Malay and, 25, 38, 40, 303n68; as minstrels, 25; as musicians, 55–56; music making of, 22, 25, 54, 67–68; oral history of, 44; St. Helenians as, 42–43, 303n66; St. Saviors and, 23; schooling of, 19, 20; segregation and, 6, 17; street bands of, 25; traveling shows of, 73. *See also* apartheid: legislation; Color Bar Act; dance bands; District Six; Group Areas Act and Amendment; Immorality Act; Population Registration Act and Amendment; Separate Amenities Act

Coloured Jazz and Variety, xxiv, 72–73

"Come Sunday," 156

Congress for Cultural Freedom, 145, 164, 168, 317n57

Coon Carnival, 26, 38

copy, xxi, 70, 73, 78, 126, 155, 223, 275, 280

copyright, 96, 133, 315n40

cosmopolitan, 13, 22, 41, 43, 61, 126, 187, 287, 291

dance bands, 12, 26, 53–57, 292; Alf Wylie's Band, 62; attire of musicians in, 63–64; Cape Corps Military Band, 61; as copies of American musicians, 27, 29, 62–64; good timing of, 62; impact of street music on, 26, 46; influence of, on Sathima's style, 64, 65, 116, 123, 223; musicians in, 24, 94; Philadelphia Rhythms, 62; recordings of, 76; Spes Bona Orchestra, 62; Tem Hawkers Band, 62; training spaces of, 24, 58–64, 68–69; varied repertory, 64, 255; wartime travel of, 61–62, 248; Willie Max's Band, 62. *See also* langarm (ballroom) dance

dance styles, 58

Davis, Miles, 84, 178, 219, 239–40

Day, Doris, 28, 32, 66, 77, 109, 252

Dedications, 111, 201–2

De Klerk, F. W., 1, 3, 208–9

de la Cruz, Francesca, 14

democracy, xviii, 246; American, 139, 168; non-racial, 50, 262; South African, 243

de Vries, Neville, 25

diaspora, xix, xx, 98, 247, 274, 284, 287, 294; living in, 9, 138, 152; musical echo in, 171. *See also* African diaspora; echo; exile; musical echo; musical surrogacy; southern touch aesthetic

Dingaka, 55

District Six, 20–22, 24, 26, 40, 42, 44, 57, 59, 63, 70, 76–77, 88–89, 264

"Don't Blame Me," 77

Drew, Kenny, 143–44

Drum Magazine, 76, 91, 128

Duerden, Dennis, 145–51, 153, 169

Duke Ellington Presents the Dollar Brand Trio, 132

Dutch East India Company, 13, 38, 100

Dyani, Johnny, 53, 116, 129, 144, 153, 156, 168, 178–80, 258

echo, 274–77

echoes of jazz: reinstatement of beauty and, 279–82; Sathima's musical echo and, 271–74. *See also* musical echo; *Musical Echoes*

Ed Samuels Orchestra, 59–60

Ekapa record company and label, 2, 10, 184, 194, 308n45; establishment of, 199–200, 206

Ellington, Duke, xiv; death of, 159; *Duke Ellington Presents the Dollar Brand Trio* recording session and, 129–32, 147, 152; presence of, in Sathima's life, xx, 2, 6, 80, 89, 95–96, 101–2, 107, 108, 164–66, 185–86, 190, 195, 198–99, 210, 215, 236, 240, 275, 279; South African knowledge of, 30, 55, 64, 76, 84, 100–101; State Department tours of, 131, 139; Tempo Music and, 149; voice of, 215

Ellington, Ruth, 148, 190

emotion: beauty and, xviii; jazz and, 33, 114, 122, 125, 126–27, 179, 221, 240; in popular music, 113, 127, 176, 185, 290; Sathima's, 9, 32, 43, 85, 89, 118, 125, 147, 159, 174, 227, 239, 245, 258–59, 273; women and, 18, 21, 127, 224

English culture, 22; hymns in, 23

Enstice, Wayne, 218–19

entanglement, 33–45; in jazz, 51–52; racial, 35–37, 46–50

Eoan Opera Group, 66, 306n15

Erasmus, Zimitri, 35–37

ethnographic listening, 50

ethnomusicology fieldwork and interracial dialogue, 49–50

exile, xxi, 3, 10, 34, 44, 99, 116, 163, 168, 181–83, 195, 203, 209, 222, 246, 259, 286, 289; cultural and political, 292

Farfield Foundation, 149

February, Henry, xxiii, 25, 32, 70, 78, 83, 101, 109, 124, 242–43, 245–47, 249, 251–52, 254, 256

Feza, Mongezi, 144

Fife, Ruth, 20, 25, 32

forced removals, 12, 21, 24, 44, 304n71

Franciscus, Joan (née Joan Benjamin), 15–25, 54, 58, 66–67, 87, 91, 156, 248

freedom, xxxiii, 116; confusion about, 120; Congress for Cultural Freedom and, 145, 164, 168; discourse of musical, xx, 137–38, 152, 163, 166, 172, 177, 185, 206, 208, 218, 220, 225, 228, 231, 239, 255, 281, 290, 292–93; Freedom Charter and, 34; "freedom dream" and, 89, 133, 197; "Freedom Now Suite" and, 121, 229; Freedom of Association Act and, 104; New York City and, 67, 185, 239; political, 210, 232, 259; possibilities of, 3, 9, 30, 47, 49, 80, 104, 224, 227, 240, 243, 259; songs of, 195

free jazz, xxi, 95, 144, 160, 163, 256, 291

Fris, Rafik, 129

Fris, Tove, 129

Gabriello, Giuseppe (aka Joey Gabriels), 66

Gabriels, Joey (aka Giuseppe Gabriello), 66–67, 306n16

Gaiety Bioscope, 29, 31

Gallo Records, 67, 74, 90, 124, 288

gendering of jazz, 217–20, 228–29; femininity and, 230–41; masculinity in, 239–40; poetics of self and, 238–41; Sathima's life story and, 221–27

George, Gambi, 73–74

Gertze, Johnny, xiv, 92, 118, 129

Getz, Stan, 143

ghoema, 26. See also *klopse* rhythm

"Gift of Love-Song for Duke," 139

Gillies, Arthur, 74, 86

Glasser, Spike, 74

Glissant, Edouard, 36–37
Gluckman, Leon, 74
Goldberg, Morris, 148, 151
Golden City Dixies, 55–56, 72, 74, 76, 86, 145, 181
Golden City Post, 76, 82, 85, 87, 89
Gordon, Dexter, 143–44
Green, Edith (Edie), 8, 66
Green, Edward, 15
Green, Evelyn, 17, 66–67, 298n7. *See also* Henry, Evelyn
Grey, George, xxv, 236
Group Areas Act and Amendment, 6, 22, 41, 44, 48, 85, 104, 183, 292
gumboot dance, 71
Gumbs, Onaje Allan, 198, 207, 233
Gwangwa, Jonas, 90, 149

Hajdu, David, xiv, 132
Harris, Corrine, 74
Hawker, Tem, 55, 60, 62
Hawkins, Seton, 210
heart, 84, 110, 193, 290; apartheid in people's, 41; broken, 28; captured, 33; -felt, 89, 208, 292; revolution of, 224–25; performance from, 78, 127, 142; Sathima's, 83, 113, 153, 166, 202, 228–29, 231–32, 235, 240, 271, 273, 279, 282
Henry, Evelyn, 14, 15
Henry, Robert, 14
Hester, Vincent, 25
"heuwel op," 26
Higgins, Billy, xxv, 110, 182, 184, 232
Holiday, Billie, 282; music of, 85; Sathima's relationship with, 110, 113–14, 229, 231; in South Africa, xx, 30, 76, 80, 105, 109; story of, xv, xxiv, 82, 114–17, 131, 174; "Strange Fruit," 196; voice of, 66, 282
home, return, 242–60
home within, xxxiii, 12, 179, 241
homeland, 6, 112. *See also* Bantustan
Horne, Lena, 29–30, 64, 76, 104, 108

Hotel Chelsea, xxi, 5, 8, 190–91, 243
Hoyt, Emily, 153, 157
Huddleston, Trevor, 103, 181
Hughes, Langston, 114, 151, 165, 190
Hujah, Jeff, 73

Ibrahim, Abdullah, xxi; *Brother with Perfect Timing*, 99–100; Cape jazz and, 53; Cape Town rhythm and, 26; contemporary African diaspora and, 103; conversion of, to Islam, 2, 152, 305n3, 311n93; Ekapa Records and, 2, 199–200; Duke Ellington and, 6, 95; music of, 1, 117, 149, 315n40; "Ntsikana's Bell" with Johnny Dyani, 179–81; relationship of, with Sathima, 21, 54–55, 84–87, 89–91, 94, 99, 104–5, 128–29, 136, 141, 144–51, 154, 177, 162, 168, 177, 180–82, 195, 199, 216, 236, 260; "Sathima" tribute of, xxxi; *Struggle for Love*, 100–101; Swaziland and, 153–58; *Universal Silence*, 156. *See also* Brand, Dollar; *Duke Ellington Presents the Dollar Brand Trio*
Ibrahim, Tsakwe, xxi, 154–59, 162–63, 190–91, 194–95, 210, 243
Ibrahim, Tsidi, xxi, 156, 161–62, 190–92, 195, 202, 210, 243. *See also* "Jean Grae"
identity cards, 43
"If I Should Fall in Love Again," 242, 250
"If You Were the Only Boy in the World," 242, 250–52
"I Got it Bad and That Ain't Good," 86
"I'll Be Seeing You," 242, 250
imagination, xix, xxxiii, 98, 104, 165–66, 216–17, 227, 236, 251, 282
Immorality Act, 6, 20, 40, 44, 84–85, 88, 104, 183
improvisation, 51, 72, 121, 138, 152, 177, 218, 239, 265, 281–82, 285, 290, 311n106
"In a Mellotone," 148

Ink Spots, 30

"In My Solitude," 136, 138, 144, 147

intuition, 189, 227, 232, 238

"I Only Have Eyes for You," 242, 252–53

Isaacs, Ayisha, 72

Isaacs, Brian, 40, 42, 73–74

Isaacs, Sam, 32, 65, 87, 225

Islam, 14, 179; in Cape Town, 38, 172, 257–58; conversions to, 152, 305n3; music and, 7, 297n1 (chap. 1)

"I Wished Upon the Moon," 25

"I Wish I Knew," 242, 253

James, Joni, 28, 32, 66, 109, 223, 252, 280

jazz: as American music, xv, 317; in exile, xix, 1, 3, 9–10, 34, 40, 99, 116, 163, 168, 181–83, 203, 222, 225, 246, 259, 288–89, 291, 294; feminine attributes of, xxi, 237–40; global travel of, xxi, 295; healing force of, xxi, 21, 155, 227, 230, 255; origins of, 52, 205, 276

jazz ambassadors, 89–95

jazz clubs: Jazz Appreciation at Kew Town library, 80; in Sea Point, 88; in Woodstock, 88; Zanzibar, 89

Jazz Epistles, 55, 90, 124, 292

jazz historiography: city and, 214, 265–70; entanglements in, 51–52; gendering of, 218; global, 51–52, 173, 241, 246, 273, 277, 279, 284–85, 287, 295; jazzwomen in, 218–21; keywords for, 288–93; as living history, 260–70; marketplace and, 97, 177, 275, 287–88; methodology for, 284–95; non-American jazz in, 12; "Ntsikana's Bell" and, 180–81; poetics of, xviii, xx, xxi, 103, 111, 197, 269; reformulation of, xix. See also jazzwomen

Jazzhus Montmartre, 142–43, 151, 314n24

jazz migrancy, 128–88; Copenhagen and, 142–44; diaspora and, 168; France and, 130–35, 141, 145; London and, 145–47; reasons for leaving South Africa and, 128; recordings with Ellington and Strayhorn and, 129–38; Sathima's early style and, 138; surviving in Europe and, 128–29; Switzerland and, 129, 152; as theoretical, 177–81. See also Congress for Cultural Freedom; exile; Farfield Foundation; Jazzhus Montmartre; Transcription Center

jazz musicians, xvii, 2, 24, 28, 32, 52, 55, 62, 69, 77, 83, 93, 95, 103, 140, 146, 149, 160, 166, 175, 210, 217–20, 222, 228, 231, 236, 279, 289, 291–92

jazz planet, 285–88

jazz self, 189, 218

jazz singer, xxxi, 70–71, 88, 123, 165, 206, 241, 279; Sathima's life as, xxxiii, 1, 3, 77, 82, 125, 194, 197, 200, 221, 227, 229

jazzwomen: biographical phases of, in Sathima's life, 221–27; book about, 218; general themes of, 219–20; Sathima's ideas about jazz and, 227–38. See also improvisation; love

"Jean Grae," 113, 192

Jephthah, Harold, 77

Jephthah, Kenny, 32, 83

"Joy, Joy, Joy, With Joy My Heart Is Ringing," 23

Julius, Elizabeth, 74

"Just a Song at Twilight," 31, 207

Just Jazz Meets the Ballet, 85, 87, 174

JVC Jazz festival, Johannesburg, 209

Kaspersen, Jan, 144

Kenilworth racetrack, 19

Kew Town, 17, 21, 48, 66, 307n31

Kew Town Library, 80, 245

Kgositsile, Melba, 198

Kgositsile, Willie, 198

Khoisan, 5, 100, 155, 163–64, 244, 248, 251, 256–57

King Kong, 55, 74, 76, 90, 102, 145, 181
klopse rhythm (Cape Town rhythm), 26, 138, 207, 247, 254, 256. See also *ghoema*
Kolbe, Vincent: as jazz and dance band musician, 26, 64, 80; jazz appreciation club of, 80; as librarian, 24, 80, 114; movies and, 30, 32, 62; as oral historian, 57, 59, 61–62, 77, 88; as organizer of first jazz concert in District Six, 76–77
Kubeka, Abigail, 73

labor, 38–39, 95; division of, 7; poetic and emotional, 227
laborers, 39, 257
Land Act, 6,
langarm (ballroom) dance, 56–57, 62, 71, 256, 259; bands, 58–60
Langa township, 55, 60
Lehner, Gerhard, xiv, xxv, 131
Lewis, Victor, 236
"Liberation Suite," 10, 121, 196, 202
Lincoln, Abbey, 222, 229, 234; "Freedom Now Suite," 121, 196–97; Max Roach and, 121
Lincoln Center, 2–3
lineage, 95–96, 257; African diasporic, 108, 127, 172, 197, 256; Coloured, 35–36, 41; Duke Ellington's, 105–9; Billie Holiday's compared to Sathima's, 110–25; Abdullah Ibrahim's, 99–101; jazz kinship and, 98, 118, 145, 218, 229, 240; media and, 248, 293; musical kinship and, xx, 95–99, 103, 177, 220, 291; place and, 125–27; popular music industry and, 98, 294; racially blended, 47; Sathima's, 34, 101–2, 191, 206, 241, 257; of South African jazz, 99, 102–5, 291
listeners, xvii, xxxi
listening: comparative, 1; in field research, 2, 5, 50; how to perform, 24, 28, 116, 228; identity and, 89; to jazz, 53, 105, 179; in performance, 237, 249; to radio, 19, 27, 125, 187, 215, 220, 223, 252; to recordings, xiii, 73, 108–9, 187; risk in, 1, 116; to Sathima, 9, 137, 139; as way of knowing, 54, 163, 166, 284
living history, xxi, 98, 258, 260–70, 289–90
Livingstone High School, 20, 29, 65
love: of city, 6–7, 125, 214–15; democratic, 224; of Echo and Narcissus, 278–79; falling in, 224–25, 239, 293; Billie Holiday and, 110, 118, 124; as human value, xv, 18, 34, 50, 90, 110, 175, 225, 238; as jazz poetics, xxi, 189, 227, 238, 245, 259, 282; lovelight and, 184, 235; motherly, 114, 116, 158; for music, xx, 2, 7, 46, 87, 116, 139, 203, 225, 245–46, 252, 254–55, 258; between and for musicians, 73, 144, 216, 229, 231, 253, 255; romantic, 32, 65, 87, 138, 205, 224; Sathima's, xxxi, 82, 85, 89, 91, 136, 153, 155, 166, 193, 201, 208, 210, 230, 234–35, 237–38, 240, 250, 271; songs of, 28, 33, 138–39, 205, 221, 259. See also *Cape Town Love*; "Gift of Love-Song for Duke"
Lovelight, 139, 184, 203, 235

Makatini, Comrade Johnny, 195
Makeba, Miriam, 1–3, 73, 76, 84, 94–95, 102–3, 126, 163, 183, 188, 197, 209; addresses of, to United Nations, 195; *Come Back Africa*, 181
Mandela, Nelson, 1, 183, 203, 208–9, 243
Mandela, Winnie, 138, 184, 203–5
Manhattan Brothers, 145, 181
Masekela, Hugh, 1, 2, 73, 84, 90, 94–95, 102–3, 108–9, 149, 163, 176, 181, 197, 209
Masinga, Ben "Satch," 76, 94
Maskanda, 71
Matshikiza, Todd, 74
McBee, Cecil, 198

McGregor, Chris, 104, 141, 144, 147, 170, 181, 256, 292

McGregor, Mary, 21

McGregor, Maxine, 168, 170, 317n58

mediated music, 26–31

Melody Five, 25

memory, memories, 265, 269–70; African cultural, 180, 187, 197, 263, 289; collective, 250, 254–55, 258; of place, 22, 172, 249, 291; ruptures in, 49, 248, 249, 257, 263, 294; Sathima's early, 33, 187, 223, 226, 248, 255, 282

Memories and Dreams, 10, 34, 202

Meyer, Paul, 84, 85, 128

Milestones Recording Studio, 244

Miller, Harry, 146

Miller, Hazel, 146

Mr. Paljas, 55

"Mr. Wonderful," 32

Mixed Marriages Act, 6

mixed race, 3, 34, 36–37, 39–40, 43, 47, 49, 51–52, 113, 179, 221, 225

modern jazz community, 76–95

Moeketsi, Kippie, 73, 90

moffie, 300n37

Mogotsi, Joe, 145, 168

Moholo, Louis, 141–42, 144, 182

Morning in Paris, A, xiii, xv, xxiv, 123, 131, 136, 139, 205, 225

Moses, Basil, 208, 242–44, 249, 251, 257, 271

movies (bioscope): apartheid and, 30–31; audiences of, 30; *Cabin in the Sky*, 29; dream palaces and, 31, 58; memories of, 273; performances at intermissions of, 31, 223, 250; romance, 32; as Saturday activity, 19, 29, 30; as source for local music, 62; *Snow White*, 29; *Stormy Weather*, 30; theaters, 29

Murray, Sunny, 144

"Music," 201–2, 227–28

musical echo, xx, xxxiii, 171, 271, 279, 288, 290, 294; book and, 278, 283; challenge of, to American music, 274, 283; traveling character of jazz as, 177, 255, 284

Musical Echoes, 271, 274; photograph of, xxi, 272–73; recording project of, 80, 123, 205, 209, 241; song, 208

musical surrogacy, 98, 174–77, 290

musical transmission, 27, 96, 176, 210, 290

music industry, 97, 176, 275, 288

music training, 24, 181, 220

"Nations in Me — New Nation A'Comin'," 10, 33–34, 196–97

Native Americans, 190–91

New African diaspora, 167, 170–74, 185, 187, 241, 260, 270, 278–79, 282, 291

Newport Jazz Festival, xxv, 96, 146–47

New York City, xiii, xxv, 1–3, 6–8, 17, 22, 34, 66, 76, 95, 99, 110, 112, 119–20, 125–26, 139, 146–48, 153, 158–61, 163–64, 166–69, 171, 179, 181, 183, 190–91, 194, 228–30, 242–43, 247, 255, 265–66, 268, 271, 279, 281, 284; Sathima and, 149, 157, 189, 195–227; as strategic retreat, xv, xxi

North Sea Jazz Festival, Cape Town, 209

Ntshoko, Makhaya, xiv, 92, 118, 129, 133–34, 136–37, 144

"Ntsikana's Bell," 179–80, 318n74

nuance, xxxi, 172, 185, 202, 227, 231–32, 258, 282

Ogun Records, 146

palimpsest, xxi, 248, 263, 265, 285, 290

Pan-Africanist Congress (PAC), 1

Parnel, Jack, 73

Pass Laws, 6

Pavitt, Vincent, 242–44

performances, live, 12, 25, 33, 171, 185, 254

Phahlane, Mike, 74, 90

Pillay, Sonny, 73

Placksin, Sally, 41, 147, 218, 254

Platt, Frank, 149

popular culture, xxi, 11, 248

popular songs, xx, 23–24, 28, 31–32, 114, 120, 138, 201, 263; archeology of, 242–53; on radio, 28, 223. *See also* Benjamin, Sathima Bea

Population Registration Act and Amendment, 39–41, 43–44

Powell, Bud, 141, 144

Powell, Dick, 242, 252

"princess for the night," 58

"Prisoner of Love," 201

Publications and Entertainment Act, 45, 94

Publications Control Board, 94

race, 47, 289; mixed heritage and, 3, 34, 113, 179, 221, 225, 302n52; racial categories and, 39, 41, 45, 105, 259; "relaxed apartheid" and, 40

radio, 9, 13, 26, 99, 299n29; Lourenco Marques (LM) Radio, 27–28; Re-diffusion Service, 27; South African Broadcast Corporation (SABC), 27; Springbok Radio, 27; Transcription Center radio programs, 131, 144–46, 148. *See also* Benjamin, Sathima Bea: radio and; Voice of America radio

Radise, Peter, 74

Ramsey, Guthrie P., Jr., 11

Rasmussen, Lars, xix, 143, 168, 216

Rathebe, Dolly, 73, 108

recordings, 9, 26, 28, 61, 63, 67, 74, 76, 78, 80, 85, 109, 121, 122, 124, 132, 142–43, 145–46, 167–68, 170, 175–76, 181, 248, 265, 267, 269, 285, 287

Regan, Steven, 60

Reprise Records, xiv, 130, 56

resonance (resonate), 109, 114, 125, 127, 231–32, 256, 274, 278, 282, 284, 290

restoration, 264, 292

rhetorical space, 8, 187, 197, 217, 276–77, 293

Rich, Basil, 25, 80, 83, 164

Riley, Ben, 184, 232

risk, xxxiii, 34, 46, 51, 85–86, 114, 116, 119, 220, 225, 228, 234, 236, 239–40, 251, 255, 288

Riverside Church, 1, 3

Ronnie Scott's Old Place, 146

"Roses of Picardy, The," 23

St. Helena, 18, 20, 22, 28, 56, 80, 87, 101, 117–18, 120; English cosmopolitanism and, 43; Population Registration Act and, 42

St. Saviors Church, Claremont, 23

Samuels, John, 59–60, 87, 164

"Sathima," xxxi

Sathima Sings Ellington, 111, 139, 200

Scarry, Elaine, xxi, 127, 274, 279–81, 292

Scott, Stephen, 208, 212, 234, 271

segregation, 40–41, 44

sense of timing, 137, 166, 235, 240

Separate Amenities Act, 6, 44, 183

separate development, 6, 40

September, Dulcie, 195–96, 319n4

Sharpeville Massacre, 5, 90, 94, 128, 153, 163, 182

shebeen, 90

Shebeen, 55

Shepp, Archie, 143–44

Sickler, Don, 104, 233

Sinatra, Frank, xiv, 130, 132, 252; South African tour of, 195

slavery, 14, 35, 38–39, 292; West African, 180, 260, 278

Snakepit, 60–61

"Sometimes I Feel Like a Motherless Child," 111, 186, 202

"Somewhere over the Rainbow," 32, 223

"Song for Winnie," 203–4

Song Spirit, 123, 206

sound recording, 9, 26, 28, 78, 109,

175–77, 248, 265, 267, 269, 278. *See also* recordings

South Africa: history of, xix, 104; listeners in, 33, 106; popular culture of, 11; studies of, xviii

South African Communist Party, 1, 88, 90–91

South African jazz, xviii, 1–2, 51–54, 90, 93, 96, 100, 104, 109, 116, 123, 138, 146, 149, 163, 168–69, 181, 256, 258, 273–74, 277, 288–89, 291; borrowed vs. belonging in, 9–10, 62, 69, 271; crossover, 60, 98, 182; as non-racial free space, 182

South African Native Affairs Commission (SANAC), 39–40

southern touch aesthetic, 184–87, 241, 292

Southern Touch recording, 184, 205

Soweto, xxi, 27, 154, 160–61, 163

Spirit of Africanness (Southern Touch), 165–66, 184–87

Sponono, 55

spontaneous, spontaneity, xxi, 121, 130, 136–37, 147, 166, 187, 189, 205, 227, 230, 232, 234, 236–38, 256, 282, 293

Stockhouse, Janice, 218–19

Stockman, Hardy, 91

Stone, Cheryl, 153

Stone, Trevor, 151, 153

Strayhorn, Billy, xiv–xv, xxi, 95, 97, 130–32, 135–38, 142, 198, 205, 216, 240

studio, xiii, xiv, 86, 90, 121, 130–31, 133, 136, 139–40, 170, 189, 200–201, 217, 221, 226, 231, 236–37, 239, 241, 247–48, 250–51, 253, 257, 284, 287

subtlety, 185, 227, 282

Tainton, Graham, 74

talent, xxxiii, 27, 31, 55, 61, 66–67, 69, 71, 73–74, 85–86, 92, 96, 130, 145, 192; source of, 232

talent contests, 24, 250; Sathima's first, 31–32, 246

Taylor, Cecil, 143–44

Tchicai, John, 144, 178

Township Jazz, 55, 74

Transcription Center, 145–47, 149, 153, 160, 164, 165, 168–70

transnationalism, 99, 102, 127, 188, 210, 277, 292; in American studies, 98, 287; of jazz, 98, 163, 285, 291; transnational community of jazz musicians and, 94, 140, 175, 291; transnational community of listeners and, 93, 126

Ulster, Dan, 65–66

University of Cape Town jazz, 76–77

U.S. Armed Services Radio in Germany, 131

van Vuuren, Hettie, 15, 21

variety shows, 24; as collaborative projects, 71; imitations in, 74; traveling, 55

voice, xvi, 2, 28, 67, 95, 98, 116–17, 126, 136, 161, 179, 186–87, 189, 209–10, 215, 217, 221–22, 263, 269, 278, 291–92, 293; Billie Holiday's, xv, 109–10, 113, 115, 123, 125, 229, 282; human, 172, 180, 264, 290; natural, 13, 24, 125; Sathima's, xxi, xxxiii, 9, 10, 15, 24, 64, 65, 82, 111, 123, 127, 131–32, 134, 136–38, 174, 206–7, 227, 230–32, 241, 247, 258, 273, 282; scholarly, 8, 110

Voice of America (VOA) radio, 152, 170

web link, 290

Webster, Ben, 143–44

Weizmann Hall, 77

"When Day is Done," 242, 248–50

white musicians' union, 77

Williams, Buster, 65, 110, 184–85, 199, 204, 207, 218, 229, 233, 235

Williams, Gene, 73

Williams, Jusuf, 74

Wilson, John, 199, 206–7

"Windsong" composition, 111–12, 160, 202–3, 233, 235, 238
Windsong recording, 110–11, 202–3
Wolf, Marjorie, 218–19
women, xix, 25, 27, 38, 54, 56–58, 67, 88, 91, 107, 137–38, 155, 169, 195–96, 202, 204–5, 209, 224, 226, 229–30, 238, 240, 258, 278, 282, 292–93. *See also* jazzwomen
women in jazz and popular music, xxi, xvii, 1, 5, 24, 28, 99, 108, 112, 114–16, 121–24, 162, 165, 171, 180–81, 209, 218, 286, 293. *See also* jazzwomen

women thinking in jazz, 217–41
"women writing culture," 7, 218
Wonder, Stevie, 153
World Wide Web, 5, 210, 287, 290

"You Don't Know What Love Is," 184
"You Go to My Head," 242, 252
"Your Love Has Faded," 135–36

Zonk! (film and show), 69–71, 306n19
Zonk! The African People's Magazine, 74–76

CAROL ANN MULLER is a professor of music at the
University of Pennsylvania. She is the author of *Focus: Music
of South Africa* (2008) and *South African Music: A Century of
Traditions in Transformation* (2004).

SATHIMA BEA BENJAMIN is a South African jazz vocalist
and composer, and the founder of Ekapa Records. Over
the course of her career she has released a dozen albums,
including, most recently, *SongSpirit* (2007).

Library of Congress Cataloging-in-Publication Data
Muller, Carol Ann.
Musical echoes : South African women thinking in jazz /
Carol Ann Muller and Sathima Bea Benjamin.
p. cm. — (Refiguring American music)
Includes bibliographical references and index.
ISBN 978-0-8223-4891-7 (cloth : alk. paper)
ISBN 978-0-8223-4914-3 (pbk. : alk. paper)
1. Benjamin, Sathima Bea. 2. Jazz singers — South Africa —
Biography. 3. Women jazz musicians — South Africa. 4. Jazz — South
Africa. I. Benjamin, Sathima Bea. II. Title. III. Series: Refiguring
American music.
ML420.B3435M85 2011
782.42165092 — dc23   2011021957